EXPLORATIONS IN BION'S "O"

Wilfred Bion described "O" as "the unknowable and the unreachable ultimate truth". In this fascinating collection, a range of authors offer their own theoretical, clinical and artistic approaches to exploring this enduring but mysterious idea.

Drawn from contributions from the 8th International Bion Conference in 2014, the book examines how "O" can be experienced in all aspects of internal and external reality and within all relationships, from an individual relating to the mother to their emotional relationship with their self. It features insights into "O" drawn from the area of faith as well as its manifestations in clinical practice, while also included is a chapter exploring the links between Bion's ideas and those of Winnicott, Lacan, Green and Freud.

Featuring contributions from some of the world's leading Bion scholars, this will be essential reading for any psychoanalyst interested in exploring the concept of "O", as well as scholars in philosophy and theology.

Afsaneh K. Alisobhani (Psy.D.) is a training and supervising psychoanalyst, a faculty member and the past Vice President of Newport Psychoanalytic Institute, and a member of the New Center for Psychoanalysis. She is a member of the faculty at University of California, Irvine, School of Psychiatry and Human Behavior and a member of the University of California/ NCP Interdisciplinary Psychoanalytic Consortium since 2002. She was the co-chair of the International Bion Conference in Los Angeles in 2014. She is the founding member, faculty and supervisor at Tehran Center for Psychoanalytic Studies (TCPS) in Tehran, Iran. She is a lecturer and supervisor in Psychoanalytic Psychotherapy program at Tehran University of Medical Sciences (TUMS) and Ruzbeh Hospital in Tehran, Iran. She is also a supervisor and lecturer at China American Psychoanalytic Alliance.

Glenda J. Corstorphine (Psy.D.) is a training and supervising analyst and faculty member and the past Vice President of Newport Psychoanalytic Institute. Prior to receiving her doctorate from NPI she received a Masters in Marriage and Family Therapy and a Masters in Theology at Fuller Theological Seminary. She is a former board member at NPI and former director of NPI's Pasadena campus. She was the co-chair of the International Bion Conference in Los Angeles, 2014. She has been in private practice in Pasadena, CA, for over 25 years.

THE ROUTLEDGE WILFRED BION STUDIES BOOK SERIES

Howard B. Levine, MD
Series Editor

The contributions of Wilfred Bion are among the most cited in the analytic literature. Their appeal lies not only in their content and explanatory value, but in their generative potential. Although Bion's training and many of his clinical instincts were deeply rooted in the classical tradition of Melanie Klein, his ideas have a potentially universal appeal. Rather than emphasizing a particular psychic content (e.g., Oedipal conflicts in need of resolution; splits that needed to be healed; preconceived transferences that must be allowed to form and flourish, etc.), he tried to help open and prepare the mind of the analyst (without memory, desire or theoretical preconception) for the encounter with the patient.

Bion's formulations of group mentality and the psychotic and non-psychotic portions of the mind, his theory of thinking and emphasis on facing and articulating the truth of one's existence so that one might truly learn first hand from one's own experience, his description of psychic development (alpha function and container/contained) and his exploration of O are "non-denominational" concepts that defy relegation to a particular school or orientation of psychoanalysis. Consequently, his ideas have taken root in many places. . . . and those ideas continue to inform many different branches of psychoanalytic inquiry and interest.[1]

It is with this heritage and its promise for the future developments of psychoanalysis in mind that we present *The Routledge Wilfred Bion Studies Book Series*. This series gathers together under newly emerging and continually evolving contributions to psychoanalytic thinking that rest upon Bion's foundational texts and explore and extend the implications of his thought.

Howard B. Levine, MD
Series Editor

---

[1] Levine, H.B. and Civitarese, G. (2016). Editors' Preface, *The W.R. Bion Tradition*, Levine and Civitarese, eds., London: Karnac 2016, p. xxi.

EXPLORATIONS IN BION'S "O"

Everything We Know Nothing About

Edited by Afsaneh K. Alisobhani
and Glenda J. Corstorphine

Routledge
Taylor & Francis Group

LONDON AND NEW YORK

First published 2019
by Routledge
2 Park Square, Milton Park, Abingdon, Oxon OX14 4RN

and by Routledge
52 Vanderbilt Avenue, New York, NY 10017

Routledge is an imprint of the Taylor & Francis Group, an informa business

© 2019 selection and editorial matter, Afsaneh K. Alisobhani and Glenda
J. Corstorphine; individual chapters, the contributors

British Library Cataloguing-in-Publication Data
A catalogue record for this book is available from the British Library

Library of Congress Cataloging-in-Publication Data
A catalog record for this book has been requested

ISBN: 978-0-367-00132-2 (hbk)
ISBN: 978-0-367-00134-6 (pbk)
ISBN: 978-0-429-44436-4 (ebk)

Typeset in Bembo
by Apex CoVantage, LLC

For our families whose support was ever present,
and patience never ending.
Life is an unfoldment, and the further we travel the more truth we can
comprehend. To understand the things that are at our door is the best
preparation for understanding those that lie beyond.
Hypatia

CONTENTS

ACKNOWLEDGEMENTS

We are grateful to all who participated in the planning and fulfillment of *psych'O'analysis: explorations in truth*, especially those who spent hours of their time meeting and dreaming the conference into being. We are especially thankful for the Organizing Committee: Ray Calabrese, James Gooch, Tom Helscher, Katina Kostoulas, Avedis Panajian, Annie Reiner, Marianne Robinson, Elizabeth Toole, Karen Willette and our advisors, James S. Grotstein and John Lundgren. Thanks to Larry Brown and Howard Levine who shared invaluable advice regarding conference planning and to the 2011 Porto Allegre conference that inspired us to tap into our creative juices.

Special thanks to Annie Reiner for editing James S. Grotstein's paper, "BION CROSSES THE RUBICON: The Fateful Course – and Curse – of "O" in Psychoanalysis and the Furies Left in Its Wake", which originally appears in *Of Things Invisible to Mortal Sight: Celebrating the Work of James S. Grotstein* (2017).

ABOUT THE EDITORS AND CONTRIBUTORS

Joseph Aguayo (Ph.D.) is a training and supervising analyst at the Psychoanalytic Center of California. A past IPA Research Advisory Board Fellow, his research specialty is the history of Kleinian/Bionian psychoanalysis, and he has published articles in the *International Journal of Psychoanalysis*. His current book, co-edited with Barnet Malin, is *Wilfred Bion's Los Angeles Seminars* (Karnac, 2013).

Afsaneh K. Alisobhani (Psy.D.) is a training and supervising psychoanalyst, a faculty member and the past Vice President of Newport Psychoanalytic Institute, and a member of the New Center for Psychoanalysis. She is a member of the faculty at University of California, Irvine, School of Psychiatry and Human Behavior and a member of the University of California/NCP Interdisciplinary Psychoanalytic Consortium since 2002. She was the co-chair of the International Bion Conference in Los Angeles in 2014. She is the founding member, faculty and supervisor at Tehran Center for Psychoanalytic Studies (TCPS) in Tehran, Iran. She is a lecturer and supervisor in Psychoanalytic Psychotherapy program at Tehran University of Medical Sciences (TUMS) and Ruzbeh Hospital in Tehran, Iran. She is also a supervisor and lecturer at China American Psychoanalytic Alliance.

Avner Bergstein is a training psychoanalyst with the Israel Psychoanalytic Society. He has worked for several years at a kindergarten for children with autism. He teaches seminars focusing on primitive mental states and on the writings of Bion, and has published a number of papers elaborating on the clinical implications of the writings of Bion and Meltzer.

Andrea Bocchiola (D.Phi, Psy.D.) graduated in Philosophy and Psychology, and is pursuing a DEA in Psychoanalytical Research (University Paris 7). He has taught Philosophical Ethics at the University of Naples and is presently professor at the Italian Institute of Group Psychoanalysis in Milan. He has finished his IPA training at the Italian Psychoanalytic Society and works as a psychoanalyst.

João Carlos Braga (M.D., Ph.D.) is a training and supervising analyst at the Brazilian Psychoanalytic Society of São Paulo and Psychoanalytic Group of Curitiba, Brazil. He is assistant professor of Psychiatry and Medical Psychology, School of Medicine, Universidade Federal do Paraná (1968–1981).

Gisèle de Mattos Brito is a full member of the Brazilian Psychoanalytic Society of São Paulo and also a full member of the Brazilian Psychoanalytic Society of Minas Gerais (Provisional). She is training analyst and teacher of the Training Institute of SBPMG where she led groups of study on the work of W. R. Bion. Since 2009 she has coordinated a Group of Bion's Supervisions at SBPSP. She has published several papers in Brazil and some abroad.

Alessandro Bruni (M.D.) was originally a biologist. He gave his dissertation thesis on "Altered States of Consciousness" with Nobel Prize recipient Daniel Bovet Prof. of Psychopharmacology at Rome's University "La Sapienza." He has been working in private practice in psychoanalysis and groups since 1980. He is now a psychoanalyst, training and supervising analyst of the Italian Psychoanalitical Society (SPI), founding member and training analyst of the Italian Institute of Group Psychoanalysis (IIPG) (of Bionian trend), member of Synaptica – Mind-Body Research Center, supervisor in Public Health Services in many Italian cities.

Nanci Carter (Psy.D., MFT) is a psychoanalyst, board member and member of the faculty at Newport Psychoanalytic Institute. Dr. Carter is certified in Jungian Psychotherapy and has practiced for over 25 years in Newport Beach, CA. She has a private practice in Newport Beach, CA.

Claudio Castelo Filho (Ph.D.) is a full member and training analyst at the Sociedade Brasileira de Psicanálise de São Paulo, Brazil. He holds a Masters degree in Clinical Psychology from the Pontifícia Universidade Católica de São Paulo, a Ph.D. in Social Psychology and is a professor in Clinical Psychology from the Universidade de São Paulo. He is a full member of the International Psychoanalytical Association (IPA)'s and the Federeção de Psicanalise da America Latina (Fepal). He has worked as a psychoanalyst at his private office since 1985. Castelo is also a painter with exhibitions and publications in Brazil, Germany and England.

Arnaldo Chuster (M.D.) is a member of the Brazilian Psychiatric Association and Rio de Janeiro Psychiatric Association; a psychoanalyst, and training and teaching analyst at Rio de Janeiro Psychoanalytic Society, IPA; professor at W. Bion Institute in Porto Alegre; has authored eight books in Portuguese about Bion's ideas; and is presenting in English the book *A Lonesome Road: Essays on the Complexity of Bion's Work*.

Keri Cohen (LCSW, BCD) has been practicing for over 20 years in Lancaster, PA. She received her MSW from the University of Pennsylvania (1991) and completed a two year post-Masters program at Bryn Mawr College. She formed and led a psychoanalytic study group for many years. She participates in a regional Bion study group.

Glenda J. Corstorphine (Psy.D.) is a training and supervising analyst and faculty member of Newport Psychoanalytic Institute. Prior to receiving her doctorate from NPI she received a Masters in Marriage and Family Therapy and a Masters in Theology at Fuller Theological Seminary. She is a former board member at NPI and former director of NPI's Pasadena campus. She was the co-chair of the International Bion Conference in Los Angeles, 2014. She has been in private practice in Pasadena, CA, for over 25 years.

Jeffrey L. Eaton (MA, FIPA) is a graduate of the Northwestern Psychoanalytic Society and Institute and a full member of the IPA. He is in private practice in Seattle, WA. He has a special interest in the treatment of autism and was awarded the 10th Frances Tustin Memorial Lecture Prize in 2006. His first book is titled *A Fruitful Harvest: Essays after Bion* and was published in 2011 by The Alliance Press.

James Gooch (M.D., Ph.D., FIPA) has been in private practice of psychoanalysis for adults, adolescents and children in Beverly Hills, CA, since 1970. He is board certified in Psychiatry and Child Psychiatry. He trained and received his Ph.D. from the Southern California Psychoanalytic Institute. In the early 1970s he studied with W.R. Bion. He was the founding president of Psychoanalytic Center of California. Dr. Gooch has been a training analyst at the New Center for Psychoanalysis, a fellow of the International Psychoanalytic Association, former Chief Psychoanalyst at Reiss-Davis Child Study Center in Los Angeles, former clinical professor of psychiatry at USC and on the Board of Representatives of IPA. He is a member of American Psychoanalytic Association, International Psychoanalytic Association and the Confederation of Independent Psychoanalytic Societies of the United States.

James S. Grotstein (M.D.) was Clinical Professor of Psychiatry at the David Geffen School of Medicine, UCLA, and training and supervising analyst at the New Center for Psychoanalysis and the Psychoanalytic Center of California, Los Angeles. He was a member of the Editorial Board of the International Journal of Psychoanalysis and was past North American Vice-President of the International Psychoanalytic Association. He has published over 250 papers and is the author of many books. In 2011, the IPA 47th Annual Congress in Mexico City featured a presentation and panel honoring his life's work.

Monica Horovitz (M.D., Ph.D.) is a full member of the Paris Psychoanalytic Society (S.P.P.) and of the IPA, and has had a private practice in Paris for 27 years. She has run a seminar for the last ten years on Bion at the S.P.P. and is the co-chair of "Bion in Marrakech." She has also written a number of international articles on Bion's thought.

Alan Michael Karbelnig (Ph.D., ABPP), a licensed psychologist, also serves as a training and supervising psychoanalyst at the New Center for Psychoanalysis (NCP) in Los Angeles. Having earned numerous awards for his teaching, he is a senior faculty at NCP and also teaches Object Relations theory (via Skype) for the Chinese American Psychoanalytic Alliance (CAPA). He practices psychoanalysis, clinical and forensic psychology in South Pasadena, CA.

Jani Santamaría Linares's (Ph.D.) credentials include Bachelor and Masters Degrees in Psychology (UIA); Masters and Ph.D. in Child and Adolescent Psychotherapy (UIC); Masters and Ph.D. in Psychotherapy (APM); psychoanalyst at The Child and Adolescent Institute (APM); child and adolescent psychoanalyst (APM); and teaching analyst (APMM3). Linares teaches at several Mexican universities, the Institute of Psychoanalysis at the Mexican Psychoanalytic Association (APM) and the Center for Graduate Studies (APM) where she teaches W. Bion, M. Klein and D. Meltzer. She has published articles in Mexican, Argentinian,

Colombian and Peruvian journals. She is currently the coordinator of the Child and Adolescent Psychoanalyst Course of the Mexican Psychoanalytic Association and a member of the Child and Adolescent Committee of the Latin American Psychoanalytic Federation (FEPAL) (2012–2014).

Guelfo Margherita (M.D.) is a psychiatrist, IPA-psychoanalyst, with training function in the Italian Institute of Group Psychoanalysis (IIPG). In his mystic trip to "O" he crossed several establishments: Psychoanalysis, Psychiatric Wards and Madhouses, Psychotic Organization of Individual and Collective Minds, Chaos Math, Meditation in Indian Ashrams. His main research interest is: How do group and institutional minds operate?

Julie Michael McCaig (Ph.D.) is a Training and Supervising Psychoanalyst and Infant Observation Faculty Member at the Psychoanalytic Center of California and the New Center for Psychoanalysis. She has a practice of Adult Psychoanalysis in Beverly Hills and she is director of THRIVE Infant-Family Program Non Profit.

Carmen C. Mion (M.D.) is a full member, supervisor and training analyst at the Brazilian Psychoanalytic Society of São Paulo, member of the Brazilian Federation of Psychoanalysis (FEPAL) and the International Psychoanalytic Association (IPA). She is in private practice in São Paulo and has published articles in Brazilian and International journals. She graduated as neurologist at the Medicine School at the University of São Paulo (USP) and was a postgraduate in the Department of Psychiatry at The University of Iowa College of Medicine from 1989–1990. She has given seminars on W. Bion's Discipline at the Postgraduate Course in Psychoanalytic Psychotherapy at the USP Psychology Institute. Dr. Mion has served as a member of the FEPAL's Education Committee (CEF) and is currently a member of the IPA's Education & Oversight Committee and co-chair on the Psychoanalytic Education & Transmission Study Group of the SBPSP.

Avedis Panajian (Ph.D.) is a licensed psychologist and training and supervising psychoanalyst at the Psychoanalytic Center of California. He is a Diplomate in Clinical Psychology, American Board of Professional Psychology. He is also a member of the American Academy of Clinical Psychology. Dr. Panajian has received several awards for his teaching including a Distinguished Educator Award from California Psychological Association. He has been a Core Faculty member at Pacifica Graduate Institute for 28 years. He teaches courses on psychoanalytic therapy, psychopathology and clinical supervision. Dr. Panajian also teaches at Psychoanalytic Center of California. He teaches the work of Wilfred Bion at Psychoanalytic Center of California. He is a frequent lecturer throughout the United States on Bion and on the French school of psychoanalysis. He is in private practice in Beverly Hills, CA.

Michael Ian Paul (M.D.) is FIPA Training and Supervising Analyst: PCC and The New Center Analysand of W.R. Bion, author of numerous papers and the book *Before We Were Young*, 1997 Esf publications and Free Associations Press.

Lia Pistiner de Cortiñas (Ph.D.) is a psychoanalyst in private practice in Buenos Aires, Argentina, full member and training analyst of the Buenos Aires Psychoanalytical Association (APDEBA) and fellow of the International Psychoanalytical Association. She has a specialization in child and adolescent psychoanalysis. She is also a psychologist (Ph.D.) and a lawyer. She gives seminars and is invited to lecture and supervise in different public and private institutions in Argentina, Paris, Rome, Sicily, Madrid and others. She teaches Theory of Technique and Psychopathology at APDEBA's training institute, and the seminar on "W.R. Bion" for the career of specialization in Psychoanalysis of the institute of mental health (APDEBA-IUSAM) and gives post-graduate seminars at the Faculty of Psychology of the Buenos Aires University. She has written two books *The Aesthetic Dimension of the Mind, Variations on a Theme of Bion*, published in Spanish and in English by Karnac, and *On Mental Growth*, in Spanish and soon to be published in English. She is co-author of the books: *Del Cuerpo al Simbolo* (from Body to Symbol) and *Bion conocido/desconocido* (Bion known/ unknown). She has also written papers published in Argentina and international publications. She was one of the speakers at the IPA Conference in Prague, where she read her paper "Transformations of the Emotional Experience," published by the International Journal and in other psychoanalytic magazines.

Darcy Antonio Portolese (M.D.) has a degree in Psychiatry from the University of Sao Paulo, a Doctorate in Psychiatry at the University of Sorbonne and at the University of Sao Paulo, and is a senior analyst at the Brazilian Society of Psychoanalysis of Sao Paulo, Brazil.

Annie Reiner (Ph.D., Psy.D., LCSW) is a senior faculty member and training analyst at The Psychoanalytic Center of California (PCC) in Los Angeles. She was profoundly influenced by the ideas of Wilfred Bion, with whom she studied briefly in the 1970s. She most recently edited a Festschrift in honor of James S. Grotstein called "Of Things Invisible to Mortal Sight" (Karnac, 2017). Dr. Reiner is also an accomplished poet; playwright; and painter, with four books of poems, a book of short stories and six children's books which she also illustrated. Dr. Reiner maintains a private practice in Beverly Hills, CA.

Cecil José Rezze's (M.D., Ph.D.) credentials include Medical School of the University of São Paulo; editor, *Revista Brasileira de Psicanálise* (1973/78); president, Brazilian Psychoanalytic Society of São Paulo – SBPSP (1979/80); co-chair, I to VII Annual Psychoanalytic Meetings: Bion, 2008 to 2014; full member and training analyst (SBPSP).

Björn Salomonsson (M.D., Ph.D.) is a training and child psychoanalyst of the Swedish Psychoanalytical Association, Stockholm. He is working in private practice and at the Mama Mia Child Health Centre. He is an affiliate researcher at the Unit of Reproductive Health, Department of Women's and Children's Health, Karolinska Institutet. His research and publications focus on psychoanalytically inspired parent-infant therapies, child analysis and the 'weaving thoughts' case presentation method. His book, "Psychoanalytic Therapy with Infants and Parents: Practice, Theory and Results" was published by Routledge (2014). A book, written with Majlis Winberg Salomonsson, was published by Routledge (2016), *Dialogues with Children and Adolescents: A Psychoanalytic Guide*, and by Erès, *A quoi pensent les enfants?*

Majlis Winberg Salomonsson (M.Sc.) is a training analyst at the Swedish Psychoanalytic Association and a member of the IPA Committee on Child and Adolescent Psychoanalysis, COCAP. MWS runs a research project at the Child and Adolescent Psychiatric Unit,

Karolinska Institutet, "Troubled babies-troubled kids, a follow-up study." She has published several papers and books on child and adolescent psychoanalysis.

Adriana Salvitti (Ph.D.) is a postdoctoral researcher at the Psychology Institute of the University of São Paulo, and candidate at the Durval Marcondes Institute of Psychoanalysis of the Brazilian Psychoanalytic Society of São Paulo.

Ester Hadassa Sandler's (Dra., M.D.) (Faculdade de Medicina da Universidade de Sao Paulo, 1974) credentials include training analyst, Sociedade Brasileira de Psicanalise de Sao Paulo; child analyst; Organizing Committee – Bion 2004 São Paulo; author of many papers on child analysis and other issues; translator of Bion and Money-Kyrle's books into Portuguese, edited by Imago ed. and Ed Casa do Psicologo, 1998–2005.

Paulo Cesar Sandler's (M.D., M.Sc.) (Faculdade de Medicina da Universidade de Sao Paulo, 1973, 1981) credentials include training analyst, Sociedade Brasileira de Psicanalise de Sao Paulo; psychiatrist at the Physical Rehabilitation Institute, Hospital das Clinicas, Faculdade de Medicina da Universidade de Sao Paulo; former director, Mental Health Program, Public Health School, Universidade de Sao Paulo; former professor in the work of Bion at the Post Graduate Program (Lato sensu) of Psycho-analytic Therapy at the Instituto de Psicologia da Universidade de Sao Paulo; author of many books published in English and Portuguese about the work of Bion, such as *The Language of Bion, A Dictionary of Concepts*, Karnac, 2005 (reprinted in 2010 and 2012), and its companion, the three volume series, *A Clinical Application of Bion's Concepts* (2009, 2011 and 2013, with forewords by Dr. James S. Grotstein, Antonio Sapienza, Rocco Pisani and Mario Giampa); and the eight volume series, *A Apreensao da Realidade Psiquica*, Imago editora, 1997–2004, a transdisciplinary study containing clinical illustrations; and many papers and chapters in books published in English, Russian, German and Portuguese; translator of Bion, Winnicott, Milner, Meltzer and Money-Kyrle's books to the Portuguese language (some of them, with Dr. Ester Hadassa Sandler).

Deborah Sherman (MS, BC-DMT, LMHC) is a certified psychoanalyst and has a private practice in Psychoanalysis, Psychotherapy and Dance/Movement Therapy in New York City. She is on faculty and is a supervising analyst at the Institute for the Psychoanalytic Study of Subjectivity (IPSS) and the Institute for Contemporary Psychotherapy (ICP) in New York.

Mary E. Sonntag (LCSW) is a graduate from the Institute of Subjectivity (IPSS- NYC) and from the Center of the Study of Anorexia and Bulimia (CSAB – NYC). She is a training analyst, supervisor and instructor at the following institutes in NYC: IPSS, CSAB and NIP. Her papers have been published in *Psychoanalytic Dialogues* and *Studies in Gender and Sexuality* and presented internationally.

Anie Stürmer is a psychologist, psychotherapist and specialist in Clinical Psychology; founder, Scientific Director, docent and supervisor of IPSI – Institute of Psychology, in Novo Hamburgo, Brazil; Docent and Supervisor of IEPP – Institute of Teaching and Psychotherapy Research, in Porto Alegre, Brazil; organizer and author of the book *Crianças e Adolescentes em Psicoterapia: a abordagem psicanalítica* Artmed Ed. Porto Alegre.

Dr. Renato Trachtenberg is a Brazilian psychoanalyst, living in Porto Alegre. He is an M.D. and psychiatrist. He did his training analysis in Buenos Aires, Argentina, and attended the seminars and control analysis at the Institute of Buenos Aires Psychoanalytical Association, being a full member of the same. He practices psychoanalysis in his private clinic and teaches Bion's work in psychoanalytical institutions and in study groups. He is a founder member of the Center for Psychoanalytic Studies of Porto Alegre and of the Brazilian Psychoanalytical Society of Porto Alegre, affiliated to IPA. In the latter, is a full member and training analyst. He has authored numerous papers on the work of Bion, published in many books and magazines. He is co-author, with Arnaldo Chuster, of the book *The Seven Capital Envy*, also translated into Spanish. Dr. Trachtenberg participated in the organization of Conferences on Bion in São Paulo (2004) and Porto Alegre (2011) and actively participates in national and international meetings and conferences on Bion's work.

Rudi Vermote (M.D., Ph.D.) is a psychoanalyst, a full member of the International Psychoanalytic Association and past president of the Belgian Society of Psychoanalysis. He's a member of the editorial board of the International Journal of Psychoanalysis, the head of the Psychoanalytic Psychotherapy Unit for Personality Disorders (KLIPP) at the University Psychiatric Centre of the University of Leuven, Campus Kortenberg, associate professor at the Faculty of Medicine and the Faculty of Psychology at the University of Leuven, and head of the postgraduate training in psychoanalytic psychotherapy at the University of Leuven. He published and presented papers on Bion's work at several congresses and wrote *Reading Bion* in the teaching series of Routledge (series editor Dana Birksted-Breen).

Tom Wooldridge (Psy.D.) is Department Chair and Miner Research Chair at Golden Gate University and a candidate at the Psychoanalytic Institute of Northern California. He has published extensively on eating disorders. His article, "The Enigma of Ana: A Psychoanalytic Exploration of Pro-Anorexia Internet Forums," was published in the September 2014 issue of *The Journal of Infant, Child, and Adolescent Psychotherapy*.

INTRODUCTION

Afsaneh K. Alisobahni and Glenda J. Corstorphine

When asked the question: "What is O?" Bion responded by saying: "Everything we know nothing about" (Grotstein, 2015). An enigmatic statement from Bion that raises more questions than provides answers. What and how are we to think about "O"? *Can* we really think about "O"? Or do we simply let ourselves have an experience of "O"? What is this experience, and how do we talk about it?

If O is everything we know nothing about then O is everywhere, all around us. There are many things we know nothing about especially when it comes to the human psyche, our domain as psychoanalysts. We human beings are wondrously mysterious, and in some ways unknowable. At the same time, when one allows oneself to be open to experiencing, the hope is that the unknown will somehow become known, i.e. the unconscious made conscious. But O is not about knowing (at least not at first), it is about "being". It is about being and becoming.

Bion gives the following qualities to O:

> I shall use the sign O to denote that which is the ultimate reality represented by such terms as ultimate reality, absolute truth, the godhead, the infinite, the thing-in-itself. . . . It can be "become" but it cannot be "known". It is darkness and formlessness . . . but it enters the domain K when it has evolved to a point where it can be known through knowledge gained by experience, and formulated in terms derived from sensuous experience; its existence is conjectured phenomenologically.
>
> *(1970, p. 26)*

James S. Grotstein speaks of a "truth instinct" (2000a) which compels one to seek the truth, to move toward O. In the same way in his paper, "On Knowing What One Knows", Donald Marcus states that

> in Bion's opinion (1967b) the mind requires the truth the way the body requires food, water, and air for proper growth and development. Lack of truth leads to stunted mental growth and, in the worst case, to death of the personality. This truth, which we all

require, refers to the truth about our emotional experience and the environment in which we live.

(Marcus, 1997)

The first International Bion Conference was held in 1997, in Turin, Italy, to celebrate the centennial of W. R. Bion's birth (8 September 1897). The conference was intended to be more than celebratory or commemorative but was a forum to keep his ideas alive and to build on and elaborate continuing thoughts. This proved to be the beginning of a tradition. Colleagues continue to meet around the world from South America, North America and Europe. In keeping with the spirit of Bion's "experience in groups" and "learning from experience" each meeting proposes a theme and focus which emerges from the organizers' group process.

The 2014 Organizing Committee was fortunate to have poets, dancers, artists and musicians as members. The theme of the conference was conceived from the aesthetic sensibilities of the group process as well as the intellectual creativity of the members along with inspirations from James S. Grotstein in an advisory capacity. Linking O and truth together led the Organizing Committee of the 8th International Bion conference to offer *psych'O'analysis: explorations in truth* as the conference theme. The conference was held in Los Angeles, CA, October 2014 and reflected not only Los Angeles' reputation for artistic creativity but also unleashed the creative capacities of those who presented workshops and papers. Los Angeles is a city with a special place in Bion's history. He came to Los Angeles in 1968, in part to escape the perils of fame in London, and he lived and worked there until a few months before his death in Oxford in 1979. In those 12 years he made a deep impact on the Los Angeles psychoanalytic community through those he analyzed, supervised, and taught. During that time he also developed his ideas and wrote many of his important works, including *Attention and Interpretation* (1970), *Brazilian Lectures 1* (1973), *Brazilian Lectures 2* (1974), *A Memoir of the Future* (Part I, 1975 and Part II, 1977a), *Two Papers: The Grid and Caesura* (1977b), *Emotional Turbulence* (1977c), and *Seven Servants* (1977d).

According to Francesca Bion (1981, p. 4) her husband was profoundly moved by music, the arts and poetry. Bion's relationship to poetry was central to his life, for he felt that both poetry and the unconscious had the capacity to stimulate awe in its readers. Francesca noted that one of his unfinished projects was a compilation of poetry for psychoanalysts. She wrote:

> The pieces were to be selected, not for the practice of psychoanalytic virtuosity in giving so-called 'psychoanalytic' interpretations, but because a psychoanalytically expanded capacity would fit the reader to have a new experience, however familiar he might think he was with previous experience of the words.
>
> (Ibid.)

Having this in mind we started the conference with recitations of poetry, which we hoped would help facilitate the creation of forms of expressions or transformations in O. This was followed by a performance of an abridged short story by Samuel Beckett entitled "First Love" with actors Alan Mandel and Barbara Bain. Beckett's work was chosen for its unique perspective on primitive mental states, which in part reflects his therapy at the age of 27 with a young Wilfred Bion.

O reflects the ephemeral reality of the mind, unknowable in verbal language, and yet experienced in all aspects of internal and external reality. It is felt in all relationships, from that of the mother and infant pair, the analyst and patient, to the individual's emotional relation-ship to his or her self. Learning through experience stimulates the turbulence and change brought about through contact with truth and is the basis for mental growth. The Organizing Committee felt that movement and dance could stimulate and help participants experience an understanding of O in a non-verbal, sensorial way. Led by Donna Gunther, Soul Motion practitioner, conference participants dreamt together in dream alpha and practiced being without memory, desire, and understanding as they moved to music, individually and as a unit.

With the help of John Lundgren, a temporary learning community with its own dynamics was created by offering small and large group learning opportunities where facilitators called attention to deeper unconscious meanings that arose in the groups from collective efforts to grapple with O. The task of the Small Group, which met twice daily, was to review the experience of the conference in a more intimate face-to-face setting. Each Small Group func-tioned as a vehicle for digesting various vertices of the conference. Group learning emerged in the here-and-now process of the group's work.

The task of the Large Group was to study the experience of the conference, both what had happened and what was happening in the group. The Large Group offered an opportunity to discover those unseen and unknown ideas from the conference that emerged in the space created by the temporary and focused lens of the Large Group. Drawing upon and extend-ing the work done in the Small Groups and paper sessions, the conference members had the opportunity to share their experiences and reflect upon the emergence of the unseen truth or "O" that was available for experiencing and learning as the Large Group unfolded. The Large Groups, facilitated by group relations experts Edward Shapiro, John Lundgren, Vivian Gold, and Barnet Malin, gave voice to previously unspoken themes of the conference as they emerged in the group as a whole, particularly themes which expressed aspects of unseen truth. The facilitators attended to the group's struggle to articulate and explore emerging themes, and tracked anxieties that may have collectively been experienced during the group's work.

Above all, Bion believed in learning from experience. This dedication to open inquiry and learning focused on Bion's concept of O and the central place he gave it in clinical work. The aim of the conference was to provide an experience of a new psychoanalytic space in which to explore the mind, through theoretical, clinical and artistic presentations. All of these diverse perspectives were designed to give voice to the mystery and power of the experiential realm of O, as well as to the controversy and confusion it evokes.

The papers in this book are assembled from presentations at **psych'O'analysis: explo-rations in truth.** Authors in this collection offer their emphases of O through their own perspectives informed by lived experience in their cultural worlds and in their clinical work. Through their writing they provide the opportunity for the reader to move toward their own experience of O. We realize that to categorize O in subsections is antithetical to the essence of O itself and that each paper is unique in its own way. However, in reading the papers we found that multiple themes emerged, and we organized the book loosely based on those themes. The book is divided into what we saw as a close approximation to a shared theme of the papers in each section.

Everything we know nothing about

Bion in Los Angeles, 2014 was Jim Grotstein's last public appearance and presentation. Like the Apostle Paul, Jim always made it his life's mission to spread Bion's ideas around the world.

It was only appropriate that his final paper and farewell speech be at the 8th International Bion conference, where he was among colleagues and friends who shared his love and devotion to Bion. Jim got to hear, one last time, from his "disciples" and lifelong friends how revered and loved he was. Almost a year later, on 8 November 2015, at Jim's memorial, a colleague who continued in case consultation with Jim until his death, approached me (Afsaneh) and told me that Jim said he felt truly loved that day. This comment was the best reward for the Organizing Committee.

Jim was an analytic father to many of us, especially in Los Angeles. He was kind, generous, and encouraging. He took pride and enthusiasm in his supervisees' and students' achievements. It was only befitting that we honor and thank him for his generosity and his spirit. We benefitted from years of Jim's contagious love for psychoanalysis and Bion; as Joe Aguayo once said about him, "Jim did not come across a theory he didn't like".

Just like Bion, Grotstein's love for literature, poetry, history, philosophy, mythology and mysticism, and his immense knowledge of world religion, was the hallmark of his papers and books, and the reader couldn't help but get a sense that he was able to easily play with them and utilize them, in ways never imagined by the philosopher or poet. The paper he presented at *psych'O'analysis: explorations in truth* is no exception, although he was dealing with not only his own illness, but the illness of his beloved wife, Sue. When he spoke with us about his paper, we couldn't help but hear the excitement in his voice. We could see that though disease may have ravaged his body, his mind and spirit were very much intact and alive; his spirit continues to live through his writings and contributions.

The paper presented at the conference, *"BION CROSSES THE RUBICON: The Fateful Course – and Curse – of "O" in Psychoanalysis and the Furies Left in its Wake (2015)"*, is no exception from his previous papers. He teases us with the title that takes us all the way to the Rubicon, the river Julius Caesar once crossed, moves us up to the peak of Darien (Keats, 1816), and speaks of O in terms of "Keter" in the "Kabbalah". He writes of the many vertices of "O", a system of masks and "curtains" that "monitors the present from the vertex of the future", O's connection mysticism, and how Freud anticipated O when he brought up the concept of the libido.

In the same vein, Annie Reiner's paper, "O-Bion's Catch-22", addresses the controversial aspects of Bion's concept of O that he related to the "mystic". She debunks the notion that aspects of O, which are often associated with mysticism and the mystic, are synonymous with religion. She states that Bion's O has little to do with religion or deity. "Bion (1992) clearly views religion as an illusion (pp. 374, 379), while the mystical view is an experience of higher truth". In her paper, Reiner sheds light on the dilemma of the analyst concerning the concept of O and compares the paradox the analyst faces with the paradoxical reality in the novel *Catch-22*. While the unknowable reality is essential to clinical work, the reality of O continues to remain unknowable. Through a detailed case presentation, Reiner demonstrates how she navigates such terrain in the consulting room.

Bion's journey towards O

In "Wilfred Bion's Los Angeles Seminars (1967b): A Gateway to Contemporary Kleinian Technique", Joseph Aguayo starts by reviewing Bion's three periods of thought prior to 1967 at which point Bion gave his Los Angeles Seminars. He describes Bion's epistemological period in the early 1960s, the development of his foundational theories up to 1965 and to his expansion of the Kleinian paradigm by "positing a variable baby with a variable mother" (Britton, 2007). In the Los Angeles Seminars Aguayo describes the impact of Bion's sugges- tion that the analyst abandon "memory and desire". By that simple aphorism, Aguayo believes that Bion shifted the focus of clinical work from a "tendency to over-pathologize" the patient, to acknowledging the significance of the analyst's subjectivity and alpha function. From there he takes the reader through the gateway to contemporary Kleinian technique and shows us how Bion's clinical method has impacted current psychoanalytic practice.

Transformation and O

Transformation in O, along with "negative capability" allows the analyst to abandon what is known, facilitating surrender to the unknown, being and experiencing reality as it appears. The authors in this section explore different aspects of clinical work that lead to transforma- tion in O, from the relationship of catastrophic change and container/contained, abandon- ment of memory, desire and understanding, and negative capability, to name a few.

In his paper, "Between Emotion and Evolution", Jeffrey L. Eaton posits that not only does transformation in O call for "a capacity to surrender of the self as knower", but also the need on the part of the analyst to welcome "an unknown evolution". If the analyst allows for this unknown evolution, she can experience a "sudden shift in perception" and the complexity of the analytic field arises. Eschewing memory, desire and understanding involves an under- standing and appreciation of the relationship between observation and intuition which Eaton suggests is the counterpart to emotion and evolution. As important a part emotion plays in learning from experience, it is the "unknown evolution" that plays the central role in the unfolding of O. He then shares his own process of eschewing memory and desire before he starts an analytic session.

In "Authentic Pleasure", Rezze and Braga write about the often neglected and at times frowned upon aspects of the human experience, pleasure. They write "We, analysts, feel com- fortable with pain and suffering, but only a few of us know what to do when authentic pleasure emerges". They start the paper with four examples of lived "authentic pleasures" in personal life as well as in the clinical setting. Authentic pleasure emerges when the awareness of a shared experience between the patient and the analyst is accompanied by "joy and satis- faction". From a theoretical perspective, they link the satisfactory aspects of authentic pleasure to Bion's model of conception which arises when a preconception is met with its realiza- tion. They then elaborate on authentic pleasure from different vertices. Although authentic pleasure is familiar to most analysts, they propose a new way of thinking about it, one that encompasses both Freud's and Bion's theories. They go on to discuss authentic pleasure as it is experienced in passionate love, awe, and aesthetic pleasure. This paper offers a fresh way of looking at transformation in O, transformation from O to K, and being at one with awe which ultimately leads to mental growth.

Adriana Salvitti, in "Writing and Transmission in Bion: Group Model, Pictorial Model and Transformation in "O" Model", poses the question: How does the analyst communicate "non-neurotic" patients' experiences through writing when representational and verbal lan- guage fail to capture archaic experiences including "fragmentation, emptiness and psychic death"? In Bion's writing he deliberately used language in such a way that the reader's emo- tional experience and expectations in the act of reading the text contribute to the meaning of the text for the reader. In focusing on three texts of Bion's, *Experiences in Groups* (1961),

Catastrophic Change (1966), and the "Commentary" in *Second Thoughts* (1967b), she proposes three models of "transmission", the "Group model", the "Pictorial model", and the "Transformation in O model".

In her paper, "Tropisms At-one-ment and Mental Growth", Lia Pistiner offers a new hypothesis that with a containing object capable of receiving the infant's projective identification through her reverie and a potential space, tropisms have the capacity of being transformed into emotional links L, H, and K. Pistiner posits that tropisms are connected to O as they need to be "rescued from the infinite formless void" and related to emotional links. She conjectures that a patient's tropisms can be redirected towards growth and development of a mind and transformed into L, H, and K links. Through a clinical example she demonstrates how a patient, who had a depressed mother and an absent father, created an autistic like barrier to communication and projective identification. She suggests that by providing a potential space (Winnicott, 1971, p. 41) and by playing an active role in preventing the patient's autistic defenses, the analyst can invite the patient to play and dream and help him create a subjective self and "an inner place where to feel that one exists and is real".

Faith and O

Faith and O, gives the reader a beginning sense of Bion as the mystic. Bion used the term faith in a non-religious sense using it more as a way to indicate faith in the psychoanalytical process, of growth and openness to O. Keri Cohen, in "Reciprocal Kindling, Emergent Life: Bion's Faith in O, in Search of Emotional Truth", suggests that the process of reciprocal kindling helps aid repair of the mind through a kinetic emotional feeling signal between two people. She posits that, guided by Faith in O, reciprocal kindling transfers a sense of comfort and healing between two life forces, furthering inner movement. She gives examples of "feeling the truth of O" and demonstrates how this non-verbal process leads to emotional growth and healing.

In "Stormy Navigation With Our 'Secret Companion' of Incredulity Towards Faith in 'O'" Monica Horovitz invites us to travel with her as she beautifully describes a case where, by drawing on "negative capability", she is able to face the excess of the patient's pain and claim the right to the need to forget. This helps her, together with her patient, to transform the monstrous sensory material that is both seen and heard into a monstrosity within the transference, opening up the hope of encountering the truth of the emotions rejected by the saturation of the senses.

Catastrophe, catastrophic change, and O

How does catastrophe and catastrophic change present itself in psychoanalysis and what is the analyst supposed to do with it? In this section the authors, each in their own style, shed some light on the issue by inviting us into their consulting rooms and sharing not only their experience of their patients but also their own experience of catastrophe and catastrophic change.

In "Beyond the Spectrum: Catastrophic Change, Fear of Breakdown and the Unrepressed Unconscious", Avner Bergstein poses the question whether the total experience of the patient is communicable through verbal discourse. While a narrow part of the patient's experience may be communicable verbally, the psychoanalytic encounter compels us to go beyond that narrow sphere, to hear, observe, and feel the patient's experience through a variety of vertices.

Through a detailed clinical case Bergstein shares the emergence of the patient's psychotic parts, as he moves to the couch, and describes the analyst's own despair and difficulty of containing the patient's fragmented selves. He then poses the question whether this experience, the patient's and the analyst's, is a breakdown or a breakthrough . . . is it a catastrophe or a caesura?

Much attention has been given to symbolization by Klein and her view of the capacity for symbolization belonging to the sphere of the depressive position. Alessandro Bruni writes about "The Girl Who Gave Me a Kiss on the Finger: How the Concrete and the Abstract Mix in Psychotic Symbolization". Starting from clinical material belonging to a 25-year-old schizophrenic patient, Bruni explores the aspects of psychotic "symbolization", as Bion views it, the capacity for abstraction and concretization. Bruni argues that while a psychotic patient may or may not be able to perceive the common meaning of a symbol, the psychotic part of the personality's perception of a sign and subsequent symbol formation that is abstracted by the patient does convey important meaning. Bruni believes this is to be explored and heard by the analyst according to and developing Bion's point of view on the matter.

In her paper "Thinking, Knowing, not Knowing, No Mind", Mary E. Sonntag discusses how trauma and how the absence of a container hinders the ability of the infant's capacity to think and symbolize. Through a case discussion of an articulate, intelligent woman, Sonntag discusses the patient's appearance of symbolization and seeming ability to learn from experience as masking the psychotic part of her personality. In addition to Bion's K and -K link, Sonntag speaks of a third possibility: no link, total absence. In the absence of a containing object, the intersubjective field is filled and identified with the absence. Through this clinical case she takes the reader on a journey of how and when the psychotic part of the personality enters into the intersubjective space, thereby opening the possibility of a different form of object relation and inviting the patient to learn from experience.

In "Dreams, Transformations and Hope" Jani Santamaría Linares writes about a difficult to reach adolescent who, at the beginning of treatment, was unable to make use of the analysis or dream any waking or sleeping dreams. Moving through choppy waters, dreams began to slowly emerge and through a catastrophic enactment the analyst was able to experience and therefore understand her patient's deepest traumas. Through the use of reverie, gathering her patient's split off parts, and containing deep anxieties the analyst began to "dream the patient into being" (Levine, 2015). This led to lasting transformation in both the patient and analyst.

Caesura and O

In his book *Two Papers*, Bion (1977b) quotes Martin Buber in *I and Thou* . . . "in his mother's womb man knows the universe and forgets it at birth". He later uses the "dramatic episode of birth" as a model to understand the challenges of a patient's movement from one state of the mind to another. He uses the analogy of the game of Snakes and Ladders, where a move in one direction leads him to the head of the snake and another as to help him get to his goal which "he may also regret", Bion then writes: "In either situation the choice that the patient makes compels readjustment to the consequences. Much then depends on the extent to which he is a victim of self-hatred or self-love". The authors in this section expand on the concept of caesura and the aftermath of the readjustments in their patient's lives. Transformation from K to O is possible when the analyst occupies the transitive space of being a psychoanalyst to becoming a psychoanalyst, the transitive space of knowing the universe and losing it.

In his paper, "Increased Hypnagogic States, Subthalamic Fears and Caesura", Arnaldo Chuster explores the hypnagogic state, the state where a person is about to go to sleep, and hypnopompic state, the state when he is about to wake up. Through mythology and clinical examples, Chuster demonstrates that in the prolonged hypnagogic or hypnopompic states, the patient's deepest fears, the sub-thalamic fears that he has suppressed in the deepest part of his unconscious, surface, sometimes in the form of mystical, super natural, ghost-like images. In the transitive caesura of awake/sleep space, when the patient has access to the sub-thalamic fear, a sense of terror that brings on primitive mental states causes internal splits and fragmentation. Chester concludes that by helping the patient transition to using his imagination, the patient ultimately makes the transformation from K to O.

Listening to Bion's lecture on *Caesura* from the 1975 recording, Julie Michael McCaig suggests that the listener has a completely different experience between hearing Bion speak and reading the text. She calls this "embodied speech", a speech in which Bion not only communicated his thoughts and ideas about Caesura, but also the "music and poetry of his mind as he thinks about physical and psychological birth".

In her paper, "Careful Emptiness and Improvisational Listening in Psychoanalytic Education: Elements of Bion's 1975 Recorded Caesura Lecture Not Contained in the Printed Version", she invites the reader to understand the Perinatal/primordial States of Mind (PSoM), that evoke memories of intrauterine life, forged in the infant just before the "pause" of birth. Listening to Bion's "Caesura" lecture, invites analysts to trust his/her own unconscious improvisational capacity to listen to gaps and pauses reminiscent of perinatal states of mind which may help promote a transformation of K to O, thereby a "language of achievement" becomes possible.

In his paper, "Caesuras and Dis-caesuras: Causality, Morality and Envy", Renato Trachtenberg elaborates on Bion's concept of caesura from the vertex of complexity in the spectral model. He states that some problems linked to the psychotic part of personality such as causality, morality, and envy, are important obstacles for the continuity and transience among different mental states and among different temporal states in the analyst or in his (her) patient. When this happens, the concept of dis-caesuras, instead of rigid caesuras or "impressive caesuras" (Freud, 1926), is useful because the absence of continuity and transience implies the impossibility of caesura. Trachtenberg believes there is no need to resort to reductionistic characterizations such as psychotic, envious, or fanatical in order to understand the difficult to reach patient. He posits that the analyst needs to focus on the fluidity or lack thereof in the caesura between the different mental states and how they are linked. In addition, he says, the analyst must tolerate the movement and maintain the transitory nature of each session.

Carmen C. Mion uses Bion's model of caesura as a transparent mirror in clinical situations in traumatic area in which the patient's and analyst's transformation in β elements doesn't belong to the verbal realm, but to transformation of O in hallucinations that are visual, auditory, psychosomatic, somatopsychotic, as well as other forms. In her paper "Conjectures about Dreams, Memories and Caesura", Mion investigates the analyst's dilemma of working with traumatized patients. In pain, the patient is experiencing nameless dread, yet the slightest attempt at putting it to words by the analyst not only doesn't provide relief for the patient, it only leads to further fragmentation and a sense of impending catastrophe. She suggests that when the patient's emotions are bereft of any psychic representations the analyst must navigate and cross the caesuras between different psychic dimensions while being aware of its infiniteness. She proposes the analyst through her/his capacity for reverie with a "mind in transit" is able to contain and dream the unthinkable terror and the unrepresentable for the patient helping the patient develop the capacity to dream.

Creativity and O

Characteristics of the creative individual include a high level of effective intelligence, an openness to experience, freedom from crippling restraints and impoverishing inhibitions, aesthetic sensitivity, cognitive flexibility, independence in thought and action, high level of creative energy, and an unquestioning commitment to creative endeavor (MacKinnon, 1962). Bion encouraged his readers to make use of his ideas by employing the characteristics of creativity. In the following papers, the authors have done just that through experiences with actors, music, poetry, and movement.

Claudio Castelo Filho takes us to the frontier of madness in "On the Verge of 'Madness': Creativity and the Fear of Insanity", by describing that during a session, he has a vision that lasts a few seconds in which he sees a man pass between himself and his patient. This vision has the quality of a real fact and it is perceived while it is happening as an actual event. He elaborates how this vision afforded the capacity of a realization and the evolution of the situation that was presented in the session. From this experience, he writes about a state of mind that is essential for the development of creative activities and for the expansion of the capacity of thinking.

Using provocative lyrics, written by Pink Floyd's Roger Waters, and quoting excerpts from Virgil's *Aeneid*, Michael Ian Paul illustrates his work with a patient who was numb and numbing. In "Selective Precise Induction of Numbing Deadening Narcosis by Primitive Superego Sources: A Method of Attacking Links by Severe Compromise of Attention", he takes us on a journey of "being one with O" to transformation from O to K in order to communicate the patient's submerged and unwanted emotions.

Deborah Sherman's paper, "Being in the Thought-Flow: Authentic Movement and Bion's 'O'", uses her experience in Authentic Movement to see her "mind in the movements" and to see her thoughts as movements of her mind. She illustrates how this experience opened the mental and psychic space between analyst and patient and helped the analyst to "unfreeze", and begin to move psychically which enabled her to think again.

Alan Michael Karbelnig, in "'The Analyst Is Present': Viewing the Psychoanalytic Process as Performance Art", views the psychoanalytic process as performance art by highlighting Bion's recommendation that psychoanalysts' work "free of memory and desire", and posits that psychoanalysts' work may be likened to performance artists in that they create transformative experiences. He believes, like actors, they use their bodies as instruments, they face each session like painters face the blank canvas or writers the blank page. Continuing in the realm of performance art, Guelfo Margherita in "A Memoir of the Future: Reading, Proof and Enactment" relates an original approach to the study of *A Memoir of the Future* (Bion, 1979b) through a group experience of reading, re-writing, and enacting their play. He writes about the experience that he and his colleagues created illuminating the depth otherwise precluded in the linear understanding of individual reading.

Freud, Klein, Winnicott, Lacan, and O

In expanding his theory of thinking Bion delved into philosophy, mathematics, and even physics. Yet, except for Freud and Klein, he hardly referenced other psychoanalytic thinkers who were his contemporaries, some interested in the same areas as he. People new to Bion are tempted, yet discouraged, to find parallels with his concepts in the theorists and analysts with whom they are familiar. The intolerance to the unknown makes that prospect safer and less anxiety provoking. It is only after tolerating this anxiety that one appreciates Bion's genius. This section is the reward for such toleration for reader and author alike.

These authors have expanded and elaborated on Bion's theory of thinking, offering new ideas built on Bion's, as well as comparing and contrasting the giants who were contemporaries who, as far as we know, never collaborated with him, most notably, Lacan and Winnicott. The authors in this section offer a comprehensive elaboration on concepts such as truth, regression, primitive mental states, and considerations in the oedipal level of organization. To borrow from Bion, the clinician has a chance of a "binocular vision" when addressing similar questions.

In "Not O and Not K. Then What is the Navel of the Truth?" Andrea Bocchiola explores the concept of O from the vertex of Freud's concept of the navel of the dream. In *The Interpretation of Dreams* (Freud, 1900, p. 111) Freud speaks of a spot in the dream that is impenetrable, "a navel, as it were, that is its point of contact with the unknown". Bocchiola draws the reader's attention to the overlap of Bion's concept of O, Freud's navel of the dream, and Lacan's concept of the Real (Lacan, 1973). By examining the very first encounter of the mouth and the breast, Bocchiola explores the meaning of O from a genealogic and semiotic point of view.

In his paper, "The Primitive Somatopsychic Roots of Gender Formation, Intimacy and the Development of Psyche with Implications for Psychoanalytic Technique", James Gooch outlines a model of mind of psychic development which grows from intimate and passionate interpersonal and intrapsychic relationships. He begins by outlining normal parental functioning and highlights both the mother and father functions. He emphasizes the parental couple as a genitally bonded, new psychophysiological unit which attains a particular suitability to perform vital functions for the baby.

In speaking about mature sado-masochism and mature bisexuality Gooch advances Freud's ideas found in *The Economic Problems of Masochism* (Freud, 1924). He suggests that immature feminine masochism and immature masculine sadism are contained by the discovery and evolution of the conjugation of mature femininity and mature masculinity, which are creative and nurturing. He believes that the growth of this mature conjugation of femininity and masculinity is essential for authentic growth and creativity.

He then applies these ideas to psychoanalytic technique highlighting use of The Grid, interpretation, and reverie. He points out that the analyst needs to be under the shelter of the mature internal couple, in generative communication with each other, in relationship to the psychoanalytic objects being experienced in the session. The patient's parental alpha function is attuned to the immature consciousness in the patient. This attuned, empathic experience allows for psychical growth in both analyst and analysand. He states clearly that the internal mature parental couple in the analyst is the psychoanalyst's instrument in tending to and analyzing the pathologic and pathogenic aspects of our patients.

In "Lost to Repetition: Hysteria From Perspectives of Bion, Lacan and Green" Avedis Panajian sheds light on the challenges faced by the psychoanalyst working with the hysteric. Panajian incorporates three points of view proposed by Bion, Lacan, and Green to work with a difficult to reach, hysteric woman. He takes Andre Green's criticism of contemporary psychoanalysis and its de-emphasis on the Oedipal level of organization, and thereby a de-sexualization of psychoanalysis to heart. In this way he places hysteria in the realm of gender identity and sexuality by integrating the pre-oedipal dyadic organization of the personality with Oedipal struggles. He accomplishes this feat partly by utilizing models of the mind proposed by Bion, Lacan, and Green with a great deal of fluidity. He addresses his patient's psychic pain and her attempt to avert the "fact of the pain" (Bion, 1970, p. 19) by utilizing Bion's "reversible perspective" and "binocular vision". With the help of the analyst's alpha function to "suffer the pain", the patient reaches a necessary developmental task. A key moment in the treatment occurred when the analyst was able to dream with the patient and experience a sense of at-one-ment with the patient. In this rich clinical paper, Panajian elucidates the invaluable insights and contributions of these theorists into the psychoanalytic approach to this clinical situation.

Truthfulness and lack thereof on the way to "O", as it can be intuited, is experienced and lived in real analysis. In his paper, "Truth, Beauty, Reality", Paulo Cesar Sandler draws on the antithetical pairs, Untruth, Ugliness, Hallucinosis, as inescapable experiences getting in the way of Truth, Beauty, Reality.

Bion and Winnicott influenced psychoanalysis in a seminal way. In his paper, "Regression in the Work of Bion and Winnicott", Rudi Vermote highlights some similarities and differences between the theoretical work and technique of both authors, specifically the place of regression in their work. Through a clinical vignette, Vermote discusses Bion's and Winnicott's approaches to regression. Regression for Winnicott is that zone close to the incommunicado self and a sacred space not to be disturbed. Bion conceptualized the link between regression and transformations. While thinking, for Bion, is linked with frustration tolerance, for Winnicott it is the result of playing. Vermote then elaborates on the effect of regression on facilitating a transformation in Knowledge and a transformation in O.

Björn Salomonsson's paper "Was Freud a Bionian? Perspectives from Parent-Infant Psychoanalytic Treatments" starts with a detailed clinical vignette of a mother and infant dyad. The mother has a hard time soothing the baby and the baby avoids eye contact with her mother. In this paper he illustrates his clinical work with infants and mothers. Through a careful reading of Freud's *The Project for a Scientific Psychology* (1895/1950) Salomonsson reintroduces the reader to Freud's views on babies, i.e. the baby's ambivalence arising when he realizes that the "first hostile object is also the first satisfying object" and soon to be discovered "fellow human-being". By going back to the German origin of the text, Salomonsson replaces "fellow human-being" with "neighbor" making the baby's experience of rage, distress, hostility, and gratitude an intersubjective one. Salomonsson observes that Freud intuited the baby's internal world and subjective experience. He argues that this is very close to the way Bion formulated a baby's experience and internal world.

O in the consulting room

Bion's theoretical formulations come from and return to the consulting room. In *Transformations* Bion stated:

> I shall . . . assume that the material provided by the analytic session is significant for its being the patient's view (representation) of certain facts which are the origin (O) of his reaction. . . . [I]n practice this means that I shall regard only those aspects of the patient's behavior which are significant as representing his view of O.
>
> *(1965, p. 15)*

and:

> No one can ever know what happens in the analytic session, the thing-in-itself, O; we can only speak of what the analyst or patient feels happens, his emotional experience that which I denote by T.
>
> *(1965, p. 33)*

The following clinical papers illustrate how the authors have applied Bion's theory to clinical practice.

Darcy Portolese in "From Knowing to Becoming and from an Informed Mind to a Nourished Mind" writes about how the attitudes and activities of analysts, through their art and their methods, make it possible to generate vital contents and developments that remain in a latent state and are unknown. The analyst seeks to detect and know the contents of the most archaic areas of the mind. He presents two cases which illustrate while in contact with this unknown, analysts can experience a certain feeling of fragility in the midst of doubts and uncertainties. He highlights that the emphasis in analysis is toward making contact with areas that are undifferentiated, incomprehensible, and ineffable, which represent the other side of caesura. The objective becomes to attain access to what Bion (1965) called "O", ultimate truth.

In "Catastrophe and Faith in Anorexia Nervosa", Tom Wooldridge states: "When working with anorexic patients, one has the sense that something catastrophic has happened". He explores the nature of the original catastrophe in patients with anorexia nervosa, discussing how the patient survives it and what drastic compromises have to be made for the patient to carry on. He illustrates what is needed for something new to take root and grow.

Majlis Winberg Salomonsson asks what makes an interpretation meaningful to the patient? In her paper, "From a Talking Hole to a Container for Growth", she refers to an analysis with a 15-year-old girl, where she discusses her work in terms of psychic space. She refers to Bion's thoughts concerning disintegration and integration elements, and the dynamic relationship between container and contained.

In "Penelope's Suitors: From Reality to Play", Ester Hadassa Sandler reports the analysis of a young girl who was able to "pour out" dream thoughts, but was not able to use them for thinking and dreaming, therefore, living in a sort of bare and raw reality, deprived of the mediating elements of dream and fantasy. She describes, in particular, the achievement of a sense of self-existence and separated-ness as a singular individual, who developed a mind of her own and was ultimately able to connect and relate to other human beings in a deep and meaningful way.

Anie Stürmer's paper, "Understanding the Reversal of the Alpha Function Through a Case", elucidates our understanding of the reversal of alpha function by analyzing the consequences of a patient's emotional development where the capacity of maternal reverie is absent. The alpha function of the therapist apprehends this failure, due to the reversal of alpha function. She discusses the Oedipal configuration and the predominant invariance of the individual relationships.

Epilogue

To close the conference the Organizing Committee sought to provide a forum in which to process the conference experience. Panelists were asked to comment on their impressions of the conference. Avner Bergstein, Gisele de Mattos Brito, Alessandro Bruni, and Nanci Carter graciously invited us into their thoughts and experiences.

References

Bion, F. (1981). Memorial meeting for Dr. Wilfred Bion. *International Review of Psycho Analysis* 8: 3–14.
Bion, W.R. (1961). *Experiences in Groups*. London: Tavistock.
Bion, W.R. (1965). *Transformations*. London: Heinemann.
Bion, W.R (1966). Catastrophic change. *Bulletin of the British Psychoanalytical Society* 5.
Bion, W.R. (1967a). *Second Thoughts*. London: William Heinemann. [Reprinted London: Karnac, 1984].
Bion, W.R. (1967b). Notes on memory and desire. *Psycho-analytic Forum* 2: 271–280.
Bion, W.R. (1970). *Attention and Interpretation*. London: Tavistock Publications. [Reprinted London: Karnac, 1984. Reprinted in *Seven Servants*, 1977d].
Bion, W.R. (1973). *Bion's Brazilian Lectures 1*. Rio de Janeiro: Imago Editora. [Reprinted in one volume London: Karnac Books, 1990].
Bion, W.R. (1974). *Bion's Brazilian Lectures 2*. Rio de Janeiro: Imago Editora. [Reprinted in one volume London: Karnac Books, 1990].
Bion, W.R. (1975). *A Memoir of the Future, Book 1 The Dream*. Rio de Janeiro: Imago Editora. [Reprinted in one volume with Books 2 and 3 and "The Key" London: Karnac Books, 1991].
Bion, W.R. (1977a). *A Memoir of the Future, Book 2 The Past Presented*. Rio de Janeiro: Imago Editora. [Reprinted in one volume with Books 1 and 3 and "The Key" London: Karnac Books, 1991].
Bion, W.R. (1977b). *Two Papers: The Grid and Caesura*. Rio de Janeiro: Imago Editora. [Reprinted London: Karnac, 1989].
Bion, W.R. (1977c). Emotional turbulence. In *Borderline Personality Disorders*. New York: International University Press. [Reprinted in Clinical Seminars and Four Papers, 1987]. [Reprinted in Clinical Seminars and Other Works. London: Karnac Books, 1994].
Bion, W.R. (1977d). *Seven Servants*. New York: Jason Aronson Inc. (includes Elements of Psychoanalysis, Learning from Experience, Transformations, Attention and Interpretation).
Bion, W.R. (1979). *A Memoir of the Future, Book 3 the Dawn of Oblivion*. Perthshire: Clunie Press [Reprinted in one volume with Books 1 and 2 and "The Key" London: Karnac, 1991].
Bion, W.R. (1991). *Cogitations*. Ed. Francesca Bion. London: Karnac.
Britton, R. (2007). The Baby and the Bathwater. Unpublished.
Freud, S. (1895). The project for a scientific psychology. *S.E.* 1: 283–294. London: Hogarth.
Freud, S. (1900). The interpretation of dreams. *S.E.* 5: 339–610. London: Hogarth.
Freud, S. (1924). The economic problem of masochism. *S.E.* 19: 159–173. London: Hogarth.
Freud, S. (1926). Inhibitions, symptoms and anxiety. *S.E.* 20: 138. London: Hogarth Press.
Grotstein, J. (2000a). *Who Is the Dreamer Who Dreams the Dream?: A Study of Psychic Presences*. Relational Perspectives Book Series (Book 19). New York: Routledge.
Grotstein, J. (2015). Bion crosses the Rubicon: The fateful course – and curse – of "O" in psychoanalysis and the furies and the furies left in its wake. In A. Reiner (Ed.), *Of Things Invisible to Mortal Sight: Celebrating the Work of James Grotstein*. London: Karnac.
Keats, J. (1816). On first looking into Chapman's Homer. In A. Allison, H. Barrows, C. Blake, A. Carr, A. Eastman and H. English Jr. (Eds.), *The Norton Anthology of Poetry: Third Edition*, p. 648 (1970). New York, London: W.W. Norton & Company.
Lacan, J. (1973). *The Four Fundamental Concepts of Psycho-Analysis*. London: Karnac. [Sééminaire XI. Les quatre concepts fondamentaux de la psychanalyse. Paris : Ed. de Seuil, 1973].
Levine, H. (2015). Dreaming the patient into being: A methodology for clinical seminars. In M. Harris Williams (Ed.), *Teaching Bion*. London: Karnac.
MacKinnon, D.W. (1962). What makes a person creative?, *Saturday Review of Literature* XLV: 6.
Marcus, D. (1997). On knowing what one knows. *Psychoanalytic Quarterly* 66: 219–241.
Winnicott, D.W. (1971). *Playing and Reality*. London: Tavistock Publications Ltd.

SECTION I

Everything we know nothing about

1

BION CROSSES THE RUBICON

The fateful course – and curse – of "O" in psychoanalysis and the Furies left in its wake[1]

James S. Grotstein

> The rising world of waters dark and deep
> Won from the void and formless infinite.
>
> *– John Milton (Paradise Lost)*

> I am not interpreting what Milton says
> but using it to represent O.
>
> *– (Bion, 1965, p. 151)*

Caveat

This contribution, as the title suggests, deals in part with Bion's change both in geographic location and, more saliently, in his theoretical stance in psychoanalytic theory and practice. He indeed underwent a "sea change" on both accounts, yet it can be argued parenthetically that his first published formal psychoanalytic contribution, "the Imaginary Twin" (Bion, 1950), convincingly reveals an unusual, complex, and unusually creative mind that precociously adumbrated a major feature of future psychoanalytic practice, that of internal psychic twins in "the here and now". His immediately subsequent so-called "Kleinian Bion" publications, in my opinion, arguably amply demonstrate "late Bion". Already one could realise that this was no ordinary Kleinian just presenting his institute graduating paper.

Rumour in addition to some substantiated truth strongly suggest that he was being subjected to gradually increasing isolation by his colleagues at the British Psychoanalytical Society because of the "mystical" nature of his new ideas, ideas which, according to many of its members, bordered on the occult. *I* believe that Bion's introduction of the letter/word "O" was critical in this reaction. I refer to the mystique of the Hebrew letter א ("aleph", Borjes, 1949) or to the epicenter of Descartes' famous chart. In very recent times, however, matters have begun to change. A significant number of the members of the British Psychoanalytical Society have now shown an amicable curiosity and positive interest in "late Bion", as his "mystical works" are called (Aguayo, 2014).

> *The old order changeth/yielding place to new,*
>   *And God fulfils Himself in many ways/lest one good custom should corrupt the world.*
>   – Alfred Lord Tennyson, Locksley Hall

Introduction

Bion's (1965, 1970) discovery of O seemed to fit in with his mathematical zeal to find unsaturated models to use in formulating and expounding some of his other similar contributions (e.g. alpha-function) that would short-cut their expedition to yet undiscovered objects of knowledge. His own first acknowledged adumbration of it occurs in his "Notes on Memory and Desire" (Bion 1967b). "O" was first published in *Transformations* in (Bion, 1965, p. 13) and then in *Attention and Interpretation* in (Bion, 1970, p. 14 et al.). As soon as it was published, it quickly attracted notice as one of the principal indicators of Bion's apparently allegedly sudden departure from traditional Kleinian thinking and his coeval immersion in mysticism and its corresponding connection with the occult. What Bion had probably been up to was taking on the task, similar to Martin Luther long before him, of obsolescing a then prevailing dogma (positivistic science, in Klein's case) that he believed was unsuitable and inapplicable for psychoanalysis. Bion's espousal of *complexity* and *emergence* theory framed in the context of what appeared to be close to inter-subjectivism went a long way in neutralising Freud's and Klein's critics as well as his own; although he and his followers and evaluators failed to note it.

What *is* O?

> Everything we know *nothing* about
>   – *(W.R. Bion)*

O is a mathematical sign of ancient Greek origin to which Bion assigned many seemingly disparate roles and functions although united by their mystery, ominousness, and premonitory terror. He does not consider it a *mental* phenomenon per se, however, because his conception and use of O's functions restrict it to the pre-mental or never achieved mentalisable state; thus, its potential for terror. Yet he does seem to regard the *analytic experience* itself as both mental (K) as well as non-mental (O). When Robert Caper asked Bion to define O, he answered: "Everything we know *nothing* about" (personal communication). It is, at one extreme, the all but inert backdrop in the scenery of our internal *and* external landscapes, but at the other extreme, it can be Poseidon's descendant, the catastrophic "god" of disruption and tumultuous change, the catastrophes of Troy, Sodom and Gomorrah, the numerous allusions to epidemics ("pollutions" in classical literature), and the frequent mention of the Furies, would seem to warrant inclusion as analogues of O.

Unmasking the unmaskable O

To my mind, O is treated by Bion as being a normal component of a system of masks which alert the personality of a forthcoming danger, but which is paradoxically perceived by the personality as the danger itself. Bion (1965) refers to *dreaming* as a *"curtain of illusion"*. The "curtain" of dreaming monitors the *past* while O monitors the *present* from the vertex of the *future* ("as in Memoirs of the Future"). Thus, dreaming and O constitute a binary-oppositional structure functioning under the guidance of adaptation. As I shall discuss later, I believe that O correspondingly functions in a binary-oppositional relationship with dreaming, constituting the Unknown about to spring invasively from the experiences from the past – and beta-elements (transformed immanently from O), originating in an internally located O (activated Plato's Ideal Forms and Kant's noumena) about to spring from behind the forthcoming future. Both together, Bion suggests, are poised collaborative to mediate the opposition between the Unconscious and Consciousness that is necessary for mental functioning.

Bion appends the following qualities to O:

> I shall use the sign O to denote that which is the ultimate reality represented by such terms as ultimate reality, absolute truth, the godhead, the infinite, the thing-in-itself. . . . It can be "become" but it cannot be "known". It is darkness and formlessness . . . but it enters the domain K when it has evolved to a point where it can be known through knowledge gained by experience, and formulated in terms derived from sensuous experience; its existence is conjectured phenomenologically.
>
> *(1970, p. 26)*

Bion also states in regard to O:

> Absolute Truth, Ultimate Reality, pre-conception (Plato's Ideal Forms), beta-element (Kant's thing-in-itself), infinity, ineffable, inscrutable, utterly unknowable, cannot be related to (objectified or subjectified), always impersonal, and curiously bipolar. O is not a mental phenomenon, nor is it an apparition; it is only the experience of the patient and the analyst, each singly, and that of the session collectively. In analysis the patient's speech and behavior are all that comprise O and constitute all that the analyst should interpret. It cannot be known, one can only *be* it. It is impersonal. The emotional situation between the analysand and the analyst constitutes . . . "the intersection of an evolving O with another evolving O" (1970, p. 118).
>
> *(1970, italics added by author)*

The collective disciplines of O

What was difficult to see in Bion's work was that he was: placing a "grid of discovery" (not to be confused with his more well-known "Grid") which was to encompass salient elements of Western wisdom from its greatest cultural dispersal and from its most ancient times and integrate them into an inchoate structure not unlike a cosmic jigsaw puzzle, incomplete but yet demonstrating a hint of a more nearly full future structure. This process of integration involved connecting the elements of cosmology, mysticism, religion, rituals, logic, philosophy, history, mythology, poetry, literature, astronomy, and philosophy from ancient to modern cultures and uniting them into a complex tapestry of meaning. Bion's conception of O became the arch symbol for the collective mystique that wrapped itself around the elements of this collective mystery of knowing and being known.

Bion conceived of O as an abstraction to use for leveraging larger models of data and thoughts about which the patient is associating ($Tp\alpha$), which then become transformed by the analyst's alpha-function from $Ta\alpha$ to $Ta\beta$. The two poles of the pair's respective bipolar

O thereupon experience the development of a third manifestation of O, the T of the session itself. O thus becomes the cryptic source and theme, in terms of its derivatives of the analytic session. *O functions by becoming a stimulus for an object by imprinting itself as a sense impression on the latter's sensory-emotional frontier (contact-barrier) as it intersects it. It is the impression that O imprints or forges on or within us that matters.* This principle underlies the over-arching importance that is assigned to *how the patient autochthonously (natively) actively*, not just *passively, receives, modifies, transmogrifies, and encodes (transforms, encrypts)*, the object stimulus.

The encoding or encryption process occurs as the patient furnishes inherent as well as acquired pre-conceptions from its own gallery in the Ideal Forms in the platonic section of the mind, and in the noumena of the Kantian section (Bion, 1965, p. 138). Put another way, the subject's experiencing of an O event emanating from an object (the object as O) has the effect of actualising or evoking images already internal to the subject as *its* O. *It is as if the object is a ventriloquist "speaking" to the subject in the latter's own imagistic language.*

The connection between O and mysticism

Bion invoked O as a simple theoretical idea, one that could represent a vast array of self↔object configurations and relationships. It constitutes the background floor of the Grid and occupies its container function. It constitutes a caesura between Cs. and the Ucs. It characteristically occupies a state of neutrality until activated by emotional disruption. Its major functions are *expectation and menacing announcement of future disruptions*, as opposed to the functions of *dreaming*, to which Bion assigns the task of *mediating the present emanating from the past* ("Curtain of Illusion", Bion, 1965, p. 147) (vide supra).

O is also associated with godhead, Absolute Truth, and Ultimate Reality. Godhead crystallises the concept of "who" (?)/which is in ineffable and numinous charge of the infinite domain of the Absolute Truth about Ultimate Reality. Bion was very interested in what he believed was a religious instinct (personal communication). He was also very interested in mysticism, the *Kabbalah*, and other religious studies.

In order to understand the connection between mysticism and the unconscious, one must consider the combined interrelations of the functions of (a) the *part-object* (Freud), (b) O (Bion), (c) the operative forces of the *infinities* (Bion) and the *symmetry/asymmetries* (Matte Blanco, 1975) of the Unconscious, and (d) beta-elements. The part-object may be conceived as another name for beta-element, an inchoate entity has been created by a disruptive stimulus on both "geographic" sides (front – O; rear – dreaming) of the contact-barrier. The part-object is now vulnerable theoretically to infinite and even grotesque expansion. If we lift these ideas and models to metaphoric transformations, we have the rudiments of mysticism formation.

Yet another combined relationship between O and religious states, according to Freud, that the part-object is the first stage of object development. Klein has placed it as an omnipotent feature of the paranoid-schizoid position. Bion has changed its appellation to "beta-element".[2] Further, Bion postulates that the beta-element/part-object arises when O intersects the emotional frontier/contact-barrier of the Unconscious, following which it "realises" its status as a conception as it mates with a pre-conception (inherent or acquired). It is my belief that this microscopic act is the forerunner of a sequential in development in which the acquired pre-conceptions enter (in personalised unconscious phantasy) joy in succeeding in achieving birth but at the price of forfeiting their unborn omnipotent status. Thus, a sacrifice – like the Eucharist and the Crucifixion – has symbolically (ritually) taken place. Further, the ritual ceremony symbolically honours God, who wishes to abdicate his deity status and become human, like Christ. Another way of looking at the difference between the normal versus the mystical view of signs is for me to take the example of the Abraxas, a triangle, atop which lies a single eye that observes in 360 degrees. The first degree is commonly used to exemplify mystical items.

I: O and the drives

Although Bion makes no mention of any connection between O and the drives, he seems to hint at one of the latter especially when he theorises that the id and its drives are mediated by the combined operations of Systems *Ucs.* and *Cs.* Moreover, he fails to list any other candidate(s) for the content of the repressed when he discusses O; Bion associates O with a beta-element (a non-mental element); Freud anticipated it under a different name, "libido".

Bion states:

> Just as Kant warned us not to overlook the fact that our perceptions are subjectively conditioned and must not be regarded as identical though unknowable, so psycho-analysis warns us not to equate perceptions by means of consciousness with the unconscious mental processes which are their object. Like the physical, the psychical is not necessarily in reality what it appears to us to be. *We shall be glad to learn, however, that the correction of internal perception will turn out not to offer such great difficulties as the correction of external perception – that internal objects are less unknowable than the external world.*
>
> *(Freud, 1915, p. 171, italics added)*

(N.B.: I include this citation from Freud – and from his study of Kant – to show how sentient he [Freud] was about what Bion would consider to be the mystic/unconscious nature of the objects of *consciousness.* I believe it is worth further study. For instance, how really *external* are the objects of consciousness, and similarly with *internal* objects and the unconscious? Additionally, by stating that "O"-ness characterises any and all objects that are yet to be encountered, then it follows that we as individuals are forever moving in a sea of beta-element [as yet unmentalised objects, ="O"].)

II: Symptoms associated with O: O → a raging verb seeking a temporising noun (verb?) or alerting protective signal?

Now I shall like to return to the discussion of Bion's self-imposed exile. Bion associates O with Kant's *thing-in-itself*, the object, which is unknowable (an entity unto itself). It is experienced uniquely differently by the patient and the analyst on one hand, and often virtually identically by the patient and analyst on the other. The symptoms which can be associated with O are all symptoms which take us by surprise and ominously anticipate immanent future difficulties. It is interesting, however, to note some symptoms that seem to have their origin in ancient fluxion: "I feel 'drained'", "destabilised", "drowning in misery", "I feel 'unbalanced'", "unstable", etc.

The briefest way to express the pathological formulations that emerge as a result of considering O function is to consider that the fundamental problem is the relationship between the container and the contained, i.e. between the object and the subject in its nascent (part-object) or mature object status – as the quality needs to be contained. The primary pathology may be thought of as destabilisation of the self, that is, there is a breakdown in the smooth functional symmetry of flexibility of self.

Solution?

While maintaining the importance of the love, hate, and knowledge functions (L, H, and K), Bion, realising that, while each of them was object-directed, they simultaneously were inherently sensory-oriented so as to sense data as well. Bion was now "crossing the Rubicon" and heading full-sail for the noumenal, ineffable, uncharted land of "The Unknown", infrequently alluded to by Jung and Freud, and located paradoxically within and around the Unconscious – and Nowhere, as in the example of "Keter" in the *Kabbalah*. O was conceived of and wrapped in mystery. Bion informed us that it constitutes an omnipotent entity by virtue of its infinite force, and that it could not be seen or heard, or, for that matter, known. It was "the Invisible Man", the "Black Hole", the One who dwelled everywhere and nowhere.

I suggest that the solution to the behaviour of O's mysterious odyssey from the memory of its future may lie in its cryptic relationship with its own nervous system, i.e. autonomic (sympathetic, parasympathetic, and enteric) when they display troublesome, excessive *cathexes*. I shall try to unpack the density of that statement: First, let us consider that the part-object (Klein) is the common denominator of O's primitive functions. Next, let us contemplate that a normal display of cathexis is present in the autonomic tree. In that situation we have the normal part-object typical of infancy. Next, let us remind ourselves that Freud's concept of cathexis, according to Bion (1965, p. 45), is empowered with *infinity*, almost identical to the way in which Freud pictured cathexis. When we experience the "hypercathected part-object", we may be in the presence of Segal's (1957) *symbolic equation*, as seen, for instance, in anxiety and panic disorders.

Standing on a peak in Darien, a sudden (seeming?) change in Bion's published works

Many of his colleagues, especially those in London, believed that Bion had become "undisciplined" (O'Shaughnessy, 2005), i.e. had replaced the quest for accepted psychoanalytic understanding with heresy in *Transformations*, where O first appeared and thereby O became the herald of Bion's new, allegedly "non-analytic venture", mysticism! As custom would have it, consequently, O inexorably became thought of as a symbol for pseudo-psychoanalytic heresy. Ironically, this series of events all too readily repeated a similar event earlier in which the British Psychoanalytic Society, already influenced from an earlier time by a growing Kleinian membership, suffered the threat of expulsion from the International Psycho-Analytic Society because of its "heretical leanings" ("Kleinian analysis").

Bleandonu (1993) has called attention to a pattern of four differing periods in Bion's works: the psychotic, scientific, epistemological, and mystical. Aguayo and Malin (2014), studying Bion's varying presentations from the psycho-historical vertex, notes that there may exist a close but hitherto mysterious affiliation between O and Bion's "Notes on Memory and Desire", a closeness that exists more than in the publishing dates, albeit that relationship is a clue. There is room to speculate, however, that Bion never really substantially changed his style, message, or thematics. If one looks very carefully at his graduation paper and other "Kleinian" papers, one will see a new psychoanalysis emerging more clearly than has been acknowledged by other Kleinians. The discussion of counter transference issues with the patient, and for that matter between Bion and Klein, cannot be omitted. Put another way, there exists a new and fresh Bionic theme in every one of his papers before his alleged change. Aguayo believes that Bion went through two defining periods, first, a "Kleinian" one and then a strictly "Bionian" one, the former dealing with extensions and modifications of Klein's theories of primitive and psychotic mechanisms (a la linear or conventional scientific theory), and the latter with Bion's own theories of "mysticism", the ineffable realm, particularly *reverie* transformations in O, and "here-and-now" in which the idea of the "once and forever infant modifies how we view the present tense".

Bion's move from London to Los Angeles in 1965 at age 70 had lent itself to considerable mixed speculation about his motives by his followers, colleagues, and readers. No one is certain why, nor did Bion ever really divulge why he had undertaken this major relocation. When asked, he would characteristically answer, half in jest, "I was so loaded down with honors in London that I nearly sank without a trace". Rumours began to abound (mainly from London, sources confidential) that, although he was highly respected for his many previous brilliant contributions, particularly the earlier ones on psychosis and on theories of thinking, which had been highly innovative extensions of Melanie Klein's work, his newer independent and creative ideas were held by many to be too "undisciplined" (vide supra), too radical, and too "mystical". But all was not lost. Although Bion's "poetic license" had been revoked in London, it was later to be renewed in Los Angeles, where he was soon thereafter and then onward to become arguably the foremost psychoanalyst that psychoanalysis has ever produced.

It was as if Bion himself had seemingly undergone a "transformation in O" (Bion, 1965, 1970) as he symbolically "stood on a peak in Darien" and began unwrapping a radically altered view of the mind and of the psychoanalytic approach to it. He had found its veritable "Holy Grail". It could also be said that he had also found and charted the "Northwest Passage" between Kleinian, classical, Relational, and other psychoanalytic schools, along with a compatible phenomenology, ontology, and cognition, on one hand, and a splendour of hitherto unknown as well as already glimpsed universes of potential wisdom hewed by multiple infinities comprising O, on the other.

O, the truth instinct, and the shift of emphasis from the past to the present via the future

The contributions of Bion have spread beyond the natural boundaries of traditional psychoanalytic thinking. His concept of O has challenged many of its canons. Reiner (2012), for instance, emphasises the importance of the "Truth-Instinct" and its fundamental relationship with O – to the point of hypothesising that they are the same function with differing names, a concept with which I strongly agree. When Bion (1967a) reassigned the instinctual drives (L, H, and K) from the prime content of the Repressed and replaced them in their influential status with Absolute Truth and Ultimate Reality, he fundamentally altered the aim and ontology, perhaps even the very nature, of psychoanalysis. *Consequently, Absolute Truth rather than the drives (LHK) from then on constituted the guiding force (of the psychical economic function) of the Unconscious in its new-found allegiance to emotions and feelings.* Bion states:

> *No one can ever know what happens in the analytic session, the thing-in-itself, O; we can only speak of what the analyst or patient feels happens, his emotional experience that which I denote by T.*
>
> *(Bion, 1965, p. 33, italics added)*

The hidden importance of the direction of O's trajectory

The spatial origin of the analyst's listening to the patient has traditionally been backwards in the direction of the patient's past history, what was putatively held to be the time of origin of the patient's illness. Bion, on the contrary, states categorically that: (a) nothing except O should ever be interpreted, and that (b) O is tracked as coming from the future immanently into the present moment, the only moment when it is experienced. This Bionic canon is implicit in his famous *A Memoir of the Future*.

The mystical stream that bore O: intimations of the origins of O before Bion

It was a delightful surprise when I found myself retracing some of the imagined steps that Bion had taken in ancient Greece, a vicarious journey for me through his readings and lectures, especially about ancient Greece, which apparently fascinated him. I recall his coming up with the name Democritus of Abdura in one of my readings and remembered how frequently Bion had referred to him (as the discoverer that the Earth was round). Bion had also mentioned Sir Isaac Newton and his debate with Bishop Berkeley over the philosophical/logical value of fluxion. (I am assuming here, by the way, that I [the author] am alone in postulating the connection between flux [fluxion] and O.)

We learn that the ancient Greeks who uncovered the concept of flux ("fluxion", flow [– of water and other fluids]) associated it with sensitivity to issues of balance (especially metaphorically), harmony, equilibrium, sense of equipoise: they collectively seem to be suggesting that a balance-centering function exists in the centre in the mind-brain. This centre of mediation involved the interaction of four functions, earth, air, fire, and water ("flux", "fluxion") (Heraclitus). Plato states: "Heraclitus . . . says that everything moves . . . and nothing rests" (Barnes, 1979). Thus, all objects, living or non-living (by *our* standards), *automatically, autochthonously move!* This idea applies to all the objects that lie on the infant's landscapes and may thereby lend themselves at first blush to becoming recognised (or mis-recognised) as actively invasive parasites.

Before I proceed with my discussion of Bion's O, I should like to allude to other possible theories for the roots of O, which, also like Bion's version, seem to have emerged in Pre-Socratic Grecian times. They deal with ancient Greek cosmogony, namely Chance, Necessity (Ananke), Strife, and Love. Chance, the polar opposite of Necessity, is unpredictable, whereas Necessity is closer to Fate (Barnes, 1979, p. 518). Other possible sources include then "humors" (body fluids), alcoholic "spirits", group baths, and other examples.

Examples of O

1   Transformations

a   Remarkably, O can easily pass as a twin relative of Bion's "Memoirs of the Future", i.e. aspects of Plato's Immortal Forms (especially inherent pre-conceptions), and whose existence always belongs to the future. They may become dangerous when they become immanent (about to intersect the object).

b   Imagine entering a penny arcade where glass-enclosed driving-booth models are located (a glass-enclosed booth with an automobile driving wheel is attached in front on the outside, and a winding-road facsimile is located inside. When the machine is operating, the road facsimile appears to approach the front of the machine where the live operator is situated – and it (the road) zigzags unpredictably. The operator's task is to "drive" up the road and attempt to remain on it. The zigzagging road has been chosen to represent O because of its relentlessness, unsteadiness, and unpredictability.

c   All examples of *entelechy* and *premonition* qualify. A classic clinical example would be that of anorexia nervosa in which then patient experiences terror upon the appearance of a dramatic and all too visible and inexorable change.

Bion (1965) first alludes to O in *Transformations* thus:

> The *sign would denote something* that is *not a mental phenomenon* and, therefore, *like Kant's thing-in-itself, can never be known.* . . . The use of these signs may be clarified by an illustration: The patient enters . . . shakes hands. This is an external fact, what I have called a *"realisation"*. In so far as it is useful to regard a *thing-in-itself and unknowable* (in Kant's sense) it is denoted by the *sign O.* . . . [T]he total analytical experience is being interpreted as belonging to the group of transformations, denoted by the sign T. The *experience (thing-in-itself) denoted by the sign O.*
>
> *(1965, pp. 12–13, italics added)*

O is derived from the things-in-themselves (beta-elements – not yet mental, according to Bion). Furthermore, it must be born in mind that O intersects the subject via its *impression* or *imprint*, not its substance.

Bion states:

> I shall . . . assume that the material provided by the analytic session is significant for its being the *patient's view* (representation) of *certain facts* which are the *origin (O)* of his reaction. . . . [I]n practice this means that I shall regard *only those aspects of the patient's behaviour* which are significant as representing *his view of O.*
>
> *(1965, p. 15, italics added)*

Bion is restating a canon of psychoanalysis: the psychoanalyst is technically restricted to interpret only what the patient thinks, believes, states, and shows in his behaviour.

Bion states:

> In terms of T, it is necessary to determine whether (patient) is characterised primarily by the need to conceal O or by the need to give as direct a representation of O as possible in view of its obscurity to him.
>
> *(1965, p. 22)*

Other sources:

2   Excerpts from Attention and Interpretation

Bion states:

> The central point appears to be the painful nature of change in the direction of maturation.
>
> *(Bion, 1970, p. 53)*

This is Bion's central theme, the close relationship between the inexorable current of reality (maturation) and its unpredictable impact on one. I shall later discuss maturation as a feature of entelechy.

Bion states:

> A psycho-analyst who remembers that A is the same person as A was yesterday indulges a column 2 element. . . . The central point appears to be the painful nature of change in the direction of maturation.
>
> *(1970, pp. 52–53)*

The relentless flow of time (the container) and of its objects (the contained) which flow in consonance with it describe the Weltanshauung (World Order) of Reality. I should have been more sanguine had Bion suggested that the objects *paradoxically also remained the same* (e.g. the *continuity* of the sense of identity.

Bion states:

> The experience to which I refer is the contact with evolved aspects of O, the realisation I have variously described as ultimate reality, the thing-in – itself, or truth. Logically, in so far as logic offers a model for the approach I am making, the absence of memory and desire should free the analyst from those peculiarities that make him a creature of his circumstances and leave him with those functions that are invariant, the functions that make up the irreducible ultimate man. In fact this cannot be. Yet upon his ability to approximate to this will depend his ability to achieve the "blindness" that is a prerequisite for "seeing" the evolved elements of O.
>
> *(1970, p. 58)*

"The irreducible ultimate man" and "the evolved elements of O"

Upon many re-readings of this passage, especially Bion's references to "*the irreducible ultimate man*" and "*the evolved elements of O*", I concluded that he may have been alluding to the presence of "multiple normal personalities (consciousnesses?)" of which O had a principal function. In support of this idea, note what Bion states a few pages later: "The *reality* of the psychic experience" – is such that the more the analyst is in contact, the more will be that part of it that he has been able to interpret. It will be clear to him that he is formulating only one aspect of a multidimensional experience (Bion, 1970, p. 71).

> [E]ach individual retains an inalienable element which is part of the deity himself that resides in the individual.
>
> *(Bion, 1970, p. 77)*

> The interpretation he [the analyst] does give is a theory, known to be false, *vis à vis* an unknown contingent circumstance, but maintained as a barrier against turbulence [O] expected to occur were it not so maintained; no statement is without a realisation to which it stands in a col. 2 relationship.
>
> *(Bion, 1965, pp. 168–169)*

This very brief citation seems pithily to sum up much of Bion's Metapsychology that is inclusive of the Grid and O.

"Bipolar O"

"His understanding of that theory can be regarded as a transformation of that theory and in that case all his interpretations, verbalized or not, of what is going on in a session may be seen as transformations of an O that is bi-polar. One pole of O is trained intuitive capacity transformed to effect its juxtaposition with what is going on in the analysis and the other is in the facts of the analytic experience that must be transformed to show what approximation the realization has to the analyst's preconceptions-..." (1965, p. 49, italics added by author. I shall discuss "bipolar O" at greater length later).

Vide supra. In this unusual dual-role for O Bion imports a *binary-oppositional function* (Lévi-Strauss [1970]) in which the expressive *and* defensive (oppositional) elements seem to work collaboratively.

A new perspective on the psychology of the double and of crucifixion

In another contribution in which I was studying dream-work (Grotstein, 2000) I hypothesised that it was the "Dreamer Who Dreams the Dream" who is the creator-architect of the dream, and the Dreamer Who Understands the Dream is the audience who proof-reads, polishes, and approves the dream. It is the first Dreamer who has the double task of handling the incoming beta-elements from the inside (Ucs.) and separately from the outside (Cs.) and the second Dreamer's task to function doubly as well. Put another way Consciousness and Unconsciousness align with one another juxtaposed on either side of a caesura known as the contact-barrier. The two domains (Cs. & Ucs.) exist in a binary-oppositional functional (mediating) state.

Now here is the difference: whereas Cs. serves only one-to-and-fro function – with Ucs. (selective absorption), the latter of which, the Ucs. of the patient, responds to (a) his own native O, (b) the O of the analyst, and (c) the combined indivisible O of the two participants. The upshot of this cycle is as follows: (a) beta-element (emotional experience T1 (Transformation)) → alpha-element (representing both internal, external O from both (re. both patient, analyst, *and* their combination)); (b) the now transformed alpha-element then mates with a pre-conception (either inherent or acquired) from the limitless warehouse of the Ideal Forms to become transformed (T2) into a union with the pre-conception to transform (T3) it into a conception, and then onward in the epistemological ladder (concept → n); in the meanwhile, n T3 a fateful and perhaps even psychically fatal reaction may have taken place – the "symbolic death" of the pre-conception, the acting representative of the "Ideal Forms" (as "godhead") can be postulated to become *incarnate* with mortal humanness and shedding their immortal "divinity".

The beta-element in line 1 is emerging from its moorings in the Ucs. – and then meta-phoroses (changes and re-forms into an alpha-element). *Meanwhile, the original inherent (immortal) pre-conception has been sacrificed.* It occurs to me that this formulation bears a haunting verisimilitude to the Crucifixion and the Eucharist: These are God's parameters: (a) God, the Eternal and Divine One, feels lonely and longs to be incarnate, to be a mortal among mortals, but this means His death or the death of himself *as* His Son or His unending grief for Him; (b) He compromises by demanding that His worshipers kill, devour, and drink Him to seal their bond, which is the sacrament known as the Eucharist.

This virtually manic ceremony may serve as a manic defense against the loss of the victim self by locating him inside one – to offset his/her being kidnapped by the infinity of eternity, as I believe constitutes one of the rituals of funerals, particularly that of the funeral wake (manic defense).

O and the Oedipus complex

Bion (1965) states:

> But the analyst must have a view of the psycho-analytic theory of the Oedipus situation. His understanding of that theory can be regarded as a transformation of that theory and in that case all of his interpretations, verbalised or not, about what's going on in the session may be seen as transformations of an O that is *bi-polar* (italics added by author). One pole of O is trained intuitive capacity transformed to effect its juxtaposition to what is going on in the analysis, and the other is in the facts of the analytic experience that must be transformed to show what approximation the realisation has to the analyst's preconceptions – the preconception here being identical with Taβ as the end-product of Taα operating on the analyst's psycho-analytic theories.

Bion (ibid.) alludes to the idea that O functions with the capacity for binocular vision (p. 66).

> I shall make three assumptions: (i) that the patient is talking about something (O): (ii) that something, O, has impressed him and he has transformed the impression by the process represented by Tpα in that his representation Tpβ is comprehensible.
>
> *(Ibid., p. 25)*

> [Concerning O] . . . the facts known to the analyst are . . . 2 people, patient and analyst, are met together in conditions of privacy. The furniture in the room, remaining unchanged, should be quite familiar to the analyst. The same should be true of features as usual sounds of the household and the neighborhood. The familiarity of the surroundings may blind the analyst to the possible significance of them for the patient, and must be on his guard against this. [These are] the constant features.
>
> *(Ibid., p. 29)*

> Amongst changing features must be listed absence of patient and analyst, or, notably during breaks, of analyst and patient. To these must be added changes in the time-table

and others likely to be significant. *All* change is a component of O, but one that's constant, namely that flows from the passage of time.

(Ibid., p. 30)

Summary-O's scattered lineage

When I linked the four irreducible elements postulated by the ancient Greeks (earth air, fire, and water), the elemental concept of *infinity* came to mind, and I recalled that it had been variously alluded to by scattered psychoanalysts but had become highlighted in the works of Matte Blanco (1975, p. 11) and Bion (1965, p. 45), each assigning its power and formidableness a model for the activities of the *unconscious*. Freud's depiction of the raw, explosive, primal nature of the id immediately came to mind. Matte Blanco's conception of *symmetry/asymmetry* applied more strictly to the *content* (contained) of the unconscious, while Bion's applied to the notion of the as-yet un-*contained* id searching for a *container*. Now we can answer the question of what might be the connection for our purposes between container/contained and symmetry/asymmetry, on one hand, and on earth, air, fire, and water, on the other. Each of these entities is immediately connected with the notion of infinity – non-containment – randomness – fragmentation – and omnipotence and can be thought of, I believe, as "linking-objects" between human beings and Mother Nature's awesomeness, ideal symbols for magic, science, and apotropaics.

Notes

1 Excerpts of this paper were presented at the 8th Annual Bion Conference in Los Angeles, CA, in 2014. The Rivista di Psicoanalisi authorises the republication of this paper, the full version of which was first published in Rivista Di Psicoanalisi, 2015, LX1, 3.
2 Consciousness presupposes existence in the third dimension of length, width, and depth. Flatness is represented by the second dimension of length and width, but no depth. Psychosis and/or omnipotence is characterised by the zero dimension, no boundaries (Grotstein 1978).

References

Aguayo, J. (2014). Los Angeles: Personal communication.

Aguayo, J. and Malin, B. (Eds.) (2014). *Wilfred Bion: Los Angeles Seminars and Supervision*. London: Karnac.

Borjes, J. (1949). *The Alef and Other Stories*. Trans. Norman Thomas di Gioanni. New York: Dutton.

Barnes, J. (1979). *The Pre-Socratic Philosophers*. London: Routledge.

Bion, W.R. (1950). The imaginary twin, read to the British Psychoanalytical Society, Nov. 1, 1950. In *Second Thoughts*, 1967.

Bion, W.R. (1965). *Transformations*. London: Heinemann.

Bion, W.R. (1970). *Attention and Interpretation: A Scientific Approach to Insight in Psycho-Analysis and Groups*. London: Tavistock.

Bleandonu, G. (1993). *Wilfred R. Bion: His Life and Works. 1897–1979*. Trans. C. Pajaczkowska. London: Free Association Books, 1996.

Freud, S. (1915). The unconscious. *The Standard Edition of the Complete Psychological Works of Sigmund Freud, Volume XIV (1914–1916): On the History of the Psycho-Analytic Movement, Papers on Metapsychology and Other Works*, 171.

Grotstein, J.S. (1978). Inner space: Its dimensions and its coordinates. *International Journal of Psychoanalysis* 59: 55–61.

Grotstein, J.S. (2000). *Who Is the Dreamer, Who Dreams the Dream?: A Study of Psychic Presences*. (Relational Perspectives Books Series, Vol. 19). London: Routledge.

Hermann, A. (2004). *To Think Like God*. Las Vegas, NV: Parmenides Publishing.

Lawlor, R. (1982). *Sacred Geometry: Philosophy and Practice*. London: Thames and Hudson.

Levi-Strauss, C. (1970). *The Elementary Structures of Kinship*. London: Tavistock.

Matte Blanco, I. (1975). Beyond object and fantasy. (A monograph on introspection, projection, projective identification, space and time.) Unpublished.

O'Shaughnessy, E. (2005). Whose Bion? *International Journal of Psychoanalysis* 86: 1523–1528.

Reiner, A. (2012). *Bion and Being: Passion and the Creative Mind*. London: Karnac.

Siegel, H. (1957). Notes on symbol formation. *International Journal of Psychoanalysis* 38: 391–397.

Tennyson, Alfred Lord (1842). *Poems*. London: Edward Moxon, Dover Street.

2

"O" – BION'S "CATCH-22"

Annie Reiner

Bion (1978) wrote, "The development of the mind has been a frightful nuisance and has caused an awful lot of trouble" (p. 53). Part of the 'trouble' he refers to in this rather amusing understatement is the ineffability of the mind and its resistance to sensory evidence and verbal description. In his later lectures in Los Angeles, Bion (1978) often raised questions about such issues, including whether or not there is such a thing as a mind, and if so what is it? It would seem obvious that analysts would agree that the mind exists, but what that mind is, Bion said, is not obvious. For one thing, his theories of thinking helped redefine the mind by includ-ing in it the experience of the transcendent reality he called "O" (Bion, 1965, 1970), beyond intellect, beyond the rational, a function of the mind more often referred to as the soul or spirit. This undefinable reality is Bion's most mysterious and controversial concept, which he nonetheless tried to define verbally as "absolute truth," "ultimate reality," and the "godhead," an experience of the infinite only partially approached by rational understanding.

Grotstein (2009) referred to O as a "truth instinct" (p. 131), an inherent human need for this kind of experience of the numinous. The dictionary defines "numinous" as "a sense of the presence of divinity," and Bion (1965, 1970) squarely places O in the realm of theology and religion. He made it clear, however, that this is a state very different from what is usually called religious. In the hope of shedding some light on this often confounding concept of O I will discuss in depth the philosophical and theological underpinnings of these differences between the reified "God" of religion and the "godhead," as Bion (1970) (after Eckhart) describes it, that is, as a metaphysical knowledge of the mind.

The ultimately unknowable nature of O presents analysts with a paradox, a kind of analytic 'Catch-22.' In Joseph Heller's (1961) satirical war novel by that name, 'Catch-22' denotes a problem for which the only solution is denied by a circumstance inherent in the problem. In the book it refers to specific bureaucratic loopholes but has filtered into popular culture to connote an unavoidable paradoxical reality. Bion's concept of O presents the analyst with such a paradoxical dilemma, for while the reality of O is unknowable, Bion (1970) makes it clear that this unknowable reality is the essential perspective in clinical work. Clearly and sim-ply he states, "The psycho-analytic vertex is O" (p. 31). The analyst is therefore in some way required to utilize a reality which cannot be understood or explained, at least not in logical or verbal terms, and this presents a significant challenge in a field which relies heavily on verbal language as a means of communication. It is a conundrum which I think contributes greatly to the enduring controversy around O. All hope is not lost, however, for while O cannot be known through reason or logic, "it is possible to be at one with it" (Bion, 1970, p. 30). The analyst can glean something of this reality by becoming it, Bion explains, and the information can then in some measure be imparted to the patient. To do so requires a capacity to break down the mental boundaries which separate the analyst from the patient, an uncomfortable, sometimes terrifying experience which neither analyst nor analysand finds pleasant. Such transgressions of mental boundaries differ from pathological ego regression in disturbed patients, although Bion's (1962a, 1970) idea of the analyst's ability to become O or become the patient's reality does rely on states of hallucinosis, as well as intuition, dream states, and "reverie." These states of mind beyond the bounds of logic, contacted by transcending the boundaries of one's own ego, differ from our "normal" experience of reality. In this realm, as in poetry, meaning is written between the lines. Bion's frustration in trying to describe the indescribable O led him to find other ways to try to convey what could not be conveyed in linear language, most notably his controversial three volume fictionalized "autobiography," *A Memoir of the Future* (Bion, 1991). These writings further fueled the controversy surrounding the complexity and ineffability of O. However, Bion did not create the confusion or complexity, he merely called attention to the scope of the challenge analysts naturally face in examining a metaphysical mind unavailable to the senses. This brings us back to Bion's question at the beginning of this paper – what is this mind, the nature and existence of which cannot be proven in our "real," sensory oriented world?

Even now, Bion remains a controversial figure. The controversy, centered around Bion's late work, with is focus on O, was recently documented in a series of articles in the *International Journal of Psychoanalysis* (2011). Bion clearly related O to mystical states of mind, and this, in my view, is the main source of controversy and confusion about his work. Vermote's (2011a) article in that series described the concept of O as an essential leap in Bion's thinking, a movement from how things are represented in the mind (thinking), to changes at a level of the mind which cannot be represented (being). As Blass (2011) points out, however, "Bion's later writings . . . are generally regarded among London Kleinians to be obscure, incoherent, mystical rather than analytically helpful" (p. 1082). Taylor's article echoes this view, describing Bion's late period as "poetic, metaphorical or frankly mystical" (Taylor, p. 1101), which "makes some of [Bion's] readers uneasy about his conclusions" (Taylor, p. 1100). Use of the word 'mystical' is implicitly negative here, which I think reflects the negative view toward the concept of O itself. It is therefore important first of all to understand what Bion means by mysticism. According to Grotstein (2007), most critics of O "fault [Bion] for what they believe is his religiosity. Nothing could be further from the truth" (p. 231). Bion (1992) clearly views religion as an illusion (pp. 374, 379), while the mystical view is an experience of higher truth.

Taylor goes on to wonder how "the average, non-polymathic reader [is] to judge" the accuracy of this new metaphorical way of understanding (Taylor, ibid.). The answer, I suppose, is that he or she can't. However, the idea of polymathic, multi-faceted knowledge certainly includes the esoteric knowledge represented by O, and one would have to ask whether it is fair to negate Bion's idea on the basis of it's not being understood. If one does not speak Chinese, for instance, it does not mean that Chinese does not exist or is somehow flawed; it just means that one does not speak the language.

Bion (1970) gave O a central position in clinical work, saying that no analytic discovery could be made "without recognition and at-one-ment with [O]" (p. 30). O seems to me to be the hub of his theories, but this is after the fact, i.e. the *meanings* of those earlier theories were all transformed by his revolutionary concept of O. In a sense all roads either evolved from or led inexorably to O. This includes his ideas about reverie, alpha function, container and contained, and the fluctuations between Ps↔D in the adult mind. Again, these theories are transformed by one's experience of O, but they all reflect mental capacities of integration and wholeness, reflecting a state of mind capable of contact with reality (O). While O is therefore a paradigm shift which brings to psychoanalysis a new foundation, the old ideas are not now false, they are simply insufficient using the old perspective and must be transformed through this new mental container, namely, O. The nature of Klein's ideas, and of Bion's own earlier transformations of Klein's ideas, is thereby transformed. While I call O a "container," being infinite, it is unlike any other kind of container, a boundaryless "container" is an oxymoron. But as past theories and ideas are transformed, the mind which contains them is also transformed. Container and contained are not static entities which stand alone; they are defined by and created in relation to each other, and each is transformed by the other (Reiner, 2012). Christ uses the parable of new wine that cannot be put in old skins because the new wine (the contained) expands as it ferments and bursts apart the old dry rigid skins (container). The same is true of new ideas – a new mind is required to hold them, a mind capable of openness to the boundaryless dream state of O. This represents an integrated relationship between container/contained (which in turn depends upon the capacity for alpha function), and each is transformed by its relationship to the other. Just as a new idea affects the container in which it is held, a different kind of container or mental space effects changes in its contents, in this case the theories themselves.

The idea of the mind and its contents in an inseparable dynamic relationship reflects Fairbairn's (1944) theory of endopsychic structure, where the structure of the mind and its energy are seen as inseparable. While Freud saw the ego as a structure which develops to deal with id impulses, Fairbairn (ibid.) called impulses, "the dynamic aspects of endopsychic structures [which] cannot be said to exist in the absence of those structures" (p. 88). The infant's impulses *toward* the object were therefore viewed as inseparable from the object.

In describing the analyst's experience of becoming O as dependent upon earlier mental development, I am not suggesting that those earlier mental integrations (i.e. alpha function or container and contained) are on a continuum with O, for O is a separate form of mental functioning. *However, these processes of integration and wholeness are needed to digest one's experiences of reality, including the experience of oneness with O.* Without a space in the mind for real thought (alpha function, container/contained) one cannot *make use of* one's experience of O (where a transformation in O results in a transformation in K). Instead, one is in the position of the infant, who has an inherent ontological sense of being, but cannot derive meaning from his experiences.

O and the integration of primitive mental states

Simply put, at-one-ment with O describes the experience of being, whose source is an experience of primitive mental states. But again, the infant's at-one-ment with his experience lacks a capacity mentally to dream about and give meaning to the experience. The ability to attach meaning to an experience of oneness with O depends on a capacity first of all to integrate primitive states of mind with higher mental functions to experience the evolution of O and its transformation into knowledge. One needs the capacity both to be *a part of and apart from* the experience at the same time. Any conscious reflection of O necessitates first of all this integration between the mind and its contents.

Bion (1970) links O to the capacity to suspend memory, desire, and understanding, as "preparatory to a state of mind in which O can evolve" (p. 33). This difficult mental discipline, a "psychoanalytic asceticism" (Bléandonu, 1994, p. 220), helps the analyst to "become infinite" (Bion, 1970, p. 46), to facilitate contact with the essential experience of the session. This breakdown of mental boundaries is a temporary disjunction from one's ego functions which Bion (1970) likened it to "an attack on the ego" (p. 48). It is nonetheless essential to the work, for the mind "preoccupied with elements perceptible to sense . . . will be that much less able to perceive elements that cannot be sensed" (ibid., p. 41). In his ideas about thoughts without a thinker, Bion (1970) makes the point that the truth exists whether we know it or not, and whether we like it or not. What's more, we are driven to know it. This idea is expressed in these words by American poet William Stafford, who said, "I don't want to write good poems, I want to write inevitable poems, given who I am" (Stafford, 2002). It reflects the same internal imperative to be one's self, to be in the truth, no matter what the consequences are, and without the arrogant belief that one knows who one is. This imperative is, in Nietzsche's (1886) terms, "beyond good and evil," for truth – O – has its own morality. Without this instinctual need for deeper truth, the willingness to endure the pain of analytic change would be unthinkable.

Patients frequently *come* to analysis expecting to be 'cured' of feelings, not to know these kinds of truths. If they *stay*, however, it may be to feed a hunger for truth which has been awakened, and it is our job to awaken it. It may lie dormant behind rigid and violent defenses which causes the person to hunger instead for the lies which obstruct awareness. Helping the patient develop a taste for truth is a critical part of the analytic process which may take years; in some it may not develop at all. This depends on the analyst's attention to this issue, and on the patient's constitutional disposition toward truth (Bion, 1992, p. 262).

Clinical example – "Claire"

Bion's ideas about the mystic may sound esoteric, but these are natural human experiences. The following clinical example demonstrates something of the importance of the concept of O, both as an analytic perspective and as a factor in mental growth. "Claire," a bright, intuitive psychologist, was raised by a psychotic mother and emotionally detached father who divorced when she was young. She is a hard worker, driven, however, by a cruel, perfectionistic conscience. After a decade of analysis, she does well in her life but suffers from anxiety around work and personal relationships. She often complains of exhaustion and has had lifelong conflicts around sleeping and eating. Preoccupations with food remain, but with symptoms of binge eating finally under control, underlying issues can now be addressed. She has recently started her own practice, which exacerbated primitive anxieties and needs.

"It's my birthday," Claire said in one session. "I have the feeling in analysis lately of really being born. . . . I feel so vulnerable." She mentioned a car accident the day before in which she'd been talking to a friend on her mobile phone. She was within the law (using a hands-free device) but felt ashamed.

> I stopped at a stop sign, a car crossed right in front of me and somehow I didn't see it . . . no damage, thank God no one was hurt, but it could have been disastrous, or cost thousands of dollars, and I have no money, I don't even have a job.

The man whose car she'd hit was "very kind, a pastor . . . it felt like a message from God to pay attention!" Though raised Christian, Claire is not religious and rarely uses such terms. She related her blind spot to having told me in yesterday's session about a painful family visit at Christmas. "I noticed where I place my gaze," she explained, "my parents are so detached, they can't see me . . . it was unbearable for me to see." I had pointed out that she had seen it long enough to feel the pain, before having "placed her gaze" elsewhere, meaning she'd become unconscious and detached. As an infant with a psychotic mother who could not "see" or hold her emotionally, Claire's gaze had shifted inward to phantasies (delusions) of a perfect mother. This hypomania, especially at Christmas, her "happiest time of year," was fueled by binges on sweets, the idea of an always available sweet mother. I had said yesterday that her "gaze" could now go back and forth between that happy internal family and the painful reality of her actual family.

In letting the details of this session wash over my mind today one statement stood out in my mind – "I don't even have a job." Superficially it referred to having left her previous job without yet having a private office, but the feelings it evoked in me – a deep sense of help-lessness, loss, homelessness – somehow set this seemingly mundane statement apart from the rest, almost like the words of a poem which seem to have more valence than other words, more intensity or weight. I recognized this quality as an evolution of O, something emerging from another mental space. Bion (1992) described it as "emotional experiences of thought about phenomena in which time is excluded" (p. 278). I took it to be the selected fact, Bion's (1962a) idea of a central element in the session around that brings cohesion to the apparently disparate facts. These facts included Claire's thoughts about her birthday, of being unseen, and her struggle to "see" her parents realistically, all reflecting what I thought was the much earlier "accident," the disastrous loss of her first difficult job of being an infant. The infant's "job" is to survive, physically and mentally, to learn to *see* with her own eyes, to attend to internal and external truths, to learn how to *be*, none of which could be accomplished in the absence of a sentient object.

This selected fact may seem incidental or arbitrary or too simple, but this notion of O is mysterious and ineffable even to those present in the room, and so much more ineffable in retelling it in words. Recounting it may also make it sound more rationally deduced than it actually feels in the session.

Being emotionally invisible to her mother had stripped Claire of her existence. It is the plight of the lost infant, in exile from her own mind, an "orphan of O," as Grotstein (1995) put it. The lost infant is then out of its natural "job," to develop and experience its existence, and such a child unconsciously undertakes a new job, working very hard to create "better" internal parents through phantasy and delusion. The infant's new job, in other words, is to create "lies," for the inherent instinct for truth has been derailed and corrupted. None of this is conscious, of course, but the lie they begin to live erodes a sense of self and being. Bion (1992) wrote, "Whatever is falsely employed as a substitute for the real, is transformed thereby into a poison for the mind" (p. 299). In having "shifted her gaze" to those lies or phantasies, Claire became blind to her own emotional existence. Unable to distinguish truth and lies, she has lived with constant doubt and confusion, exhausted by a meaningless job which she does not know she is doing.

I interpreted that Claire seemed to have been working hard all her life to avert her eyes from what she felt, and was unsure now who she really was. I had enough confidence in this to say it, but in order to convince myself I needed more evidence, which I thought emerged in her dream.

I was in my car with Jerry [her estranged brother, a drug addict]. We pulled up to the house where we'd lived with Dad when my parents divorced. I got out of the car. A Mexican guy was lurking at the front door and I thought he might be a killer so I wondered if I should get back in the car. It felt dangerous, although not like the total terror I feel in some of these kinds of dreams.

Living in that house was a painful time, Claire said. "My father was oblivious to me and my brother." She had just heard that her brother was on drugs and refusing treatment. After enduring years of his paranoid attacks when she tried to help him, Claire had finally gained enough mental space to tolerate a boundary between her and her psychotic brother/mother, and could tolerate the pain of letting him go. She said "Mexicans" were "hard workers . . . often gardeners". . . . I liked the gardener at my apartment. The inconsistency of her positive associations and this apparent killer struck me immediately, and deepened my earlier hypothesis. Linking the potentially scary killer and "hard work" seemed to reflect her fear of doing the difficult work of 'shifting her gaze' from phantasy to reality. Since I am helping Claire with this difficult work, I am experienced as a frightening killer who is threatening her idealizations and detachment. She wonders if she should "get back in the car" – return to that childhood method, and the "safety" of that deadened state, fused with her mother. As she said, however, she was not really terrified, so she is somehow aware that the killer is not me but this addiction to her mother. She is then faced with a choice – go back to a perfect mother/womb of deadened feelings, or be born and re-experience the real terror of her infancy. Apropos of this, we need to recall that the first thing she said in the session is that it is her birthday. Something is being born, and although she considers retreating in the dream, at least for now she doesn't.

Discussion

I am aware, as suggested above, that my detailed verbal description after the fact may give the false impression that my experience of the session derived from logic, when in fact it felt, as usual, chaotic and confused. Only after *feeling* my way *without thought* did I have any ideas at all. I had intuited something in her simple statement about not having a job that felt essential, and which allowed me to begin to dream further into its meaning (Transformation in O gives way to transformation in K). As we see in the hardworking Mexican in her dream, the session did prove to cohere around the idea of work, the infant's authentic "work" of being.

How does O reveal itself in the flood of material we often hear in a session? It may be a feeling, an aura or, as here, a few words which begin to give shape to the rest of the material, usually in a seemingly simple, even mundane but idiosyncratic way ("I don't even have a job"). However, it has a quality as if having poked up from the "formless infinite." What emerged in this session helped me to understand an obstacle I'd faced in Claire's treatment, for despite her unrelenting suspicions of me for the last few years, she also valued and worked diligently in analysis. I had not found a way to address this split effectively, for at this deeper level she does not know what our work is. We see here how her *secret* work directly opposes everything we do, as any real work with me is quickly obstructed to fulfill her old job of fixing her internal parents.

In supervision, Bion often asked the enigmatic question, "What language is this patient speaking?" This unanswerable question, like a Zen Kōan, forced us to consider the patient as a unique culture, in whose language we must learn to communicate. This is not a new idea. As analysts, we are not meant to reinvent analytic principles but to find a language to speak to the patient. So while Claire's material may be recognized as a split, one needs to experience the nature of that split anew at any given time. What might be read as resistance, envy, or a negative therapeutic reaction actually reflected a much more primal lack of existential experience. In this session I got a new perspective on an ambivalent transference in which I was the feared or idealized internal mother, and a clearer sense of the deep confusion about what we are doing together. Increasing awareness of her struggle to exist as a real person is slowly emerging, and in this dream, her feeling of "not [being] totally terrified" indicated a slight opening toward the hard work in which we are actually engaged.

O, mysticism, and the selected fact

The criticism of O as religious is debunked by Bion's (1970) statement that the tendency to view religious feeling as supernatural may simply reflect "a lack of experience of the 'natural' to which it relates" (p. 48). O, mystical and arcane, is the natural human experience of intuitive states able to reach a level of truth beyond the senses. Such experiences are always fleeting, emerging from the patient's dream-like state to be apprehended by the waking dream state of the analyst.

There is some overtly religious *content* in Claire's material – her references to the pastor and the "message from God" which shifts her gaze to a new place. It raises interesting questions as to whether these are expressions of a primitive religious idea of God or an expression of O, the Godhead. The latter is the instinct for truth, an internal experience of metaphysical knowledge described in the Gnostic gospels (Pagels, 1989), while the former reflects Freud's idea of religion as a neurosis or illusion, a primitive view of God as the exalted father (or mother). For the Gnostics, Christ is not a reified external God, but an *internal* teacher of metaphysical knowledge (cf. Reiner, 2009, 2012). I see both factors at work in Claire's struggle between her desire for a mind capable of knowledge and her reliance on the magical mother/ God to assuage the terror of an infant for whom real internal development was unavailable.

On this, her birthday, Claire hovers between the supernatural belief in an omnipotent parent/God and the metaphysical striving toward knowledge and real mental development. Like so many 'orphans of O,' her life has been a fulfillment of the myth of Christ, a baby whose job it is to save the whole family of man through the growth of consciousness. For the Gnostics, consciousness requires inner knowledge of one's 'sins,' although these 'sins' might be viewed analytically as thoughts and behaviors that obstruct truth, and life. Claire fears having to revisit the terrifying emptiness of an infancy without a mother to help her mind to grow. What she does not realize is that she retreats to this emptiness over and over again, a comforting deadness which keeps her split between devotion to that absent mother who invalidates her existence, and her devotion to our work of developing a true sense of being.

Summary

There are far more questions about O than answers. The answers we have are mutable, quickly and easily morphing into their opposites in the blink of an eye. Analysis deals with a mind, enigmatic and ephemeral the constant flux of life expressed by Keats on his gravestone in Rome: "Here lies One whose name was writ in Water." He did not even want his name on the tombstone (although it is there); he wanted just a symbol of a broken lyre, the symbol of the music of poetry, his now silenced. Even to have a name, he implied, belied that unconscious flow of inspiration from a transcendent realm of being, beyond the ego's knowledge. Words themselves impose limits on the resonant meanings of what can actually be experienced in at-one-ment with the myriad aspects of O. From this perspective the field of study in analysis is also writ in water. Is it possible then to overcome the essential Catch-22 of O, to communicate something impervious to being clearly communicated? Is it possible to speak to the patient, or to our colleagues, about these realities which cannot be seen or proven? Apparently Bion thought it was worth trying to do so, despite the very real challenges of finding a language in which to speak to patients and to each other. He focused on language – the language of Achievement, the tower of Babel, the transformations of O or transformations of the pictorial mythological language of dreams into a language capable of being shared – because of his awareness of the difficulties, and necessities, of creating a language that might bridge the gap between people's minds. He never concluded that we are able to do it, but I agree with his presumption that the effort is worthwhile.

The criticisms of Bion's later work on the grounds of its being 'mystical' seem sometimes to lack understanding of what Bion meant by this term. Some critics admit they are not conversant with the reality which corresponds to his ideas about the mystic, a term Bion used interchangeably with 'genius' and 'extraordinary individual.' I am among those who see Bion himself as that kind of extraordinary individual, who was moved to think and talk about these ideas impervious to verbal understanding. In so doing, he called attention to the very real difficulties of communication, not only with others, but with ourselves, and with truth itself, the real and substantive difficulties, that is, in having a mind.

References

Bion, W.R. (1962a). *Learning From Experience*. London: Basic Books.
Bion, W.R. (1962b). A theory of thinking. In *Second Thoughts*. New York: Jason Aronson, 1967.
Bion, W.R. (1965). Transformations. In *Seven Servants*. New York: Jason Aronson, Inc., 1977.
Bion, W.R. (1970). *Attention and Interpretation*. London: Karnac.
Bion, W.R. (1978). *Lecture*. Los Angeles. UCLA, NPI.
Bion, W.R. (1991). *Memoir of the Future*. London: Karnac Books.
Bion, W.R. (1992). *Cogitations*. Ed. F. Bion. London: Karnac.
Blass, R. (2011). Introduction to "On the value of 'late Bion' to analytic theory and practice" *International Journal of Psychoanalysis* 92: 1081–1088.
Bléandonu, G. (1994). *Wilfred Bion, His Life and Works, 1897–1979*. London: Free Association Books.
Fairbairn, W.R.D. (1944). Endopsychic structure considered in terms of object relations. In *Psychoanalytic Studies of the Personality*. New York, Great Britain: Brunner-Routledge, 1952.
Grotstein, J.S. (1995). Orphans of the "Real." *Bulletin Menninger Clinic* 59: 287–311.
Grostein, J.S. (2007). *A Beam of Intense Darkness: Wilfred Bion's Legacy to Psychoanalysis*. London: Karnac.
Grotstein, J.S. (2009). . . . . *But at the Same Time and on Another Level . . . Volume I*. London: Karnac.
Heller, J. (1961). *Catch 22*. New York: Simon & Shuster.
Nietzsche, F. (1886). *Beyond Good and Evil*. London: Penguin Books, 1973.
Pagels, E. (1989). *The Gnostic Gospels*. New York: Vintage.
Reiner, A. (2009). *The Quest for Conscience and the Birth of the Mind*. London: Karnac.
Reiner, A. (2012). *Bion and Bion: Passion and the Creative Mind*. London: Karnac.
Stafford, K. (2002). *Early Morning: Remembering My Father*. St. Paul, MN: Graywolf Press.
Taylor, D. (2011). Commentary on Vermote's "On the value of 'late Bion' to analytic theory and practice." *International Journal of Psychoanalysis* 92: 1099–1112.
Vermote, R. (2011a). On the value of "late Bion" to analytic theory and practice. *International Journal of Psychoanalysis* 92: 1089–1098.

SECTION II
Bion's journey toward O

3

WILFRED BION'S LOS ANGELES SEMINARS (1967)

One gateway to contemporary Kleinian technique

Joseph Aguayo

Introduction

To those relatively unfamiliar with Bion's clinical thought, I review his theoretical and clinical development prior to 1967, the year he gave the first in a series of clinical seminars in the Americas, the *Los Angeles Seminars*. One reason we should care about this work is besides standing the test of time, it also stands as one gateway to understanding so much of contemporary Kleinian technique (Spillius, 1988). Contemporary interest in Bion's clinical thought has also received a considerable boost from the recent publication of 16 volumes of his *Complete Works*, edited by Chris Mawson (2014). Besides Klein's work itself, Bion's work informs much of what passes for contemporary Kleinian work today (Grotstein, 2009). I will touch on some of these contemporary off-shoots at the end of this paper.

To recap Bion's three periods of thought to 1967: there was the group period, the psychosis period and the epistemological period (1947–1967). To summarize the three periods of thought to 1967, Bion tackled the practical problem of how to rehabilitate neurotically incapacitated soldiers by studying intra-group tensions in their hospital facility. With his colleague John Rickman, Bion treated neurotic disability as a social problem, a problem of the group – neurosis was the 'common enemy' and the group was to be treated in terms of processes that either facilitated or hampered their 'solution' to this common problem (Hinshelwood, 2015).

Bion (1952a) then took his group work into peacetime practice at the Tavistock Clinic after World War II, but now applied a psychoanalytic methodology to the study of 'intra-group' tensions. He delineated a facilitating group process – the 'work group' and an inhibitory/task-defeating process – the 'basic assumptions' group. He importantly delineated 'binocular' vision (a term incidentally that Bion borrowed from Hugh Crichton-Miller, founder of the Tavistock Clinic) where he saw the individual as individual and the individual as group member. Just as the individual psychoanalytic patient had a defensive structure that lessened his potentiality for a more wide-ranging self-exploratory attitude, the group could instigate irrational, task-defeating processes driven by obstructive defensive structures. In his group work, Bion leaned clinically on his direct emotional reactions to the group as a preliminary to understanding his countertransference. This experiential aspect also occurred before the other important task of gathering together a 'feel' for what the pooled transference fantasies of the group was towards its leader.

Bion carried forth into his third period, or Kleinian phase – and never forgot his group work – as he then took up Klein's (1946) proposal that psychotic states of mind were both understandable and treatable. Here Klein challenged Freud's (1914) view that proclaimed that while some analytic understanding could be rendered in cases of psychoses, i.e. the Schreber case (Freud, 1911), as a group, these patients were not psychoanalytically treatable. Along with collaborators Herbert Rosenfeld and Hanna Segal, Bion fleshed out ideas that explicated a Kleinian understanding of psychotic states, particularly keying around a core defense mechanism, *projective identification*. Klein's (1946, 1952) multi-faceted concept had many aspects: the patient-as-infant projected despised aspects of the self into the analyst-as-mother; it also represented a way of differentiating the 'me' from the 'not me'; it could represent a fantasized relationship established with external object, for example, an ideal self projected into the object so as to remain fused with it or an aggressive intrusion into the object so as to control it. Lastly, projective identification is a psychotic mechanism found in primitive object relations (Aguayo and Malin, 2013).

There were further refinements, mechanisms such as the 'massive confusion of self and other,' where the 'me' and 'not me' remained chaotically unintegrated (Rosenfeld, 1947, 1950); 'symbolic equations,' where things were concretely confused with what they represented (Segal, 1950); and 'attacks on one's mind,' where the patient attacked the very apparatus of perception (Bion, 1959). These Kleinian ideas then formed an emerging clinical approach that was applied to psychotic patients. While the treatment success was modest, this research provided the groundwork for two developments: the positing of a 'psychotic' core to the human personality (Bion, 1958, 1959) and provided the building blocks for the examination and treatment of near-psychotic states, emblematically represented by borderline and narcissistic states of mind.

In his fourth and last period, the epistemological period in the early 1960s, Bion took the findings from the previous two periods and expanded the Kleinian conceptual paradigm by completely re-working it. He wrote dense works on a psychoanalytic theory of thinking, primarily concerning himself with how to bring order to the diverse number of analytic theories vying competitively (as had that other product of 'inter-group tensions,' the three training tracks) at the British Psychoanalytical Society. With so many conflicting theories at war with each other, Bion (1965a) searched for the 'invariant' or an over-arching method that encapsulated truthfully so much theoretical difference. While the findings from the Kleinian period provided the basis for his understanding of psychotic disorders, Bion (1962) expanded the model in a variety of different directions: he took up the normal developmental processes inherent at the outset of life in the actual mother-infant relationship, which he now termed 'container/contained.' Winnicott privately complained about Bion's conceptual maneuvering here, as he himself had long discussed the importance of the 'real' or 'environmental' mother. That however is another story (Rodman, 2004).

Bion also added in a new factor, namely the subjectively processing capacity of the analyst, which he now termed 'alpha function.' Melding this idea with the Kleinian emphasis on the pathologically projecting infant, he evolved the notion of a variable infant in the presence of a variable analyst. In summary, while Klein had posited a variable baby in the presence of a constant mother and Winnicott had posited a constant baby in the presence of a variable mother, Bion expanded the Kleinian paradigm by positing a variable baby with a variable mother (Britton, 2007). It was now a model of *both* pathological and normal development.

This model of container/contained incorporated the effects of a psychically fantasizing infant (and its analogue in treatment, the patient-as-infant) interacting with a psychically and emotionally receptive analyst-as-mother. Her maternal 'alpha function' capacities absorbed the infant's communications, metabolizing and distilling their essence, so that a resonant understanding could be rendered. The formerly Kleinian two-bodied model, which focused treatment attention on pathological activities of the patient-as-infant – what it projects, or evacuates into the object; and what it takes in or introjects from the object – was now expanded to include the similar processes in the mother-as-analyst. In this new interactive, *inter-psychic* model, Bion focused on the to and fro transactions between patient and analyst. He expanded the notion of projective identification in a variety of ways: it served a normal, communicative function, where the infant communicated via gestures, guttural utterances, its needs to the maternal caretaker, who in turn via reverie and attempts at metabolization, signaled back to the infant its understanding of its primitive forms of communication.

Of course, Bion's emphasis on theory by the 1960s had essentially precluded examples of his clinical work – as he demonstrated in *Second Thoughts* (Bion, 1967). To extrapolate what I think of as the essence of Bion's *method of clinical inquiry* with psychotic and near-psychotic patients: first, these clinical vignettes were given as a series of existential episodes in the journey of the clinical situation. The protagonist is neither the patient nor the analyst. The protagonist is the *clinical situation* itself, which moves along of its own accord, with its own generative core. The failure of movement – and negative therapeutic reactions – is potentially revelatory of what Bion has failed to understand. Bion detailed how insight into this core emerges unpredictably and retrospectively. Previously revealed features of the patient's mental functioning and elements from the current material suddenly combine into a pattern, one that he now termed the 'selected fact' (Bion, 1967). The loose system of linkages moves into a *temporary* coherence: the analyst articulates the meaning of this occurrence. One reason why reading Bion's clinical papers is so difficult is because Bion is writing experimental prose – he is looking for a form that will do justice to the complex movements of the clinical situation. Another reason is that when things come together and cohere, his prose becomes correspondingly condensed. We are in the domain of systemic rather than direct causation. Bion tacks back and forth between the particularities of emotional experience and corresponding abstract formulations at the same time. He is attuned to the primitive origins of the patient's mind – its development in the clinical encounter and its failure to develop. Like Freud and Klein before him, Bion had the capacity to abstract from the particularities of the clinical situation and thereby postulate factors that either facilitated or hampered the development of the patient's mind (Dermen, *unpublished*).

Bion's method of inquiry is useful precisely because he demonstrates repeatedly how to avoid foreclosure. His fundamental presumption is: 'I am missing something.' James S. Grotstein used to say that Bion was more preoccupied with what was *absent* than what was *present* in the clinical situation. Bion did not treat *any* insight, however hard gained and temporarily illuminating, as a final resting place. As a matter of fact, he never seemed to be at rest in the clinical situation. What matters is what happens next. His capacity to live with the uncomfortable premise that every gain in analysis will come at a cost – to patient and analyst alike – is remarkable. Insight is a way station on the hazardous mountain climb that is psychoanalysis.

There is scarcely any need these days to argue that Bion's theoretical contributions, like those of Freud and Klein, have stood the test of time. The less examined question is whether clinical Bion also has contemporary relevance, something that I illustrate by way of examples from contemporary Kleinian work.

Bion's *Los Angeles Seminars*

We now come to 1967 when Bion shifted his ground to distill the essence of his clinical technique precisely at the time when London Kleinians, such as Hanna Segal (1967a), took pains to define what legitimately passed for 'Kleinian technique,' as it was now called. The monumental consequences of his brief 1967 sketch, 'Notes on Memory and Desire,' could not have been anticipated. Given first almost in the form of an impromptu lecture at the British Society in 1965 (Bion, 1965b), it seemed that he merely distilled what many British Object Relations analysts had practiced for years, namely that all analytic sessions needed to be conducted in the present moment. When Bion stated that analysis needn't be overly concerned with what *had* happened any more than what *would* happen, it might have appeared to be another way of saying what Melanie Klein's work with young children had demonstrated for decades – and James Strachey (1934) had implied: *all analysis occurred in the present moment*, as the analyst simultaneously uncovered the unconscious mental processes dominating the patient's conflictual life, while simultaneously being the object of those very psychically primitive processes.

So when Bion gave the second and more well-known 1967 Los Angeles sketch, 'Notes on Memory and Desire,' we now have an informing context for understanding why Bion's ideas about technique, so relatively commonplace in London, created such controversy in a foreign analytic culture – that of the Los Angeles Freudian community dominated by ego psychology. Bion instigated a radical departure from years of theory-laden work, making his ideas on technique and clinical work accessible to a new audience of American Freudian analysts, some of whom were incredulous that Bion could so seemingly and easily dismiss genetic reconstruction. To their ears, it was at the heart of the analytic endeavor, as they had long practiced the slow and careful reconstruction of the patient's infantile neurotic history, which in turn became the basis of transference interpretations (Aguayo, 2014).

In the *Los Angeles Seminars*, Bion introduced a new distinction when he differentiated the work that occurred *inside* the analytic session itself and the conceptual 'thinking about' its significance *outside* the session, particularly with patients who came to be known as 'difficult to treat' or make 'emotional contact with,' the near psychotic and psychotic (Joseph, 1989). Bion's clinical examples now showed a *practical* aspect serving as prods, so that the analyst could keep on interrogating his understanding of the intransigent clinical situation, with the end of finding a new direction which could open up a fruitful line of inquiry.

So, what did Bion mean to say by abandoning 'memory and desire'? By way of the analyst's subjective processing 'alpha' function capacities, the analyst (ideally) began each session by clearing his or her mind, emptying it of all preconceptions, wishes, agendas and recollections of past sessions, so that one could make clear observations (the 'K' link) that allowing a spontaneous evolution of the patient's material to occur. By listening patiently and attentively in the here and now, paying close attention to what feels most emotionally urgent in the patient's expression, there lies a potential for increasing a working collaboration, where new patterns of meaning can occur. This expansion of awareness optimally veers in the direction of the unknown or infinite (the "O" link). Put differently, while allowing for the operation of free-floating attention, the analyst operates in the preconscious like a sensitive receiving set, all while attending to what one heard internally and spontaneously as one listened to the patient.

But what about the other way around when this injunction was ignored by the analyst. He or she enters the session with preconceptions, agendas or wishes that were overlaid on the patient's material. The analyst can alternatively be activated by the patient's transference, responding inappropriately or irritably, as both Freud and Klein had noted in their articulation of the personal interference or 'narrow' countertransference. In the worst-case scenario, the analyst imposes his own preconceptions or agenda on the patient's material. Negative therapeutic reactions arise from these types of countertransference difficulties. Impasses can develop as a function also of a reiteration of old, recycled interpretations, perhaps born out of theoretical prejudices. For instance, too much preoccupation with the patient's past can foreclose on the analyst being actually present to the changes occurring in the living moment (Aguayo, 2014).

I think here Bion quietly corrected for a bias he had experienced with his London Kleinian colleagues, namely a tendency to over-pathologize the patient, while simultaneously underemphasizing the shaping influence of the analyst's own subjective, processing capacities. Perhaps this was one of the lessons of Bion's (1950) paper on 'The Imaginary Twin,' where his own countertransference left him in a confused state, from which he had to muddle his way through an experience of therapeutic ineffectuality. One epiphany came with the realization that much of what the patient had discussed in session was more 'imaginary' than 'real' – and this then resulted in more emotionally connected and incisive interpretations. Bion discovered and disturbed a patient living inside a secret lair, where he was adhered more to a fantasied object relation than the one he had maintained with his analyst. While the ensuing emotional contact made by the analyst stirred up intense retaliatory and persecutory fears in the patient, emotional contact and greater meaning resonances had been established. It was only with his gradual realization that a pseudo-patient had misled him into becoming a pseudo-analyst that Bion was able to put the analysis back on a proper track.

I now move to some clinical examples from the material he presented at the Los Angeles Seminars. At the outset of the 3rd Seminar, Bion gave a case illustration – I call him patient 'A,' legally certified as a schizophrenic. In the midst of the patient's generally unintelligible communications, so much 'incoherent stuff,' 'A' suddenly and quite uncharacteristically recalled a dream from the previous night:

> 'I was walking along the river bank with my children, when they fell into the river, and they were carried by the very strong current towards the weir, the waterfall that was in the river. Before getting to this, they came to an overhanging part of the bank, which covered some kind of diversion. The water was canalized off, and this terrific current would just disappear underground, is what it came to.' He said, 'I jumped in to rescue the children, and was at once carried with them towards their weir, towards this sluice, this channel, which disappeared underground. I can tell you,' he said, 'I never woke up so quickly in my life.'
>
> *(Aguayo and Malin, 2013, p. 56)*

In this and other clinical vignettes, they were all given without any background or early history, but in a here and now fashion. After telling the dream, 'A' lapsed once again into incoherence and simply went under. This moment of coherence, reflected by the telling of the dream was quite exceptional in the patient's communications. In the midst of this account, Bion may have startled his listeners with his next statement about 'A':

> I had nothing to interpret to him. I did not know what to say about this. But it made the focusing point for a good deal of thought because one felt that (as I felt about this) I'd simply been handed it on a plate, and had failed to understand, and had failed to be able to make any contribution.
>
> *(Aguayo and Malin, 2013, pp. 56–57)*

This clinical material might illustrate a number of points made by Bion in his published work, such as the idea of 'ideo-motor activity,' a way of demonstrating an idea through physical and emotional expressiveness; or the patient's violent projective evacuation of 'beta-elements,' when the patient attains a momentary coherence, best represented by his capacity to report a night-dream, but then attacks the link, and lapses back into incoherence (Bion, 1959). But in this vignette, what do we make of the analyst's inability to digest and metabolize the meaning of the enactment in order to make an interpretation? Bion pointed out the curious paradox between what is verbally expressed yet simultaneously remains in a sort of infrared spectrum of the non-intelligible (Aguayo and Malin, 2013, p. 63). Here Bion put into bold relief problems of conscious comprehension and unconscious indecipherability, aspects that enabled the analyst to think about how these two related to one another. He sought to integrate the sequence of comprehensible and incomprehensible elements within a session. He also examined the varying effects of the incomprehensible upon the analyst's mind, a phenomenon that at times could leave both participants wondering about the possible sources of incomprehensibility (Aguayo, 2014).

In the face of momentary incomprehension, it seemed as if Bion was also self-identifying as an analyst who could be baffled by psychotic forms of communication. Was this also a technique of persuasion, when a so-called expert in the field of psychotic disorders confessed to feeling stumped? Could it have been a subtle means of exhorting his colleagues in Los Angeles to identify with him in the face of how indecipherable psychotic communications could be? I think so and further maintain that this type of clinical example veered away from what now passed as London Kleinian technique that maintained its focus on the patient's pathology, while very rarely ever discussing how the analyst's subjectivity or lack of awareness might be influencing the proceedings. For instance, Herbert Rosenfeld (1952) might have invoked his conception of 'massive confusion of self and other' in order to tap the source of the patient's most urgent anxiety, namely the raging river that symbolized his chronic confusional tendencies. The 'weir' actually represented a 'we're' – in brief, the patient's profound terror that the analyst was gravely risking his own sanity by attempting to jump in and help the patient. This is expressed by reversal in the dream: the patient is the analyst; and the endangered children represent the patient's insane state of mind.

By taking up the subjective, processing capacities of the analyst, Bion allowed for the importance of a transmission from the patient's unconscious to his own. Deploying his crucial distinction between work done *within* the confines of the analytic session itself and the kind of thinking we do about our patients *outside* the session itself, Bion here drew upon his 'direct emotional experiences' *within* the session as a necessary first step in arriving at a 'wider conception of countertransference' *outside* the boundary of the session. Here, Bion's conception of countertransference always included Klein and Freud's 'personal interference' perspective, but after Heimann (1950), he added to it the unconscious to unconscious dimension, the so-called wider perspective. This definitional expansion Bion maintained for the rest of his career.

This 'wider' view – I call it the Heimann/Bion view – of the potentially informing nature of countertransference also quietly rooted itself firmly in the workaday armamentarium of London Kleinians, so that by the 1970s, Betty Joseph (another one of Heimann's analysands, who also drew extensively upon Bion's work) adopted it as well. Bion's work also was elaborated upon by Joseph Sandler's (1977) view of the role-responsive aspects of the countertransference. To put it in his terms, later adopted by Betty Joseph (1989), the patient 'nudged' or organized the analyst to be role-responsive in relationship to some of his archaic wishes and object relational patterns. The Heimann/Bion view has prevailed: the analyst must both 'sustain' his direct emotional reactions, no matter how problematic and conflictual they feel, before he could 'subordinate' them by means of understanding. This in turn made a pertinent interpretation possible. Later on however, Heimann (1960) was adamant, as was Bion, that an analyst could not simply say: 'I base my interpretation on my countertransference feeling,' especially if they 'seemed [to be] disinclined to check their interpretations against the actual data in the analytical situation.' For the remainder of his career, Bion rigorously differentiated his direct emotional experience from conceptual discussions of countertransference outside the confines of the analytic session.

To reiterate Bion's point: he advocated 'no memory, no desire, no coherence, no understanding,' a radical technical innovation in which the analyst ideally entered the session with patience and security. He exposed himself to the full blast of the patient's communications, which in the workaday situation might produce feelings of persecution and depression. Gradually however, a pattern would form, one that he likened to a kaleidoscope that would eventually form a 'selected fact.' Inquiries about the patient's past were marginalized, all in favor of a resilient contact in the living present moment. Explorations of the past were marginalized in favor of what Bion termed the 'past presented,' or that aspect of the conflictual past that refused to stay past. Bion's abiding concern was now the irreducible reality, the only one that could be sensuously and intuitively apprehended, so that inferences could be made about the patient's truthful psychic reality.

Bion's clinical method as a gateway to contemporary Kleinian technique

So how does an understanding of Bion's method of clinical inquiry inform us about contemporary Kleinian technique? I have maintained that it was Bion's clinical thinking that served as a main source of inspiration for Betty Joseph's work on technique (Aguayo, 2009). While she had originally trained in the classical Kleinian method – interpretations at the point of greatest emotional urgency, the linking of conflictual, infantile past to present by way of transference interpretations – she gradually grew somewhat dissatisfied with this approach, particularly when she felt she could not 'reach' or make contact with the patient.

By 1971, Joseph began to implicitly question the usefulness of making past-to-present transference interpretations. With a particularly sexually perverse patient, she wondered why her interpretations did not reach the patient. She surmised that it was the past-to-present transference interpretations that were the problem. She shifted focus to the patient's directly lived experience, taking up directly how her patient defensively maneuvered, pretending to listen as a way to deaden off dependency feelings. Joseph concluded that what was retrospectively deduced mattered less than what the patient directly experienced.

By 1975, Joseph marginalized past-to-present links and drew upon the patient's report of his past in a different way. She now emphasized the communicative impact of projective identification with particularly 'difficult to reach' patients sequestered inside of defensive enclaves. Joseph evolved a method of accessing countertransference that also emphasized a group aspect, something also inspired by Bion's group work. Recall here that Bion had remarked that he assessed countertransference in group work as a primary source of orientation. Betty Joseph dealt with the analyst's informing countertransference in a group setting. Analysts learned the difference between the analyst's narrow-subjective reaction and the wider, unconsciously induced reactions by the patient, gradually displacing the old past-to-present transference work. It was now a 'you and I in this moment' type of interaction over and above abstract-sounding, experientially distant body part language, like the mouth and breast. I maintain that Bion (1967) was an important influence here – no memory or desire should interfere with the analyst's even hovering attentiveness. One directly observed the patient's material in the here and now, allowing neither desires about the past or wishes for the future to intrude.

In Betty Joseph's consolidation of Kleinian technique, she consolidated many of Bion's more implicit ideas about technique, focusing on the patient's structure of internal object relations, as they were projected into the past. The remembered history and unconscious past were now part of a deeper psychological/experiential structure. That which remained un-metabolized and unconscious was projected in the 'here and now.' Now the analyst could do a history of the analysis in terms of the patient's internal object relations.

Betty Joseph's distillation of Bion's clinical ideas also influenced the work of Michael Feldman (2004) who elaborated a theory of psychic change; the analyst attends moment-to-moment as he tracks the patient's living experience – and as a result, widens the patient's field of perception. Psychoanalysis helps the patient to identify with the analyst's understanding and containing function. These small micro-movements within the session gradually can add up to a change occurring beyond the boundaries of the analytic relationship: the macro changes as a function of micro tracking.

In Feldman's view, the analyst was now an active participant-observer engaged in an existential encounter with his patient. Of necessity, he had to carry a greater burden of clinical responsibility for his subjective and objective countertransference – which mirrored the patient's wider or total transference communications. As such, enactments were a matter of daily course for the analyst – and the emphasis struck here was for the analyst to identify, delineate and recover from their effects, so that the analysis might be kept on track. And while more work was published on countertransference during these years, the disclosures were made to colleagues at conferences and in print, but not to the patients themselves.

Like Betty Joseph, Feldman drew upon J. Sandler's concept of 'role responsiveness,' when the analyst was enlisted to enact certain wish-fulfilling roles, mainly in the service of the patient's defensive equilibrium. Feldman's (2004) theory of psychic change represented a reformulation of a theory of the patient's internal object relations now structuralized similarly to Bion's notion of 'past presented.' If not handled sensitively, they could infiltrate the analytic relationship to the point where the analyst could remain blind to its unconscious organizing impact and thereby lead to therapeutic impasses. Feldman also struck a distinctive note in the area of *introjective identification*, when the analyst now listened intently to how his interpretations were listened to by the patient – the 'analysis of the analysis.' He also contrasted this approach with the classic countertransference model elucidated by Heinrich Racker, saying that the latter's 'past-to-present' model lacked the wider communicative intricacies of projective identification (Feldman, 2007).

Needless to say, I have only taken up one fertile offshoot of Bion's clinical thinking. There are, of course, many others, too many to elaborate within the space of one paper – Ferro (1999, 2009), Civitarese (2013) and Ferro and Civitarese (2015) – many post-Bionian elaborations and contributions that have proliferated in our tiny psychoanalytic universe. These contributions are testimonies to the pervasive impact Bion had on contemporary Italian psychoanalysis that date back to his Italian Seminars given in Rome in 1977. Likewise in Brazil, where starting with the work of Grinberg et al. (1975) much of Brazilian psychoanalysis took a Bionian turn, one that survives today in the work of Paulo Sandler (2009, 2010, 2011). And of course, here in the United States, there has been burgeoning interest in Bion that has emanated almost single-handedly from the torrent of publications from Jim Grotstein (2009) and San Francisco's own Thomas Ogden (2012).

In fact, all these diverse elaborations of Bion's thought aptly reflect the openness and exploratory attitude of a psychoanalyst for the 21st Century.

References

Aguayo, J. (2009). On understanding projective identification in the treatment of psychotic states of mind: The publishing cohort of H. Rosenfeld, H. Segal and W. Bion (1946–1957). *International Journal of Psychoanalysis* 90: 69–90.

Aguayo, J. (2014). Bion's notes on memory and desire – its initial clinical reception in the United States: A note on archival material. *International Journal of Psychoanalysis* 95: 889–910.

Aguayo, J. and Malin, B. (Eds.) (2013). *Los Angeles Seminars and Supervision*. London: Karnac.

Bion, W. (1950). The imaginary twin. In *Second Thoughts*. New York: Basic Books.

Bion, W. (1952a). Group dynamics: A re-view. *International Journal of Psychoanalysis* 33: 235–247.

Bion, W. (1952b). Group dynamics: A re-view. In M. Klein, P. Heimann and R. Money-Kyrle (Eds.), *New Directions in Psychoanalysis*, pp. 440–477. London: Tavistock, 1955.

Bion, W. (1958). On Arrogance. *International Journal of Psychoanalysis* 39: 144–146.

Bion, W. (1959). Attacks on linking. *International Journal of Psychoanalysis* 40: 308–315.

Bion, W. (1962). *Learning from Experience*. London: Karnac.

Bion, W. (1965a). *Elements of Psychoanalysis*. London: Karnac.

Bion, W. (1965b). On memory and desire. A talk given at the British Psychoanalytical Society, 1965. In *Complete Works of Bion*, Volume VI.

Bion, W. (1967a). *Second Thoughts*. New York: Basic Books.

Britton, R. (2007). The baby and the bathwater. Unpublished.

Civitarese, G. (2013). *The Violence of Emotions: Bion and Post-Bionian Psychoanalysis*. London: Routledge.

Dermen, S. (unpublished). Panel contribution on "Clinical Bion today." A paper given at the IPA Boston Congress, July 25, 2015.

Feldman, M. (2004). Supporting psychic change: Betty Joseph. In E. Hargreaves and A. Varchevker (Eds.), *In Pursuit of Psychic Change*. London: Routledge.

Feldman, M. (2007). Racker's contribution to countertransference revisited. *Psychoanalytic Quarterly* 76: 779–793.

Ferro, A. (1999). *The Bi-Personal Field: Experiences in Child Analysis*. London: Routledge.

Ferro, A. (2009). *Mind Works: Technique and Creativity in Psychoanalysis*. London: Routledge.

Ferro, A. and Civitarese, G. (2015). *The Analytic Field and Its Transformations*. London: Karnac.

Freud, S. (1911). Psychoanalytic case notes on an autobiographical account of a case of Paranoia. *S.E.* 12: 3–82. London: Hogarth.

Freud, S. (1914). On Narcissism: An introduction. *S.E.* 14: 67–102. London: Hogarth.

Grinberg, L. et al. (1975). *Introduction to the Work of Bion.* London: Clunie Press.

Grotstein, J. (2009). . . . *But at the Same Time and Another Level: Psychoanalytic Theory and Technique in the Kleinian/Bionian Mode.* Volumes I and II. London: Karnac.

Heimann, P. (1950). On countertransference. *International Journal of Psychoanalysis* 31: 81–84.

Heimann, P. (1960). Countertransference. *British Journal of Medical Psychology* 33: 9–15.

Hinshelwood, R.D. (2015). Panel contribution on "Clinical Bion Today." *Paper Given at the IPA Boston Congress,* July 25, 2015.

Joseph, B. (1989). *Psychic Equilibrium and Psychic Change: The Papers of Betty Joseph.* Ed. M. Feldman and E. Spillius. London: Routledge.

Klein, M. (1946). Notes on some schizoid mechanisms. *International Journal of Psychoanalysis* 27: 99–110.

Klein, M. (1952). Notes on some schizoid mechanisms. In M. Klein, P. Heimann and R. Money-Kyrle (Eds.), *New Directions in Psychoanalysis,* pp. 292–320. London: Tavistock, 1955.

Mawson, C. (Ed.) (2014). *The Complete Works of Wilfred Bion.* London: Karnac.

Ogden, T. (2012). *Creative Readings: Essays on Seminal Analytic Works.* London: Routledge.

Rodman, R. (2004). *Winnicott: Life and Work.* Cambridge: Perseus Publishing.

Rosenfeld, H. (1947). Analysis of a schizophrenic state with depersonalization. *International Journal of Psychoanalysis* 28: 130–139.

Rosenfeld, H. (1950). Notes on the psychopathology of confusional states in chronic schizophrenia. *International Journal of Psychoanalysis* 31: 132–137.

Rosenfeld, H. (1952). Transference phenomena and transference analysis in an acute catatonic schizophrenic patient. *International Journal of Psychoanalysis* 33: 457–464.

Sandler, J. (1977). Countertransference and role responsiveness. *International Review of Psychoanalysis* 3: 43–47.

Sandler, P.C. (2009). *A Clinical Application of Bion's Concepts. Volume I: Dreaming, Transformation, Containment and Change.* London: Karnac.

Sandler, P.C. (2010). *The Language of Bion: A Dictionary of Concepts.* London: Karnac.

Sandler, P.C. (2011). *A Clinical Application of Bion's Concepts. Volume II: Analytic Function and the Functions of the Analyst.* London: Karnac.

Segal, H. (1950). Some aspects of the analysis of a schizophrenic. *International Journal of Psychoanalysis* 31: 268–278.

Spillius, E. (1988). *Melanie Klein Today.* Volume I and II. London: Routledge.

Strachey, J. (1934). The nature of the therapeutic action of psychoanalysis. *International Journal of Psychoanalysis* 15: 127–159.

SECTION III
Transformation and O

4

BETWEEN EMOTION AND EVOLUTION

Jeffrey L. Eaton

Many readers consider Bion's work to be abstract, frustrating, and intimidating. It helps to read Bion in a group and to discuss his ideas together. If you read Bion slowly, as if in a dialogue with him, his ideas begin to open up many new possibilities.

Over time, Bion developed his own models for describing and questioning the complexity of psychoanalytic experience. His concerns are rooted in the work of Freud and Klein, but, perhaps more importantly, they arise from what he encountered in trying to comprehend his own experiences with his patients. In this essay, I will share some of the ways that his ideas inform the way I listen as a psychoanalyst.

What an analyst selects and draws to the patient's attention involves tremendous complexity. Gradually, as Bion accrued more analytic experience, he shifted his investigation to the analyst's capacity to think about emotional experience, and to the vicissitudes involved in the patient's development of functions of the mind that allow for elaborating contact with psychic reality and its complex interdependence with external reality.

Bion explored the development of mind, thinking, and learning in his major books. The result of this exploration is not a set of answers or recommendations on technique, but instead an enlargement of the analyst's imagination. In his late work, Bion became increasingly concerned with the quality of the analyst's experience and the ability of the analyst to use her imagination in the service of understanding the patient and the analytic process.

I'm going to focus on one strand of Bion's elaborate tapestry: a tension between learning from emotion and from experience of what Bion (1967) calls *evolution*. By evolution, Bion means a surprising moment of sudden direct experience, one that may take many different forms that neither analyst nor patient can anticipate or predict.

In "Notes on Memory and Desire" (Bion, 1967) Bion differentiates an evolution from ordinary remembering. An evolution may have the quality of an insight, an intuition, a recognition, or a flash of memory or understanding. An evolution does not guarantee progress or change, but it warrants close attention and is often overlooked, ignored, or rejected. My intention is to highlight an attitude characterised by openness to a sense of oscillation that moves back and forth between awareness of emotion and sudden recognitions of evolution (emotion ←→ evolution).

Particularly with regard to his later work Bion is sometimes accused of mystification. I believe his intention is the opposite. Bion's work enacts a search for clarity about extremely complex processes that, when looked at carefully, reveal a great deal of uncertainty.

In his later work, Bion enlarges the analytic focus beyond reified self–other interactions towards a much greater awareness of the epistemological complexity of the analytic process. He believed that an important change in point of view occurs if the analyst can allow for a wider view of reality and its complexity as part of a psychoanalytic attitude. He indicated the need for this larger view by his use of the symbol O.

The first task of a psychoanalyst is to create a setting within which a psychoanalytic process can develop. The job of the analyst is exceedingly complex because she participates in the same process that she intends to observe and describe. Additional tasks involve gathering the data of experience, sorting and exploring them, digesting them emotionally as much as possible, and describing patterns as they emerge. Through these processes the analyst can lend plausible meanings to emergent patterns and offer them as interpretations.

Bion was humble about what he thought that an analyst can claim to know. He emphasised the problems in observation and the need to make disciplined and informed guesses about the nature of the patient's experience. These guesses come not from theory but from a sincere attempt to describe something that is alive in the moment shared with the patient. This process inevitably involves the analyst's own use of self as a disciplined instrument of analytic perception.

Bion (1963) introduced a complex idea he called a *psychoanalytic object* to describe an experience potentially shared in a session. According to Bion, a psychoanalytic object has extension in the domains of sense, myth, and passion. Another way to say this is that the analyst has an embodied experience (sense); is able to put it into a description, a story, or a narrative of some kind (myth); and this emotional experience is shared with the patient as an expression of something unconscious that is evolving into awareness. This last extension is of particular importance because Bion defines passion as always involving the meeting of two minds. In this way, an analytic couple, and even an analytic field, is gradually constellated.

Bion (1965) then attempted to develop a notational system that he called "transformations" in order to track and describe the complexity of the interaction between an analyst and patient. What this project revealed was ultimately the limitations of representation with regard to the complexity of interactions between analyst and patient. The symbol O stands in part for this ultimately unknowable and incompletely representable complexity.

Another way to put this would be to say that in every analytic session there is an unknowable excess or background of experience. Whatever can be felt, said, observed, inferred, or intuited cannot exhaust the possible descriptions of factors and forces that combine to create the unique analytic field that evolves as two minds meet.

In his last lectures, Bion would use the electromagnetic spectrum as a model, emphasising the problem of how we might extend our senses in order to investigate a wider range of influences. This model suggests that while many important forces may be invisible to our ordinary senses, they are nonetheless real in their influence on the field shared between patient and analyst.

How is an analytic attitude enlarged by including the symbol O? I shall offer an example: the question of the nature and creation of consciousness. This topic is actually a giant open question. There is no single agreed-upon theory of consciousness today; instead there are many competing models. While consciousness, in one sense, is a very ordinary experience, it is also, from another point of view, a mystery, an example of O.

A distinction must be made between the experience of consciousness and the question of what it is. Psychoanalysis is a strong method for investigating the experience of consciousness, although it has no particular authority in explaining how it comes into being or what it is. From this perspective one can see the utility of Bion's use of the symbol O. It helps the analyst to refine his observational skills, especially through the function of differentiation between K (knowledge or curiosity) and O. It is not a departure from the reality principle but a deeper expression of it.

Bion urges an expansion of the analyst's attitude in order be able to listen more openly, to use imagination in a disciplined way, and to get to know the patient's *idiosyncratic view* of the world, not some preformed idea about what is healthy or pathological. The symbol O goes together with another key idea that Bion emphasised, which is the importance of the process of "getting to know".

Bion (1962) called the impulse to explore a *K link*. This is a shorthand term for an *attitude* of observing, inquiring, attending, and investigating. In other words, a K link stands for a *process* of getting to know.

K represents an attitude towards experience and is a crucial motive force that requires one to bear the frustration that is inherent in learning. It is not about gathering information in a materialistic way. A K link involves real curiosity, perhaps even a sense of wonder and awe.

For example, if you picture a young boy listening to a lecture on biology at his desk at school and learning to memorise facts from a book you are not really dealing with a K link. Instead, you should picture that same young boy kneeling in the mud by the edge of a pond and carefully but with excitement studying the way tadpoles swim in a sunlit patch of water. The feeling of deep curiosity (which is close to wonder) is the real motivation for exploration. It involves an aesthetic dimension of experience that Bion was deeply sensitive to.

Getting to know is a part of emotional experience and involves what Bion (1965) called a *transformation in K*. This kind of transformation is about an emotional link between self and other. The link can be assigned to a domain characterised by love, hate, or curiosity. Bion also proposed a sign for negative L, H, and K, which increase the possible combinations of links that can be hypothetically observed and noted.

As an analytic process opens up and deepens, a transformation in K will touch upon the awareness of the unknown. According to Bion, contact with the unknown can give rise to many different forms of transformation. If this space can stay open rather than become saturated by preformed habits of knowing, a transformation in O may take place. I believe this is one kind of evolution.

A psychoanalytic process can be seen, in large part, as the investigation of everything that obstructs the awareness of transformation in O. A transformation in O cannot be willed. Instead, the analyst must be able to surrender to becoming at one with an emerging experience. A transformation in O reveals a sudden sense of truth, a deeper pattern that connects many otherwise disparate elements. This kind of insight is deeply intuitive and difficult to symbolise because it comes as a sudden, direct awareness of complexity that requires the analyst to temporarily disappear as a knower intentionally making meaning in order to welcome it.

Using dreaming as a model may help to clarify this elusive description. When you dream, most often you are at one with the dream experience. Rarely do you recognise within the dream that you are dreaming. Instead, you flow along with the direct emotional experience arising within the dream. Sometimes you may recognise yourself as a character within the dream, while at others you *are* the dream experience as it unfolds.

Later, after waking, when the experience can be reflected upon, you might find words for it, yet, as with telling any memory, the description of the memory of a dream is never the same as the experience itself. This difference helps us to understand, I think, what Bion called a transformation from O into K. The dream is no longer unknown, but there remains an unknowable background or dimension to it. Grotstein (2000) asked, "Who is the dreamer who dreams the dream?" and differentiated this figure from the one who understands it.

To summarise so far, transformations in K take place in the realm of emotion and are characterised by links between self and other. Transformations in O involve a capacity to surrender the sense of the self as knower and require a moment of welcoming an unknown evolution. One becomes, rather than knows. From a subjective process point of view, the insight is not created by a knower, but received by an open awareness. The differences I am describing are not theoretical; more properly, they are phenomenological. They involve the development of a careful and disciplined capacity to notice different dimensions of the psychoanalytic task of observation.

In the realm of emotion and the K link we learn about the complexity of the patient's anxiety, his defences against anxiety, the consequences of relying on those defences, and about the way these deeply unconscious patterns can be externalised and lived out in the patient's life and in the transference to the analyst.

In the realm of evolution, if the analyst can register and welcome it, she can become at one with some emergent aspect of complexity manifesting in the analytic field and a sudden shift of perception may be possible. This may generate a moment of terror, or a moment of grace, but it often changes the view of things profoundly, not just for the analyst, but also for the patient if the analyst has the courage to risk describing the evolution. A new view can alter the analytic field shared between the two as a couple.

According to Bion (1967): "The only point of importance in any session is the unknown. Nothing must be allowed to distract from intuiting that" (pp. 17–18).

The development of a model of psychoanalytic intuition remains an incomplete challenge, but there is no doubt that Bion believed that intuition was a vital aspect of the mature psychoanalyst's experience. I believe that a creative psychoanalytic experience involves an oscillation between emotion and evolution, between opportunities to learn in K and moments of learning from O evolving.

I have taken Bion's instructions to eschew memory, desire, and understanding to heart, and I try to put them into practice in each session. I treat his instructions as guidelines for an experiment. They are directions on how to sit and on how to get in touch with my own mind and its activities as I listen to my patients. Bion is clear that this is a discipline and that this experiment must unfold over time. It is not an experiment to be conducted over a few hours for a few days or weeks, but hour after hour, five days a week, for years and even decades.

One problem that quickly arises from performing this experiment involves the new levels of awareness of the complexity of the task of psychoanalytic observation. Bion's instructions to eschew memory, desire, and understanding must be understood within the context of trying to define conditions that allow one to hone and sharpen the relationship observation ←→ intuition, which can be seen as a counterpart to emotion ←→ evolution. Understood in this way, they are fundamentally practical instructions that are related to the practice of what Bion will call "real psychoanalysis", a method designed to register the evolution of the unknown (see especially Sandler, 2005, pp. 605–633).

Bion's apparently extreme advice to eschew memory, desire, and understanding is not about creating an experience or willing a certain state of mind. Instead, Bion is advocating an experiment in *subtraction*. By bringing disciplined attention to all that we expect (desire) or believe that we already know or can come to know (memory and understanding) Bion hopes to increase open awareness of the barriers and obstacles to noting novelty in the moment to moment clinical interaction.

People who have practiced any form of mindfulness meditation will appreciate that by bringing attention to one's own mind you suddenly become aware of a great deal more activity than you are ordinarily conscious of. When you have an open focus or a capacity for choiceless awareness you can note all kinds of unfamiliar activity. This is part of what I call learning to "welcome" experience at increasingly complex and nuanced levels.

On the other hand, when you concentrate your attention on a specific task you create the unintended phenomenon of inattentional blindness. This means that your concentrated focus makes you unable to register many elements in the field that are unconsciously screened out through hyper focusing. It is in fact dangerous to observation to set yourself any specific goal in the clinical setting. Freud (1912), of course, famously advised against this and encouraged an attitude of "evenly hovering attention", which he said, "will be sufficient for all requirements during the treatment" (p. 112).

Bion's instructions, then, are neither naive nor mystical. They are intended to help acquaint the analyst with his own habits of thinking and feeling in order to realise conditions suitable for deepening observation and refining perception.

In *Attention and Interpretation* Bion (1970) explores the implications of disciplining certain habits of thought, habits of feeling, and habits of experiencing that are structured by habits of time, space, pleasure, and sensation. This does not mean that one enters some kind of mindless void. Instead, it is more like a practice of repeatedly learning to clean (some of) the layers of grime and dust from a window in order to see more clearly through it.

Bion implies that the biggest barriers people face in recognising an evolution in a session come from the unconscious ways we cling to stable habitual pictures of the world built out of memory, desire, understanding, and preferred sense impressions. These unconscious habits orient us. When we can bring aspects to awareness, recognise and bracket these kinds of experiences we can begin to attend to other data that appear on the outskirts of our awareness. Gradually one can begin to realise a new kind of perceptual space in which to intuit and welcome other emergent aspects of clinical experience. Perhaps you can recall vignettes from your own clinical experience that may provide examples of the way contact with O involves a realisation of the difference between relating through concept and opening to awareness of direct experience.

Becoming O involves a different form of perception, one that relinquishes subject knowing object in order to become at one with an emergent experience. Bion suggests that if we practice, if we make it a discipline, supported by Faith, we can transiently experience freedom from the tyranny of memory and desire. Sometimes we can intuit complex psychic events that come as an aesthetic surprise (or even shock) through the significance they bestow. We can glimpse a fragment of a pattern that connects.

Though this experience seems to come from out of the blue, in fact, it comes from the disciplined immersion of the analyst in the experience of the details of the clinical moment. A practical theory of psychoanalytic intuition would start from this immersion in the listening process while also recognising that the intuitive moment, the moment of insight, is not a matter of analytic will or adherence to any particular theory or stance.

These experiences of analytic intuition are linked with beauty, terror, and truth. Terror because the analyst will feel that he suddenly loses his habitual forms of orientation and identification; beauty because he suddenly glimpses an aesthetic evolution revealing a pattern that connects; and truth because, just for an instant, he feels himself part of the presence of a complex integrity transcending his will that gives rise to an imperative to leave the situation just as it is.

By taking Bion's descriptions and my own experiences seriously, I realise that there is often a caesura between working with reverie in the realm of LHK, and working with Faith in the realm of O. Both domains are important, and in fact they are always in relationship. Repeatedly crossing a caesura between emotion and evolution reveals that O is always already present in every moment. Every moment is O, but one can habitually withdraw in gross or subtle ways from welcoming its impact and from elaborating it symbolically.

I think this caesura is an artefact of the habits of memory and desire. Reverie deals mainly with the life of the emotions and how they are structured by memory and desire, self and object, and only by eschewing these habits can one begin to really experience memory and desire as barriers to transformation in O. I think Bion implies the necessity of going "beyond reverie" at certain moments, and that this is best formulated in observing the movement from emotion to evolution (emotion $\longleftrightarrow$ evolution).

How do you prepare yourself to become radically open? Preparation before meeting the person coming to therapy was made clear by Bion when he wrote, in *Attention and Interpretation*,

> Anyone who considers it possible to achieve a suitable frame of mind by a few minutes of psychological tidying up before starting work cannot have grasped the nature of the discipline necessary to be an analyst or the nature of the insights that become available to the analysed analyst if he brings "artificial blindness" to bear on his dark spots.
>
> *(1970, p. 67)*

By bracketing the categories of memory and desire I notice over time that I feel more embodied, more sensitive, more vigilant and relaxed at the same time. I am increasingly aware of my filters, biases, limitations, and dependence on familiar sensations, images, thoughts, feelings, concepts, and habits of mind that help me to remain oriented. I notice how quickly one can become distracted, even entranced, in fleeing from the concrete details of the moment as it is unfolding.

Instead of seeking an idealised state of empty receptiveness, I become more keenly attuned to how many barriers and obstacles exist to deeply welcoming my patient as an embodied mystery. It is hard to stay in touch with the reality that every session is actually a radically open question. But this is what Bion asks us to turn our minds back to, over and over: the reality of contact and encounter as profoundly open questions.

When we listen to a patient we hear many kinds of stories. We hear stories about the past (memory) and stories about the future (desire) and stories about the present (understanding) as well as stories full of emotion (LHK links). Some people have trouble narrating their stories, and some stories are terribly fragmented (PS $\longleftrightarrow$ D). Some stories are dead, and some people tell many conflicting ones. Some stories are repeated over and over. All stories are evidence of alpha function, of the ability to process emotion, to dream it, and to communicate about it. But not all stories show evidence of evolution. Some stories are barriers to change.

At a certain point, Bion decides that he must go beyond stories. Then he is making the path while walking, crossing into a new open frontier. The late Bion challenges the conventional analytic attitude, especially the sense of the analyst's role as the meaning maker or knower. Bion's O implies that all stories eventually trap us. There is experience before the story and beyond the story, and we ignore this fact too easily. We are seduced by stories, and at some point the words no longer carry the energy and emotion of lived experience. And, perhaps most importantly, there is direct experience, in contradistinction to the story of experience.

Consider, once more, the experience of dreaming. While you are dreaming your experience is vivid and direct. When you wake, the dream experience vanishes. You can never actually tell a dream. The best you can do is to narrate bits and pieces of the dream, and perhaps in doing so evoke some of its fugitive significance.

How different is our waking experience from dreaming? The ephemeral nature of direct waking experience is obscured by reliance on the satisfying organising power of all the concepts and stories we make and tell to each other. Yet being without a story for an experience does not mean that the experience is without significance or meaning.

★★★

Now, let me tell you a story:

One rainy afternoon I was driving home from my office when I noticed out my window a wide, colourful rainbow in the distance. Immediately, I was impressed by its radiance and beauty. I thought, "Oh, I wish my wife could see this, she would love it too". Then I thought, "It will be gone before I get home and I will never be able to describe it to her". I felt a little bit sad noticing the gap between my experience and my capacity to describe it and share it.

To my delight, when I arrived home the rainbow was still vivid and fully visible from our front yard. I ran into the house and called my wife out to the front steps in order *to show her the rainbow*. As I had imagined, she was delighted by *seeing* it.

I do not think telling her a story about seeing the rainbow would have delighted her nearly as much as being able to *show* her the rainbow. While the story of the rainbow contained emotion and meaning, the story could not really *share* the experience itself.

I think our job, as psychoanalysts working after Bion, is to notice the rainbow that is evolving in the session and to direct our patient's attention to it. In our best moments we are able to show the patient a rainbow and share that experience with them. I have used the image of the rainbow to help you picture an evolution. Of course, we do not know what form an evolution will take. We do not know what to watch for. We cannot make O an object of our attention. We have to be open to anything evolving.

I am trying to make clear the difference between our stories about experience, which can carry real emotion, and the direct experience itself, which has a different kind of quality. Our stories are necessary, but they are also obstructions to direct experience and to contact with O. Some stories become barriers to O while others are the animated attempt to share the experience of O. We must learn to sense the difference in the patient's use of language.

In conclusion, I am highlighting an oscillation between observation and intuition, and between emotion and intuition. I'm suggesting that taking the later Bion seriously helps us to consider a complex interdependence between observation of self getting to know another, and the sudden direct experience of "seeing the rainbow" in the session.

Attention to O does not involve idealisation or mystification. Interest in intuition is legitimately part of psychoanalytic practice. These issues are neither unnatural nor supernatural. O is a symbol for the fullness of the ordinariness of daily life and its often unnoticed dimension of mystery. We contact O through a disciplined process of learning to open to a wider field of reality. This involves the intersection of the body encountering with the world, others, and the mystery of our own ongoing being and its unconscious receptive transformation through the dreaming processes. Close attention to moments of evolution in a session or in dream life helps to reveal a deepening pattern of interaction between emotion and evolution, observation, and intuition.

References

Bion, W.R. (1962). *Learning from Experience*. London: Heinemann [Reprinted London: Karnac, 1984].

Bion, W.R. (1963). *Elements of Psychoanalysis*. London: Heinemann [Reprinted London: Karnac, 1984].

Bion, W.R. (1965). *Transformations*. London: Heinemann [Reprinted London: Karnac, 1984].

Bion, W.R. (1967). Notes on memory and desire. *Psychoanalytic Forum* 2(3): 271–280 [Reprinted in E.B. Spillius (Ed.), *Melanie Klein Today: Developments in Theory and Practice (Vol. 2)*, pp. 17–21. London: Routledge, 1988].

Bion, W.R. (1970). *Attention and Interpretation*. London: Tavistock [Reprinted London: Karnac, 1984].

Freud, S. (1912). Recommendations to physicians practising psycho-analysis, *S.E.* 12: 109–119. London: Hogarth.

Grotstein, J.S. (2000). *Who Is the Dreamer Who Dreams the Dream? A Study of Psychic Presences*. Hillsdale, NJ: The Analytic Press.

Sandler, P. (2005). *The Language of Bion: A Dictionary of Concepts*. London: Karnac.

5

AUTHENTIC PLEASURE

Capture of moments of Unison with reality

Cecil José Rezze and João Carlos Braga

Our aim in this study is to discuss a form of pleasure that Rezze (2011) named *authentic pleasure*, which is distinct from *pleasure* as usually discussed in psychoanalysis. *Pleasure* is a concept that ranges from satisfaction of the senses to satisfaction of the spirit, such as aesthetical or ethical pleasure. *Authentic* adds several connotations to the word *pleasure*, which we will clarify along the text.

The concept *authentic pleasure* emerged from experiences with clients and followed a necessity of the authors to contain and develop these experiences in the psychoanalytical work. It is a breakthrough in the strong tendency in the psychoanalytical tradition to consider satisfaction, joy, or even a smile from the client as an evasion or a hallucinatory manifestation. The same tendency applies to pleasant experiences of the analyst in the psychoanalytical work.

The point in discussion, therefore, is that *authentic pleasure* opposes the general psychoanalytical view of observing and working with *pleasure* as a symptom. Even when we examine psychoanalytical theories today, it is easy to recognize that they continue to be permeated with a strong tendency to consider the client's manifestations from a pathological perspective. This tendency is an inclination of psychoanalysis to follow its medical roots for which cure is the main goal.

With the concept *authentic pleasure*, we have an instrument of investigation and an opportunity to question this concept. In this context, we will not adopt the classic opposition *pleasure vs. reality*, nor will we use *pleasure* as a symptom or pathology; we will rather use *authentic pleasure* as reference to new theorizations. In order to achieve that, we must separate *pleasure* from the meanings it receives in primary processes and pleasure principle derivatives. We then have *pleasure* as an entity that deserves rethinking, since with this proposition a new paradigm may emerge that can give new dimensions to our practice, characterizing a paradigm break.

And how can we accomplish that? We will try to keep our proposition as open as possible instead of defining the concept. To achieve this goal, we will favour the level of descriptions and analogies proper of the status of an observational conception evolving towards a more abstract understanding – a concept. This choice enhances the phenomena associated with the concept, delineates its limits but leaves it open to be apprehended by others through resonance with their own experiences.

Following this proposition, we will rely on some resources. We will start from the synthetic formulation *the grace and the enchantment of living* (Rezze, 2011), try to expand it with descriptions of experiences of everyday life and of the psychoanalytic clinic, offer a few glimpses of its theoretical background, and hope that the concept of *authentic pleasure* will be apprehended by a combination of the reader's personal knowledge and impersonal reality.

Four approaches to *authentic pleasure*

Let us start with the description of four situations experienced by each of us individually.

1   (CJR) The other day, my granddaughter and her mother were chatting during breakfast about something that I do not recall exactly what it was. The 5-year-old girl manifested with sweetness to what her mother was saying. I then had one of those rare opportunities in life of feeling a profound tenderness and a desire that the moment would last forever, although deep inside I had a vague feeling of a future colouring the present.

2   (JCB) During the discussion of a study about *authentic pleasure* (Marra, 2011), I made a few comments about the proposal of this concept and approached it from the classic psychoanalytical view of sexuality, resorting to André Green's observation about the current marginalization of the concept of sexuality in psychoanalysis (Green, 1995). During the discussion, the proposer of the concept (CJR) questioned this approach and alerted us to the need of knowing with clarity the conceptual field in which we reside when we make a formulation; if the field is that of the prodromes of mental life, signalling the evolving of an emotion towards its representation, we would in fact be outside the classic referential of instinctual manifestations of sexuality. At that moment, I realized that I was treating the subject without this discrimination and experienced the emotion of achieving something new. I felt startled, touched, as if I had received a valuable gift. For a few hours, my mind worked in an uncommon way, as though trying to overcome an excitement emerging from a turmoil of ideas, with a need to develop what I had just apprehended. What stood out was not only the feeling of an insight, but mainly the pleasurable emotions of facing a development that opened new perspectives to me.

3   (CJR) Let us consider the contribution of a colleague (L.F. Nóbrega) about a client. While describing, during a scientific meeting, a particular session with a client, this colleague mentioned that after his interpretations the client repeated emphatically, "Perfect!" The analyst considered this manifestation something like an idealization, since he could not be all that perfect, so he made some remarks about that to the client.

Later on, after another intervention from the analyst, the client repeats, "Perfect!" The analyst works hard to clarify again the same aspect. On a third movement, the client says, "Perfec . . ." and starts laughing. The analyst highlights how the client becomes aware of the situation with this movement and ends the description.

I understand that the analyst is telling us that the client had an insight, and it seems to me that the client manifested a great satisfaction.

Thinking about the satisfaction, I ask the colleague how he conducted the situation. Surprised, he tries to find an answer to the question. I clarify that I was referring to the satisfaction that the client manifested and I question if that could not also be taken into context.

The colleague, very collaborative, adds that the client frequently complains exactly of not having satisfaction in life.

In the context of this work, I consider that this moment is unique because the client not only becomes aware of what happens between him and the analyst, but does that with joy and satisfaction. I should therefore highlight this fact since it is something new that occurs within the pair. And *what is psychoanalysis if not the opportunity to allow the birth of something that was not yet born, to create what was not yet created, or to favour development of resources that will allow the client to have pleasure or satisfaction on his or her existence?*

We, analysts, feel comfortable with pain and suffering, but only a few of us know what to do when *authentic pleasure* emerges. We work diligently to help the client have a new view of life, but we lack the attention when this goal is achieved because we are not prepared for something of this nature.

4   (CJR) During a session, an analysand complains of not sleeping well. He attributes that to his habit of mulling over things. He comments that his ex-wife makes demands and that he, not knowing what to do, is unable to stop these demands. He mentions,

> "If the car breaks, she demands that my office takes care of that. She does not pay for car insurance or taxes. If I make a comment about that, she says she does not receive invoices from the insurance company and justifies that the car is used to drive my children. She makes demands all the time, demands more money and, soon after that, we fight. Why do I stand that? Why don't I make it stop?"

Following the same path, he complains about the son and an uncle, each one making clear what they want which opposes what he wants.

He goes on:

> "I keep all that in my head, don't sleep well, as if I were a blotter that absorbs everything."
> The reference to the *blotter* is like a bell ringing in my mind, calling attention to something that I do not know what it is, but which seems to be very important.
> I feel as if I should say something and he seems to be waiting for me to do so.
> I mention that he thinks of me as someone in his favour, someone who will help him put a stop on that situation. But the situation is unclear because it is actually a blotter.
> I am still thinking about the image of the blotter.

He goes on:

> "Yes, blotters were applied when quill pens were used for writing. They removed the excess of ink left by the pen. Also, when there was a blot, when ink spilled, it was used for cleaning."

He becomes interested and we begin to talk as in a casual conversation.

I: "Yes, with the blotter, the writing is preserved and the blotter is left with an impression."
      The conversation about the blotter continues free and spontaneous and I question myself what that could be. Was it psychoanalysis? Maybe.
I: "With its use, everything becomes smudged on the blotter because the writings overlap. So, they look as if they are different elements. The writing stays clear and preserved, leaving the blotter with all accumulated and overlapped."
HE: "That's how I feel, everything overlaps in my head and I can't distinguish anything."

Everything then seemed to have come together and the story of the blotter, which developed spontaneously, made sense.

I THEN SAY: "Now I'm thinking about what you told me in the beginning of the session. It seems like each person defines their own writing: the ex-wife, the uncle, the son. With the son, in the beginning, you even do the writing as in the example of the soccer and its foundations, like the pass, the kick to the goal and so on. But then comes the blotter."

HE COMPLAINS, RIGHT AWAY: "But you think it is easy. I am here listening to you saying all these harsh things to me."

I: "Hey! You have now inverted the situation. The writing was yours, the one of the blotter that I developed with you. Now that you can read it, you don't want to know about it. You passed on the writing to me and you became the blotter."

He becomes surprised and laughs intensely:

"That is it, indeed!"

Time was up and he then stood up and shook my hand with an affectionate and satisfied smile.

Any clinical material leaves grounds for several meanings, but I believe that the moments when he *becomes surprised and laughs intensely*, and says *that is it, indeed*, are the best approach that I can make to *authentic pleasure* and its essentialness to the analytic work.

The comment above may cause surprise, but if one considers his or her own work, he or she may observe how many weak theories are used and how many times *pleasure* may be highlighted as an essential element, possibly when *the grace and enchantment of living* is stressed.

Delineating the concept *authentic pleasure*

In order to accomplish this task, we will discuss below *authentic pleasure* from a theoretical and a clinical perspective.

Theoretical perspective

When we initially approached the concept of *authentic pleasure* from a theoretical perspective, we realized that we lacked a proper organization to give consistency to the concept because it is not part of the main body of consecrated psychoanalytical theories. To face this problem, we resorted to a previous development, the concept of *weak theories* (Rezze, 2010). In this concept, we take as *ad hoc* theories the events that take place during a session which may or may not be verbalized to the analysand, such as cause-effect theories, descriptions or narrations, dawns of creativity, premonitions, and associations made by the analysand that touch us significantly, such as the one mentioned above about the blotter.

Taking this concept into consideration, *pleasure* would be regarded as a weak theory. This change in perspective would be possible, since we have separated *pleasure* from the basic psychoanalytic theories – those of recognized status in psychoanalysis, such as Freud's pleasure principle and the instinctual pleasure, a point that we discuss in this study. We see this movement as a breakthrough in the psychoanalytical thinking, since in this universe it is not possible to approach *pleasure* without considering Freud's pleasure principle and the instinctual theory. It is not our intention to disregard or substitute them. However, if we consider *pleasure* within a context proper to emotional experiences that evolve in the analytic situation, either in thinking processes or in movements to put himself or herself at one with reality, we tackle a different problem than the one studied by Freud.

In this condition, the concept *authentic pleasure* has the status of a theory – a *weak theory* – based on the theory of psychoanalytic observation that emerges to help identify an experience that is common in the analytic situation, allowing the discrimination of *authentic pleasure* from other forms of pleasure. *Pleasure* can then be perceived not only as a symptomatic manifestation of instinctual base – a manifestation of sexuality – but as an evidence of an experience of mental growth.

In the psychoanalytic literature, a reference to *authentic pleasure* would be Bion's "A Theory of Thinking" (1962a, p. 129). In this theory, Bion highlights *satisfaction* and proposes that conceptions emerge as a result of the encounter of pre-conceptions with their realizations. The model he used was the fulfilment of the innate pre-conception of the breast with the real experience of finding the breast and then allowing the emergence of the conception *breast*. Following that, Bion observes, "The conceptions, therefore, will always be associated with an emotional experience of satisfaction."

Clinical perspective

Even without ignoring the classical theories, we are able to develop *authentic pleasure* with a system of observation to operate a clinical situation with practicality. The descriptions of the four experiences mentioned above are pertinent illustrations, particularly the one that refers to free associations with the *blotter*.

After refining our personal and clinical experiences, we feel confident to state that:

Authentic pleasure is not a state of ecstasy, even though it can be.
It is not a state of pain, even though it can be.
It is not a state of contemplation, even though it can be.
It is not an insight, even though it can be.

Looking at *authentic pleasure* from a wider perspective

When we attempted to discuss *authentic pleasure*, we felt as if we were trapped in a paradox, with the impression of approaching something new in the psychoanalytic universe but, at the same time, probably familiar to all analysts. We consider this a condition proper to our object of study.

The way we ended up dealing with this paradox was prioritizing the delicate and shifting balance between personal experience and shared knowledge. By doing that, we are able to discuss *authentic pleasure* through its elastic and imprecise boundaries with established concepts from Freud's and Bion's theories.

Passionate love and *awe* emerge as natural choices. We add to them *aesthetic pleasure*. All three concepts refer to *emotional experiences*. They overlap so extensively that we wonder if they would not be similar emotional experiences transformed in three different media: our insignificance in the face of Nature's magnificence (*awe*), our enchantment for an artist's creation (*aesthetic pleasure*), and our joy when we live the experience of being in unison with reality (*authentic pleasure*). In contrast, the concepts of *pleasure, pleasure principle*, and *hallucinated pleasure* also correlate with *authentic pleasure*, but indwell different universes.

Authentic pleasure *and passionate love*

Bion states that "passionate love is the closest I can get to a verbal transformation that 'represents' the thing-in-itself, the ultimate reality, the "O" as I denominated (1981, p. 183)."

If we rely on this statement, we can get a glimpse of the convergence between *authentic pleasure* and passionate love as a presence of feelings of pleasure, joy, enchantment, and tenderness. *Authentic pleasure* and passionate love also represent experiences of being in unison with reality.

Authentic pleasure *and awe*

Awe is generally thought of as *reverential fear*. In Bion's writings, this meaning is found in *Experiences in Groups and Other Papers* (1961, p. 85) to refer to a state of mind that prevents thinking and evolution of the group. Within this meaning, *authentic pleasure* and *awe* would be non-converging concepts.

In Bion's writings, probably after Second Thoughts, *awe* achieves the condition of an indispensable step to a harmonious mental growth (Rotenberg, C., 2013). This is clearly the meaning that Bion gave to the word *awe* in an introduction that he wrote for a book of poems for psychoanalysts which was never published. The book was unearthed by his wife who cited the introduction during the Memorial Meeting (Bion, F., 1981):

> It is easy at this age of the plague – not of poverty and hunger – but of plenty, surfeit and gluttony – to lose our capacity for awe. It is as well to be reminded by the poet Herman Melville that there are many ways of reading books, but very few of reading them properly – that is, with awe. How much the more is it true of reading people.

The meaning of *wonderment, authentic pleasure* and *awe* point to the same issue: mental growth.

Authentic pleasure *and aesthetic pleasure*

In our understanding, *authentic pleasure* and *aesthetic pleasure* are very close mental experiences. Observations of these emotional states suggest that both experiences overlap in many ways. Both are forms of emotional experiences; *authentic pleasure* may be attained through an aesthetic experience, and mental growth may be lived as an *aesthetic experience*. This is probably due to the importance of aesthetic experiences in the processes of knowledge and communication, as well as in the process of living an experience of being at one with reality. In an abridged synthesis, the artist's emotional experience is "lived" and "communicated" through works of art, leaving to the observer the possibility of intuiting the artist's emotional experience lived as an aesthetical pleasure.

In areas where both concepts do not overlap, we are able to identify that the objects apprehended from aesthetic and psychoanalytic experiences are different. The same applies for the media in which both are apprehended. In psychoanalysis, we rely on a direct inter-course between two minds, while in arts, a transitional space is created between the involved minds.

Authentic pleasure *and emotional experience*

In Bion's thinking (1962b), emotional experiences and their destinations are the core of men-tal life. The decision to lean towards thinking, hallucinating, or being is accompanied by an emergence of different emotional states. Even though *authentic pleasure* can be the experienced emotion, most of the time it is not.

Pairing *authentic pleasure* and *emotional experiences* may help us tune with the moment in which mental life emerges, when the emotional experience provided by a container/contained relationship allows the emergence of meanings. Within this context, we think of *authentic pleasure* as a mutative emotional experience of enchantment, proper to the integra-tion between the psychic and the material faces of personal reality (a finite universe) and to the experience of being reached by evolutions of the impersonal reality (an infinite universe).

Pleasure, pleasure principle, and authentic pleasure

According to Freud (1911), the pleasure principle is one of the two principles that guide our mental functioning: the psychic activity has the objective of preventing pain and providing pleasure. It is an economical principle in the sense that displeasure is considered to be con-nected to an increase in excitement, whereas pleasure is linked to its reduction. Later on, in *The Economic Problem of Masochism* (1924), Freud deems incorrect the statement that all unpleasure must coincide with an elevation and all pleasure with lowering of the mental ten-sion caused by the stimuli.

What we want to highlight with these initial references is that we should not confuse *pleasure* and *pleasure principle*, because the meaning of pleasure extends beyond pleasure prin-ciple and its derivatives. In human beings, *pleasure* is not opposed to *reality*; it is instead part of it, although the change from energetic consideration to a qualitative one gave Freud the possibility to consider both pleasure-unpleasure and reality principles master structures in his thinking.

In psychoanalysis, the word *pleasure* achieves a meaning of something unreal, such as in a dream, and expands as if connected to the pathology, that is, a symptom that usually refers to the hallucinatory dimension. One has always to consider the derivatives of pleasure principle permeated with a moral or religious meaning.

Following these observations, we may claim that *authentic pleasure* is inserted into another conceptual universe than that of Freud's reasoning about pleasure. Similarly to *awe* and *aesthetic pleasure*, *authentic pleasure* belongs to a psychological universe of mental processes that allows us to be in touch with reality. The Freudian thinking, in contrast, relies on a biological approach to the mind.

Authentic pleasure *and hallucinated pleasure*

In *Formulation on the Two Principles of Mental Functioning* (1911, p. 219), Freud observes that a young child is in a situation in which she maintains a system of low tension that is undifferentiated from pleasure when it comes to quality. As a result, the child has no access to proper experiences of satisfaction, nor enchantment with the existence or any quality of this nature *(authentic pleasures)*. Only when accompanied by maternal care the child can achieve a condition of not being governed by the pleasure-unpleasure principle. In contrast, when the child faces increased tension, she tries to discharge this tension under the pleasure principle through hallucinatory activities such as crying or moving her arms and legs. When the child experiences that, she accomplishes the hallucinatory experience that aims at decreasing the tension.

Bion's early investigations on this same issue (1962b, p. 48) are based on Freud's ideas on the development of thoughts. Bion enriches our understanding about thinking by linking the hallucinatory dimension with the evasion of emotional experiences, substituting the painful generated meaning for a supposedly painless one.

In a nutshell, we may affirm that while *authentic pleasure* points to a moment of being at one with reality, hallucinated pleasure points to its denial, to the dominance of the pleasure-unpleasure principle.

We may say that *hallucinated pleasure* is a creation of the pleasure-unpleasure principle, in accordance with Freud, turning undistinguished thoughts and sensations, whereas *authentic pleasure* represents states of being at one with reality. Each one not only is part of a different conceptual universe, but both result from different psychic movements and are lived as different experiences. The differentiation between both experiences turns out to be a task for the analyst, who must rely on his awareness of his own emotional experiences.

Summary and review

Adopting as our starting point the motto *the grace and the enchantment of living* and deliberately using *pleasure* with a connotation of *authentic*, we discriminate it from the spectrum of manifestations of the pleasure principle. In doing so, *authentic pleasure* emerges as an essential element to mental growth, both in the dimension of knowledge, as well as in the dimension of being in unison with reality. These are descriptions on a psychological level of Freud's biological hypothesis of facing an instinctual manifestation. Due to its primordial condition to mental development, it imposes the conjecture of possibly being the founding experience of what we later experience as mental pleasure. One of the consequences of this approach is a fundamental change in the psychoanalytic view: the pleasure of sexuality would no longer be seen as the only prototype of pleasurable psychic experiences.

If we consider psychic quality, both *pleasure* and *unpleasure* are part of it. With some exaggeration, we could say that psychoanalysis took the path of pain as the sole foundation to all its developments and, *ipso facto*, to the mental development of the individual. Therefore, if we take the *pleasure* approach and add the connotation *authentic*, we will have another foundation for the emergence of thoughts, as we can consider with *awe* and *aesthetic pleasure*, in convergence with the idea of Bion about *satisfaction* emerging after pre-conception of the breast matching with its realization (1962a, p. 129).

In a broader view, we abandon the economic (metapsychological) point of view, leave aside questions raised by Freud such as libido accretions and discharges, consider the context of the observation that comes with the theory of transformations, and recognize the experience of *authentic pleasure* as the moment in which O enters the domains of knowledge and promotes a pleasurable experience of mental growth.

We are not proposing the abandonment of pain as our founding path to mental develop-ment. We are instead widening the way we look at it. Even for Bion, who abandons the biased curative approach, mental pain is occasionally prioritized via correlated concepts such as "nameless dread" (1962a), "catastrophic change" (1970), "thalamic or sub-thalamic fear" (1976), and "primitive conscience" (1978). In these conditions we are confronted with pain in moments of development; pleasure is buried under tons of scary hallucinated constructions.

Along these lines, Bion mentions on the last page of *A Memoir of the Future*, probably parodying Dante's *The Divine Comedy*, "Abandon Hope all ye who expect to find any facts – scientific, *aesthetic* or religious – in this book." After this warning, he continues, "All these will, I fear, be seen to have left their traces, vestiges, ghosts hidden within these words; even sanity, like '*cheerfulness*' will creep in." With *authentic pleasure*, would it be possible to see a movement to free and legitimate *cheerfulness* in the psychoanalytical work?

Wrapping up: back to our empirical base

We examined from a ground perspective a concept dear to the psychoanalytical tradition, the concept of *pleasure*. It is easy to conceive that this new treatment unveils the pre-existence of a non-traditional psychoanalytical thought. Specifically, the appreciation of states of mind, in the analyst or the analysand, devoid of previous theorizations, even those consecrated in the main body of psychoanalytical knowledge.

This condition grants a foreign perspective to the analyst that is favourable to surprise him and bring discoveries of what the knowledge hides, a condition that Rezze (2011) points to as

> A system of observation to operate with practicality the clinical situation.

Acquiring equality with theories that are part of the psychoanalytical tradition, the theory of observation of the analytical situation grants freedom to the analyst to conjecture and hypothesize in the spur of the moment and to describe the singular situation that is being experienced. The formulations thus produced, *weak theories*, will combine with the strong theories that are the founding elements of psychoanalytical thinking. By doing so, we rep-licate the pair invention↔tradition or clinic↔theories that has proved so enriching to the psychoanalytical method.

With this new perspective – *weak theories* – we operate in clinical practice with theories that we create about each specific moment of the analytical situation. The theories that compose the accepted body of psychoanalytical knowledge continue to be present, offer-ing support similar to a picture frame, but no longer organizing the analyst's thoughts. We ceased to *apply* the consecrated theories, refined from filtered elements of decades of analytical experience from privileged authors, to operate with our own condition to perceive and to formulate mental and non-mental phenomena, accessible to the analyst at each moment in the consulting room.

This was our background to develop the concept of *authentic pleasure* from clinic and per-sonal experiences. It names a specific emotional state, proper to getting in touch with reality through the experiences of *knowing* and *being*; subjectively it can be experienced as *the grace and enchantment of living*, either by the analyst or by the analysand. It has the condition of an invariant, a sign of psychic change and an evidence of an experience of mental growth ($\female\male$ transformed), a moment of integration between the psychic and material faces of reality.

In agreement with Bion, since the capture of moments of unison with reality is an evolution of the infinite, it is not possible to know *authentic pleasure*. What we may do is identify *authentic pleasure* when it reaches the phenomena level, and then live it.

The success or failure of this paper will be evaluated by the matching – or not – of the concept *authentic pleasure* with the reader's own experiences. That's what may bring to life what we have drafted here.

References

Bion, F. (1981). Tribute to Dr. Wilfred R. Bion at the Memorial Meeting. *International Review of Psychoanalysis* 8: 3–5.

Bion, W.R. (1961). *Experiences in Groups and Other Papers*. New York: Routledge.

Bion, W.R. (1962a). A theory of thinking. In *Second Thoughts*. London: Heinemann, 1967.

Bion, W.R. (1962b). *Learning from Experience*. London: Heinemann, 1962.

Bion, W.R. (1970). *Attention and Interpretation*. London: Karnac.

Bion, W.R. (1976). Evidence. In W.R. Bion (Ed.), *Clinical Seminars and Other Works*. London: Karnac, 1994.

Bion, W.R. (1978). Supervisions A5, A6 and S12, held in São Paulo in April, 1978. Audiotape transcriptions by José Américo Junqueira de Mattos.

Freud, S. (1911). Formulations on the two principles of mental functioning. *S.E. 12*. Toronto: Hogarth Press, 1975.

Freud, S. (1924). The economic problem of masochism. *S.E. 19*. Toronto: Hogarth Press, 1975.

Green, A. (1995). Has sexuality anything to do with psychoanalysis? *International Journal of Psychoanalysis* 76: 871–883.

Marra, E.S. (2011). Prazer-Amor-Psicanálise? *Scientific Meeting at the Brazilian Psychoanalytic Society of São Paulo*, November 19, 2011.

Rezze, C.J. (2010). O Dia a Dia de um Psicanalista. Teorias Fracas. Teorias Fortes. *Revista Brasileira de Psicanálise* 44: 127–144.

Rezze, C.J. (2011). Limites: Prazer e Realidade. Objetivos da Análise: Prazer Possível? Realidade Possível? *XXIII Brazilian Congress of Psychoanalysis*.

Rotenberg, C. (2013). Bion e o Sentimento de Encantamento ("Wonderment") como Depuração do Impulso Religioso Primordial. *XXIV Brazilian Congress of Psychoanalysis*.

6

WRITING AND TRANSMISSION IN BION

Group model, pictorial model and transformation in "O" model

Adriana Salvitti

Introduction

The discussion regarding the possibilities of psychoanalytic transmission beyond the analyst's office is an old one. Since the time of Freud the teaching of psychoanalysis, the conditions for analyst training, and the challenges of clinical and theoretical writing have all been rendered problematic at one time or another.

This debate became especially acute with the reporting of non-neurotic material and of events beyond verbal language and the representational realm. However, this only radicalises a difficulty that is intrinsic to psychoanalysis. The nature of the unconscious productions, the inadequacy of language and the distortions of memory preclude recreating the psychoanalytic object and the experience in which it is formed even for the analyst himself.

Wilfred Bion (1897–1979) addressed the problem of transmission in several works and created different writing styles as a way to deal with the issue. This was due to his clinical practice with psychotic patients, as well as his great sensitivity to communication challenges, and his concern with theoretical controversies among psychoanalysts. But a much further step was taken when he introduced in psychoanalysis the concept of an ultimate and unknowable reality named "O" (Bion, 1965).

From his earliest writings, Bion used language to show the theorising process of the analyst as part of a thinking apparatus. He also used language to create several effects on the reader. Expectations, impressions and emotional experiences generated in reading should take part in the construction of the text's meaning. These elements that go beyond verbal discourse and the literalness of the text are actually very closely linked to clinical practice; this is particularly true for patients for whom the analyst's role and mental functions matter more than the words themselves.

But if writing and the demands made on the reader have a strong clinical dimension in Bion's work, the fact is that the writings of many great psychoanalysts, beginning with Freud, have this literary appeal (Mahony, 1993). The contribution of Bion, however, included deliberate attempts to use language to invoke an analytic attitude while reading (Ogden, 2004). Therefore, Bion's writing is fundamentally a communication about method. This, however, is not readily apparent.

Our proposal is to closely follow how Bion handles challenges in transmission in three of his texts. We will indicate how he creates different models of writing and reading based on the theories that were being presented. To do so, we will advance in chronological order, starting with *Experiences in Groups* (Bion, 1961) and then moving to his late works, "Catastrophic Change" (Bion, 1966) and the chapter "Commentary" in *Second Thoughts* (Bion, 1967b).

Through these works it is possible to outline three models of transmission, namely the "group model", the "pictorial model" and the "transformation in O model". Although they have a close relationship with the ideas presented in each work, the models are not a reproduction of these ideas nor are they restricted to the cited texts. Since they are models rather than theories of transmission, they do not apply to Bion's entire work. However, they reflect his attempts to create bridges among an analytic event (which is no longer present at the moment of writing), a means of thinking about it and its communication. Loosely speaking, this represents for the reader what is at stake in clinical practice when emotional experiences must be thought about.

Group model

In the 1940s, Bion created and participated in various groups with the goal of understanding their emotional tensions. His reports and theoretical findings were brought together in the 1961 book *Experiences in Groups*. Bion offered detailed descriptions of experiences and the manner in which his theories were formed. He also talked about the illusory beliefs and expectations that were placed on his work, accompanied by feelings of opposition that emerged both within and outside his groups, including reactions of the reader:

> If my description of what it is like to be in a group of which I am a member has been at all adequate, the reader will have experienced some misgivings, harboured some objections, and reserved many questions for further discussion.
>
> *(Bion, 1961, p. 39)*

Many interpellations were made to the reader during the construction of his arguments. Rather than seeking agreement, offering results or proof of his proposals, Bion intended for the reader to utilise the descriptive material "in reaching his own conclusions" (Bion, 1961, p. 40). Despite Bion's efforts to describe what he observed in groups and to indicate theoretical findings, the procedure quickly seemed doomed to failure. In the second chapter of *Experiences in Groups*, he gave up on offering further examples of a feature of group mentality, as he had not yet encountered a method to describe it. And he concluded with the following statement: "I suspect that no real idea can be obtained outside a group itself" (Bion, 1961, p. 52).

About 20 years later, he continued to make the same statement about the formulation of an experience. "What has to be communicated is real enough; yet every psycho-analyst knows the frustration of trying to make clear, even to another psycho-analyst, an experience which sounds unconvincing as soon as it is formulated" (Bion, 1967a, p. 122).

This frustration also included attempts by Bion to expose his methods of group observation and to create analogies which soon appeared inadequate. One may assume that this difficulty would be reinforced by Bion's lack of clarity regarding the phenomena in question. The fact is that Bion's observations do offer information on the elusive and non-sensuous dimension of the reality that presents itself in the clinical situation. Some years later, in referring to reality in its final or fundamental dimension, Bion (1965) coined the term "O" and went on to highlight its impermanent and fleeting character, which is untamable by any form of language.

Nevertheless, the search for more appropriate formulations about group experiences and observation methods produces a sense of vagueness in the reader in terms of meanings and definitions. This certainly creates a state of confusion and, in the best case scenario, leaves the reader intrigued. Additionally, Bion incites the reader to access his impressions about what it means to be in a group and sometimes tries to establish complicity, especially when wishing to express highly difficult issues.

Alongside with the concepts that were being presented, Bion summons the reader's participation expecting him to follow the thought process of clinical situations based on his (the reader's) own experience. Bion therefore creates a group with the reader and shows what it is to participate in a group of which he (Bion) is a member. In being included in a common field of experience, albeit not identical to the one experienced by Bion himself and the members of his groups, the reader is awarded more than results and explanations. After all, the reader is offered the possibility of live contact with the object of knowledge.

To conclude, the parallel between Bion's analytical attitude and the reader's attitude with respect to his experiences situates within the scope of writing and reading the relationship with knowledge *per se*. The process of investigation and curiosity is often accompanied by feelings of catastrophe and hostility, leading to a group effort to preserve its *status quo*. In this case, there is an impediment for the emergence of new ideas, in addition to rivalry with the analytic method and a tendency to take hold of the truth. Hence, this poses the question of how a group created with the reader would favour the opposite movement, directed at the expansion of emotional experiences and learning from them.

The implications of these ideas for writing and reading in psychoanalysis will be deepened in "Catastrophic Change" (1966) and the chapter "Commentary" in *Second Thoughts* (1967b).

Pictorial model

In 1966, Bion presented his work "Catastrophic Change" at the British Psychoanalytical Society. He intended to describe an emotional configuration frequently noted in analysis, represented by the image of container and contained, and by the symbols ♀ and ♂.

To illustrate this configuration, Bion used examples ranging from clinical observations to narratives of historical events. Contrary to what one might think, the historical narratives and case reports were not supposed to be considered as historical facts. They are what Bion called "C category elements", that is "descriptions made up of sensuous images derived from a background of experience or reported experience reassembled for my purposes" (Bion, 1966, p. 27). They should evoke different reactions in the reader. For Bion, historical narratives and clinical accounts are at their most interesting when they facilitate the analyst's ability to think emotional experiences, instead of being used to offer proof of clinical results or to consolidate the theories which support them.

The formulation of "C elements" was coined in *Elements of Psychoanalysis* (Bion, 1963) to address mental phenomena that are manifested as dreams, dream thoughts and myths.[1] When Bion states in "Catastrophic Change" that he seeks illustrations for the pattern "container-contained", classifying them into the "C category", he indicates the close relationship between this search and the analyst's dream activity in the session (Bion, 1962). As for the reader, Bion expected the contact with these formulations to stimulate his imagination, mobilising his pre-conceptual, preverbal and nonverbal repertoire. However, the formulation proposed by Bion also carried some risk.

Although the "container-contained" configuration could be related to known theories, Bion did not intend to give "C category" descriptions the status of a concept and avoided including them into the established body of theory. He aimed to give them maximum openness to facilitate the analyst's investigation and recognition in different situations. Bion's own writing is a living example of this configuration and shows the process involved in the search for meaning:

> Indeed what I am describing is a good example of the meaning ♀ in which is embedded the unknown word or formulation ♂, for what I *would like would be* to find a word that most people *would* regard as appropriate to represent the meaning I want to convey.
> *(Bion, 1966, p. 29. Emphasis added.)*

In this quote there seems to be an uncertain and indeterminate quality in Bion's intention, revealed by the conditional tense of the highlighted verbs. Certainly he was willing to find appropriate formulations, but he also leaves room for the reader to ask if there is an ideal combination between ♀ and ♂ that would provide the exact word Bion hoped to find. Would this combination not put an end to searching and investigation? In transposing these issues to clinical practice, one wonders if this search would not be doomed to failure, given the impermanent nature of the psychoanalytic object. In *Transformations* (1965), Bion emphasised that the ultimate dimension of all experience is unknowable and unnameable. In this case, the supposed appropriate word implies a failure in communication and obstruction of the analytical process. This is because, instead of stimulating thinking (which depends on the experience of frustration), the appropriate word would lead to satisfaction and gratification of desire.

In fact, these issues are based on the quality of the link between ♀ and ♂: in this case, between word and meaning, but also between the author and his text, between the text and the reader, and by extension between patient and analyst, or between the patient and himself. Bion identified at least three links between container and contained: the commensal link, in which container and contained coexist independently; the symbiotic link, in which interaction generates change and development in both; and the parasitic link, where interaction destroys one or the other.

The greatest concern with the quality of communication lies therefore in the parasitic link. An excess of meanings, where everything seems clear whether by translations into images or references to what is already known, leaves little room for indetermination, lack of precision, doubt and, consequently, for the creation of new meanings. In this case the descriptions produce, according to Bion, "so great a penumbra of association that the formulations become saturated and narrow the analyst's perspicacity" (Bion, 1966, p. 31). It may also be the case that a meaning to be communicated is so intense that no formulation is capable of containing it, or the formulation encountered would be rigid to the point of depriving the meaning of vitality.

Problems like these seemed inevitable, and would put Bion's contribution at permanent risk of losing its clinical potential. However, the reader's ♀ is put to the test at every moment by other formal qualities of the text as well. Although Bion discriminates a common configuration in various human situations, descriptions overlap and are greatly expanded in an infinite mirroring game between the formulations presented, the writing of the text, the experiences of the author and of the reader. Moreover, the fact that Bion does not make any connection between his ideas and psychoanalytic theories contributes to a sense of instability. The effect that is generated is very well described by colleagues who attended the scientific meeting where the work was presented. In the interesting commentary by the editor of the *Complete Works of Bion*, we learn that Meltzer felt sort of drunk and anchorless, but was also delighted with the freshness of the subject (Bion, 1966, p. 22).

The discomfort caused by the lack of a known theoretical base that would better situate the reader reveals the audacity, but also the potential, of Bion's proposal. Certainly there was an expectation that the reader would reflect on the way he reads and uses ideas or how he welcomes (♀) and employs the text (♂). This amounts to a communication strategy, in which Bion tries to access the reader from inside his experience, in a way that is analogous to what the analyst could do in his practice.

Now, we will examine how Bion (1967a) discusses the method and its transmission by making use of the concept of transformation in "O" in his reading of his own work.

Transformation in "O" model

In 1967, Bion compiled most of his writings from the 1950s and 1962 in the book *Second Thoughts* (Bion, 1967b). For this publication, he wrote a critical commentary, comparing his previous ideas with recent conceptions about the method. However, in addition to explaining and describing this new approach, Bion showed its characteristics in the text itself, promoting a close and direct overlap between theory, writing and reading.

In Bion's early articles, narratives were regarded as factual accounts and there was great concern for clarity and consistency. In his new approach the recording of patient or analyst conversations and biographical data were considered to be irrelevant from a psychoanalytic point of view. What matters is the reality of the session and what could be seized from it. Without a proper means to register them, miscommunications become inevitable, even when author and reader are the same person.

In the book *Transformations* (Bion, 1965), the issue of transmission and the recording of experiences had become particularly acute with the notion of "ultimate reality". Bion discussed the impossibility of reaching the ultimate truth and the definitive meaning of any experience. He created the term "O" to refer to a reality that is unnamable, unfathomable and unknowable. With this term, Bion indicated that psychological and emotional growth occurs not only as a function of the knowledge acquired about an experience, but also in contact with the reality of an experience. Access to such reality would never be direct and would depend on different transformations of an original experience that is inaccessible in itself. Just as the discourse of the patient and the analyst can be conceived as the result of transformations of an experience, narratives and psychoanalytic theories would amount to a transformation of what had already been transformed in clinical practice.

Thus, two of the transformations identified by Bion are "transformation in K" and "transformation in O" – henceforth represented by T(K) and T(O). T(K) refers to all the knowledge that can be obtained in or out of a session *about* the reality of an experience. However, in addition to knowing, one can *be* the reality that presents itself; this is because reality is also given to us through the experience of "being", or what Bion named T(O).

If in the "early Bion" there is an appreciation of T(K) and the ability to give meaning to reality, in "late Bion" – characterised by works from the second half of the 1960s – there is an emphasis on the importance of abandoning what is already known. This does not mean the mere suspension of knowledge, but rather the abandonment of an inclination to know, and to avoid filling the space of ignorance with memories or any prior understanding.

Bion described T(O) in different ways, all of which try to cover different aspects of "being" and "becoming". With a play on the word "atonement", he deconstructed it as *at-one-ment*, changing its meaning to express the act of being-at-one with the reality of an emotional experience. But that would also entail coming into contact with undifferentiated layers of reality or its radical otherness, eliciting amazing and astonishing experiences. Vermote (2011) points out that this would also represent a realm where creative potentials can arise. And Grotstein (2000) points out the existing paradox in T(O), since its realisation is only possible if we give something of ourselves to what is impersonal and elusive in "O".

These views were taken up in "Commentary" (Bion, 1967a) through the examination of the transformations that were operating in the text and which should be part of the reading process. As we have seen in the pictorial model, a writing format valued by Bion would be the "C category" statement. Its evocative potential would generate images and impressions that give shape and meaning to emotional experiences. This requires an ability to tolerate a wide range of thoughts and emotions, and indicates the existence of a container (♀) which is responsive, which is capable of producing meanings and does not become threatened by the contained (♂).

We have also seen how these same formulations could impede the expansion of the analyst's capacity to think. In this case, ♀ would be filled with ideas, images, theories and knowledge, and without the emptiness necessary to create new meanings. There is also the risk that the formulations would be considered as a literal description. They could thus acquire a concreteness that would be typical of the mental functioning of psychotic patients. These failures in thinking were discussed by Bion in relation to these patients, but also in relation to the analyst's own ability to think (Bion, 1962). All these considerations belong to the realm of T(K), in which the meanings generated can favour or obstruct thinking. However, this would also indicate defensive reactions to T(O), for example, when the sensation of incompleteness is eliminated.

Regarding the reading process, Bion thought that the reader should adopt an attitude that would provide an antidote to the parasitic link with the text. To this end, he suggests that reading should be made under the same conditions in which psychoanalysis is conducted, that is, without an attempt to fill in an experience with memories, desires and theories, without the reader wanting to be an analyst like Bion, and without seeking understanding.

In this way, Bion's hope is that the reader does not cling to the meaning and to what is known, but becomes capable of moving from T(K) to T(O). For that to happen, it would be necessary to abandon what was read, and to allow a certain emotional experience to re-emerge in a spontaneous and authentic way. This was the same attitude that Bion claimed to have in relation to the authors of his own tradition, such as Melanie Klein and Freud. Only in this way, Bion says, "it is possible to produce the conditions in which, when it is next read, it can stimulate the evolution of further development" (Bion, 1967a, p. 156). Otherwise, T(K) could be part of a defensive reading and replace the experience of reading.

In order to weaken these defensive readings, Bion repeatedly emphasised in his "Commentary" the failure of his own communication, indicating how descriptions do not represent the patient's state of mind, and that an experience that led to an interpretation cannot be accessed. However, he also believed that the analyst would not doubt the reality of the description, as long as he were to use the same method and experience what became real for Bion in his practice. He says: "If two analysts are successful in minimizing the operation of memory and desire, they minimize the danger of collusion and increase the chance of sharing the same experience – 'seeing' the same mechanisms at work" (Bion, 1967a, p. 152).

When Bion wrote *Transformations* (1965) and "Catastrophic Change" (1966), he had not yet used Keats' expression "negative capability" (Bion, 1970). Identified as the ability to be in uncertainty, in doubt and mystery, this notion was already present in Bion's statements on the analyst's attitude, as well as in the demands he was making on the reader through his writing style. It is precisely this capacity, associated with the abandonment of memory, desire and understanding, which gained ground in his theorisation process.[2]

Final considerations about the reading of Bion's work

Our goal here is not to reach a conclusion about what it means to write about clinical practice and to read psychoanalysis texts. We shall conclude with some brief considerations about Bion's writings.

Bion's writing frequently disturbs the reader, generating feelings of helplessness and confusion, as he is constantly showing the transitory and impermanent nature of clinical experiences as well as of his own ideas. Difficulties are also experienced by the reader due to the dryness of his discourse, the imprecise and hermetic character of some passages, and the trite way in which he discusses highly complex ideas, drawn from different areas of knowledge.

However, if Bion's writing incites and demands an active emotional involvement in reading, it also provides tools to investigate the experiences generated. In receiving not only knowledge, but also an experience to be experienced, the reader is encouraged to return to practice, not by adopting the author's ideas but rather by developing and taking possession of his own ideas.

Notes

1 "C" corresponds to the position occupied by this element in what Bion called the "grid". The grid is a set of lines and columns that expresses types of uses and degrees of development of a psychoanalytic object, from the most concrete ("A") to the most abstract ("H") (Bion, 1963).
2 Bion deepened the discussion about the meaning of T(O) in writing and reading in his subsequent book *Attention and Interpretation* (Bion, 1970). A detailed and sensitive examination of this topic was conducted by Ogden (2004).

References

Bion, W.R. (1961). *Experiences in Groups*. London: Tavistock, 2004.
Bion, W.R. (1962). *Learning from Experience*. London: Karnac, 1991.
Bion, W.R. (1963). *Elements of Psycho-Analysis*. London: Karnac, 1984.
Bion, W.R. (1965). *Transformations*. London: Karnac, 1991.
Bion, W.R. (1966). Catastrophic change. In C. Mawson (Ed.), *The Complete Works of W. R. Bion. Volume VI*. London: Karnac, 2014.
Bion, W.R. (1967a). Commentary. In *Second Thoughts*. London: Karnac, 1993.
Bion, W.R. (1967b). *Second Thoughts*. London: Karnac, 1993.
Bion, W.R. (1970). *Attention and Interpretation*. London: Karnac, 1993.
Grotstein, J. (2000). *Who Is the Dreamer who Dreams the Dream?* Hillsdale, NJ: Analytic Press.

Mahony, P.J. (1993). Freud's cases: Are they valuable today? *International Journal of Psychoanalysis* 74: 1027–1035.

Ogden, T.H. (2004). An introduction to the reading of Bion. *International Journal of Psychoanalysis* 85: 285–300.

Vermote, R. (2011). On the value of "late Bion" to analytic theory and practice. *International Journal of Psychoanalysis* 92: 1089–1098.

7

TROPISMS[1] -AT-ONE-MENT AND MENTAL GROWTH

Lia Pistiner de Cortiñas

I will take as a starting point the hypothesis about the pre-natal, protomental aspects of the mind and the failures of the process of symbolic transformations. I will include Bion's conjectures about **tropisms** as pre-natal, protomental functioning and its transformations from the perspective of mental growth. This will be the frame to make a differentiation between the failures of the process of symbolization in the frozen autistic desert and in the world of psychotic emotional turbulence.[2]

The development of thinking implies creating instruments. With patients who have failures in their symbolization process, we meet with problems due to the lack of development or deterioration of these mental tools. And if we don't have tools we don't have the necessary instruments to think and solve our problems. So a first technical approach is that in the treatment of patients with autistic or psychotic disturbances, first the patient needs to repair or develop functions.

The Greek word "symbolon" means sign of acknowledgement, password; this sign was represented by an object split in two. Each participant kept one half. After an absence, one of the participants presented his half and if it matched with the second half of the other participant, the relationship between the two became evident. *The symbolon is a tangible object, that in absences reminds the participants of the relationship. The symbolon is a combination of an emotional experience of presence that reminds the absence and vice-versa, the symbolon represents the relationship. It also implies a third: the interpreting subject.* Symbolism doesn't work through imitation but through analogy. To use analogies demands a differentiation between the "thing" and the "no-thing" – tolerating the relation between the absence and the presence. An idea is a no-thing. The analogy shows the relation. Meaning implies differences, and there can be no meaning in a completely homogeneous field.

To understand how in our species this capability of making relations evolved I want to get back briefly to our evolution and to a characteristic of human kind, which is to be *born prematurely* and at the same time having many potentialities for development, different from other species that are born with all the knowledge they need for surviving encrypted in their DNA. The premature birth was an *autopoietic*[3] evolution. The human being is born with pre-conceptions (Bion, 1962). The premature birth also implies that, in the relationship mother-infant, a psychological counterpart of the nutritious breast is needed – a mind to be able to grow and develop needs another mind.

In her autobiography *In Praise of Imperfection*, Rita Levy Montalcini (1988)[4] says that the imperfection she praises is that of man, who is born premature and incomplete, but with great potentiality for development, unlike other species such as insects. In the evolution of our species and of our brain it could grow and also transform through mutations. What is interesting about these mutations is that they mostly affected the cortex, the grey matter associated with reason, our intellectual side, which also besides mutations can continue evolving because of cultural influences. But there is another system, an older one: the limbic system. Bion calls it thalamic or subthalamic and speaks of subthalamic terrors. The limbic system cannot mutate because it regulates both emotions, and their biological anticipation – such as the adrenaline discharge – as well as such vital mechanisms as breathing and heartbeat.

The relationship between the evolved cortex, which receives the influences of culture, and the limbic system is not pre-determinate and there may or may not be established connections, connections which can also have different characteristics.

Bion speaks about tropisms in his posthumous book *Cogitations* (1992), and in his published work he only refers to this hypothesis under the name of narciss-ism and social-ism, in Chapter 6 of *Transformations* (1965), as two opposite poles of mental functioning that coexist. In *Cogitations* there is no date so we don't know when he wrote about these ideas, but as I see it they are related to the ideas of an embryonic mind, which he describes in his paper "Caesura" (1977), with the hypothesis of somatic anticipations of what will later become transformed into emotions; this notion of tropisms also has a strong kinship with all those conjectures of pre-natal and proto-mental elements that we find in his writings from *Experiences in Groups* (1961) onward and in the Vol. 3 of *A Memoir of the Future: A Dawn of Oblivion.* (1979).

The hypothesis of tropism is also related to the investigation of the characteristics of the primitive mind, and its evolution from a primitive form of communication, realistic projective identification and the environmental circumstances that it meets. As we will see, these circumstances refer to a human environment that we also find later under the name of maternal reverie, alpha function, etc., and which contribute from a psychoanalytic vertex towards understanding mental growth and its obstacles as a relationship between two minds. In *Cogitations*, Bion says that tropisms are seekers of objects, objects that can receive and transform this primitive communication. Therefore, tropisms can be communicated.

In this paper I will be referring to mental growth regarding the development of potentialities, through the transformation of primitive proto-emotional, pre-natal aspects, and I will approach this subject from the perspective of tropisms. This development is an evolution which can fail or be achieved in different ways.

These ideas have significant implications in psychoanalytical clinical practice. Psychoanalysis has studied the primitive mind from its inception and, like other hypotheses, this one is disturbing and creates turbulences.

To develop the ideas I will take some of Bion's hypotheses which contribute to the understanding of his journey from the first notions about primitive mechanisms – already present in *Experiences in Groups* – and disturbed functioning – the psychotic and non-psychotic part of the personality – to his formulations about learning from experience and the elaboration of a notion of the development of the personality through transformations towards mental growth. This will be the vertex from where to understand the different alternatives in the transformation of tropisms and its consequences for the personality.

In *Cogitations*, Bion says:

> Tropisms may be communicated. In certain circumstances they are too powerful for the modes of communication available to the personality. This, presumably, may be because the personality is too weak or ill-developed if the traumatic situation arrives prematurely. But when this situation does arise, all the future development of the personality depends on whether an object, the breast exists into which the tropisms can be projected. If it does not, the result is a disaster which ultimately takes the form of loss of contact with reality, apathy, or mania [. . .]. If such an object exists, a breast capable of tolerating projective identification which are thrust into it (for it is to projective identification in relation to the breast that I have now returned), then the outcome may be supposed to be more favorable, although in suspense.
>
> *(Bion, 1992, p. 34)*

Why "in suspense"? Because the result depends on the transformational quality of the breast-object-container: if it is or is not an object with reverie that can accept projective identifications and transform them so that they become tolerable for the infant's personality, who will then be able to reintroject that part of its personality made tolerable. My hypothesis is that tropisms are linked on one hand with **O**, since Bion says that they need to be rescued from the infinite formless void and on the other hand there is a relation with their development as emotional links. *My conjecture is that tropisms become links, emotional links **L** (love), **H** (hate) and **K** (disposition towards knowing) through the mediation of a breast that is capable of receiving and transforming them, giving them a meaning.* This conjecture is a bridge to understand certain technical considerations in clinical practice, and to develop an adequate container-contained relationship with our patient.

From *Learning from Experience* (1962) Bion presents his *theory of emotions as the core of psychic life and so the K link, the disposition towards knowing, is a primary and fundamental link as love (L) and hate (H).*

Under this conception of the K link, several psychoanalytical ideas are reassessed and even changed, due to his theory of reverie and alpha function. The hypothesis of a K link, as an emotional link, as the disposition to know and not as the possession of knowledge, differs substantially from the Freudian conception of knowledge as the outcome of sublimation of the childhood's sexual curiosity, and from an epistemophilic instinct as in Klein's formulation. *Can we conceive a tropism as the disposition towards knowledge that is transformed into a K link through a containing object that provides meaning?*

With this change of the vertex of observation, the first object relation (and the analyst in the analytical process) becomes an object that provides containing and meaning for what evolves from **O.** In the development of the personality, the encounter with this meaning-providing object is fundamental, through maternal reverie or the analyst's alpha function.

Meaning and truth are the nutrients of the mind. The infant's personality, and the patient's in analysis, may be too weak for these primitive powerful means of communication. If they don't find a psychological counterpart of a nourishing breast, that can receive the tropisms and transform them, or if it is hostile to this primitive communication, the situation becomes traumatic[5] and may have disastrous consequences, as we will see. The containing object that provides meaning provides understanding, learning from experience and wisdom. It is an object that contributes to the development of the mental equipment the human being needs to face psychic change, to grow and contain the turbulence implied in this process.

This object that provides meaning is different from the breast provider of services, such as the toilet-breast (Meltzer, 1967) or the gratifying or frustrating breast (Klein, 1952). It also is not the integrated breast of the depressive position, although to my understanding, if everything goes well, the evolution of the relationship of the mother's mind and the infant's mind includes both, the capacity for integration as well as the tolerance for moments of depression and for the moments of uncertainty: the PS↔D function.

The container-contained relationship plays a central role here. *With the idea of maternal reverie as a container of the primitive projective identifications of the infant and as a psychosomatic channel of communication, through which the mother conveys what she feels for the infant and the father, the environmental factor acquires a psychoanalytical meaning.* The notion of tropism complements this psychoanalytical understanding of the environmental factor as the emotional atmosphere. Under this conception, the counterpart of the nourishing breast is a breast whose function of being receptive to primitive communications and providing meaning is fundamental for the process of humanization and mental growth. This is the context in which the description of a catastrophic anxiety arises, possibly the most fundamental state of helplessness of the human being: the fear of an impending catastrophe. When reverie fails in the transformation of the primitive emotions, this anxiety becomes a *nameless dread*.

Tropisms can be communicated. To describe this communication one can conjecture that the infant launches a primitive emotion into the outer space, through projective identification. Through its crying, its screaming, its kicking, its gaze, the infant sends the emotion, like a probe seeking an object that can contain and transform it. Freud had already stated in the *Project* that the infant's crying, when in contact with a Fellow Human being, becomes communication (1895).

Once again, why does Bion say "in suspense"? As the infant with the mother the patient needs the analyst to be receptive to his/her modes of primitive communication and to be able to modulate his/her catastrophic anxieties. If this communication meets an object with reverie that can accept and transforms projective identifications he/she will be able to reintroject that part of his/her personality, now made tolerable; otherwise the situation becomes traumatic because it is too premature. When the personality is too weak or underdeveloped, this increases the probability of the situation becoming traumatic. In clinical practice, the patient depends on the analyst's alpha function to receive and transform the traumatic situation with all its defensive deformations.

What is interesting from a clinical vertex is that out of the three tropisms that Bion describes, parasitism, murder and creation, he suggests that the one that predominates in the patient who comes to analysis is creation, which is seeking an object with which projective identification is possible as a realistic method of primitive communication. In *Cogitations* he also states that the infant's tolerance of frustration is not of primary significance, because I suppose that it also depends on the modulation made by reverie, but it is a factor for clinical practice: a patient who has little tolerance of frustration will have more difficulties in a psychoanalytical treatment that inevitably implies frustration, and will need more of the analyst's alpha function to modulate the catastrophic anxieties and traumatic states of helplessness.

In human beings, the tropisms described by Bion are greatly dependent on their transformations. They can evolve towards transformations in dream-thoughts, or they can turn more virulent or even wither or freeze. Obviously, it is not the same to dream a murder, or write a novel or paint a picture of a murder, than carry out the act of murder itself. When tropisms freeze, as it is my hypothesis regarding autism, the patient can sometimes express it from a non-autistic part of his/her personality, such as my patient Paul did when he could describe that he felt that he was "withering" and he associated this mental state with what he read in *Steppenwolf* by Herman Hesse (1927). The consideration that the tropism that predominates in the patient who seeks analysis is the tropism of creation is of great clinical significance because it means that the patient wants to recover his/her vitality. In a dream Paul could represent this rejecting object as a woman who had the skin of a hippopotamus.

Unlike instincts or drives, tropisms are not theoretical hypothesis, they can be observed: taking phototropism as a model, it is obvious that plants seek light and roots seek the earth. One essential trait of tropisms is that they are sensible to environmental changes. A flower has certain expectations regarding light, temperature, etc.; if it does not find them, it withers.

I now come back to my hypothesis of the relationship between transformation of tropisms and emotional links, which are channels of communication with external and internal reality (Pistiner de Cortiñas, 2007). *My hypothesis is that the encounter with this containing object that provides meaning, transforms tropisms into emotional links of love, hate and the disposition to know.* I come back to this idea because I am now interested in describing the relationship between tropisms and the *self* and the *disastrous consequences when containment and transformation fail* (Bion, 1992, p. 34). Regarding the *self*, what is interesting – and in line with Winnicott's notions that there is not such a thing as an isolated infant and about the development of the true self – is that Bion gives priority to the emotional links with the self: this first transformation of tropisms into links of love for the self, hate for the self and self-knowledge is necessary. These L, H and K links with the self are priority; Bion calls them narciss-ism and according to how they develop, they reflect in the object relations (what Bion calls social-ism). *The discovery of the other and the nature of object relations have as a precondition the development of emotional links with the self.*

The development of mental equipment and the matrix functions of thinking are directly related to the "environmental" circumstances, in the tropism model. A primordial source of catastrophic anxiety for Bion is that the infant has no notion of absence, so the absence of meaning is experienced not only as a nameless dread but it is also perceived as if the source of all meaning, the breast, has been lost. In Chapter 6 of *Transformations* (1965), Bion says that if the infant does not find this transformational object for which the infant has a meaning, it seeks a God for whom it has a meaning. This God, as I see it, is the primitive super-super-ego that usurps the ego functions, the moral conscience without morality. This primitive super-ego, hostile to primitive communication, is described by Bion as an assassin of the Ego and is one of the central obstacles to a creative transformation that may stimulate a new evolution towards mental growth. Moreover, the object that rejects these primitive means of communication is internalized by the infant, and becomes an internal object that is hostile to this kind of communication. This causes many difficulties and misunderstandings which are a challenge in psychoanalytical clinical practice. The infant's or the patient's personality also rejects the tropisms, or at least in part, and as we will see, they can remain enclosed in the means of communication, which paradoxically prevent them from being useful for communicating. We meet with evacuative speaking or looking, etc. This adds to the clinical difficulties, since a psychoanalytical treatment depends on communication. In psychoanalysis, discovering these obstacles and helping the patient to develop authentic Ego functions clears the way to dismantling crystallizations, the autistic encapsulations or the exoskeletons, and to become more authentic with his/ herself. This means becoming in at-one-ment.

So a significant question arises, representing a true challenge for psychoanalytical theory: Is the tropism hypothesis a different way of defining the object relationship – at a very primitive, protomental level – as the seeking of an object? Is this what Bion later includes in the concept of innate pre-conceptions, clearly a much more complex scheme? Are tropisms what he will later describe as the links that form the matrix of contact with reality? My hypothesis, which I have already forwarded, is that in these descriptions included in *Cogitations* we find a precedent idea of **O**, the infinite formless void from which something evolves, and this evolution is of the tropism (matrix of mental life) that can be transformed into a link, in the primary relationship with the breast with reverie, or in the session, through the analyst's alpha function. It's the evolution of $O \rightarrow K$, *evolution in which what is formless is transformed in an emotional link.* In my opinion, the notion of the whole personality could be included in **O, as what is not yet transformed**, and the personality must evolve towards mental growth, therefore these transformations are always necessary to prevent deterioration. The evolution towards growth implies to win from the infinite formless void a meaning, a narrative container skin, as are the function of dreams, myths and models. But in order to dismantle what is crystallized or the disastrous consequences that Bion refers to and so opens the possibility of evolution and mental growth, there is another step: the transformation of $K \rightarrow O$ in order to become that which was obtained through K. *This implies for the patient developing functions to enable him/her to develop a mental skin, creating a potential space where to exist and feel real and become more authentic. Therefore, a new step is the transformation of K to O, becoming that which one has discovered, and being in at-one-ment with it.*

The psychotic world has a violent turbulence with attacks on linking and a hypertrophied primitive means of communication, which was realistic in its origin but became hypertrophied. When the rejection is produced, which also can become worse with the reversion of the reverie channel – the mother's projective identifications circulate towards the infant – [6]in this case we will see the consequences of psychotic turbulence or psychosomatic disorders. What prevail are **projective transformations.** It is also possible for tropisms to remain at a somatic protomental level: as perhaps happens with the mysterious auto-immune illnesses that still require investigation.

I want to differentiate between patients with predominant **projective transformations** and those who function mostly with **transformations in hallucinosis**. In projective transformation, the violence of the projective identifications that have not been contained and given meaning by reverie, do not tolerate ideograms, which are the sensory impressions formed by the images, the "furniture of dreams". Ideograms are evacuated through a hypertrophied projective identification, so the means of communication, of contact with internal and external reality are invaded by the tropisms, because they are rejected both by the infant's personality and the object, as we have seen. The eyes are not used for seeing, the ears for hearing, etc., but in reverse, for projective identification.

A vicious circle arises, in which there is no distinction between the sense impression and the object of the external world. But if what prevails is the tropism of creation, the analyst's alpha function can transform them into alpha elements, while the analysis stimulates an adequate container and the patient can start reintrojecting what he/she evacuated, transformed into tolerable aspects of his/her personality and at the same time developing their own alpha function. A potential space for dreaming is created. The patient begins to differentiate between psychic and external reality. In this case, we find that patients start to dream, to value their dreams and to generate a space in their inner world for dream-thoughts, which provide emotional meaning, nourishment of the mind, and are a very significant factor for mental growth.

In transformations into hallucinosis, what predominates is envious rivalry and the arrogant super-super-ego, the method of transformation into hallucinosis is considered superior to the psychoanalytical method. Contact with reality is more damaged than in the projective transformations of tropisms; possibly what predominates are the tropisms of parasitism and murder that have not been transformed into dreams and stimulate an intolerable terror and mental pain along with a toxic system of lies. However, when this kind of transformation predominates, the first task in analysis is to consider and modify this rivalry of methods, as far as possible; if this is not achieved, instead of a space for the development of dream-thoughts we are left with a hallucinotic space. In the hallucinotic world, dream-thoughts have been substituted by lies and hallucinosis; it is a toxic world not only for the mind of the person who is generating it, but also for the mind of those who come into contact with such toxicity.

Another possibility is that the answer to the seeking of the tropism of an object with which projective identification is possible may be a *non-response, an apathy, such as in autism*; in this case, my conjecture, as I already pointed out, is that the tropism withers or freezes, as is the case in the autistic frozen desert.

Psychoanalytical exploration in autistic children reveals conditions of "non-contact", a halt in projective identifications, substituted by adhesive identifications linked to a particular fusion of their own body with the body of the object, with predominance of the tactile sense, the use of autistic sensation objects, which is different from an object relation. For the autistic child, a toy is not to play with, it's something hard to hold on, which stimulates tactile sensations that enable the child not to feel separated. Autistic infants have intolerance to be aware of separation between tongue and nipple; they experience the separation as a hole in their own body.

These factors contribute to a terrifying experience of separation, felt as a hole in their own body, and lead them to develop spurious soothing sensations that condemn them to disconnection.

The way in which a body that is felt with holes protects itself from terrifying experiences, is by wrapping itself in whirlwinds of self-generated sensations, which strengthen the lack of attention to shared realities and becloud the awareness of normal sensations. *Disconnections leave holes in the place of relationships.*

I want to illustrate these ideas with a clinical experience. John was born at a time when his mother had lost her own grandmother, who had raised her, because her own mother had suffered from depressions all her life. John's cesarean birth and the death of this grandmother happened at the same time. The mother first believed that John had died. Then she became very depressed and could not tolerate the infant's intense gaze. The father was absent most of the time and John only started breastfeeding when the father returned and they went together on a family vacation. However, the mother's depression and fragility continued, as well as the father's absences. The infant at last fell into autism, avoiding all visual contact. In his analysis he began to show a capacity for contact playing and communication, from a non-autistic part of his personality, while at the same time falling back time after time into clinging to autistic maneuvers (Tustin, 1990) and autistic sensations objects, inanimate objects that stimulated spurious sensations. These maneuvers and objects belong to a lifeless world that's different from the psychotic world. In the evolution of his analysis, John oscillated between moments of playing and moments of seeking the sensations of his autistic world, such as turning his back and licking the window, disconnecting himself from all human contact.

Maternal depression and paternal absence combine with the baby's high sensitivity to the object's mental states; the response of the breast-object that nourishes mental life is not rejection but apathy, a non-answer. This absence of reverie is a disconnection of reverie (as a communication channel) and in this case, tropisms face a void, a lack of vitality, not a rejection such as in psychotic turbulence. In the autistic zone of non-transformation, tropisms are stripped of vitality, they freeze or wither and the development of embryonic thought stops and this truncates the development of a consciousness capable of awareness. Among the functions that are most affected by disconnection, annulment and isolation are memory, attention, judgment and curiosity. These undeveloped, arrested functions, the isolation, and the emotional and cognitive disconnection allow the conjecture of frozen tropisms and their lack of transformation into **L**, **H** and **K** links.

A fundamental question for clinical practice is how to help these patients to get out of this frozen, inanimate world to gain access a creative transformation of their tropisms.

In my book *The Aesthetic Dimension of the Mind* (Pistiner de Cortiñas, 2007), I discuss that we need to create a potential space for playing and dreaming and other technical resources such as the personification of emotions and the need for a more active prevention of autistic maneuvers (such as John's licking of the glass of the window) which keeps the child or the adult in that arid world and with untransformed terrors. This potential space implies also creating subjectivity and an inner place where to feel that one exists and is real (Winnicott, 1971).

Leaving that arid world where tropisms remain frozen by creating a space for playing provides the possibility not only to transform tropisms into playing, but also opening a space for the oedipal pre-conception to be vitalized and thereby enable the exploration of the real relationship between the parents. This exploration allows transcending caesuras between the autistic part of the child and a more mature understanding, from another vertex. Both dreaming, in Bion's extended definition, and playing are vital factors for the differentiation between psychic and external reality and contribute to the vitalization and transformation of tropisms. They are potential spaces of projection in which, as is the case with reverie, dreamlike images, personification and games return parts of the personality with a meaning, which now being more tolerable, can be reintrojected. These children or adults provoke in the analyst tenderness, unlike the violence of psychotic turbulence, which requires other technical resources. Furthermore, in my clinical experience I've observed that when they leave the autistic world, they very often develop towards aesthetic achievements, such as painting, music or theater.

The same goes for the patients in which "over-adaptation" to external reality works as an exoskeleton; when they can leave their prosthetic devices and generate an endoskeleton, often through dreams, playing and personification, the evolution towards mental growth is to find more poetry and more life in their life.

As for psychotic turbulence, if we are dealing with problems arising from hypertrophied projective transformation, then although we sometimes face a toxic atmosphere and misunderstandings generated by transformations into minus – *K, of active disavowal*, the analyst's alpha function slowly enables tropisms to be transformed by creating a relational space, a field in the session for dreaming and playing and prevents tropisms from becoming parasites of the means of communication with internal and external reality. This space, related to the development of mental functions, also opens up the field to substitute atonement[7] – thanks to the alpha function which enables us to discern between dreams, outer and inner reality. Atonement is related with the primitive super-super-ego in contrast with at-one-ment, to become one with oneself, described by Bion. The development of the matrix functions of thinking, starting with embryonic thought, also opens up a space in which the patient can exist and feel real. The development of this space and the notion of time as a fourth dimension, a linear time of life, also opens up the possibility to grow up assuming limits and responsibilities, tolerating the relation infinite – finite.

Notes

1 Definition of tropism: plants can detect changes in the environment and respond to them. The most frequent response for plants consists of growing slowly in a certain direction, as defined by the stimuli.
2 To illustrate emotional turbulence one of the models Bion proposes is the reflection of a tree in the water of a lake. The degree of deformation of the reflection depends on the atmosphere, calm or stormy, that can agitate the lake. Emotion, representation and object relation and its interaction are the elements that we need to consider.
3 *Autopoyesis:* a neologism that designates a system capable of reproducing itself and maintaining itself. It was proposed by the Chilean biologists: Maturana and Varela in 1972. Autopoyesis is the condition of existence of the living beings in the continuous production of themselves.
4 An Italian doctor who won the Nobel Prize for her discoveries on neurotransmitters.
5 In the context of Bion's hypothesis of container-contained, an undigested fact can be traumatic.
6 Let us not forget reverie as a psychosomatic channel of communication.
7 In my opinion, Bion is playing with words when he suggests at-one-ment is like being in unity with oneself, in contrast with atonement, a word which means expiation and which I relate to the super-super-ego.

References

Bion, W.R. (1961). *Experiences in Groups.* London: Tavistock Publications Ltd.
Bion, W.R. (1962). *Learning from Experience.* London: William Heinemann.
Bion, W.R. (1965). *Transformations.* London: William Heinemann.
Bion, W.R. (1977). Caesura. In W.R. Bion (Eds.), *Two Papers: The Grid and Caesura.* Rio de Janeiro: Imago Editora. [Reprinted: London: Karnac, 1989].
Bion, W.R. (1979). *A Memoir of the Future: The Dawn of Oblivion.* London: Karnac.
Bion, W.R. (1992). *Cogitations.* Ed. F. Bion. London: Karnac.
Freud, S. (1895). Project for a scientific psychology. *S.E.* 1: 283–346. London: Hogarth.
Herman Hess (1927). *Steppenwolf.* Berlin: Fisher Verlag.
Klein, M. (1952). Some theoretical conclusions regarding the emotional life of the infant. In *Writings.* London: Karnac.
Meltzer, D. (1967). *The Psycho Analytical Process.* London: William Heinemann.
Montalcini, Levy, R. (1988). *Praise of Imperfection.* New York: Basic Books.
Pistiner de Cortiñas, L. (2007). *The Aesthetic Dimension of the Mind.* London: Karnac.
Tustin, F. (1990). *The Protective Shell in Children and Adults.* London: Karnac.
Winnicott, D. (1971). *Playing and Reality.* London: Tavistock Publications Ltd.

SECTION IV
Faith and O

8

RECIPROCAL KINDLING, EMERGENT LIFE

Bion's faith in O, in search of emotional truth

Keri Cohen

Bion spoke of Faith in O, in the unknown. Is there knowledge in Faith? Faith rests partly in the emotional process to carry us forward in the face of tragedy. Certainly there are signals of faith, communication among the life forces on this planet. Bion spoke of a need to grow the capacity to receive what is offered emotionally. Likely, he was ahead of his time, intuitively knowing that the brain, the soul had to be ready to receive emotional nourishment, somehow having developed the innate capacity to do so. Within the last few years articles on the brain and on the signals snap pea roots send to each other underground, seem to bring his thoughts to scientific fruition. The snap pea's root can send a warning signal about drought, to another snap pea root, so that the plant can prepare or store the information for a later time. The brain clears toxins during periods of rest, sleep. The brain grows the capacity, makes necessary preparations before it is able to take in new signals.

The concept of kindling in mental health began in the 1990s, with the theory that emotionally charged events in succession could lead to a manic episode. The episodes or life stress eventually are not needed, and one's autonomous inner being becomes enough to trigger mania (Bender and Alloy, 2011). The kindling about which I speak uses this concept to suggest that kindling can promote calm and healing between life forces, rather than dysregulation and mania. When space opens enough in search of the truth in O, the process of kindling transforms into a new layer of emotional truth. Faith in the process, whether that be analytic, healing from trauma or grief or protection from destruction, becomes possible. Examples I provide link Bion's faith in O, bringing about a kindling process between life forces that promotes healing and a new emotional truth.

When discussing reciprocal kindling, I imagine a non-verbal transfer of a state of being from one life force to another, and back again, however this is only possible when internal space is open. Energy within one force transfers to another, promoting healing and a new emotional truth feeling. Bion spoke about experiencing the thing-in-itself, aiming for O (Bion, 1963). By bringing his concept together with scientific discoveries, we can begin to see scientific proof that his intuitive methodology for analysis was truly healing, full of repair. Further, adding the concept of reciprocal kindling allows for the concrete application of his intuition. Reciprocal kindling between two life forces, influencing the birth of an emotional truth through Faith in O, is applied to reach new depths.

The energy to create kindling seems kinetic from within, but there is an external kinetic energy signal that exists between people, animals and plants. Science seems to be bearing witness to this in plant life. Science also teaches that the brain is busy at work while it rests, detoxifying, making room for repair. Perhaps reciprocal kindling can heal, help life forms cope and soothe one another. The energy becomes shared, dispersed and reabsorbed by the other as a way to heal. Although internal kindling can be destructive, manic, the kinetic transfer of kindling can warm up a frozen soul after loss, or help prevent one from falling into a state of withdrawal.

Bion spoke about the ability to experience O and find the emotional truth in O. If the mind is saturated with memory, "such a mind is one who is incapable of learning because it is satisfied" (Bion, 1970). He says, "The exercises in discarding memory and desire must be seen as preparatory to a state of mind in which O can evolve" (Bion, 1970). Bion's capacity for O can be joined by what science is discovering in the natural world. Through this lens, we can observe that mentally and physically, forces are at work to make room for a powerful experience enabling new emotional truths in and through our relation to O. Further, these experiences are not limited to one participant, as something happens in this emotional truth that sparks the concurrent transfer of positive kindling between life forces, leading to repair and soothing emotional truth in O.

I suggest that the process of reciprocal kindling helps aid repair through a kinetic emotional feeling signal between two people. In addition, it can possibly act as a buffer for future pain. Perhaps too, reciprocal kindling can help us to stay present focused, not frozen from trauma, if we are able to create emotional space and clear the toxins, in order to receive its bounties. I think it possible to have positive, healing reciprocal kindling.

We can get overloaded, flooded with experience, traumas, secrets, situations, daily pressures of just being. Destructive kindling has the potential to ignite an explosion, make us bleed out – kindling gone wild. Held inside a personality structure that digests limited amounts at a time, one tries to cope but is limited. It takes a different kind of kinetic movement to spur the brain to share the inner workings of the soul with another.

Recently, in an online discussion group, someone posted about their friend's sudden loss of an older child. As she described the pain of the news from her friend, she spoke of the emergent life she heard in the background on the other end of the phone line. She spoke about how incredulous it was to lose a child, wondering how her friend could possibly go on living. During the phone call, her friend was cooing with her new baby granddaughter, emergent life. Death and life co-joined; emergent life peeking out from loss.

Michael Eigen writes, "If we put repair and emergence together, we have moments in which coming through something (difficulty, trauma, loss, defeat) can couple with an unexpected learning or opening, or taste of a world to come here and now, even, at times, tragic growth and learning" (Eigen Workshop, Yahoo! Forum).

This woman's friend, in present time, demonstrated exactly this sentiment, coupling life and death with grief and emergent life, as she cooed with her granddaughter. In that moment, she chose to focus on what was, rather than what was not, emergent life in front of her. Perhaps this reciprocal kindling repaired part of the tragedy. She stayed with life. She taught through doing, about the living. She was living through tragedy, discovering the reality of tragic growth and learning.

Science tracks this idea. The brain removes toxins when we sleep, sweeping away material that could clog our life force. The journal *Science* carried an article in October 2013 that spoke about this discovery.

The research discovered that the brain has limited energy and must choose between two states of being, "awake and aware or asleep and cleaning up" as Dr. Maiken Nedergaard explained. This research builds on a 2012 discovery of the brain's own ability to discard its own toxins through an internal system called the glymphatic system. Special cells in the brain, which keep nerve cells alive, literally shrink during sleep, which produces further space between brain tissue, thus allowing more fluid to be pumped in that can wash away the toxins. Dr. Nedergaard said that this was a "vital" function for staying alive, but this function did not appear to be possible while the mind was awake. In order for humans to stay alive, the brain must discard toxins. Perhaps this is how, quite literally, people die from psychological trauma, if they cannot take in positive life energy.

The personality cannot always contain the grief and trauma of the human condition. Our very being puts demands on our psyche that seem too much to handle. Our faith in surviving grows dim unless we are able to not only tolerate, but offset the inherent pain life provides. The article spoke of the brain as a living organ, yet our sensory and feeling psyches function as our spiritual and psychological faith organs. How much can they bear before they shut down from overload? Our spiritual selves may mirror the brain's capacity to pump out toxins to make room for reparations.

Somehow, this woman's friend was able to pump out enough toxins from her child's death to enjoy the energy provided by her granddaughter. Life forces filled the space before more toxins could infiltrate. Perhaps her granddaughter kindled her brain into reparation. Or maybe her unconscious just sensed more room needed to be cleared for repair of the tragic. The elasticity of the sensory feeling organ of the human personality structure seems aligned with science, albeit in a softer more beautiful way.

Winnicott (1988) speaks about the unknown background support in terms of a mother and the baby. The baby cannot survive without the background support of the mother, yet the baby is not aware that the mother provides the sensory, feeling temperature. The reverse could be true in times of loss. The loss this grandmother experienced, the loss of her child, was met with an unknown background support of her new baby granddaughter. Could a baby provide an unknown background support for a grieving relative? The space made in the brain or in the emotional soul, after the toxin washout, is filled with emergent life force feelings and energy. A reciprocal unknown ability to rekindle life exists.

Somehow, plants are able to do this in a similar way to humans, possibly more successfully and proactively, through a conveyance and momentum of signals through their roots.

In 2012, an Israeli team found that snap peas have the ability to send warning signals through their root system when risk of drought emerged. The researchers, headed by plant biologist Ariel Novoplansky of the Mitrani Department of Desert Ecology, exposed five garden pea plants to drought conditions. They found that the stressed plant closes its leaves to prevent water loss. Meanwhile its roots release signals that caused neighboring plants, which were not exposed to drought conditions, to react as if they had been. The study showed "the unstressed plants transmitted the information on to other healthy plants" (Novoplansky, 2013).

Preliminary results indicate that plants that receive the distress signals will survive better if exposed to drought at a later stage in their life. Novoplansky says,

> The results demonstrate the ability of plants and other "simple" organisms to learn, remember and respond to environmental challenges in ways so far known in complex

creatures with a central nervous system. . . . In some cases the immediate response helps healthy plants to deal with distress that has not yet affected them directly.

Could our language center mask our ability to feel and sense one another in our relationships? What if we could not speak to communicate, only could sense, feel, like plants. Maybe we would be able to mitigate the severity of our emotional force field more creatively; maybe we are able to do this sometimes. The plants seem to store signals for the future. The plant receives a distress signal and has a better chance of survival if exposed to drought, trauma, later in life.

Often, when humans receive distress signals or experience severe stress early in life, it sets up an incapacity to handle stress later, setting the scene for internal kindling to ignite damaging fire in the personality and soul. It seems that plants can protect against future stress, whereas humans often experience compounded trauma resulting in a decreased ability to cope. Humans sometimes are set on a trajectory for recovery rather than proactive prevention to ward off stress.

The brain has plumbing to pump out the toxins; person to person contact has the ability to absorb another's pain. The grandmother I mentioned was able to coo with her granddaughter and perhaps the kinetic energy absorbed by the baby will help build future coping mechanisms, like what the Israeli scientists reported about plants. Maybe intuitively the grandmother knew that if she expressed the stress of grief from the loss of her child into her granddaughter's field, her granddaughter would be set up for destructive kindling and a need for recovery rather than energized with positive nurturing kindling, the preventative love needed to fight stress. Science tells us the brain requires rest to remove toxins. It has to sleep in order to do this work. Rest and work coupled. Maybe cooing with her granddaughter allowed the traumatized part of her being to slumber while her kinetic energy transferred into her granddaughter's psyche. Maybe the granddaughter's emergent life force was reciprocal for the grandmother and served as an unknown background support to enable the grandmother to coo with her. Perhaps lack of language helped the process, a lack of language associated with O.

The human condition, the inability to solve problems of our psyches continues. For all of our sophistication, structures, medical interventions and inventions, we cannot seem to master our overwhelming emotional field. Plants seem to be ahead of the game in this ability to protect damage to their internal regulation system. Plants do not have language, just signals. Signals are their language.

To extract a little from an Emmanuel Levinas quote that Michael Eigen uses in his book *Emotional Storm*:

> Beyond dialogue, a new . . . *maturity and patience for insoluble problems*. . . . Neither violence, nor guile, nor simple diplomacy, nor simple tact, nor pure tolerance, nor even simple sympathy, nor even simple friendship – that attitude before insoluble problems. . . . The presence of persons before a problem . . . to go toward the Other where he is truly other, in the radical contradiction of their alterity.

Sometimes, we signal each other without language. We speak through transferring our energy soul feeling fields.

I have worked with children who have lost a parent at a young age. One youngster told me that she comforted a friend after her father quickly succumbed to a terminal illness. Several months later, she found herself joining her friend on the swings at the playground one day, away from the other children. They sat in silence. Her friend broke the silence and spoke about not having her father, that she missed his hugs and smell. The girl nodded. They sat together for a few minutes in silence. Spontaneously, the moment ended and they ran to play. There were no words, yet, they sensed the emotional field lifting or the kinetic energy they had between them working. Perhaps the girl and her friend experienced reciprocal kindling. There was room in her friend's psyche to take in the feelings, "The presence of persons before a problem" left with no words.

One could say that the friend's personality structure was forced to expand rapidly to try to take in the death of her father, the finality of it. No language exists to replace this feeling of loss. Yet language could destroy it.

Thoughts come of the peas that signal each other through their roots, the part that lives underground. What lives unseen in the human spirit kindles the connection to bear witness to another's inherent suffering. Somehow signals were passed between the girl and her friend. Reciprocal energy led to a moment of repair and growth. Joined were grief and a life force. Something grew from the company of feeling souls sharing a moment, which sparked spontaneous play. No words, just feelings, a new truth emerging from a faith in O.

Is there a courageous kindling that takes place between two or more people when one expresses grief or trauma? Can the kinetic energy be reabsorbed by those who share the loss? Could it potentially stop reclusive states after traumatic loss or experience? The courage of the girl's friend to sit alone on a swing, on a playground full of her peers, seems profound during a developmental stage when children naturally play together in groups. Maybe, too, toxins were filling her psychic being and she needed the rest; this coupled with the girl's feeling the signal to approach her in such an alone state of being, creating an external kindling opportunity. The grieving girl had the capacity to take in the presence of an Other and the sensory experience, void of initial language was key.

A lot was in play; a distress signal may have been sent out (like the plants send), a sense was felt to draw near, a background support was created, external kindling led to reciprocal kindling, toxins were washed away during the period of rest as the girls sat together, and space was created for spontaneous play; an active aliveness resumed. Much can be gleaned from the courage of two children on a playground – an emerging new life force.

I want to offer a brief clinical example from my practice to further illustrate Faith in O, in search of emotional truth. I began seeing a man who was referred to me after the trauma of waking up next to his girlfriend who had passed away in her sleep. I saw him for an initial session and when he returned the following week, he shared that he had held a loaded hand gun to his head two days before our second session. He was broken, guilt ridden, hopeless. His girlfriend, he realized, had opened a door to the reality of a world he had never before experienced. This was a seasoned man, formerly married, a good father, working in a sophisticated job. One day, after some silence, he shared with me that while he grieved her loss, he grieved the internal feeling of trust and love that was generated from his interactions with her. For the year they dated, he felt something deeper, richer, more emotionally truthful that led him to literally trust the world more. His interaction with the world around him had changed, softened. He struggled to put this feeling into words, but he intrinsically knew that something was different when he was with her, something emotionally salient. Something in her being kindled a response in his insides that relaxed him, soothed him, and he felt fuller with her. It was a new feeling that he was then able to send back to her and the reciprocal kindling generated an F in O that he used to interact with the world around him. He felt less suspicious of others in his interactions with them, in every area of his life. What a gift, to feel this emotional truth for the first time in his life. After his girlfriend died, convinced that the Truth would never be experienced again, he nearly ended his life. Powerful life forces at work gave him the gift of F in O and an unmatched sense of emotional truth. Unfortunately, the kindling could not be sustained in her absence. He had no warning to prepare, like the snap peas, for trauma. We continue our work together and his effort to find his own Faith in O. Is it possible to have reciprocal kindling within the relationship you have with yourself? He is on a journey to find out, wrestling with loss in the process.

I suggest that the process of reciprocal kindling helps aid repair through a kinetic emotional feeling signal between two people. In addition, it can possibly act as a buffer for future pain. Perhaps too, reciprocal kindling can help us to stay present focused, not frozen from trauma, if we are able to create emotional space, clear the toxins, in order to receive its bounties.

Reciprocal kindling seems to transpose time. It helps us to live in the moment and stretch the structure of our personalities, our inner gauge of emotional endurance, running on its fuel.

Reciprocal kindling, emergent life, a never ending soul feeling process.

References

Bender, R.E. and L.B. Alloy (2011). Life stress and kindling in bipolar disorder: Review of the evidence and integration with emerging biopsychosocial theories. *Clinical Psychology Review* 31(3): 383–398.

Bion, W. (1963). *Elements of Psychoanalysis*. William Heinemann Medical Books, Ltd. London: Heinemann.

Bion, W. (1970). *Attention and Interpretation*. London: Jason Aronson Inc.

Novoplansky, Ariel, Omer Falik, Yonat Mordoch, Lydia Quansah, and Aaron Fait. (2011). Rumor has it . . .: Relay communication of stress cues in plants. *PLOS One*. Mitrani Department of Desert Ecology, 2 Nov. Web. 15 Nov. 2013.

Winnicott, D.W. (1988). *Human Nature*. London: Free Association.

9

STORMY NAVIGATION WITH OUR "SECRET SHARER"

Monica Horovitz[1]

Negative capability, as described by Bion, permits consciousness not to be invaded by sensory data, it frees intuition and opens up the ineffable dimension of the psychoanalytic object. This ridge line is difficult to follow, but we must have faith in the method which opens us to the infinite spaces of the unconscious. The psychoanalytic attitude short-circuits and transcends our need for control and makes it possible for us to experience the impact of emotional reality so that it can then really evolve and be transformed into growth.

For Bion, faith and catastrophe are oscillating movements and include oscillations between PS and D. Faith in the psychoanalytic method, moreover, is the adequate and primordial response to catastrophe, while psychoanalysis presents itself as a catastrophe for the diverse systems of security that we have set up over the abyss of the unrepresentable.

This catastrophic change that Bion compares with an explosion is linked to a transformation into O. It tells us that we are no longer in the presence of a disaster, as with a buried world, but of an evolution where nothing will ever again be as it was before. Catastrophic change is thus a deep emotional situation occurring during a moment of psychic growth.

Catastrophic change, discovery, evolution is only possible once our own world of closely knit structures has been unfrozen, once the analyst has torn himself away from his own theories and can tolerate uncertainty, which will give birth to a new process of transformation. This transformation is evocative of the link between Bionian mysticism and other mystical experiences accomplished by going through the obscurity of the night: doubt, mystery and psychic pain, that is to say, negative capacity.

The log book of my journey with John

Just as we speak of "extreme sport" to refer to a dangerous sports activity which may result in serious injuries in the case of error, the case of John may be described as an "extreme psychoanalysis". It was a matter of trying to communicate the non-communicable by making use of the model of field, navigating without memory and desire as compasses, in spite of the emotional storms, which, like sea currents or violent winds, are moved by powerful invisible energies.

The limits of this analytic navigation reside fundamentally in our faith in what both the method and the patient bring, making us experience the truth of Bion's maxim that "our patient is our best colleague": John was the "secret sharer" described in the short story of that name written by Joseph Conrad in 1910.

The narrator of this sea story is a young and inexperienced captain of a ship that has to make the voyage to England from the Gulf of Siam. While he is taking the anchor watch until 1 o'clock in the morning, he discovers a sailor, exhausted from spending hours in the water, holding on to the rope side ladder. He takes him on board clandestinely and hides him in his cabin, without the crew's knowledge. A fascinating confrontation then takes place between them behind closed doors: "*Anyone bold enough to open [the door]stealthily would have been treated to the uncanny sight of a double captain busy talking in whispers with his other self*". The captain and his "secret sharer", accomplices in spite of themselves, then concoct a highly risky plan for him to flee the ship and swim to safety: the captain orders the ship to deviate from its course and to sail close to the shore. Each of them trusts in his own capacities to achieve an extremely uncertain goal. Their success will hang by no more than a thread.

Likewise, it is the combination of the knowledge of the patient and of the psychoanalyst which – in turns – saves the situation. Everything I have learned from the "extreme psychoa-nalysis" with John has not only opened up a new universe in me, but enormous gratitude to him for having put his trust in the sharing of our capacities in order to overcome the impossible.

So, in the same way, I invite you to come on board the ship of this analytic experience to share my feelings of inadequacy, of incomprehension, of being overwhelmed, feelings which – if we are honest and authentic – lie in wait for us each time we meet a patient.

In fact, the visual image I had of my patient was such that it created in me a traumatic absence of representation which made it vital to establish a space that was not saturated by his disfigured face and the few things he said. Faced with the danger of being fascinated by terror, I had to process within myself the need to forget.

John was in his 40s when he had his first appointment with me. He is an American artist who has lived in Paris for the past 15 or so years. Four years ago, he was treated for mouth epi-dermal carcinoma, the result of his addiction to smoking and alcohol – surgery, radiotherapy, followed by reconstructive surgery. For that treatment, he went back to New York, staying there for some 18 months until he recovered.

He lived with his partner for about 20 years, but she left him after the operation. He has no children. He himself is the youngest of three children, and the only boy. I would later learn that his parents had belonged to the liberal Jewish upper-middle-class in Poland. In 1939, when Poland was invaded, his father was sent to a forced labor camp, a munitions factory, where he remained until the end of the war. In 1945, as the Allied armies were advancing, the Germans sent him, along with 2,500 other prisoners, on a forced march in the bitter cold and with no food. Only 80 of those prisoners survived. The patient's father learned that his entire family had been deported and wiped out; in Stuttgart, he met an old friend of his – she too was the only surviving member of her family. They married, and ten years later emigrated to the USA, where the patient's father became well known in his professional life. They died soon after their son was diagnosed with cancer.

One evening, a phone call – in English; not easy to understand – I thought that there was some kind of technical hitch on the phone line. A male voice, with some kind of speech impediment, asking for an appointment and mentioning the name of a colleague of mine of whom I have a very good opinion. We agreed on a date, but already I had some doubts in my mind: was he depressed, on medication?

It was snowing on the day of that first appointment. When I opened the door, I saw a very tall man, who was also very thin, wrapped in a cape but wearing clogs, with his feet bare. It was only then that I looked at him and saw his face. He came in, sat down and started to speak with considerable difficulty in articulating. I managed to understand that his parents were dead and that his partner had recently left him; at the same time, I felt overwhelmed, as though in the grip of a wish to wake up from a nightmare. It was a terribly complicated situation, how was I to cope with it? If I had known, I would not have given him an appointment – but to whom could I have referred him? Why me? Fascinated by his clogs, I avoided looking at him directly.

For the first few months, I saw him in a face-to-face setting three times a week, then on the couch, four times a week. During the face-to-face period, I could feel just how important it was for me to "face up to" his face, and not wipe it out, for example, by having him lie on the couch. I realized also the extent to which the human face is an implicit reference to the core of someone's personality, like a mirror. It was therefore through the experience of my own face as a mirror, and thanks to the rhythm and stability of the analytical setting, that we were both able to read and talk about our joint attempts at processing, thereby developing our ability to be together. That also helped him to express his acute aggressive feelings towards me – he saw me as being insensitive to his pain, as if I hated him. Nevertheless, I represented not only the hate that he felt at seeing himself, but also his capacity for observation and his courage in taking a good look at himself. A feeling of otherness began to evolve, in the shape of an externalized self-image and the image of the face of the internalized analyst, supportive and enduring, that enabled him to have access to the couch.

I shall begin my clinical description with these words: "The patient arrives and looks elsewhere. . . ." The patient reaches my door and that in itself is a real victory: wanting analysis, finding an analyst, coming for therapy. Coming, coming back once again and keeping on coming back. For many people, that is never the case – they do not seek the help they need, or else they cannot do anything with it, or perhaps they leave before they manage to find it. With this patient, we are already beyond that stage: he comes and he keeps on coming.

John arrives, but he looks elsewhere, he breaks off all contact. For the time being, coming is all that he can do: making contact, entering into a relationship – that is just too much for him. He and his body manage to find ways of being present without committing himself, without opening himself up to anything. Appearing and making visual contact at the same time are too much for him. He therefore modulates his sensitivity with respect to contact without letting himself be overwhelmed by fear. By curbing his fear, he can make the first move and actually enter my consulting-room. Looking elsewhere is an indication that I must not expect too much of him, I must not ask for too much. It could be said that to some extent he cancels out the psychoanalyst, treating me as if I were not there, but that is only a hypothesis – perhaps he is putting me at a safe distance in order to be there in spite of everything. In such circumstances, breaking off contact is one way of enabling the tiniest degree of bearable contact. Unconsciously, the patient is creating a connecting link between tension and attachment, as though references to pain or to potential pain were accompanied by a feeling of not being there: cutting himself off from the situation by breaking away from what is being felt, or almost feeling nothing, becomes second nature to him, a permanent state of being. His face expresses an almost physically acute pain, accompanied by deep weariness. As if his mind and body were in a paroxysm with no way out, clinging together, knotted together, yet at the same time letting it all go, letting himself go. The body becomes the grave of a senseless and incurable pain. Being tense is for him a suit of armor, like an alarm bell that might take the edge off the somatic and emotional memory of never-ending pain.

All the same, John does try to speak: "There's something I'd like to say", then he starts to stammer. The feeling is that there is something that he wants to say, that his mind needs to express, something about the truth of his life, about what it means to be him – but the trauma of existing cannot yet be put into words. Only little fragments can be unveiled. I can feel the strangulated state of his existence. An image suddenly appears of the psychosomatic tension that rises and falls again with respect to the nuclei of pain expressed indirectly through the movements of his body and by the disjointed fragments of what he says, their destiny and temporality aborted.

In another session, John speaks of "cutting the branches": the word "cutting" is here a reference to traumatic pain. He talks about "being broken", "being cut short" – the language of wounds. Freud (1893–95) pointed out that words or a look may be experienced as a slap in the face or as a stab to the heart, and he stressed the fact that this is not just a metaphor – there is a real emotional pain that may have somatic consequences. The patient makes use of a vocabulary of wounds that refers to his emotional pain and his failure to nourish himself emotionally: "Cut off, bad taste, no home. I couldn't stand that". He cannot stand the pain of existing, the cuts, the emotional state of being, as it were, without a shelter, the horrible taste of his life. He accentuates my feeling of helplessness by adding that it is a matter not only of his ability to tolerate pain or wounds, but also of his inability to communicate these to me. The despairing futility of the process of communication. Not only do his attempts at communication fail in their task, they even exacerbate his wounds. I share his despair, his vain furiousness, his inability to cut me off from the painful feeling of not being able to be in contact either with the other person or with myself.

A shared experience

The feeling of "not being able . . ." is our only link – and I cannot tolerate it, because it is such a direct expression of pain.

John says, "Shut up", and I feel that shutting-up in my mind, my body, my whole being. It's almost like shouting: "Clear off!" Freud (1955) said that the initial trauma is that of being inundated with too much excitation. We feel a need to turn down the volume and perhaps even to switch off, but the problem is that when we shut ourselves off from emotions, we are shut off from ourselves too. To whom or what was that "shut up" addressed? To the mother, the source of care and food? To the analyst? Or, more deeply, to his own self? A "shut up" that runs through all the violence of existence. A feeling that something is not right, a cry that is frozen and chronic, soundless – the session itself. I cannot talk about my own frustration; nothing that he says allows me to do so, and I draw the conclusion that it is itself part of the emotion that he is communicating to me. The link is frustration. I am forced into an emotional experience which I do not understand and from which I cannot learn anything, because it is precisely the visible absence of any change or of learning. Nevertheless, I think that learning to stay with such an experience implies being on the verge of learning something. It is at such times that, as analysts, we can feel how important it is to stick with the feeling of getting nowhere for as long as it takes, in order for the world of emotions to open up. In fact, it is strange, but there is also some pleasure in going through such an experience together, sharing that "other time". What brings us together is endurance, courage, patience, anger, fellow-feeling and love – i.e. everything that patient and analyst go through together. If there is some frustration, it is a highly vivid one, at the heart of which lies a great deal of love, and it links us together over the years. It is as though, all that time, we were both banging our heads against a wall: "Something's not right" is part of our relationship. Together we observe the pain that is life.

With John, the fundamental communicating of pain involved many changes of direction, disguises, devices and camouflaging, but it always survived in his body as a kind of spasm. We cling to words as a kind of lifeboat, which to some extent is a good way of putting it because they themselves are part of the shipwreck. Emotional pain is frozen in the body and in our language, like a fossilized wound.

Communication can be deeply meaningful but it also may be a way of sending out an SOS message: something to which the individual concerned no longer has access. Patient and analyst are faced with a situation from which apparently there is no way out, but the fact of putting up with it together brings other capacities into play.

One final point: John's pronunciation was so distorted that, for the whole of the first year, I was unable to understand the words that he said. I could only feel them.

Faced with the risk of being fascinated by terror, I had to process within myself the need to forget. That is how we were able to communicate and give shape to what, until then, had no shape. After about a year, there came a point at which, for me, his face and his speech became regenerated, as it were, so that I was able to discover the face beyond the face, the face which, behind the disfigurement, was not affected by it and which contained some hope. In addition, John, who had lost all sense of taste and smell, once again began to take pleasure in cooking sophisticated meals for his friends, and he offered me a present. One day, he arrived for his session carrying a box covered in multicolored gift-wrap, inside which were two mangoes. He said that he had discovered a place that was alive and full of warmth. John added that he was offering me "the breasts of his mother from the South, so different from the ice-cold breasts of his Polish mother".

In concluding this paper, I would say that the memory that Bion was referring to in the phrase "without memory or desire" is the distractedness of the mind when it is saturated with sensory elements and unpleasure. That intentional memory looks into the past for something that will give shape to what is currently being observed.

I would also like to say a few words about forgetting, in the sense of the deployment of the analyst's negative capability. What Bion (1970) called negative capability, with its links to the denial of reality, is neither repression nor the need for not remembering. Negative capability is not a loss of memory; it is a denial of reality that opens up a potential space for encountering emotional psychical states through the new links created by what is presently being said. In such a case, the denial of the concrete reality of John's terribly mutilated face made it easier to experience "monstrosity" as being part of our relationship. A path opening onto a process in which the traumatic experience is no longer an eternal present – the absolute opposite of a traumatic hypermnesia that can never forget. Memory linked to forgetting, as I have described it here, is not an automatic and involuntary discharge; it is an evocation connected to thinking and a symbol of absence. In his rendition, with some poetic license, of what Freud wrote to Lou Andreas-Salomé, Bion said that, instead of trying to focus a bright intelligent light on obscure problems, "one should cast a beam of intense darkness into the interior so that something that has been hitherto hidden in the glare of the illumination can now glow all the more in that darkness" (Grotstein 2000, p. 687).

Note

1 Translated by Andrew Weller.

References

Bion, W.R. (1970). *Attention and Interpretation*. London: Tavistock [Reprinted by London: Karnac, 1984].

Conrad, J. (1910). The secret sharer. *Harper's Magazine*. New York: Harper & Bros.

Freud, S. (1955). Studies on Hysteria. *S.E.* 2. London: Hogarth.

Grotstein, J. (2000). Notes on Bion's "Memory and Desire". *Journal of American Academy of Psychoanalysis* 28: 687–694.

Catastrophe, catastrophic change and O

10

BEYOND THE SPECTRUM

Fear of breakdown, catastrophic change, and the unrepressed unconscious[1]

Avner Bergstein

To what extent, Bion (1967a) asks, can we rely on the luxury of sticking to a part of the total experience which is verbally communicable? Bion makes use of the spectrum of the electromagnetic waves as an analogy for emphasising the limits of our sensory apparatus which receives only a small part of the spectrum. The wavelengths visible to us fall in a narrow strip of visual perception in between the infrared on the one end and the ultraviolet on the other. We cannot see the ones that fall off these ends, but they are nevertheless there. Using that as an analogy, Bion proffers that thanks to verbal capacity, there is a certain realm of mental life which we can speak of in terms like personality, mind, and so forth. This is the small part of the spectrum in which one could talk about it as being verbally communicable. However, the psychoanalytic encounter compels us to observe and meet those areas of the mind that lie beyond that narrow sphere. We see a patient who seems an ordinary neurotic patient, Bion says, but as the analysis goes on, he seems to have what one might call a psychotic breakdown. Alternatively, the analysis takes a turn and what we are accustomed to regarding as psychotic elements, become much more visible. "Can we make some corresponding extension of our . . . mental capacity, to take in a little bit more of . . . the invisible aspects of the spectrum?" (1967a, p. 60).

★★★

Guy, aged 30, is a good-looking, suntanned, and muscular young man. He usually arrives wearing shorts, a sleeveless vest, and clogs, and his body is very exposed. From the very start he became very attached to me, perhaps in an undifferentiated manner. He finds it hard to leave at the end of the session, asking, allegedly humorously, if there's no 'double session'. I feel him to be very adhesive, intrusive, always arriving early, walking around my backyard, once even standing at the door when I opened it for the previous patient to leave. He talks very emotionally, weeps, moves incessantly. He wants to tell me of the panic attacks he had experienced some years ago but cannot find the words. He's afraid the attacks might re-appear, and he'll do anything to prevent them from coming back. He remembers his greatest fear was of falling. Fainting and falling. He relates the panic attacks to his use of drugs at the time of their onset. Up until then, he says, his life was terrific: he fell in love twice a week, smoked grass, and felt great; organised parties for all his friends, and everybody sought his company. He says he was in touch with his feelings, and there was no sign of anxiety. The first panic attack came out of the blue. He describes a clear 'cut' between his life until the age of 20 when he began using drugs and life after the first panic attack. He says he hasn't had a meaningful relationship with a woman since then.

In one of our initial sessions he tells a recurring dream where he's in a stormy river with his mother, and he fears she's about to harm him. He explains that his mother is very emotional and stormy. In the past she was depressed. She is very attached to him, very offended if he doesn't call often enough. Father is described as more practical, and blocked.

Guy is intensely involved in various extreme sports, even though he feels these activities no longer suit his age, and I realise he needs these thrills and that he is also afraid of growing up.

In time, I hear more about his nocturnal activities – he drinks a lot, picks up a girl and takes her home. The girls seek him out, but none of them really interest him. He says: "I'm good at beginnings but not at relationships". He's afraid of getting bored, afraid of endings, of death. He says: "I want to stay with you here in the room for hours". Although his enthusiasm seems histrionic, it is contagious, and I too look forward to our sessions. After a few weeks, I offer him the use of the couch and propose he come four times a week. He accepts.

But the move to the couch brings along a dramatic change.

The sessions become surprisingly deadening. He recounts over and over the load he has on his shoulders, the disappointments from close friends, the despair and hopelessness he feels of any possible change. He stops taking girls home, stops drinking, says he masturbates several times a day, needing to feel alive.

I realise that the masturbation, much like the physical and mental over-activity, is not an expression of pleasure but an excess of excitation. He is compelled to unburden himself of the unbearable, unmentalised stress he has inside of him. 'A slave of quantities' (de M'Uzan, 2003).

He keeps arriving exactly 2 minutes early for his sessions. I feel it drives me crazy. He moves constantly on the couch, bounces his legs frantically, stretches them as if to feel the limits of his body, incessantly puts on his glasses and takes them off. At the end of the sessions the couch looks like a battlefield. The napkin is wrinkled beside the pillow, the small mat is crumpled, and the pillow is upside down. During the sessions he picks his nose, his ears, takes out secretions from his eyes and puts it in his mouth, scratches himself, digs into wounds in his skin, peels off scabs and re-opens them. Lying down, his body is even more exposed than before. His vest is pulled up, his shorts stretched down, and his pubic hair is revealed. He seems to need to adhere to me and can't bear any gap or barrier between us, not even the napkin or any clothing.

And amidst all this movement, I can hardly keep my eyes open. I feel an unfathomable sleepiness descending on me. At first, I assume I am trying to defend myself, or silence the hostility I feel, or perhaps the rejection, disgust, homosexual anxiety or excitation. Perhaps I'm trying to preserve my boundaries from being breached. I don't want him to come anymore, and I feel immense guilt over the harsh feelings I have for him.

The analysis is hard for him too. He despairs, and yet the time between sessions feels to him like eternity. I think that he might be better off going to another analyst, someone more competent who could bear him.

From time to time he wants to sit. He goes over to the chair, or sits up on the couch, and miraculously, the experience returns to what it was at the beginning. He goes back to being moving, attractive, fascinating, and my heart goes out to him. My fatigue completely disappears.

As soon as he goes back to lie on the couch, the deadness prevails.

I realise this is a crucial communication, however in the state I am in, I can hardly think. My thinking is anaesthetised and I'm barely alive – not even dead, just in a kind of stupor.

The months go rapidly by, and his condition deteriorates. He feels utterly desperate. Nothing interests him anymore, and he hardly works. I'm surprised to realise that he's already three years in analysis. It seems hardly a year. I feel guilty for not being able to help him, and even more than that, I feel that the analysis itself is responsible for the worsening of his condition.

In one of the sessions, after speaking and weeping, while I remain silent and immersed in a state of opacity, I hear him ask: "Are you dead?"

I startle and 'wake up'.

I think I may have unconsciously become identified with the deadening mother who couldn't stand his aliveness. Alternatively, I think of him as saturated with his mother's total presence, which completely imbues him, drowning and deadening him. I feel him inducing a feeling of death all around, and I realise he has to move incessantly so as not to feel his deadness, and mine. It seems I'm both the dead and the deadening mother. Transference here is not a kind of displacement as it is traditionally described, but a form of turnaround that the patient inflicts on the analyst, that which he has been subjected to without being able to integrate it (Roussillon, 2013).

For months I struggle with sleep threatening to overwhelm me. I succeed in not falling asleep, but once in a while I drift into a dream, perhaps a day-dream, and leap in a startle, trying to get hold of a shred of the dream, sensing that something very valuable is concealed in it, if only I could capture a glimpse of it. But the dreams quickly dissipate. I get tired of struggling, and it becomes clear that the very effort to keep awake is in fact what prevents me from encountering something deeper in Guy's inner world. I feel more and more convinced that I must let go, and whatever will be – will be! And yet I am afraid it might lead to catastrophe.

I feel a growing aversion to Guy, to his pungent body odour, to the way he slides his bare feet over the couch, or peels off dry skin from his feet, letting it drop on the couch. He leaves a large oil stain on the couch after a visit to the garage, and I feel him adhering to me and suffocating me. He, or his residues, remains on the couch, which has become the place where he lives. I'm reminded of the dream from the beginning. I seem to have become the mother who wants to harm him, perhaps abort him? And yet I think this is what must probably happen. He will have to fall, to collapse, to be dropped, but I dare not.

The sessions I'll describe are obviously the ones in which I was able to be more attentive, or the ones in which we could transform something from the psychotic part of the personality to a symbol, a verbal formulation, or mentalise an unmentalised experience (Mitrani, 1995).

GUY SAYS: "I'm in chaos! I don't have a clue as to how to deal with my feelings! I feel I so much want to connect but every time I try – I panic!"

He sobs, frustrated, and moves agitatedly. He tries to describe his feelings but gets stuck, becomes very frustrated. "I feel I'm dissociated, 'besides it', and I get into a loop. Phew! How can I explain it??!"

He presses hard on his temples; his whole body is on the move. He's in a terrible distress, sighs, sobs. I say only a few words, just to help him go on.

He weeps but succeeds in describing his attempts to connect to his feelings and the panic that upsurges every time.

I SAY: "You feel something begins to come into being and you sever it at the root. . . ."

HE SAYS: "Yes. I don't want to let it in. It's bad. I don't want it to happen but I can't control it".

And then he begins to speak coherently about a specific time when he began to feel the fear spreading inside him, and he succeeds in articulating a fear of going mad. But the affect has changed. He doesn't move restlessly anymore, and I feel he's more connected, and calmer. I realise that the effort to capture what he is – drives him mad, and yet the capacity to put this amorphous experience into words, is plenty for now. The fact that I managed to keep him in mind is an indication for me that his speech was more meaningful – not a beta-screen but rather a contact barrier that has been constructed from alpha-elements and dream-thoughts.

Guy seems to be immersed in a strenuous struggle between trying to communicate his amorphous experience, an inner experience of *non-existence*, and the fear of the recurrence of this terrifying experience; the fear that if he succeeds in connecting to the feeling he is trying to describe, and articulate it, he will collapse and fall. But then I think, as Winnicott (1974) says, that the breakdown he and I are afraid of has already occurred. Perhaps now, it can be *experienced*. I realise that the amorphous experience may be that same experience of non-existence Winnicott writes about. This is his greatest fear. This is an experience he is living for the first time in the analysis – an experience that has already occurred, encapsulated in the *un*repressed unconscious, an experience of a world where it is impossible to feel. This is an amorphous, meaningless world, in which the threat of falling into an infinite and formless void lurks at every minute.

I feel we've come a long way. The amorphous experience is present in the here-and-now of the analysis. However, we've still not encountered something essential that we both seek to meet and yet we also both seem to dread. The session described above is an exceptional one amidst the experience of deadness and nothingness that governs the analysis with Guy. I still struggle not to drop him, still have to make an enormous effort to remain attentive, to find words, to make sense, and not to hate him.

At times I feel that I'm getting to the limits of my capacity. Guy doesn't give up. He keeps arriving early, soiling the couch, and anaesthetising me.

It was at that time that I came across a poem by Octavio Paz:

> . . . listen to me as one listens to the rain,
> without listening, hear what I say
> with eyes open inward, asleep
> with all five senses awake . . . (1975, p. 134)

These words echo Bion's (1976) who writes that in order to be able to pick up signs of some archaic, irrepresentable psychic element

> we have to be in a peculiar state of mind; the margin between being consciously awake, able to verbalise one's impressions, and being asleep, is extremely small. It is easy to be in a state of mind where you slip over into sleep, actually . . . when you are supposed to be working. It is equally easy to slip over into a state of being horribly intellectually awake. The border between the two . . . is very difficult to achieve. . . . Being on

the right wavelength, which has to be experienced to be recognised, is unfortunately comparatively rare.

(p. 288)

Nevertheless it is there we must strive to.

Perhaps that's how I must be: 'agree' to sleep "with eyes open inward", to relinquish the demands of the super-ego, to agree that what will be – will be, to stop grappling with the numbness and the amorphous experience.

Another session

I arrive at one of the following sessions in utter despair. I feel I can't struggle any more. If a catastrophe has to happen – then so be it! I feel the analysis is stuck anyway.

Guy arrives early as usual, with a smile that seems to me silly. I feel a great turbulence, my heart is pounding, and I don't understand how I've come to this. I hate him, I hate my work, my professional identity is subverted, and I feel all hope is lost. I sink heavily in my chair.

Surprisingly I'm wide awake.

HE SAYS JOKINGLY: "I had a crazy dream. I was somewhere with a friend and another girl. I look out of the window and see a pool and many stairs leading down, like some sort of a resort, and the only way down is through the stairs outside. I follow my friend till we reach the end of the stairs. The rest are all broken. No way through. You can't reach the pool. But *he* succeeds. He jumps and makes some kind of a somersault. *I* am too scared and I also don't want to lose the girl. I'm afraid that if we go there she'll never find us. He hangs onto the railing and passes easily, as if it's something he does daily, but *I* couldn't. Then mum called and I woke up. She told me that A died. It was really weird".

"Weird?" I ask.

HE SAYS: "When we went down to the pool, we arrived somewhere else, a big piazza. The railing led us *further* than the pool, *beyond* it. What amazed me was that I said to the other guy 'How will she find us? We're not at the pool', and then he magically disappeared for a second, jumped over to the other side and fetched her.

"I know what I think about this dream" he goes on. "This guy is sure of himself, he has money, he has everything. When he slides down the railing, he overcomes the obstacle in a second. But *me*, I just see it all from above. I arrive unnaturally, and even then, I don't get to the pool. I pass from one level to another lower one, and the pool is in between – and up there everything was good, and down there, everything was . . . well, rock bottom, nowhere else to go.

I like piazzas. You can sit and watch people go by. That's how it is with me – I can only see but not touch. When I arrived at the piazza I felt lost. I didn't know where I was".

He's silent for a minute and then begins to sigh deeply, inhaling and exhaling intensely, as if he's having trouble breathing.

HE SAYS: "After I heard A died, I thought 'what if I die like that?' Alone at home?"

We're silent for some minutes. In my mind, I associate the dream to birth more than death and I feel very turbulent. I want to interpret but I fear it's only an overvalued idea I latch onto.

BUT THEN I SAY: "I actually thought more in the way of birth . . ."

He's reflective for a while and then he says: "I know it took a long time till I was out, at least twelve hours. Finally, I arrived unnaturally because my mum had to have suction. I was born quite small. It was a hard delivery. My dad wasn't there because he suffered from diarrhea. My mum used to smoke a lot but not during the pregnancy. She just got fatter and fatter".

"Why did she get fatter?" I ask.

"Because she ate . . ." he replies cynically.

"And why did she eat?" I ask.

"Why did she eat??! Because she was hungry!! Because *I* was in there! . . . After that she began eating and throwing up . . . I feel uneasy talking about my mum".

He becomes silent. After a few minutes he goes on: "It wasn't normal the way she threw up all the time. One day when I was little, I told my grandma and she grasped her and sent her to get treatment. Damn illness! . . . It doesn't feel right talking like that about my mum".

"Why?" I ask, "What are you afraid of?"

"My mum had a fucked up life" he cries out loudly. "All her life she's had to deal with all this shit! She's always worried about her looks. Whatever I do, she's always pessimistic and unsure of her looks! She's getting old, almost sixty. Soon I'll have to deal with her wanting plastic surgery!"

"*You* will have to deal with it??" I ask.

"It's just a way of speaking", he says.

I SAY: "It sounds like when a mother talks about her child".

HE YELLS: "Because my mum is a baby! That's it! I said it! There's nothing I can do about it!! My mum is an insecure little baby! It's getting harder and harder for me to deal with it. It's hard to deal with an apathetic dad and a four-years-old mum!"

CRYING FORCEFULLY HE SAYS: "You know what just went through my head?! I thought what would happen to me when my parents die. Sometimes I think I'll get into a crazy breakdown that I won't be able to deal with. I'm weak!! I have no one except my family! I'm sick of it all!"

He breathes heavily, sighing, and he says: "I'm panicking a little now. I feel I'm going mad!"

He presses his temples, exhaling, trying to organise his breath, inhaling and exhaling heavily as if he's suffocating. He moves restlessly on the couch, crying, unable to speak. He stammers, chokes, and says: "I must calm down! I can't go on anymore! I'm trying to stop my thoughts and that only makes me panic more. I'm disconnecting again!"

"What is it that you don't want to think?" I ask.

He doesn't reply, just exhales forcefully. I fear he might be having a heart attack. I'm very tense but after a few minute he says: "I've just had a panic attack like I haven't had in years! I was scared I was going mad. I couldn't think what I was thinking. The very fact that it happens *here* only amplified the panic. That's it! Enough! I can't go on anymore!"

It's time for us to stop. He asks for a glass of water. He drinks and leaves relatively organised.

The caesura between breakdown and breakthrough

Is Guy having a breakdown or a breakthrough?

What would we think, Bion (1976) asks, if we knew someone carved holes in human beings – if we couldn't excuse the behaviour on the grounds that he was a surgeon? And what would we say when this successful surgeon who has done surgical operations for years had what we call a 'breakdown', and can't face the operating theatre? Is it a 'breakdown', he asks, or break-up? Break-in? Or break-out? Or breakthrough? Might we think that the surgeon is seeing something he has never allowed himself to see before – how cruel, how brutal, how violent he is?

Analytic transformation is possible through a 'break-up' of the familiar meaning and a 'breakthrough' of the new discovery. Often, this entails a threat of catastrophic 'breakdown' (Bion, 1977). Bion suggests we observe from different and unconventional vertices. What looks like a breakdown from one vertex may be a breakthrough when looked at from a different vertex.

One might therefore ask if my despair and difficulty in keeping and bearing Guy in my mind is an expression of a breakdown and a collapse of my analytic capacities, or might it be a caesura on the way to encountering the deadness in Guy's inner world? Could we think that my struggle to keep thinking, to stay awake, is actually an expression of my resistance to encountering the emotional truth present in the room, and to my attempt to defend against a formless and chaotic experience, against 'becoming O', and as an attempt to prevent Guy's inevitable breakdown?

To my mind, Guy's panic attack is saturated with meaning and is the most meaningful event at this stage of the analysis. A breakdown is no doubt a tragedy, but it can become a transformative experience leading to a breakthrough (Bollas, 2013).

To this day I cannot say what exactly precipitated Guy's anxiety attack in this session. Nevertheless I think that my utter and absolute despair, my very renunciation of the struggle against sleep and detachment, my mere collapse, are the elements that created the conditions for Guy to get in touch with himself, with the roots of his being and with the primitive agonies in him. One does not encounter primitive agonies in themselves but rather their shadows (Eigen, 1999), much like our limited capacity to only *approximate* at-one-ment with O, unknowable, absolute truth.

The analyst's participation

Winnicott writes: "At length, dependence becomes a main feature, and then the analyst's mistakes and failures become direct causes of . . . the outbreak of fear of breakdown" (1974, p. 103). I propose that "the analyst's mistakes and failures" are not a mishap in the analytic process, but may rather be an expression of the analyst's receptivity to the patient's illness and his primitive communication. The patient 'knows' his analyst's state of mind. Only when the patient senses the analyst's receptivity to the emotional experience in its entirety, does he know that the analyst has relinquished his own method of verbal communication, and has opened himself to the *patient's* method of primitive communication. Only when he perceives the analyst's internal struggle to bear the unbearable, does he know that he has touched the analyst deeply, and only then does he feel capable of encountering something unbearable and encapsulated within himself. Bion (1967b) stresses that a patient will only accept an interpretation if he feels that the analyst has passed through an emotional crisis himself as a part of the act of giving the interpretation. When confronting the psychotic parts of the personality, the analyst's experience is an integral part of the patient's material. It is the analyst who must feel in his flesh the fear of breakdown and the fear of potential catastrophe *in the present*. We are thus required to take upon ourselves a dissociated part of the patient's psyche of which the patient cannot as yet assume authorship. At this phase of the analysis, it was the psychic dead-ness inside Guy's inner world, the deadness that existed but was not experienced, but most of all, the hateful, deadening aspects of the inner object. Receptivity to this facilitates something from the unrepressed unconscious to emerge – not something that has been mentalised and repressed, but something that has never been registered "for want of a poet . . . [Since] as yet the poet hadn't turned up; so the recording tape was a blank!" (Bion, 1975, p. 120). The ana-lyst's tolerating the countertransference involves his making links (as well as breaking links) in *his* mind, and it is this which allows the patient to do likewise (Carpy, 1989). It seems that the link *I* made between the dream and the experience of birth, albeit being *my* association, created a profound and as yet unformulated link in Guy's mind.

The following session

The following session Guy arrives pale and sits in the chair. He says he can't lie down. He breathes heavily and says that since our last session he hasn't functioned. He says he felt he was losing it and was scared of going mad. He says he told a friend about our previous session and that the friend thought it might be a breakthrough(!).

He describes his experience of disconnectedness, talking very excitedly, his body trem-bling. He says: "I'm cautious – I try not to be too happy, not to get too excited, to keep very still! I'm scared to think. Scared of anything that might disrupt my equilibrium. I'm scared of drinking (alcohol). I'm scared something might happen to me!"

> He goes on describing his feelings and after a while he says: "I'm beginning to feel the anxiety rising".
> I'm aware that my mind has drifted, that I had lost him.
> HE SAYS: "I lost the thread of thought".
> And I think that it is *I* who has lost the thread and that he had been dropped.
> I SAY: "Perhaps you lost the thread of thought because you didn't know where I was. You were alarmed because I didn't look at you and you felt I wasn't there, that I didn't keep you in my mind, that I'd dropped you – and then you felt you were losing the thread of thought, and began to feel anxious".
> He's quiet.
> A FEW MINUTES LATER HE SEEMS CALMER. HE SAYS: "Somehow now, I managed to get over the panic. It was about to erupt, and then I felt I was back in place. I'm a little relieved now. I can breathe a little. I heard you and I felt safe again".
> I think he felt safe being back in my mind.

★★★

For the neurotic, the couch can be symbolical of the mother's love. However, when encoun-tering the psychotic parts of the personality, it would be more true to say that the couch *is* the analyst's womb or lap (Winnicott, 1947). The earliest anxiety, Winnicott (1952) says, is related to being insecurely held. I now realise that lying on the couch, Guy was regressed to a primor-dial and primitive state, feeling unheld in an actual womb or lap. This state awakened primary catastrophic anxieties of unintegration, falling forever, and death. Sitting face to face, we again meet the neurotic parts of his personality, and the experience is then entirely different – for both of us. This may be a reflection of the acute split he makes between his life up until the first panic attack, when he held himself with his intellectual and social skills, constant activity and an efficient false self organisation, and the life *after* the panic attack and the collapse of the omnipotent self-holding.

The unrepressed unconscious

Both Winnicott and Bion echo Freud who maintained that our psychoanalytic investigations have directed our interest too exclusively to the repressed. Freud (1923) writes:

> "We recognise that the *Ucs.* does not coincide with the repressed; it is still true that all that is repressed is *Ucs.*, but not all that is *Ucs.* is repressed. A part of the ego, too – and Heaven knows how important a part . . . undoubtedly is *Ucs.* And this *Ucs* . . . is not latent like the *Pcs*. . . . [W]e find ourselves thus confronted by the necessity of postulating a third *Ucs.*, which is not repressed" (p. 18). Later on he says: "Pathological research has directed our interest too exclusively to the repressed".
>
> *(p. 19)*

Freud (1920) referred to the tendency "to repeat the repressed material as a contemporary experience" (p. 18). However, in light of his reservation that "not all that is *Ucs.* is repressed", it would be more apt to speak of the tendency to repeat the *unconscious* material as a contemporary experience, and the unconscious in this context is rather the *un*repressed unconscious.

Winnicott writes of the fear of breakdown and the pull towards it, and Bion writes of catastrophic change and the fear of it. Both meet in the realm of the *unrepressed unconscious*. Both focus on the dread of encountering emotional truth encapsulated in the unmentalised, unrepressed unconscious, threatening the mind with a psychotic state. Yet both contend that this encounter, facilitating the integration of remote and unmentalised parts of the self, can save the personality from mental catastrophe, or alternatively from psychic death as a defence against it (Bergstein, 2009, 2013).

Winnicott refers to a fear of breakdown that has already happened, an unthinkable fact encapsulated in the unconscious. "The patient needs to 'remember' this but it is not possible to remember something that has not yet happened, and this thing of the past has not happened yet because the patient was not there for it to happen to" (1974, p. 105). Furthermore: "The unconscious here is not exactly the repressed unconscious of psychoneurosis. . . . In this special context the unconscious means that the ego integration is not able to encompass something" (p. 104). In this thinking, the traumatic experience is *that which could not be elaborated psychically* (Botella and Botella, 2005). An essential characteristic of the fear of breakdown is the compulsive pursuit of an event from the past – in the future.

Bion seems to be concerned with the individual's capacity to dare to communicate with those unconscious, irrepresentable areas of his psyche. In fact, he says,

> We [are] dealing with people who . . . dare to come to a psychoanalyst, but who really need some sort of assistance which would enable them to penetrate their own resistance, or which would enable them to penetrate whatever this thing is which seems to get in between themselves and themselves.
>
> *(Bion, 1975 in Aguayo, 2013, pp. 65–66)*

And this thing is not something that has been repressed, but rather that inaccessible part for which Bion adopts the metaphor of the caesura of birth and the mental events that lie *beyond* it.

The capacity of an individual for becoming at one with oneself is experienced as a catastrophic change. It is catastrophic because it subverts psychic equilibrium. However, when it is contained in the analytic setting, it may be controlled without bursting the mental container. It can thus lead not to catastrophe but rather catastrophic *change*.

It is my understanding that catastrophic change is capacitated through an encounter with the unrepressed unconscious *in the present*, in the transference. One cannot get in touch with these remote parts of the psyche through interpretation alone. Since it is unconscious and yet unrepressed, it cannot be *known* but must first be *lived* in the present. This is a transformation in O, a paradoxical, caesural experience in the here-and-now of the analytic setting, echoing a past experience, which has occurred but as yet not been experienced. It is an experience entailing a loss of identity, simultaneously enabling psychic growth.

Returning to Bion's metaphor of the spectrum of the electromagnetic waves, we might think that Guy's anxiety attacks appeared from somewhere beyond the spectrum. The attempts to understand or interpret them dynamically and verbally led to an impasse. Guy's anxiety seems to have been an expression of a surplus of unbound and intolerable quantity of excitation, originating in primitive unmentalised experiences (Mitrani, 1995) that the mental container could not contain due to its embryonic, primitive, and immature nature and/or the absence of an external object able to facilitate the transformation and elaboration of the experience.

★★★

The traumatic situation then, seems to be an excess of excitation, unable to be transformed even in the form of a neurotic symptom. The individual remains condemned to the dominance of quantities of excitation he cannot monitor or elaborate mentally. The individual is left in extreme helplessness, franticness, agitation, and confusion which can only acquire meaning *in retrospect* through the mind of an analyst.

Hence the way to psychic transformation is pinned in the possibility to experience the past in the present, for the first time, in the transference. This, I propose, is possible primarily through the analyst's capacity and willingness to experience the agonies of breakdown in his flesh. It is the analyst who must 'agree' to experience a catastrophic change, to lose his identity, even if momentarily, hence enabling the patient to dare to approach the breakdown that has already occurred and encounter the psychotic part of his personality. Hence, both patient and analyst can experience catastrophic change.

Speculative imagination[2]

Could we speculate that Guy is compelled to repeat a primal trauma that has been burnt and encapsulated in his psyche before it could be experienced or registered as an emotional experience, perhaps even before he was born? Could the dream in which he's in a stormy river with mother, fearing she is about to harm him, tell of his mother's death wish at the time of his coming into being? Could it be that being immersed in psychic deadness herself, she had no space inside her for a foetus experienced as too greedy and needy? Alternatively, could the dream tell of an unconscious phantasy of his?

Reflecting on the way in which Guy severs his nascent thoughts, forbidding them to sprout and develop, I wonder – is he living, over and over again an experience of disruption? A phantasy of abortion? Are we, Guy and I, compelled to repeat and re-live the trauma – I as the aborting object and him as the aborted foetus? Could this be an unthought thought captured in the unrepressed unconscious awaiting a thinker to think it? Or is this my overvalued idea (Britton and Steiner, 1994), an anchor protecting *me* from drowning in the raging river of caesura?

I assume we will never know what 'really' happened then and there, and it is probably of no importance that we shall. Nevertheless, neither one of us, Guy nor I, have any doubt about the experience in the here-and-now of the analysis.

Notes

1 This is a modified version of a paper published in *Rivista di Psicoanalisi*, 2014. 60: 847–868.
2 Speculative imagination according to Bion is an expression of the analyst's dreaming and a means of capturing something from the ineffable, irrepresentable emotional truth. "These speculative imaginations, however ridiculous, however neurotic, however psychotic, may nevertheless be stages on the way to what one would ultimately regard as scientific, psycho-analytic formulations" (Bion, 1977, p. 41).

References

Aguayo, J. (2013). Wilfred Bion's "Caesura". In H.B. Levine and L.J. Brown (Eds.), *Growth and Turbulence in the Container/Contained: Bion's Continuing Legacy*, pp. 55–74. London: Routledge.

Bergstein, A. (2009). On boredom: A close encounter with encapsulated parts of the psyche. *International Journal of Psycho-Analysis* 90: 613–631.

Bergstein, A. (2013). Transcending the caesura: Reverie, dreaming and counter-dreaming. *International Journal of Psycho-Analysis* 94: 621–644.

Bion, W.R. (1967a). Third seminar. In J. Aguayo and B. Malin (Eds.), *Wilfred Bion: Los Angeles Seminars and Supervision*, pp. 55–79. London: Karnac, 2013.

Bion, W.R. (1967b). Reverence and awe. In *Cogitations*. London: Karnac, 1992.

Bion, W.R. (1975). *A Memoir of the Future*. London: Karnac, 1991.

Bion, W.R. (1976). Four discussions. In *Clinical Seminars and Other Works*, pp. 241–292. Abingdon: Fleetwood [Reprinted London: Karnac, 1994].

Bion, W.R. (1977). Untitled. In *Taming Wild Thoughts*, pp. 23–51. London: Karnac, 1997.

Bollas, C. (2013). C. Bollas interviewed about new book "Catch them before they fall". www. routledgementalhealth.com/psychoanalysis/articles/christopher_bollas_interviewed_about_new_book_catch_them_before_they_fall/

Botella, C. and Botella, S. (2005). *The Work of Psychic Figurability*. New York, NY: Brunner-Routledge.

Britton, R. and Steiner, J. (1994). Interpretation: Selected fact or overvalued idea? *International Journal of Psycho-Analysis* 75: 1069–1078.

Carpy, D.V. (1989). Tolerating the countertransference: A mutative process. *International Journal of Psycho-Analysis* 70: 287–294.

Eigen, M. (1999). Shadows of agony X. In *Toxic Nourishment*, pp. 159–170. London: Karnac.

Freud, S. (1920). Beyond the pleasure principle. *S.E.* 18: 3–64. London: Hogarth, 1955.

Freud, S. (1923). The ego and the id. *S.E.* 19: 1–66. London: Hogarth, 1957.

Mitrani, J. (1995). Toward an understanding of unmentalised experience. *Psychoanalytic Quarterly* 64: 68–112.

M'Uzan, M. de (2003). Slaves of quantity. *Psychoanalytic Quarterly* 72: 711–725.

Paz, O. (1975). *A Tree Within*. Ed. E. Weinberger. New York: New Directions Books, 1988.

Roussillon, R. (2013). The function of the object in binding and unbinding of the drives. *International Journal of Psycho-Analysis* 94: 257–276.

Winnicott, D.W. (1947). Hate in the countertransference. In *Through Paediatrics to Psychoanalysis*, pp. 194–203. London: Tavistock [Reprinted London: Karnac, 1984].

Winnicott, D.W. (1952). Anxiety associated with insecurity. In *Through Paediatrics to Psychoanalysis*, pp. 97–100. London: Tavistock [Reprinted London: Karnac, 1984].

Winnicott, D.W. (1974). Fear of breakdown. *International Review of Psycho-Analysis* 1: 103–107.

11

THE GIRL WHO GAVE ME A KISS ON THE FINGER

How the concrete and the abstract mix in psychotic symbolization

Alessandro Bruni

Gianluca was 25, tall and stately, a very clever young man. He had an identical twin brother and a much younger sister. His parents were especially inadequate and poor, both in economic and in psychological terms. His father was a waiter, totally absent and unable to manage a psychological relationship with his children. The mother managed the whole family. She was small and very religious, in a way that led to a highly symbiotic relationship with her sick child.

Gianluca was studying statistics at the university and had successfully taken some exams when he decided to leave with his brother and work as a volunteer to relieve victims of an earthquake in northern Italy. That experience of a sudden break with his ordinary family life must have been like an earthquake for his inner world. Among other things, an event that had troubled him was having witnessed sexual intercourse of two young persons sharing his tent. A few days later he had a psychotic breakdown that progressively projected him into a labyrinthine world, an overlapping of his internal and external worlds. Gianluca was projected into a medium of obscure and dream-like meanings, floating in an altered state of consciousness characterized by hallucinations.

After the crisis, Gianluca and his brother had to go back to Rome, and during his return trip by train he apparently met "the girl who kissed me on the finger".

His communications to me were always suggestive and allowed access to analytic reverie. For example, during a certain period of his therapy he used to say, "I live in Narcissus' house and somebody moved the mirrors in it". And he often mentioned "Snow White and the seven dwarfs" which he transformed into the Italian anagram of that phrase, "Snow White and the seven years" by changing the word *nani* or dwarfs into the word *anni* or years. From this transformation, a traumatic memory resurfaced: When he was 7 he had to undergo surgery for squinting eyes and was suddenly separated from his mother and cared for by nurses. He remembered he had woken up with a bandage, intense anxiety and a feeling of being lost.

Unfortunately, Gianluca's psychotherapy had to be interrupted because I could not find adequate support for the family in the national health system. The family and especially Gianluca's mother strongly opposed his therapy. I had felt a serious risk of homicide and/or suicide and I could not go on alone without that support.

When Gianluca told me the phrase: "Then . . . the girl on the train gave me a kiss on the finger. . . ." I realized that the real event was connected with the accustomed gesture of asking for silence but instead it seemed to the patient very obvious that I should have understood the general category of "girls who gave kisses on the finger".

W. R. Bion, expressing a more comprehensive position on symbolization than Melanie Klein's, wrote:

> The psychotic patient does not always behave as if he is incapable of symbol formation. Indeed he often talks or behaves as if he is convinced that certain actions, which to me are innocent of any symbolic significance, are obviously symbolic. They mean apparently obviously, some message which is of personal and particular concern to him. This "meaning" is quite different from the meaning one assumes to lie behind a constant conjunction that is public and not private to one individual. . . . The symbol, as it is usually understood, represents a conjunction which is recognized by a group to be constant; as encountered in psychosis it represents a conjunction between a patient and his deity which the patient feels to be constant.
>
> *(Bion, 1970)*

Thus the psychotic patient can share the meaning of the Greek etymology of the word "*symbolon*". The verb "*sym-ballo*" in fact means to keep together, to unite. It oddly has the same meaning as "*religion*", which probably derives from "*re-ligo*" (to tie again) and the same as "*Yoga*" which means the yoke which holds together two oxen.

But the "symbolic reunion" realized by the psychotic part of personality does not support a meaning shared by a group, i.e. abstract and general enough. It rather reveals an esoteric agreement between the subject and a dark part of himself, felt as a highly private demon.

In this sense, it is quite interesting that, as compared to the "symbolic religion" supported by common sense, psychotic functioning at times seems to the subject embodying it and to his listeners like an inversion of perspective from "devilish" characteristics.

As opposed to "*syn-ballo*", the verb "*dia-ballo*" from which comes "*dia-bolos*", devil, means to scatter. Here we can find an analogy with the integration/non-integration polarity, Melanie Klein's depressive position and paranoid-schzoid position and even better with the most abstract and general position suggested by Bion, i.e. the PS< − >D oscillation (Bion, 1962). But this description can immediately prove inadequate in explaining the patient's experience since it is formulated within the non-psychotic way of thinking and symbolizing. When we think of "non-integration" or "disintegration" or "splitting" we ourselves risk to "demonize" the devil, i.e. to reify it. We unconsciously give the patient, who is often conscious of our subconscious, the label of possessed by a demon and challenge him to absorb our super-egoic stigmatization, thus feeding the "para-noid" spiral.

I don't know if this is a contemporary chapter of the never ending story of the fight between God and Devil or of the apparently inescapable need for any God to create a poor devil.

"Devilish" integration or dis-integration can be the result of rebellion against an excessive and unbearable "symbolic" pressure, supported by an arrogant and monolithic super-ego that has no respect for sexuality. Could it be that Lucifer and Icarus paid, with their fall, for the omnipotent lust of their ego ideal? Or that the tower of Babel should be seen as a proto-theory of schizophrenia?

Mythological-religious suggestions allow further reflection. One of the reasons of the dispute between God and the Devil concerns, in fact, the diverging evaluation of what is most important in life. Whereas God champions faith in inner spiritual values, along with superior but deferred gratification, the Devil champions material, concrete and sensual goods and immediate pleasure.

Behind this dispute we see the polarity between abstraction and concretization, i.e. between the psyche's sophisticated evolution, which establishes within itself a virtual world of abstract mental objects, and the need to recover a more and more efficient contact with the material and sensual world.

Bion paid a great deal of attention to this polarity deriving from the emergence of thinking. The English term "abstraction", he says, means both "abstraction" and "extraction" (Bion, 1962). To obtain abstraction in fact, we must extract from a particular experience some arbitrarily selected elements and test whether the new more abstract entity deriving from it can be used to represent or explore many concrete facts different from what caused the original experience.

Thus the process of abstraction requires some sort of "spoliation" of the most material and sensual aspects of experience. This means it implies, when not a real loss, at least an "eclipse" of many apparent aspects of the sensual substratum where it operates.

This "diminishing" is however offset by a gain deriving from the "vitality" of the abstract product, if it turns out useful as a means for knowing new facts. In order for this to come true, it is necessary that the arbitrary selection of "extracted" elements is proper and adequate to its aim in quantitative and qualitative terms (Bruni, 1993).

When an "abstract" position also holds the privilege of being considered "general", this means it is inserted in the "normopathic" thinking process compatible with the group's common sense. On the other hand, the "material" and "sensual" dimension is related to the individual's private and particular dimension.

From these premises it should be clear that the dynamics of abstraction is deeply rooted in the emotional dimension and the genesis of thinking.

To produce an abstraction, in fact, it is necessary to be able to tolerate the feelings emerging from the eclipses of the concrete and sensual aspects of the real object. In psychoanalytical terms, this means loneliness and abandonment, fear of losing the object and at times appearance of its persecutory phantom.

The very likelihood of the birth of a thought as an extracted mental object as opposed to the "thing in itself", for example the idea of breast, depends on the ability to tolerate the emotional emergence related to the "not-being-there-of-the-real-mother's-breast-for-a-certain-period-of-time".

As human beings we still find it hard to trust in the ability of the mind to let us sail to and fro from concrete to abstract, from things to thoughts. In the "normopathy" of everyday life we have instances of imbalance towards hyper-concrete or hyper-abstract.

The frequent inability to understand math or the Saint Thomas syndrome whereby one must touch to believe are examples of this emotional distrust in abstraction that philosophers called entanglement in the concrete (Einaudi, 1977).

By contrast, the clear propensity for abstract thinking of mathematicians is often related to shyness and bashfulness, and to a more general wish to keep away from the concrete aspects of emotional relations. The cliché of the absent-minded scientist who through abstraction is absent from contingent reality is a good example of what I called "flight into the abstract" (Bruni, 1993).

In Gianluca's choice we can see that these extreme positions seem paradoxically to coexist in his "symbolic" construction. In fact he tries to extract and promote to general symbol a non-ordinary meaning anchored to the graphic reading of the girl's gesture. He thus flees into the abstract, but reifying a whole category of sensually and bodily laden gratifying elements: "girls giving kisses on the finger". The result is a fore-closure or a by-pass of the more ordinary and generally shared meaning "Be silent!" that would have required recalling painful and unbearable emotions related to the mother.

In a first approximation we could then say that Gianluca "psychotically" denied the obvious fact that the girl had asked him to be silent. But the subtly hopeful smile with which he said this indicated that he knew at some level the traditional meaning of this gesture, but was asking me a riddle about a proposition with a double meaning: "I can't register the thought that someone wants me to be quiet, i.e. denies my separate individuality, at the same time I need someone to gratify me and restore my wounded narcissism".

Gianluca "extracts" his "symbol" from a vertex located in a borderline position between the theoretical prospects that are now oddly opposed, in my opinion wrongly, in the psychoanalytical domain. I mean the opposition of the so-called "drive" theory and the "relational" theory. With one single formulation, in fact, on the one hand he shows the evidence of a psychotic disorder of thinking, on the other he invites us to consider his need for narcissistic support to be able to repair it.

Maybe the schizophrenic patient tries to get out of the labyrinth of "*parà-noia*", or deviated, lateral and circular thought, and invites us to build together a "*metà-noia*", or transformational thought.

Building and crossing bridges together, it is possible to look at both sides of the field and share the exercise of perspective inversion in order to revitalize or regularize the breathing of thinking.

References

Bion, W.R. (1962). *Learning from Experience*. London: Tavistock.
Bion, W.R. (1970). *Attention and Interpretation: A Scientific Approach to Insight in Psycho-Analysis and Groups*. London: Tavistock.
Bruni, A. (1993). "c∑ | ⟨ |∑⟩∑⟩ ". *Vicissitudini dell'astrazione*. In C. Neri and G. Di Chiara (Eds.), *Psicoanalisi futura*. Borla: Rome.
Einaudi (1977). *Dizionario enciclopedico*. Torino: Einaudi.

12

THINKING, KNOWING, UNKNOWING, NO MIND

Mary E. Sonntag

"The U. N. is Kafka on a good day" was a statement sarcastically tossed off by my patient Sarah in one of her many entertaining monologues. Sarah is an intelligent 38-year-old woman who works at the United Nations in Peace Keeping. She entered therapy three years ago due to a heartbreaking relationship with a schizophrenic man. Sarah fills the session with descriptive narratives full of wit, humor, and sarcasm but eventually returns to bouts of despair, wishing she were dead. She articulates what seem to be insightful, coherent reactions/thoughts to situations in and out of therapy. The work feels deep and generative of ideas and meanings firing rapidly back and forth. It has taken me a long time to realize that behind her creative language and satirical quips is a mind that cannot hold on to meaning or what Bion refers to as knowledge K (Bion, 1962). Just because there are symbols does not mean they are used symbolically and thus, for Sarah, language often replaces thinking. I mis-recognized, in the psychotic parts, an emotional quality that was masked by her speech and was not (maybe could not be) acknowledged by either of us. You might say, I was the wrong analyst talking to the wrong patient.

I have come to hear her speech more often as a signal (sign) and less as a symbol. A signal that something catastrophic has happened or is about to happen. Since she defends against what is malformed or unformed in her capacity to think about, use, or know her emotional experience, she is unable to bear her effects of frustration, envy, shame, or guilt. But this is not just an evacuation of what cannot be tolerated; it is also a mode of communication. I decode her communication in search of the affect. I listen as if it were a dream, as Ferro (2002) has described, hearing the narrative derivatives of the patient's waking dream thoughts. My attention focuses on how and when her mind turns upon itself. It is less about attacking links with others and more about a deficiency in her capacity to think, attacking links to herself – a repetitive eradication of her own meaning.

In this paper I consider how and when psychotic processes slip into the intersubjective space, using Bion's ideas about different forms of psychic thinking and the limited capabilities of thinking and coherence in the patient's most primitive levels of mental functioning. Although the intersubjective is always present and is a relevant component of the analytic relationship, my concern here is the patient's relationship to herself and to how her mind works – to notice what parameters, functions, and activities are linked to mental activity (both enhancing it and/or disrupting it), such as time, trauma, capacity to tolerate frustration, responsiveness, attunement, etc.

Bion's theory of thinking or how the mind works presupposes that knowledge of the psychological precedes knowledge of the physical world. In his theory, the earliest form of thinking seeks to know psychic qualities and is the outcome of early emotional events between a caregiver and infant which are decisive for the establishment, or not, of the infant's capacity to think (O'Shaughnessy, 1981). Thus in this sense, the developing mind or capacity to think and integrate knowledge is relational. The three phenomena in his theory are: 1) the emotional experience of trying to know the self and others – K; 2) the cruel denuding link of misunderstanding/misrecognising the self and others and of experience and meaning – Minus K; and 3) the psychotic state with No Mind able to know the self or others – No K.

I am aware that there may be various influential factors and conceptualizations to consider, such as relational systems theory, Piaget's developmental theory, mentalization, dissociation, intergenerational transmission of trauma, and so forth. However, Bion's concept, I believe, is more primary because his concern is with the very first moments of an infant's curiosity, which is not only pleasure seeking but also **object** seeking. From a Bionian viewpoint, thinking is a fundamental link between human beings and a significant constituent in the divergence of psychotic from normal functioning. Via the clinical vignette, I would like us to consider how we might "think about thinking" or how the mind works when our patients shift into psychotic states; how to think about what happens to the mind at the point of an unbearable or unrecognizable experience; and how to perceive the coming and going of the mind and its attempts to find ways to mend itself.

I begin this discussion with Kafka, not from my own associations, but because Sarah brought him into the room. Is this coincidence? It is interesting she refers to Kafka since I experience her at crucial affective moments to have a collapse of thought and coherency, not unlike the characters in a Kafka story. He is best in describing objectless guilt and the futile pursuit of unattainable goals that cancel coherent interpretations, leaving one feeling depersonalized and alienated. In Kafka's world the mind is imprisoned, a torturing instrument in a functionless vacuum. There are absurd laws, rules, punishments, having nothing to do with human concerns and from which no one knows why, where, or how they were constituted, rendering them unintelligible. The sense of the real is inexorably being lost; true reality lies elsewhere in the inaccessible. He takes us into the guts of humor and horror at a level where life is felt like a "brute happening bare of meaning" (Kafka, 1995).

Sarah describes an unyielding guilt and shame. She searches to find the "why" and the "what," but there is no comprehensible answer, and despair and hopelessness set in. The first two years of her treatment centered around the psychotic boyfriend and her attempts to make sense of his delusions and paranoia, much of which were aimed at her. At times I felt as if I were "losing my mind" when she would come up with justifications or rationalizations for his horrific behavior and crazy accusations. But she could not leave him. She felt a sadness bigger than life by the thought of leaving him. What would leaving him leave her with? Was she describing her boyfriend's psychosis as an unconscious communication of her own state? Her academic, professional, and social brilliance lured me away from sensing her own psychotic parts, shielding a reality that she was yet capable of knowing and I was yet able to discern. What comes to mind is the concept of a personal bastion (Baranger and Baranger, 2008). The risk of Sarah losing this relationship/this man would leave her in a state of vulnerability that she believed she would not survive; she would "go mad and never come back." As the treatment progressed, I came to understand how her bastion was linked with earlier histories, namely her mother's history of trauma that could not be known. Although she was rational and well-organized in most of our interactions, my queries and curiosities into this relationship, her bastion, roused a childish rage that blocked my words/thoughts entry into the space. Speech, mine and hers, no longer informed or signified meaning. Language was insufficient, ripped up and torn apart. The narrative was more of a tool or method to get to the emotional experience underlying her words.

In these moments there was no room to play with thoughts and ideas. No fantasy. No dreaming. No reverie. No link. No mind. She was in a psychotic process where there was no understanding or knowing. An emotional problem arrives but there are no words or thoughts yet found. The psychotic part of her personality would take over and in this more primitive state I felt useless because she could not hear reason. One cannot make psychosis go away with interpretation. But there is plasticity and multiplicity and it can be transformed by enhancing and developing the patient's capacity to think and by promoting abstraction and symbolization. When she was in an unrepresented state of suffering I would offer links between emotional states and events/descriptions. She would give me a brief glance but never paused from her rant. My voice, my words were an interruption; nothing could penetrate. Many times I would utter a reflection or interpretation just to let her know I was in the room. For a long time, our only link was the repetition and endurance of the treatment.

Her dreams carried a theme of "screaming out" but no one hears. What was I not hearing? Why could I not understand that she **had** to be with her insane boyfriend? Why could I not see that her guilt and shame were deserved? She begged for recognition of her guilt, shame, and due punishment, but what was the crime? There we were, in the room, not knowing together. What is Sarah telling me about how my mind functions? How might I be failing in our relationship? What dimensions of experience have I been unable to give voice to?

I am aware that there exists a tension in the room between knowing and not knowing, between great doubt and absolute certainty, in me, in her, and in our relationship. I recall a description Mike Eigen (personal communication, 2012) has expressed many times in his Bion seminar: "Watching my own psychotic process watch my patient's psychotic process." This allows for a shift in attitude, stance, query which opens new pathways and fields of experience. Thus, little by little, Sarah became more of an observer to her own process and primitive thinking, as I became more comfortable observing my own psychotic process. Sarah's quality of "coming through" depended on my quality of "coming through."

Her dreams about "screaming out and no one hears" express an emotional truth about her experience that she was not yet capable of knowing. She talks of her childhood with an idyllic nostalgia, but her dreams reveal a catastrophic aloneness and desperate need to be recognized. Sarah was not able to tolerate this dreaded affect long enough to make sense of a subjective truth. She struggled to give expression to self states and to reflect on them. She was in a winless race, running from her pain and trauma. She often described events and experiences in the third person placing it outside herself into another. In the psychotic mental states, it is not the material that is unconscious but the **ownership** of the material. As I described earlier, she spoke rationally and had a sophistication in mulling over the material, masking her primitive states and her inability to synthesize the emotional impacts and possible meanings. The lingo was a kind of pseudo-thinking. The links between thinking and feeling are repeatedly being destroyed. But in some ways destruction always fails. The awareness that something awful has happened pushes on the psyche and one can never get rid of the pain by trying to destroy it. Her over-burdened mind dumps the material into my lap for me to feel, know, and make sense of.

Thus, the therapist-I take on the paranoid-schizoid process for the patient but in a manner that is not wholly identified with the position to be able to synthesize all that is going on in the treatment. Her undeniable belief that she is fraudulent, guilty engenders a perpetual state of shame and a paranoid fear of "being found out." She engages in projective-identification (PI) and splitting to avoid taking in emotional experience or to evacuate it, which ultimately protects her from self-knowledge. The capacity to learn, as Bion (1962) sees it, is the ability to tolerate the paranoid-schizoid (P-S) position, the depressive (D) position, and the dynamic and continuous flow between the two and to help our patients tolerate the perpetual vacillation between not knowing and knowing, the unconscious and conscious, reality and fantasy.

There was little movement in the treatment for a long time, and I had to tolerate Sarah's ceaseless "undoing of herself" either by an inability to let anything in or by an eventual destruction of that which was taken in. Sessions often ended with her declaring, quite victoriously: "I understand everything you are saying but it doesn't matter, it changes nothing about how I feel or the meaning in my life." She throws away the session in order not to feel, to think, or be aware of feelings she is not yet able to manage. She understands analytic interpretations but quickly deprives them of life and meaning. So over and over again her mind fractures and thinking breaks down, whereby something becomes nothing, knowing becomes not knowing, here becomes not here, past becomes now. And the trauma remains un-named, because her psychotic part will not allow it to be named, will not allow it meaning.

There is a part of Sarah that does want to know and link the different dimensions of her experience – experience waiting for her to find it. She is curious about her shame, guilt, and fraudulence. But it is not a loving curiosity. It feels more dangerous and threatening. Bion (1962) believed that one's basic feeling of guilt was hiding a state of intense terror, a nameless dread. Sarah's conscience manifestation of her guilt and shame often surface in the sessions as self-hatred and self-punitive attacks. Her curiosity and creativity are quickly shut down by a guilty conscience that would tell her what she should not do or think but never possibilities of what she could do. It is my hope that via the treatment and our relationship she will build up tolerance to be in the gap between her emotional experience and her capacity to think about it, know it, and use it. Instead, she is more apt to fill the gap with tormenting thoughts that are barriers to a more observing and creative aspect of her personality. I want her to know she is both a traumatized being and a creative being and that she can give testimony to both; that one does not have to occlude the other; that she can be fully impacted by an emotional experience and at the same time be outside of it, having freedom to roam and observe it from various positions.

Sarah is beginning to bring in more details and remembrances of her childhood and family. She knows that much of her sadness is connected to her mother. She recollects her mother also experiencing shame, guilt, and depression. Her idyllic childhood is melting and a more expansive narrative is evolving, revealing difficult memories and emotional experiences. What Sarah knows about her mother is sparse.

It is an obscure and impenetrable history, one where no one and nothing can get out or in, including Sarah. The mother delinks from her past and what she excludes is not lost but expands and multiplies within Sarah's psyche constituting what Gerson (2009) calls the "dead third" or the presence of an absence. Bits of her mother's history are surfacing. A story recently revealed by Sarah's father is that when her mother was 5, her father left for work one day, never to return. Every day for one year, the grandmother, with her two children, would wait at the train station for her grandfather's arrival. He never arrived. Years later they were informed he died in the Crimean Offensive, fighting for the Nazis.

It is a story that is frozen in time whereby one is not able to mourn, mother nor daughter. A story of trauma and shame/guilt-laden secrets held unconsciously over generations. There is catastrophe that is displaced and removed from original catastrophe. Sarah searches for the original disaster, as well as defends against it. As in Kafka, she is filled with a shame and guilt that brutally punishes and to find peace she needs to find justification. This would mean relinquishing her bastion to find that what is behind it is criminality, or in Bion's terminology to transform β elements that are fragmentations of the knowledge of the horror of the war. What is at stake is not merely her own psyche, but the psyche of the mother as well. She would repeat over and over "It's killing me" or "I feel erased" when faced with the tragedy of her boyfriend's psychosis. Without her personal bastion, she felt she would die or worse that her mother would be lost to her forever.

She tells me of an incident that happened when she was 8 years old. There was an old swing in the countryside near her home that was off-limits because her parents felt it was not safe. Sarah, disobeying, would secretly sneak off to play on the swing. On one of these secret escapades she fell off the swing breaking her arm. Terrified of "being found out" and full of shame for not abiding her parents' rules, she never told anyone and lived with an unattended broken arm for one week until finally her teacher noticed. It is remarkable how alone she was . . . the degree to which there truly was no one to witness or confirm her external and psychic realities was so great that not even the pain of a broken arm could be shown or expressed, but even more remarkable were the unobservant and unresponsive parents. Hers was a world constituted by generations of absence.

As she retold the memory, I wondered if Sarah was letting me know that I have failed to see her "broken arm." She entrusts in me her secrets/disobediences, but have I not recognized her pain? Or is she fearful that if she doesn't abide by my rules she will be punished, "found out" and rejected? I ponder her communication silently and wonder if this relates to her anguishing breakup with the boyfriend, where I too often concentrated on helping her get out of the relationship missing crucial underlying emotions. A few sessions later Sarah tells me she continues to be in contact with the boyfriend, but only as a friend. She then reveals

> that being with him transforms me to a different reality. It transforms me out of my shame. It is my secret garden. I step into a separate world, it's lovely. It is comforting because I can unload the burden of myself when I am with him. It is both exciting and annihilating.

I know now that this relationship is her "secret swing."

Two weeks before my summer break Sarah cancels a session due to a medical procedure . . . she was having her eggs frozen. The session following her procedure she was in a good mood declaring, "I produced plenty of eggs and most were healthy and viable . . . having gone through with this makes me feel good about myself." There is hope and desire even if it has to be on ice for the time being. Nonetheless, I wonder about all that has been frozen . . . time, trauma, terror, me, us, the treatment and her evolving capacity to thaw out? I also know there are some traumas that cannot be worked through, leaving destroyed broken parts. . . . I hope that Sarah will someday be able to thaw out some of her frozen parts knowing that others will forever remain on ice.

References

Baranger, M. and W. Baranger (2008). The analytic situation as a field. *International Journal of Psycho-Analysis* 89: 795–826.

Bion, W.R. (1962). *Learning From Experience*. London, UK: Heinemann.

Eigen, M. (2012). Personal communication.

Ferro, A. (2002). Some implications of Bion's thought: The waking dream and narrative derivatives. *International Journal of Psycho-Analysis* 83: 597–607.

Gerson, S. (2009). When the third is dead: Memory, mourning, and witnessing in the aftermath of the holocaust. *International Journal of Psycho-Analysis* 90: 1341–1357.

Kafka, F. (1995). *The Complete Stories*. Ed. Nahum N. Glatzer. New York: Schocken Books.

O'Shaughnessy, E. (1981). A commemorative essay on W.R. Bion's theory of thinking. *Journal of Child Psychotherapy* 7: 181–192.

13

DREAMS, TRANSFORMATIONS AND HOPE[1]

Jani Santamaría Linares

In his private notebook entitled *Cogitations* (1992), Wilfred Bion presents dreams as emotional experiences which a person has not allowed him/herself to experience during waking hours and stresses the transformation of alpha (alpha dream work) as essential for their own formation. According to Brown (2012), alpha function is the agent which carries out the operation that produces transformations and therefore, following Grotstein (2000, p. 7), dreams constitute emotional thought.

Dreams reveal and conceal aspects of the internal world and mental function; they are mental images of emotional states. As Cassorla states:

> During the analytic process, the analyst is included in the patient's sleep through transference. The analysis, in a specific operational sense, then becomes an 'observing system' through which unconscious processes, whether or not originating from what is repressed, acquire the conditions to be represented and transformed.
>
> *(Cassorla, 2008)*

Clinical experience with patients who manifest primitive aspects of the mind (Caper, 2000) allows one to reflect upon the role that dreams and transformations play in this very specific mental function.

In this paper I will elaborate on the vicissitudes of emotions experienced by the analyst in working with difficult to reach patients. One such patient, Esperanza,[2] the embodiment of hope itself, will be presented here.

Esperanza is a 25-year-old girl, who began analytic treatment at 16 years of age, to work through her emotions. She felt it was very difficult to deal with the separation process with her parents. She was filled with pain and hopelessness, since she felt the only attachment between her and her mother was the hate (H) bond. She felt bad for being her dad's favorite.

Esperanza is the youngest of three sisters. At the time she lived with several college roommates and was about to start work on her PhD. We agreed to work four times a week in order to create as much intimacy as possible.

When Esperanza came to treatment, there was a hardness to her, like a shield, yet she was so fragile that a little external pressure, such as separation from her parents, a small fluctuation in her emotions, was enough to plunge her into emptiness. This psychic pain, a part of her being, like a ripe fruit, could easily fall from the tree with the blowing winds of fate.

For several years, we struggled with parts of herself that were attached to an internal object built from hate. This hate expressed itself in different dimensions and made her feel very persecuted. Within this highly parasitic and symbiotic bond with her mother (a professional psychologist) she delivered her own prognosis: "End up as an addict, commit suicide or become a prostitute." Esperanza had a strange ability to live in a transparent world un-knowing to herself (-K) (Bion, 1962). She attacked her own mental functions (Aguayo and Malin, 2013) by building a "hallucinated" relationship with her precarious perceptions and communication through actions (Aguayo, 2009) such as using drugs and exposing herself to situations with a great deal of violence and abandonment. She felt the projective identifications as though they were bursting into a limitless space, without any coordinates that could serve as guides.

Growing up and facing the psychological, physical and emotional changes of adolescence is very difficult for most teenagers. For Esperanza, the challenge was excruciatingly painful and almost impossible to manage. Her mother was very angry because Esperanza had started a "homosexual" relationship with a friend named Ana. When I informed Esperanza that I was going to be away from the office for a period of time, she told me that her "girlfriend/friend" was also going to be out of town. These separations made her very depressed. The pain which she did not speak of but whispered silently in her heart led to a breakdown.

While I was away, her mother had her hospitalized for one month in a psychiatric hospital. The treatment took a tragic turn due to the interruption. From this moment forward, her mother became hostile toward me and threatened not to pay for treatment. She demanded that I contact Esperanza's psychiatrist and get a confirmation of her diagnosis . . . bipolar disorder. The turbulence of the psychotic part of the personality (Bion, 1962) attacked and violated the therapeutic territory.

When we resumed treatment the emotional space, which had been dynamic, transformed itself into something static. The flow of the sessions was frozen through reversal of perspective (Bion, 1957). Esperanza accused me of wanting to have her "locked up" in the office. She turned to "projective transformations and transformations in hyperbole" (Bion, 1965) and decided that the "only" solution was to leave her mother's house and the analytic treatment. Each fragment of the session was converted into a missile threatening to overpower the analytic texture. Through projective transformations, a kind of psychotic transformation, she assigned me cosmic responsibility for all that happened to her. The actual quality of her thoughts transformed my words into things, into symbolic equations (Segal, 1957). Thus, despite my attempts, she decided to quit treatment.

Klein (1946) showed that when the patient gets rid of what she has projected onto the analyst, she has the illusion of getting rid of this splitting; Shakespeare explained it best in *Hamlet* (Act III, 4 Scene) when he said, " Oh, throw away the worst part of it, and leave the purer with the other half." This was what happened – she dumped me and left.

After two years of absence, Esperanza returned, telling me she found herself scared because she realized that "evil" lived in her. Therefore, we reestablished the process with the same setting.

One day, she started a session by saying:

> Ana died . . . she was murdered by her boyfriend at a party, he stabbed her 15 times in the face. I have a boyfriend but if I had gone to the party, she would be alive. We were

like Siamese [twins] and we made a pact to always be together and think the same thing. I betrayed her because I came back to treatment with you and left her; I'm angry at you but I'm also grateful that you saved me.

Hearing this took me to a state of torpor and pain, which deterred me from dreaming. Mendizabal (1998) and Ferro (2012) emphasize that the analyst is sometimes touched by the patient at her deepest and most vital part and sometimes she is touched in death. I could not stop thinking about the murder scene, the painful reality turned into a nightmare and could not be digested.

The following session, she told me her first dream:

I dreamed I came to session, but you, you were two, one was like you, and the other one was younger. She was about 16, I laid on the couch with both of you, and once I got up I was able to cry. It was like I was trapped; but, when the "other you" arrived, who was younger, things changed. . . . I woke up very upset.

She questioned herself about her bisexuality/homosexuality. She had not had sex with Ana because she felt her body was like something sacred. All she had been looking for was loving strokes and skin-to-skin contact. When her parents separated, she recalled feeling "warm while sleeping in bed with her mother." I felt in some way, she was angry with me and I began to feel that she might abandon the emotional experience. She then started missing sessions and occupied those time slots to have sex with women.

Esperanza needed to keep this painful experience dissociated. So, she resorted to manic defenses. The constant use of splitting, penetrated me like a pungent odor which on many occasions hindered my ability to think. At the same time, but on a different level, I observed a change in her for the first time since she had shared the dream with me.

In the following session, she told me that Luis (her boyfriend) rejected her need to have contact with a woman, she said:

I keep thinking about the dream I had about you. It troubles me. It's like, at the same time I dreamed about you, I was sleeping with Luis. He was hugging me around my neck and I felt he was choking me. I do not know if what woke me up, if it was the distress of dreaming about you or that Luis was choking me.

She continued to process the dream:

I was anguished to be stuck on the couch, but everything changed when the "other you" was there; the one who looked happier, the one who you are, and thanks to this third person I could sit down, get up from that couch and talk. I always wanted to be at "one" with someone, and this was the way it was with Ana. She had given me a mirror and it broke when she died. I felt that she was angry [with me] because I was in bed with Luis. Why doesn't Luis understand that I need a woman and a man?

She mentioned that her mother had problems; she likened her with the mother in the book *Sybil*, an intrusive, imposing and violent figure. She remembered the time when her mother had her hospitalized at a psychiatric clinic when she found out that she was dating Ana.

The material that was coming down like rain gave rise to theoretical concepts; I struggled not to get caught up in an intellectual endeavor.

The exercise of "negative capability" (Bion, 1966) nurtured and helped me navigate the storm. I pointed out to her the constant conjunction between omnipotence (being male and female) and psychic pain. She became angry and shouted that she deserved to have everything, "my boss has two girlfriends and they live with her." After shouting, she sobbed with passion and in the next day, she told me with an air of triumph and arrogance: "Luis agreed to my having a girlfriend, you see, yes you can have it all, this was how it was with Ana, the boyfriends always accepted our relationship."

I felt very silly, I wondered if I was being infiltrated by moral prejudices regarding homosexuality/bisexuality; I felt I was beating around the bush with a theme that had no end: homosexuality. The field was saturated (Baranger and Baranger, 1961–62) (Ferro, 2009).

Esperanza came to the subsequent session. She mentioned that as a child, she slept in bed with her parents and both of them caressed her. She said:

> I dreamed that I was in between my parents, my dad stroked my chest and I felt good . . .
> but in reality, Luis was stroking me while I was dreaming. It's like that dream I had with
> my mom where she was choking me and so was Luis. Oh No! It was not my mom, it
> was you, and "the other you" saved me.

The concept of confusional state came to mind – this mixture which Cassorla (2008) calls "dream and not dream." I asked her if something was going on, and she answered

> Yes, for the first time I became angry and it was because I broke the dream barrier.
> Sometimes when I'm alone, I imagine that I move your image and that of others within
> me, so that it does not hurt me.

I asked her: "Do you feel that this barrier is breaking? Like when that mirror broke when Ana died? What is going on, Esperanza? Where are we going?"

She cried and interpreted this confusion as a warning that something inside of her was breaking up; she mentioned that the crisp and clear dreams meant that she could not get over Ana's death; she added: "I'm terrified that something is pulling me and it wants to take me with her, there is something inside attacking me." This story was the expression of a psyche overwhelmed with pain. I observed a young woman navigating in an inland sea, on a fragile psychic raft, built with logs of hope and with ropes of desire, and I had the feeling that this time the analytic treatment would work.

In the following session, while I was reading an article about the Claustrum (Meltzer, 1992), Esperanza arrived. She began:

> I've been thinking that what psychiatrists call "fleeting thoughts" is what is happening
> to me now as I write my thesis; an idea comes to me and another and another and
> another, the difference is that now this "madness" is helping me write.

She laughed and went on

> "Maybe being crazy is not so bad, it's all a matter of knowing how to fit the craziness
> in. This sixteenth century theme is fascinating, the women locked up in a convent. . . .
> I think this is how I felt when I was with my mom.

She was silent and then said,

> I had a dream: I was in the lounge of a psychiatric hospital. My psychiatrist was sitting in a wheelchair, and so was Dr. José who smiled at me but no one could see him. In the dream, I thought to myself that the psychiatrist always told me that we were all crazy and thought, "Now it's his turn."

She went on:

> The strange thing in this dream was that there was a lady who had a thread in her stomach, like a circle close to where the belly button is. I didn't get this. I remembered that as a 4-year-old girl, I tied a string to my finger. Like in the dream, I tied it to the door handle and I'm not sure how, but I managed to lock myself in my room; the door closed, it was horrible. They had to break through a window in order to get in and I cried and cried.

She continued: "This dream also reminded me of when I was locked up in a psychiatric hospital. Dr. José told me that I became crazy in order to remain faithful to my mom. I think this is true."

Esperanza cried when she remembered Dr. José; she kept on talking about the experience of loss, the hospital admission, her "manic" episode, the sexual promiscuity and climbing on chairs and tables at the hospital to avoid getting an injection. The story had comic and tragic touches . . . 5 minutes before the end of the session, the image of the lady in her dream with the thread near her belly button came to mind. There was so much information! I realized I was saturated. Many configurations in forms of equations were brought to my mind: the thread connected to the umbilical cord. I thought: "It's now my turn to be paralyzed" like the psychiatrist in her dream. The prevailing anxieties of confinement and separation were also clear.

I wished to extend the session because I felt I needed more time to digest all those scattered particles, those beta elements (Bion, 1962); I felt there was "something" loose in the atmosphere . . . but the reality principle, time, made me end the session, I remained restless as I climbed the stairs to walk her to the door. I knew that the transferential meaning of the dream was clearly suggested in the material but I consoled myself thinking that this issue would come up in the following session.

I was shocked when I returned to the office and found the office door locked. Esperanza shut my door, and I had no key to open it. I felt time "like a devil"; I only had 5 minutes until I would see the next patient. I called the security guard; he jumped through the window into the office and opened the door.[3] I could not believe what had just happened; Esperanza "had locked the office itself" and she had locked me out of my workplace. Until then I had felt mentally imprisoned by her but now I thought to myself: "I have no key to leave the physical and mental state of this prison . . . (hers and mine)."

Bion (1965) speaks of transformation in "O" and says that "true knowledge" is something that "has been and is unknowable." I thought then that it was not only about "knowing" (K) the history of confinement, I have "been" ("O") the confinement (the claustrum).[4] In this way, Esperanza wished to show me the terror and confinement that accompanied every act of her life. The transformation in my emotional state from this shocking bitter pill not only helped me connect with Esperanza's inner world but also with my own thinking apparatus

(Bion, 1962). I turned to my "internal colleagues" to recover from this state of mind. I tried to capture, through what Sapienza (2001) calls "intuition analytically trained," the other "threads" that remained loose in this experience and under the L, H and K links, I established the "key" of the session.

I remembered the importance of a new character, the office security guard who jumped through the window and opened the door.

In her first dream, Esperanza had mentioned that there was "another part of me" (analytic function) which intervened as a third part and "helped her out of a mental state." I thought she was referring to the appearance of the father figure (Nick, 2013). The transition to the oedipal constellation and the gathering of the split parts was a difficult and painful process; it was time to integrate the coordinates of the paternal function.

In this caesura (Bion, 1977) the door became a contact and separation point. A door was shut and another opened; Esperanza compelled me to train my ears to differentiate the notes in the transformations.

The catastrophic change (Bion, 1966) was vitally necessary. From it, transformations were born, the transformation from O to K (Bion, 1965) helped me survive the confinement. The transformation from K to O led us both to grow mentally although this growth still carried the "catastrophe." I observed the construction of her mind through the digestion of the life lessons in truth. This story seemed to oscillate between a two-dimensional and a three-dimensional functioning, in slow and fast motions (Meltzer, 1975).

In considering transformation, Grotstein (2007, p. 231) said:

> Bion invoked the concept of transformation to move psychoanalytic thinking from stasis to flux – that is, the constancy of movement and change – and to help us to understand the intermediate processes by which we "learn from experience": how we "digest" experiences and "metabolise" them into emotional meaning and objective significance.

Transformations, then, need to be considered in context with evolution – specifically the evolutions of "O" which can be understood as the inexorable flux of circumstance, life, from both the internal and external vertices. Transformations constituted Esperanza's ultimate moving backdrop. Finally, her academic projects and relationships found their respective space, and she started to show curiosity about her dreams. As Bion wrote: "The theory of transformations is intended to illuminate a chain of phenomena in which understanding of one link, or aspect of it, helps in the understanding of others" (Bion, 1965, p. 34).

The analyst's *reverie* (Bion, 1962) as a therapeutic tool was important for my work with Esperanza. It allowed me to capture the analytic object and regulate the temperature of the connections. Additionally, it allowed me to observe myself and not lose the ability to have a mind of my own. Daydreaming allowed me to "dream for two" (Cassorla, 2008), and I followed the method that Levine (2015) called "dreaming the patient into being."

On the other hand, the dream function and the "whole dream" (Grotstein, 2007) deserve special attention. I believe that dreams have a stake in the digestion of the truth; they go through various combinations. Sometimes they are evacuative dreams (Cassorla, 2014), others are traumatic ones like Esperanza's unfolding dream on the couch (Garma, 1990), or they are expressed as acts like the thread and paralysis dreams. In this way, the dream function symbolizes something, i.e. the oneiric life (Meltzer, 1983). It is expressed as a theater – a window, generator of meanings.

Grotstein (1992) considers the study of dreams as an abstraction through which a sense of existence is achieved or sought to be acquired. Sandler (2009) believes that dreams are tools to know and be known. Dreaming then appears as a primary analytic function of the mind (Santamaría, 2000; Schneider, 2011).

The fluidity in her associations provided her with a cascade of memories (contents) that had held her back. The scent of the depressive position introduced her to a new emotional landscape. She was now capable of giving psychic qualities to non-mental facts (Transformations from $T\beta$ to $T\alpha$) (Bion, 1965). Hope became a point on the horizon.

Esperanza kept alive the desire to know and be known – K link (Bion, 1962). Ana's loss as a real attachment figure became bearable when she was able to connect with the "Ana-Esperanza" figure of her childhood. The last dream she shared with me illustrates the seed of germination of a nascent thought.

> I dreamed I saw Ana in the hospital, she was alive, her face was split in half, she had reconstructed only half of her face. ". . . It hurt to see only a part of the destroyed face, but at the same time, it gave me hope that the other half was already in recovery."

In contrast to the failure of dreaming and the feeling of being dead, as it happened in the first part of the process, it seems to me that this dream confirms what Bion mentions in *Cogitations*, "the real dream is felt as the promotion of life" (1992, p. 67).

Every session opens itself to infinite possible developments, patiently waiting for the birth of a transformational dream in the direction of mental growth and an opportunity for an encounter with the truth.

I end convinced: *Each session is an act of hope.*

Notes

1 The original title in Spanish is "Sueños, Transformaciones y Esperanza."
2 Esperanza is both a female name and the word for hope. This clinical case is about a girl named Esperanza. The double meaning is inferred in the original title.
3 Two months prior, I had changed consulting rooms and I still did not have a key for the door because the door was always open when I was not working. On this occasion, Esperanza closed it when she walked to the exit.
4 The subsequent sessions brought about memories of that "claustrum" (the psychiatric hospital, her childhood home, transference, the sixteenth century "convent" thesis.

References

Aguayo, J. (2009). On understanding projective identification in the treatment of psychotic states of mind: The publishing cohort of H. Rosenfeld, H. Segal and W. Bion (1946–1957). *International Journal of Psychoanalysis* 90: 69–90.

Aguayo, J. and B. Malin (2013). *W. Bion Los Angeles Seminars and Supervision*. London: Karnac.

Baranger, M. and W. Baranger (1961–62). The analytic situation as a dynamic field. *International Journal of Psychoanalysis* 89: 795–826.

Bion, F. (Ed.) (1992). *Cogitations*. London: Karnac.

Bion, W. (1957). Differentiation of the psychotic from the non-psychotic personalities. In *Second Thoughts – Selected Papers of Psycho-Analysis*. London: Karnac.

Bion, W. (1962). *Learning from Experience*. London. Jason Aronson.

Bion, W.R. (1965). *Transformations*. London: Heinemann.

Bion, W.R. (1966). Catastrophic change. In *Attention and Interpretation*. London: Karnac.

Bion, W.R. (1977). *Two Papers: The Grid and the Caesura*. London: Karnac.

Brown, L. (2012). Bion's discovery of alpha function: Thinking under fire on the battlefield and in the consulting room. *International Journal of Psychoanalysis* 93(5): 1191–1214.

Caper, R. (2000). Psicopatología y estados mentales de la mente. *Libro Anual de Psicoanálisis* XIV: 129–140.

Cassorla, R.M.S. (2008). The analyst's implicit alpha function: Trauma and enactment in the analysis of borderline patients. *International Journal of Psychoanalysis* 89: 161–180.

Cassorla, R.M.S. (2014). Personal communication.

Ferro, A. (2009). Transformations in dreaming and characters in the psychoanalytical field. *International Journal of Psycho-Analysis* 90: 253–258.

Ferro, A. (2012). Traslados A y desde el inicio inconsciente: Reveries, transformaciones en el soñar y sueños. *Revista Psicoanálisis*, No. 10.

Garma, A. (1990). *Tratado Mayor del Psicoanalisis de los Suenos*. Ed.Technipublicaciones: Madrid., S.A. Grupo Editorial Julian Yebenes. Colección Continente/Contenido. Dirigido por la Dra Mercedes Velo.

Grotstein, J. (1992). The Psychoanalytic session as a dream, as improvisational theatre and as sacred drama. In *But at the Same Time and on Another Level: Psychoanalytic Theory and Technique in the Kleinian/Bionian Mode*. Vol. I., London: Karnac.

Grotstein, J. (2000). *Who Is the Dreamer, Who Dreams the Dream?: A Study of Psychic Presences (Relational Perspectives Book Series) (Vol 19) First Edition (US)*. Abingdon-on-Thames: Routledge.

Grotstein, J. (2007). *A Beam of Intense Darkness: Wilfred Bion's Legacy to Psychoanalysis*. London: Karnac.

Klein, M. (1946). *Notas Sobre El Mecanismo Esquizoide: Tomo III Obras Completas*. Buenos Aires: Paidós.

Levine, H. (2015). Dreaming the patient into being: A methodology for clinical seminars. In M. Harris Williams (Ed.), *Teaching Bion*. London: Karnac.

Meltzer, D. (1975). *Explorations in Autism*. London: Karnac.

Meltzer, D. (1983). *Dream Life: A Re-Examination of the Psycho-Analytical Theory and Technique*. Strath Tay: Clunie.

Meltzer, D. (1992). The *Claustrum*. London: Karnac.

Mendizabal, A. (1998). Alucinaciones en las Neurosis: trabajo presentado en el *XXXVIII Congreso Nacional de Psicoanálisis*.

Nick, S. (2013). El padre, el dolor psiquico y el desarrollor de las psicosexualidad *Trabajo plenario presentado en las XX Jornadas Interregionales de Ninez y Adolescencia de FEPAL, Mexico 2013*.

Sandler, P.C. (2009). *Dreaming, Transformation, Containment and Change, a Clinical Application of Bion's Concepts*. Vol. I. London: Karnac.

Santamaría, A. (2000). Los sueños como fuente de creatividad. *Cuadernos de Psicoanálisis (APM)* Julio–Diciembre: 3–4.

Sapienza, A. (2001). O trabalho do sonho alfa do psicanalista na sessão: intuição-atenção- interpretação. In M.O.F. FRANÇA et al. (Eds.), *Transformações e invariâncias: Bion -SBPSP: Seminários Paulistas*. São Paulo: Casa do psicólogo.

Schneider, J.A. (2011). Del trabajo del sueño de Freud al trabajo del soñar de Bion: la concepción cambiante de soñar en la teoría psicoanalítica. *Libro Anual de Psicoanálisis* XXVI: 47–60.

Segal, H. (1957). Notes on symbol formation. *International Journal of Psycho-Analysis* 38: 391–397.

SECTION VI

Caesura and O

14

LONG-LASTING HYPNAGOGIC STATES OF MIND, SUB-THALAMIC FEARS AND CAESURA

Arnaldo Chuster

Two kinds of experiences constitute the caesura between the sleeping state of mind and the awake state of mind:

1 before sleeping (hypnagogic state)
2 before awakening (hypnopompic state)

Usually they are very fast and, therefore, not perceived. However, we may observe some situations when they last longer than usual. This paper is about those states of mind and their relationship with psychoanalytical practice.

In such experiences, **all senses** may be involved, and although the **visual** images are the most cited, because they cause a stronger impression and are more time-consuming, the **auditory** experiences are the most frequent. It is very common to find someone who has experienced being in a mental state, almost asleep, and hear his name being called and then awakening. In other words, the output of the hypnagogic state occurs by the call of "some-one" who was over there taking care of the individual.

There are two important defining aspects of the hypnagogic state: 1) stimulation of only **one sense** and 2) the contact with a **protective object** (alpha function).

The less protective the object, the more time-consuming the hypnagogic state can be. That is, the hypnagogic state could be a kind of reluctance to sleep because sleeping means to meet the failing protective object (bad object). Sometimes due to a massive failure, going to sleep means to meet the **vacant object** and with it comes envy, greed, hostility, omnipotence. Insomnia could frequently appear in such a situation. It is a defense against contact with the **bad object**.

One should also note that the longer lasting the hypnagogic state there is an increased pos-sibility of assigning **veracity** to it. Instead of recognizing that the individual was almost asleep and was awakened by the "illusion" that, for instance, he heard the voice of someone calling him, he feels to have had an experience that often acquires a mystical, religious or supernatural interpretation. A kind of "Ghost" was present.

Such was the case of a 38-year-old patient who was experiencing many conflicts due to a divorce. She reported that while lying in bed at night she saw her late grandmother staring at her. The grandmother was standing there, smiling, without saying anything. She felt scared and at the same time a sense of comfort. She tried to talk, but Grandma did not say anything and walked quickly away.

When she was very young this patient used to have frequent problems with a psychotic mother. In extreme conflict situations, she used to run away to Grandma's house. She recalls becoming intimidated while going from her apartment to her grandmother's apartment nearby. She recalls being so small that she could not push the elevator button. Then she climbed the stairs to get to Grandma's apartment, usually arriving there so tired that she fell asleep in Grandma's arms.

The patient said very anxiously that she could not admit that the experience was a dream. *It was so real.* The ghost of the grandmother came to visit her.

Our position, as psychoanalysts, should not be to fear ghosts, poltergeists, spirits, demons, feelings, ideas and thoughts. Our position is not to argue or prove it is not true. This patient thinks that it is reasonable to feel it is a ghost.

However, it may be part of the job to add another interpretation while reinforcing the intention of not trying to prove that the psychoanalytic point of view is better than the patient's point of view. We have to be careful with transformations in hallucinosis (Bion, 1965).

The analyst said that the experience could signify a meeting with an idealized protection that she needed at that time. Maybe she was feeling insecure and didn't feel a sense of protection she might be needing.

She added: "That is right, I feel very insecure except during our sessions, I feel secure here to say those things. Only a psychoanalyst would not consider me a crazy person for having such experience".

One could notice that there is a caesura: much more continuity between what I have said to the patient and what the patient said to me.

I see here the possibilities of K link in the direction to O. I can say this in the following way: confidence creates sincerity, and sincerity creates confidence. It is a circular argument. As those elements gradually increase in the link, the diameter of **psychic intimacy** also increases. Therefore, one may have confidence + sincerity + intimacy = mental development (Chuster, 2014).

The psychotic mother of the patient always rejected her by decreasing the value of her personal achievements. The patient got married to a man who repeated the same pattern of relationship as the mother.

Another patient reported that he got home late one night and found an old friend in his living room after hearing nothing from her for many years. She was there sleeping on the couch. He was very surprised and started thinking how she could have gotten into the house. Was it the housekeeper who opened the door for her? No, this is not the day of the housekeeper. Then he tried to wake her up by calling her name. She stared at him but did not say anything. When he went to the next room to hang up his jacket, he heard her saying that she was about to leave at that moment, because she was late to meet her son. He said, "Please wait a few more minutes, let us talk a little about your life". However, when he returned to the living room she had already left. He ran to the elevator but the elevator was at the floor. He ran to the stair entrance but he did not hear any sound of steps.

The next day, deeply intrigued with the visit and this friend, he decided to phone her son. He said to him: "Three days ago I saw your mother in my house, but she left suddenly without talking to me". The son said very shocked: "My mother died six months ago".

Of course, the patient was shocked too! He was very scared of the experience. He was afraid that it was a sign that he was becoming mentally ill, but he also considered that he had a kind of supernatural experience, although he was not a man of religious beliefs.

I asked him if he was too tired when he was driving back home that night. He confirmed and said he had to stop for a few moments at a gas station to sleep. Then he associated that the gas station was located in a street with the family name of his friend. They used to meet there when they were teenagers.

This patient was having a deep conflict with his teenage daughter. His daughter was using drugs and had a "bad trip" the previous weekend that put her in the hospital. His woman friend used to be a lovely and caring friend when they were young.

Therefore, when I proposed that he could think of this experience of contact with many meanings in a state of mind near sleep, he felt relief and cried. I could add many free associations that brought this patient to his childhood conflicts, but it is not the purpose of this paper.

Another patient, one week after his father's funeral, was driving back home from work feeling very sad and tired. He had been having insomnia and although his physician had given him sleeping pills they did not work properly. He hadn't been to work for two weeks and this was the first day he got back to his office. Of course, during the day many problems came up with no solutions at all. He was deeply frustrated when he stopped for a moment to refresh himself at a gas station courtyard. It was then he heard his father talking to him from the radio. His father was counseling him in many aspects of his work. However, the voice was too low to hear clearly. The patient felt scared and at the same time comforted.

I said that he probably knew how his father used to think. That made sense to him. Nevertheless, he said that he was afraid that I would say that he should go to a mental institution. I added that there is an aspect of cruelty in not trying to understand some facts in a broad range (which was quite his father's way of thinking). I also said that he had lost the protection of the good father and was about to meet the cruel object in his dreams. I think this is the reason for his insomnia. The bad object is the absent object.

Of course, there is a lot more information about this case in order to explain why I gave that interpretation. The reader will note that in all three cases there was a deceased person representing a container that was prone to fail. Just part of the communication was going through.

In a general way, situations of insomnia are produced when the individual does not feel himself to be a confident container for his own experiences. The container which deals with the conflicts during the state of sleep (HYPNOS) is a persecutory and punitive container, therefore unable to properly digest the conflictive facts that occurred when he was awake. Those facts certainly represent a repetition of a **failure**, but also the perception of the impossibility of something between the individual and his mother, or also between the individual and his parents. The impossibility to have confidence, sincerity and intimacy.

Body reactions are sometimes present in these states as for instance a hypnagogic jolt (a sudden tensing of the body or a feeling of falling). These are frequent descriptions. They last less than a second.

The initial periods of paradoxical sleep (REM sleep) link to sensory images and may be associated with a state of mind described as not being able to act; this is because in reality the body is sleeping.

Usually, the hypnagogic and hypnopompic phenomena are not indicative of dysfunctional or pathological processes. But when they last longer than usual, they may be indicative of a state where sleeping instead of being a container for the mind has turned into something scary or threatening. This is when **sub-thalamic fears** (**terror**) may appear. Primitive mental states usually follow these feelings and require a good deal of imagination to put all the split experiences together.

The way the container functions is related to the initial experiences of life with the mother. In those hypnagogic experiences the process of **reverie** is perceived as flawed or flawing, and consequently, as an experience in which there is something **impossible** to be accomplished with the mother. Such impossibility is the main factor that increases **the feeling of terror**. In other words, the impossibility is a consequence of an extensive failure of alpha function.

One can also note how these ancient experiences are transferred to other relationships in life, to a greater or lesser degree, and can affect the emotional and sexual life in intense or episodic forms.

Once again, one of the features of the hypnagogic state is that it reaches **only one sense**. That is, if the experiences reported refer to hearing, there is no other sense involved. The ghost is talking but cannot be seen or if the ghost is being seen, it does not talk. This differentiates the hypnagogic state from a pathological hallucinatory state.

The hypnagogic state sometimes is reported as being deeply creative. During its occurrence one could have access to unconscious inspiration as we often see in poetry creation.

Therefore, the hypnagogic state is sometimes considered a kind of creative state of mind without any boundaries or limitations. In this state, one may have access to unconscious resources without superego restrictions. Thomas Alva Edison used to value this state so much that he developed his own technique to keep it turned on while he was working through his inventions. He used to sit on a special chair trying to relax and meditate in order to reach a hypnagogic state. He used to grasp a snooker ball with his fist turned upside down and his arm resting on the chair. He then placed a metal plate on the floor. In case he fell asleep, the ball would fall down and make a noise that would wake him up. He then repeated the procedure many times searching for a "wild thought".

Extreme situations often produce hypnagogic states, like **situations of war** or near-death states or near coma states. It may happen when someone has had surgery and is coming back from anesthesia, or some situations in Intensive Care Units.

I will use the **model of war** to dialogue on the subject.

The central problem is to cross the caesura between one mental state and another state of mind that has completely different features, i.e. going from war to life in society and vice versa. The individual needs to handle the caesura that occurs in his day to day life, and for this he depends on his psyche being able to digest the experiences and for such task needs to have a trustable container.

In other words, soldiers who must go to war deal with death. They take life away from others. This is normally the role of God. Asking young soldiers to take that role without adequate psychological preparation can lead to damaging consequences.

Yet there is a point where soldiers must go back home. They should cross a **caesura** between the world where they are acting in the role of God and the world where they are acting in an ordinary societal role.

Killing someone without splitting oneself from the feelings that the act engenders requires an effort of supreme consciousness that is beyond most humans' capacity. Killing is what warriors do for society. Yet when they return home, society does not generally acknowledge that the act it asked them to do created a deep split in their psyches, or a psychological weight most of them will stumble beneath for the rest of their lives. Warriors must learn how to integrate the experience of killing, to put the pieces of their psyches back together again. For the most part, they are left to do this on their own without the proper instruments.

War is the antithesis of the most fundamental rule of ethics – not to do unto others what you would have others not do unto you. When called upon to fight, we violate many codes of civilized behavior. To survive psychically in the proximity of Mars, the god of war, one has to come to terms with stepping outside conventional moral conduct. This requires coming to terms with guilt over killing and maiming other people.

Reconciling ethics and moral conduct taught in childhood, with brutal actions of war has been a problem for warriors of good conscience for centuries. It is also a problem for society throughout history. When a warrior goes to combat, he loses the protection of society. When he comes back, he may be suspicious of society, because it was society that sent him to war, therefore he feels unaccepted or dangerous.

Bion tried to describe such a situation in which he himself was involved in World War I by quoting the *Mahabharata*, the classic Indian epic. The original "author" was Vyasa who tried to tell about the Great War between the Pandavas and the Kauravas – cousins who claimed to be the rightful rulers of a kingdom.

Krishna was the cousin of both parties, but he was a friend and advisor to the Pandavas, became the brother-in-law of Arjuna, and served as Arjuna's mentor and charioteer in the Great War. Krishna is portrayed several times as eager to see the war occur, and in many ways the Pandavas were his human instruments for fulfilling that end.

At first Krishna tries to buck up Arjuna by appealing to his reason, explaining how critical the situation is. This fails. Then he appeals to pride, chiding Arjuna for letting his feelings get the better of him. This fails too. Finally, Krishna taunts Arjuna about his manhood. Arjuna is not swayed.

One can see here the same situation described at the crossroads in the myth of Oedipus. On one side, there is Laius in a chariot driven by a charioteer, on the other side, Oedipus walking towards his tragic destiny. The dialogue is quite the same. Should I step aside to let the other carry on in his path or should I fight because I have the right to be number one? Who is going to be ready to let the other continue and not be arrogant or too proud of his own qualities?

Even two or three thousand years ago, appeals to manhood and social duties were not sufficient to stop killing our equals on the other side. Krishna presses forward appealing to religion, usually a surefire persuader. Krishna says:

> Believe me, the eternal soul is imperishable. No one can comprehend it. . . . You do not kill and your victim is not killed. . . . Weapons cannot hurt the soul; fire cannot burn it; water cannot wet it. It is eternal and it is the same forever. Once you realize this truth there is no need for you to grieve.

Religion is still misused to get men to kill their brothers. But saying it's all right to kill my own equal because, just maybe, the universe is a vast recycling plant, had about the same effect on Arjuna that it would on any of us today – none.

Any warrior has to be very careful about whom the politicians make out to be devils. Sometimes we have to choose sides with limited information and limited self-knowledge.

History is full of examples of decent citizens making big mistakes while defending ideas based on false premises. For instance, the Germans during World War II committed crimes against humanity killing the "devils" created by the false premise of the existence of a plot of the international Jewry.

Krishna tells Arjuna that there are two paths to realization, the path of knowledge by meditation and the path of work by men of action. The same paths are identical to those portrayed in our Western mythology, for example the story of the knight Parsifal, which is part of the Grail legend. There the fisher king's brother represents the path of knowledge. He is a monk and religious contemplative whom Parsifal meets just before reentering the Grail Castle. Parsifal himself shows us the path of action, the same path put forward by Krishna to Arjuna.

In *Oedipus Rex* the conversation between Oedipus and Tiresias follows the same pattern, as well as the conversation between Oedipus and the Sphinx.

One can say that there are many times when people are at war with themselves and others. During this state of mind, they might have "*wild thoughts*". The problem, should such a thought come along, is what to do with it. Of course, if it is wild, you might try to domesticate it. However, how to do it? How to manage a wild thought in a path free from moral impulses and religious standards?

Bion pointed out that it seems to be simplest to try to tackle the problem by considering what this strange thought is. We might get a clue about it by wondering in what frame of mind or in what conditions this wild thought turned up and became enmeshed in our method of thinking. It could be that it seemed to occur to us when we are asleep.

Moreover, one must use a kind of a model to develop more hypotheses to work with the situations that arise from those states. In summary, one must respect the complexity of mental functioning (Chuster, 2014).

I suggest that for the **hypnagogic states of mind** one can use *The Death of Palinurus* (Virgil 29–19 B.C.) quoted by Bion (1977).

Virgil, in Aeneid, wrote that everybody in Ulysses' fleet went to sleep. Palinurus was on duty, fully awake, monitoring the weather conditions. The god Somnus disguised as Phorbas, assuming a human form (as Krishna did), said to him: "Don't worry; I can take care of the situation". However, Palinurus said: "No! I am not going to be tricked by the placidity of the Mediterranean Sea". Then he tied himself to the helm of the boat. This made him very helpless. Somnus was narcissistically wounded with Palinurus's denial. Who is this arrogant human being, who is defying a god?

Could an analyst who is "tied up" to a theory be a representation of Palinurus's helplessness? Could the god be his own omnipotence or the patient's omnipotence? Could the boat represent analysis?

The god became free to act through Palinurus, collected some drops of water from the *Lethes* (the caesura between the world of the living and the world of the dead) and spread them over his eyelids. Palinurus fell asleep tied up to the helm. The god threw him into the sea with fury.

Drugged by the god of sleep, Palinurus falls overboard with a loud splash. Aeneas, captain of the fleet, wakes up and takes over the helm. Unaware of the god's influence, he accuses Palinurus of complacency. This can also happen with a psychoanalyst who uses memory, desire and need for comprehension. Using those elements, he will not see and therefore cannot help the patient. He can also become drugged with a transformation in hallucinosis (Bion, 1965) trying to prove some psychoanalytical point of view. Moreover, by its turn the patient can act as the god Somnus (omnipotence).

The brief exchange of speeches between Somnus (Hypnos) and Palinurus is carefully composed and finely characterized by Virgil. Each is given four lines, but of sharply contrasting tone. Somnus begins by courteously addressing Palinurus by name and patronymic, followed by three parallel clauses that reinforce their message with incantatory echoic effects: *aequera … aequaetate … aurae … hora quieti*. The sea is calm.… The first line is ordering Palinurus to "steal his tired eyes from his toil" and offers to take Palinurus's place. Palinurus replies in a very different tone with three indignant rhetorical questions. Palinurus's indignation is roused by the thought that he could be negligent in service to his leader Aeneas and devotion to the post in order to allow Aeneas to proceed on his sacred path.

Palinurus is **the sacrificial victim** in an ultimate vertex: "The death of the victim will save many", which constitutes one of the most terrible fantasies amongst all, **the death of the child**. Could that be the source of terror in those hypnagogic states?

References

Bion, W.R. (1965). *Transformations*. London: Heinemann.
Bion, W.R. (1977). *Two Papers: The Grid and Caesura*. London: Karnac.
Chuster, A. (2014). *A Lonesome Road: Essays on the Complexity of W.R. Bion's Work*. Imago: Rio de Janeiro.
Virgil (29–19 BC). *Aeneid (Book 4)*, London: Penguin Classics, 2010.
Vyasa (c. 4th century CE). *The Mahabharata: Complete and Unabridged* (set of 10 volumes). Trans. Bibek Debroy. India: Penguin Books, 2015.

15

THE CAESURA

Careful emptiness and improvisational listening in psychoanalytic education: elements of Bion's 1975 recorded Caesura Lecture not contained in the printed version

Julie Michael McCaig

Much has been written about Bion's Caesura which was first published as: *Two Papers: The Grid and Caesura in 1977*. This workshop focused on the *recording* of his lecture in 1975. The transcript may be found in: Levine and Brown (2013, pp. 55–74).

Workshop participants endeavored "to turn ourselves into resounding song-boxes carving out careful emptiness like those in cellos and violins" (Umberto Eco, 1973). Workshop members listened to selected sections of Bion's Caesura Lecture recorded in Los Angeles in 1975. While it was a lively discussion – far ranging and insightful – the hoped-for result of the workshop was to experience Bion thinking while speaking in his Victorian-tinged speech. His speech stuck my "modern ears" as more like a "species of art". [He was] "imagined and conceptualized cognitively as a living being" (Brandt, 2009). That was how I first experienced the listening. I have come to understand I was also experiencing Bion's capacity for an invitational, embodied communication: being present in a conversation with oneself while thinking and speaking with another/others. This is psychoanalytic, improvisational communication. The experience then is not unlike listening to music and resonating with the mind of the composer/musician as well as their emotional presence.

We hear Bion speaking from another century in Los Angeles. This was a time of great theoretical and political conflict in American psychoanalysis as represented in his audience. At the heart of his communication, Bion leaves us the Caesura Lecture in 1975, an additional memoir of the future: as he is present, in the moment, thinking while he is being recorded into the future. The recorded version of the Caesura differs significantly from the written version. I have listened to this memoir over many years almost like supervision. He also communicates to us the music and poetry of his mind; I will call this embodied speech: thinking and creating while being physically present in the moment, as differentiated from reciting received ideas, or repeating prior conjecture. This form of communication offers an *invitation* to the listener. I find this very similar to jazz musicians' capacities for musical improvisation. Bion is *being* a psychoanalyst; *his* "neural lyre" as suggested by Turner and Pöppel (1983), tunes *our* neural lyre to a unique opportunity for learning from experience. This is an emancipation of psychoanalysis from theory alone and reflects his capacities for technique in reaching the patient who is "difficult to reach". As I have a great interest in the aboriginal, perinatal aspects of life, this Caesura Lecture has captivated my interest since I found it in early 1980.

Bion is improvising with his audience and communicating across time, every time one listens. Our neural lyre and capacities for listening and thinking focus anew, each time, to Bion's presence/lyre. This improvisational, unconscious, elemental capacity of the analyst is key for transformations in O to occur and is impossible to teach, except by example. Bion has left us an excellent example in this Caesura recording.

His title "Caesura" conveys two ideas he incorporates in his embodied speech. The first element is the sense of a gap/caesura in time/space present in every session and every moment of our lives.

The word caesura is, as we are informed, from Latin, *caes* – means to cut, hewn, from the verb *caedere*. Caesura (in Greek and Latin verse) refers, of course, to a break between words within a metrical foot, or in modern verse, a *pause* near the middle of a line (Oxford English Dictionary). He quotes Freud to make his point about the impressive caesura of birth and the continuity of our experience at the beginning of his lecture. "There is much more continuity between intra-uterine life than the impressive caesura of the act of birth would have us believe". From: *The Ego and the Id* (Freud, 1926).

This "Caesura" is more about the seismic, poetic "pause" between intrauterine life and birth. Bion transcends the idea/belief that this is an unbreachable gap. He thinks aloud about how to reach across this *pause* in our experience. What he is prescribing is a careful emptiness, "without memory or desire" and perhaps, even without the distinct awareness of life before birth *vs.* life after birth. It is a *pause*, albeit, an *impressive* one, as Bion, and Freud, before him, articulated. This caesura also provides the pause for the analyst and patient to develop the capacity for thinking while experiencing emotional turmoil. My experience of using Bion's guidance in this manner has led me to the fleeting, transcendental nature of what psychoanalysis holds for the patient and the analyst who can approach this careful emptiness: Bion's Kantian conception of "O".

In this unique communication, he articulates two impressive observations. The first is that there is normal splitting in the primordial world of the womb where the "muchness" we share with all the other animals cannot be fathomed by the fetus and he must break it into "packets". The second notion is a prescription of technique: "To have a hallucination may be the only way the analyst who is not too difficult to reach" may reach the patient who is very "difficult to reach" (Bion, 1975). Bion makes note of the importance of theory but also emancipates psychoanalysis from theory alone. He provides us with his notes on technique, including accessibility of the analyst's mind in relation to the primordial muchness of the patient's intrauterine and perinatal experience. He also expresses hope that the analyst's analysis has been extensive enough to provide a safe receptor site for projections and hallucinations in her patient and herself. Bion does not make a specific prescription in this lecture about transmutations, transformations/transubstantiations of these experiences into mutative interpretations: these are understood in light of his other works and grid.

★★★

As psychoanalysts, then, we may use these neural elements and strive to develop *careful emptiness* to embody the resounding, transitive turbulence inevitable when working in Perinatal/Primordial States of Mind (PSoM). These PSoM are "reminiscences of intra-uterine, perinatal/physical events that transform into *psychological* events" (Bion, 1975): pressure is an example, as articulated by (Paul, 1981). In my experience, these states are consistent in premature and full-term infants and adults, and can also be located in the non-verbal, gestural language of patients who may have a resonance with experience before the "pause" of birth or elements of early experience that welds into protective structures for survival. These states require *careful transient insanity* to find language for the un-say-able and the "unknown knowns".

This thirty-five-year attempt to understand the Perinatal States of Mind (PSoM) is an ongoing research project suggested by the Caesura Lecture. We do not know the language for the experience so patients may use tonal intensity, gesture or musical references, etc., and, of course, dreams. One becomes the instrument, the player and the played in these experiences of essence meeting essence (Lipovetsky, 2010, and Eshel, 2012).

Primordial, Perinatal States of Mind (PSoM) seem to predate and insinuate into Primitive Mental States (PMS): PSoM ↔ PMS.

Primordial, Perinatal States of Mind – PSoM are also reflective of a time of non-pathological splitting as the fetus and infant cannot take in the world of the uterus or even the uterine world of mother to begin: so experience is broken into "small packets" as Bion tells us in this lecture. These Primordial, Perinatal States of Mind (PSoM) underlie Borderline and psychotic states and seem prevalent in the neglected. The previously non-pathological split-ting may become violent projective identification while the PSoM search for a containing mind. Repeated experiences of mourning the absence of a containing presence may provide a containing, thinking presence in the mind of the patient if the transference can endure the grief, loss and despair or occasions when hope is used like a shield against the depth of despair.

What may appear to be an obstructive object is revealed to be the accidental structure designed by a fetus/infant/toddler to avoid primordial turmoil. The ever-present, perinatal, unconscious experiences of seeking, panic, grief, rage, lust, fear and care that Panksepp (2012) explicates in his studies of Affective Neuroscience, betray our relations to the primordial world that are forever alive. We are always, presently in danger of death and abandonment seeking care and relief from panic and grief that may transform into rage alongside our dual track of adult accomplishment. Developing a mind that can think/alpha function while under the sway of these primordial experiences is the goal. If you are born prematurely and it is painful to breathe from the first, why would you trust anything human life has to offer? Some do (McCaig, 1997).

Placental physical relations are sometimes the only stable experiences many neglected, abused/traumatized children of Narcissistic/Borderline/Dual Diagnosis and Psychotic par-ents may have. They seem to attempt to recreate these implanting/ placental/parasitic/peri-natal, physical experiences (reminiscences of physical events that have become psychological and sometimes perverse) in adult relations to tragically disappointing results.

One may provide an infinity of interpretations of idealization, destructiveness, defensive-ness, encapsulation, etc. But, *in the moment* it appears that only "having a hallucination or a delusion" (as Bion suggests in the Caesura Lecture) opens the transitive space of the gap/cae-sura. Then, an unborn idea, feeling or experience may be "incarnated", leading to increased alpha functioning. This is, as Bion suggests, risky business – as analyst and patient alike fear insanity from these "transient delusions". The patient hates the analyst for having this tran-sient PSoM sensitivity, including the understanding of "un-metalised" PSoM communicated in movement and gesture (Bloom, 2006, 2009). The patient fears and hates the experience and keeps attending sessions to have more hated experience until there is a moment when there is only slightly more gratitude than hatred/envy. It often comes just when the analyst and patient feel as if all the work is wasted, useless, delusional or failing and they both have absolutely had enough! This is a moment of psychic weaning when the patient has developed a more separate mind. It is *this* moment in the analysis when the patient may restart development in an area of his mind due to an increase in alpha function: he may have a new idea that opens her work of art, starts a business, or finishes a project, and the transitory hallucinations/delusions recede. A psychological birthing has perhaps occurred. The patient may use hope as a shield against despair or be thrilled (even hypo-manic) until there is a shift back to another round of PSoM <-> Ps <-> D<->PSoM. It may be an exceptionally hazardous time with those who evidence underlying psychosis or an actual or psychic failure to thrive that underlies their adult accomplishments.

★★★

This single contribution has led me to study the gap/caesura in many aspects most notably the impressive caesura of the Neonatal Intensive Care Unit where "maximally naive infants" (as Trevarthen and Reddy (2006) refer to premature infants) require extraordinary intervention in the Netherworld between intrauterine life and viability.

Psychoanalysis with adults and infants who were born prematurely has informed me how penetrable the caesura is. The Caesura Lecture and *A Memoir of the Future* articulate (Bion, 1990) pedagogy for working in these transitory states of turbulence.

As Jacobus suggests in *The Poetics of Psychoanalysis in the Wake of Klein*:

> For the later Bion, the psychoanalytic encounter was itself a site of turbulence, a mental space for further ideas which may yet be developed. . . . If we accept that Bion introduced a new form of pedagogy in his writings, we may conclude at least that he achieved his stated goal therein: To prevent someone who KNOWS from filling the empty space.
>
> *(2005, p. 257)*

Being in a state of knowing *about* these primordial/perinatal states forecloses possibilities of transformations in "O". Nothing is known absolutely in this experience of "presencing" as Eshel (2012) suggests in her work with sex offenders. Eschel's ability to open her analytic instrument to the perpetrators of violence comes to mind as evidence of range, repertoire, capacity and emotional fortitude. Ordinary, transitive violence is our background music, the underscore of variations of annihilation anxiety as evoked by the possibilities of catastrophic change and informed by the generations in both analyst and analysand. The turbulence of ordinary mental life is remarkable!

We develop aspects of our Analytic Instruments in concert with our patients, sometimes to an astonishing degree as we find ourselves, as T. S. Eliot (1974) suggests: "At the still point of the turning world". Analytic training, with a focus on careful emptiness and improvisational listening, equips analysts and candidates for this invitation to a caesura: it may be a kind of disciplined, "transient, hypo-frontality" as hypothesized by Dietrich (2003) that is evidenced in endurance running, meditation or what we call psychoanalytic "reverie", that is less guided by cognition than multi-modal processes. This invitational listening, taught by example, may be like learning to play an Indian Classical Raga from a Raga Master learning a tonal framework for composition and improvisation. Or musical improvisation with other jazz players, trading fours – a pattern in which two solo instruments alternately play four measures each.

In addition to personal relations, experiences of war and loss of his wife in childbirth, I wonder, for example, if Bion (or any psychoanalyst) could be the same person at the end of life if we had never met our analysands. A psychic mosaicism develops in the well-tempered, carved-out, song-box of the analyst and may be parallel to the patient's development or lack thereof.

A plea for psychoanalysis for the twenty-first century becomes evident

If Bion's 1975 Caesura Lecture could reach a future 2015 target, I imagine he might agree that it is well past time for psychoanalysis to reach our most underserved population – the *actual* infant. How would this change theories/enhance our understanding of capabilities of the infant from the beginning? My work in Pregnancy Accompaniment, prematurity in the NICU, and Perinatal States of Mind (PSoM) in adults and infants provides more questions than answers (McCaig, 2013).

It is an astounding truth that psychoanalysis can sometimes reach back through the caesura of birth to the primordial aspects in adults and perhaps restart development – even in the elderly. It is even more astonishing how rapidly psychoanalysis may reach the *actual* infant and her mother through work in pregnancy and states of postpartum depression, traumatic birth, multi-generational transmission of pathologies and trauma, as the crucible for growth may never be more available than in these early experiences. For examples of work with babies and their families see: Houzel (1999), Norman (2001), Salomonsson (2014) and Bradley et al. (2012). There are many, many more excellent papers attending to psychoanalytic work with infants.

Working in the "aboriginal sensible muchness", as William James (1916) called intrauterine life and the perinatal period, immediately informs one of what psychoanalysts have long known:; humans are the only animals who find shame in our need and dependency and erect complex, defensive psychic architecture to obscure our vulnerability. The Caesura informs our careful emptiness to elements of the patient's authentic states of being and becoming or "O" no matter the age of the patient.

References

Bion, W. (1975). *Caesura Lecture* recorded in Los Angeles: The Los Angeles Psychoanalytic Institute.
Bion, W. (1977). *Two Papers: The Grid and Caesura.* London: Karnac.
Bion, W. (1990). *A Memoir of the Future.* London: Karnac. Revised Edition.
Bloom, K. (2006). *The Embodied Self: Movement and Psychoanalysis.* London: Karnac.
Bloom, K. (2009). Embodied attentiveness: Recognising the language of movement. In *Infant Observation: International Journal of Infant Observation and its Applications* 12: 175–185.
Bradley, B., J. Selby and C. Urwin (2012). Group life in babies: Opening up perceptions and possibilities. In C. Urwin and J. Sternberg (Eds.), *Infant Observation and Research: Emotional Processes in Everyday Lives*, pp. 137–148. Hove and NY: Routledge.
Brandt, P.A. (2009). Music and the abstract mind. *The Journal of Music and Meaning* 7: 1–15.
Dietrich, A. (2003). Functional neuroanatomy of altered states of consciousness: The transient hypofrontality hypothesis. *Consciousness and Cognition* 12: 231–256.
Eco, U. (1973). *Travels in Hyperreality.* New York: Harvest Books.
Eliot, T.S. (1974). Collected poems 1909–1962. In *The FOUR Quartets*, p. 189. Faber and Faber Limited.
Eshel, O. (2012). A beam of "Chimeric" darkness: Presence, interconnectedness, and transformation in treatment of a patient convicted of sex offenses. *The Psychoanalytic Review* 99: 149–178.

Freud, S. (1926). Inhibitions, symptoms and anxiety. *S.E.* 20: 138. London: Hogarth.

Houzel, D. (1999). A therapeutic application of infant observation in child psychiatry. *Infant Observation* 2(3), 42–53.

Jacobus, M. (2005). *The Poetics of Psychoanalysis in the Wake of Klein.* Oxford: Oxford University Press.

James, W. (1916). *Some Problems of an Introduction to Philosophy.* Longmans, Green, & Co. (150).

Levine, H. and L. Brown (2013). *Growth and Turbulence in the Container/Contained – Bion's Continuing Legacy*, pp. 55–74. London and NY: Routledge.

Lipovetsky, V. (2010). Womb speak in. *The Psychoanalytic Review* 97: 21–44.

McCaig, J. (1997). The use of infant observation in the treatment of a clinical neonate. In S. Ahlanati and K. Kostoulas (Eds.), *Primitive Mental States Across the Lifespan*, pp. 53–81. New Jersey, London: Jason Aronson.

McCaig, J., K. Bloom, E. Grumbach, N. Lieberman, and V. Lipovetsky. (2013). The study of embodied attentiveness and communicative movement in infant observation and psychoanalysis: Developing a language of somathematic elements of observation, pp. 1–27 (unpublished).

Norman, J. (2001). The psychoanalyst and the baby: A new look at work with infants. *International Journal of Psychoanalysis* 82: 83–100.

Panksepp, J. and L. Biven (2012). *The Archaeology of the Mind: Neuroevolutionary Origins of Human Emotions.* New York, London: W.W. Norton & Company.

Paul, M. (1981). A mental atlas of the process of psychological birth. In J.S. Grotstein (Ed.), *Do I Dare Disturb the Universe?*, pp. 551–570. Beverly Hills, CA: Caesura. Reprinted 1983 with corrections by H. Karnac (Books) Limited.

Salomonsson, B. (2014). *Psychoanalytic Therapy with Infants and Parents: Practice, Theory and Results.* London and New York: Routledge.

Trevarthen, C. and V. Reddy (2006). Consciousness in infants. In M. Velman and S. Schneider (Eds.), *A Companion to Consciousness*, pp. 41–57. Oxford: Blackwell.

Turner, F. and E. Pöppel (1983). The neural lyre: Poetic meter, the brain, and time. In *Poetry. 142,* 5, pp. 277–309. Chicago, IL. : Poetry Foundation.

16

THE IMPRESSIVE CAESURAS

Some thoughts about complexity and paradoxes

Renato Trachtenberg

About caesuras

Inspired by Freud's famous sentence – "[T]here is much more continuity between intrauterine life and earliest infancy, than the impressive caesura of the act of birth would have us believe" (Freud, 1926, p. 138), Bion developed the concept of "caesura" into a fundamental precept in his theory of mental functioning and the clinical encounter. The concept of caesura was first described in a quotation from Freud (Bion, 1976a).

Historically, it appears as an answer from Freud to Otto Rank and his notion of birth trauma (Chuster, 2012). With his sentence about caesura, Freud somehow included the notion of continuity (which is not present in Rank). However, to Freud it arose despite the "impressive caesura". Bion will later say that the continuity is part of the caesura, and it does not happen despite the caesura.

In Civitarese's opinion, the text *Caesura* "assumes the significance of a spiritual testament" (Civitarese, 2008, p. 1129). For Bion, "The caesura of birth is the model of the birth of every new thought" (Civitarese, 2008, p. 1130).

Sandler (2005) emphasizes the paradoxical nature of the concept of caesura as an event that simultaneously unites and separates, defines it as functioning in the mode of the contact barrier, of transformations and of invariants. Quoting Civitarese, Sandler writes:

> [T]he caesura becomes a split [a shibboleth, as I conceive it] when it is not tolerated: it is the intolerance of frustration that establishes the cut and which renders a viewpoint absolute and conceals continuity. (. . .) It is for this reason that Bion, in *Caesura*, makes himself the theoretician of continuity – because the dis-union is already by itself. Sandler is therefore right to point out that, notwithstanding its twofold, paradoxical nature as latent continuity and manifest discontinuity, the concept is used and rendered commonplace, in the sense of interruption. Bion's starting point, on the other hand, is, precisely, continuity.
>
> *(Civitarese, 2008, pp. 1132–1133)*

And Bergstein pointed out:

> In a footnote to Freud's paper, Strachey notes that the word "caesura" is a term derived from classical prosody, and means a particular kind of break in a line or verse, after which the verse continues. In music it is a pause or breathing at a point of rhythmic division in a melody. So "caesura" seems to bear the meaning of a break *and* continuity.
>
> *(Bergstein, 2013, p. 622)*

That is why ideas like calcified or ossified caesuras, or, in the opposing direction, transcending the caesura, although used by Bion himself, seem inadequate to express the paradox of simultaneous separation and continuity.

I want to emphasize this point: transcending the caesura is an expression that is not adequate because it implies that it is possible to think of a caesura without continuity. Caesura and its transcendence or traversal are redundant. The same is true about impressive caesuras: impressive caesuras are not caesuras. Caesuras are only impressive in their impossibility.

Bion marks the caesura with a slash, the sign "/", indicating the gap between the apparent binary oppositions or between two mental states (internal/external, unconscious/conscious, past/present, patient/analyst, light/dark, hate/love, etc.), signifying a potential dynamic change.

The vertex provided by the caesura fosters the difference between mental states without comparing them. Transience becomes visible. This position avoids the transformations in hallucinosis that create values scales of superiority/inferiority. Comparisons and values scales of superiority/inferiority point to the presence of morality, envious activity and rivalry between mental states.

The caesuras allow us to live simultaneously in at least two worlds (mental/protomental, symbolic/non-symbolic, psychotic/non-psychotic, finite/infinite, sensorial/imaginative, knowing about psychoanalysis/being a psychoanalyst, being a psychoanalyst/becoming a psychoanalyst, etc.), even if one of them predominates as an observational vertex. These two worlds are coupled phenomena. The different sides of the same phenomenon are like two poles, two vertices of a possible approach. Each pair implies a caesura, and each caesura implies the possibility of a spectral perspective.

The "impressive" caesura

Bion substantially modified the implications and meaning of the Freudian sentence when he declared:

> So (...) [i]nvestigate the caesura; not the analyst; not the analysand; not the unconscious; not the conscious; not sanity; not insanity, but the caesura, the link, the synapse, the (counter-trans)-ference, the transitive-intransitive mood.
>
> *(Bion, 1977, p. 56)*

For Bion, then, caesura becomes the vertex through which analyst and analysand may observe the phenomena that occur in the psychoanalytic session, which may become an object of observation itself. Bion said that he was impressed by the "impressive" in Freud's dictum. In Bion's words:

> I am impressed by the fact that the physical birth is so impressive (. . .). The fact of birth certainly impresses the individual and the group. But it seems to me that it is too

limiting to assume that physical birth is as impressive as many people suppose it is (. . .). I think the lack of discussion of this point is a blind spot. Freud developed this idea of "the impressive caesura of birth" of our being too impressed by it. He didn't investigate it deeply – a great mistake from our point of view.

(Bion, 1976b, p. 271)

In analysis we are seeing a total personality who has at some time, consciously or unconsciously, chosen a particular view or vertex from which to observe. This always involves inhibition of the capacity to see the views that one does not want to see (Bion, 1977, p. 52).

In many instances, Bion used the expression "impressive" caesuras to show the difficulty of transcending the different caesuras. I think that this idea of an "impressive caesura" often produces misunderstanding, mistaking caesura simply for an interruption.

Yet, at the same time it became clear to Bion that presence and absence, gain and loss, life and death, body and mind, somapsychotic and psychosomatic, etc. were only different sides of the same phenomenon, and that the difficulty of sustaining these opposites at the same time reflected the human difficulty in maintaining a paradox, a caesura.

Caesura and spectrum model

In Bion's work, the spectral model originates from the narcissism/social-ism spectrum from his book *Experiences in Groups* (1948).

The notion of spectrum helps us understand why the caesura is not a place or any definitive or definable spatiality. Caesura is movement and agent of movement. It implies an idea of movement, which is defined by its possibilities of oscillation, and with its absence producing developmental inhibition. In a previous text (Trachtenberg, 1998), I used the seesaw as a metaphor of this oscillation: this toy sustains itself by instability, not by balance.

In his previously mentioned paper, Bergstein wrote:

> The psychoanalytic quest is not traversing the caesura so as to arrive at a safe harbor, but rather widening the capacity for motion and free flowing between the two river banks, between the two rims of the caesura. The mere movement and transition are what matters and not its *direction*, hence there is no notion of moving forward towards a goal, or cure. *The movement itself* is what expands the mind and facilitates psychic life.
>
> *(Bergstein, 2013, p. 625, italics in original)*

According to Chuster (1997, 2002), the spectral model defines itself as the indefinite and undetermined extension of phenomena from which one can extract or build an indefinite number of concepts. It is, however, a whole that can never be fully rebuilt through the sum of its parts, because the spectrum is in a permanent state of expansion and expresses the irreversibility of time. In order to be recognized and preserved, it implies the need to refrain from seeking "answers" and implies a condition in which there is a constant creation of interpretations without reaching the finality of explaining. In the spectral configuration there is no place for causes or results.

> I find it somewhat easier to think of envy and gratitude as being on the same linear progression; they are not really separable, but one is the extreme of the other, as

if they were polarized, as if these sorts of feelings could be spoken of as polarized activities.

(Bion, 2005, p. 91)

In Chuster's words:

The creative aspects of the mind, resulting or representing the psychoanalytical function of the personality, are revealed in the radicalism (. . .) of the caesura concept. In any given moment, if we do not let ourselves be impressed by the elements of memory, desire, need of comprehension and the sensorial perception, our minds recover the plasticity of movement, moving about temporal splitting, establishing unsuspecting links, generating conjectures, exercising, in the end, imagination.

(Chuster, 2001, p. 106)

The "Complexity of Evil"

In my paper for Bion in Boston 2009 (Trachtenberg, 2013) I said that envy, morality and causality are important phenomena related to caesura's denial. They obstructed the sense of continuity, the necessary condition, as I already said, for occurrence of caesura. I will now describe it more accurately. The mental states of envy, morality and causality "work" together; they are different sides of the same phenomenon. We (Chuster and Trachtenberg, 2009) have called them *The Complexity of Evil*.

One can observe that envy does not tolerate differences and insinuates itself in the form of comparisons. Comparison is a superego product dominated by envy in which the categories of right/wrong, better/worse, superior/inferior, etc. are used as indicators of differences. People cannot be compared; not even the same person can be compared to his or her self in different moments. Even mental states cannot be compared. Doing so reflects a kind of superego dominated by moralistic thinking. On the other hand, tolerating differences requires caesuras in activity, complex thinking and complex ethics (Morin, 2005; Trachtenberg, 2008, 2013).

The influence of the envy factor can be detected even in Bion's early works. Starting with *Attacks on Linking* (1959), envy as a function of relationship starts to arise as a typically Bionian idea.

Oelsner reminds us that Bion says:

The patient's hatred contributed to the murderous attack on *that which links the pair, on the pair itself and on the object generated by the pair* (the analytic cure in this case). Here the envy and the envious attack is launched not against an object but the creative link between two objects.

(Oelsner, 2010, italics in original)

From the moment Bion starts focusing on the Oedipus myth as a problem of knowledge, truth and arrogance of the characters, it becomes clear that envy appears "directed against the individual's capacity to negotiate Positions" (Bion, 1992, p. 208).

With regards to the role of Positions, Bion states:

The Positions, as a vital factor for the dialogue between the unknown and the known, will indicate the individual's learning capability throughout his entire life. His/her ability to tolerate them and the continuous and dynamic interaction between the two would be permanently harassed by envy.

(Bion, 1992, p. 199)

There is an attack on the Positions because they are a vital factor in the conversion of the unknown to the known; the individual's capacity for learning depends, throughout life, on his ability to tolerate the two positions and the dynamic and continuing interaction between the two. Bion pointed out that the Oedipus myth itself embodies the problem of knowledge in as much as a question it poses, demanding an answer. But what was the question posed by the sphinx? Envy plays a role in this fundamental problem: "This envy is directed against the capacity of the individual that makes him able to negotiate the Positions" (Bion, 1992, p. 201). Perhaps, it is for this reason that in *Learning from Experience* (Bion, 1962) envy appears as a crucial factor in K. The envy that destroys knowledge in K has moral qualities derived from the "super" ego's quality of minus ♀ ♂ relation. It asserts the moral superiority and the potential superiority of "un"-learning.

Bion himself, approaching a more aesthetic model of the mind, modifies his concept of envy. However, it is only at the end of the book *Transformations* (1965) that Bion proposes a theory of envy that becomes part of an ethical-aesthetic model of the mind in relation to the ethical-aesthetic problem of growth and development. If envy was previously limited to the transformations in "K", to the conflict between "K" and "-K", it now presents itself as a problem in the transformations in "O" and, as a consequence, with an indefinite origin.

In *Attention and Interpretation*, he wrote:

> In the parasitic relationship [of container-contained] the product of the association is something that destroys both parties to the association. The realization that approximates most closely to my formulation is the group-individual setting dominated by envy. Envy begets envy, and this self-perpetuating emotion finally destroys host and parasite alike. The envy cannot be satisfactorily ascribed to one or other part; in fact it is a function of the relationship.
>
> *(Bion, 1970, p. 78)*

Chuster and Trachtenberg (2009) illustrate this through the use of the cancer model (as Bion did in *Attention and Interpretation*), showing how a cancer-infected cell refuses to die, and, through a kind of "anti-reproductive reproduction", eliminates the death "information", destroying the organism in which it "lives", in search of perpetuation.

If the psychoanalytic method is conceived in a limited way, consisting in the accumulation of knowledge (possessiveness), divorced from the processes of maturation and growth, it becomes a potent stimulus of envy (Bion, 1970).

At the end of *Attention and Interpretation*, Bion writes:

> The model for cancerous growths is not splitting of the object but splitting of the envy, each "bit" then growing independently of every other "bit". Ostensibly these "bits" appear as "different" ideas (. . .) Sometimes this state is described as a negative therapeutic reaction when it would be more accurately described as "proliferation of fragmented

envy". If the envy were to assume an aspect of whole object it could be seen as envy of the personality capable of maturation and of the object stimulating maturation.

(Bion, 1970, p. 128)

In this affirmation, we observe the linking concept already present in his previous comments, and that now includes the aesthetic problem of maturation (either development or growth). Besides the knowledge problem, we come in contact with the matter of being. The developmental inhibition is defined as the envy of the personality that is able to grow, and from the growth-stimulating objects: "The impulse to inhibit is fundamentally envy of the growth-stimulating objects" (Bion, 1970, p. 129).

The *growth-stimulating objects* (fertilizing objects) favor growth through the negative capability when promoting contact with frustration and with truth. The growth criteria will be given by the aspirations of internal objects. Envy, thus it is understood, would be motivated by the tension between what the subject would like to be and what he/she is not able to be. The envious mental state of a patient cannot stand not being the person he/she will never be. Envy produces remarkable facts; they are impressive stimulators of memory. In a state of envy, the analyst is loaded with memory. Lie is also an important "creator" of memories, facts that mitigate the feeling of envy while expressing it at the same time. The mental state impregnated with memory, desire and understanding, which prevents the development of a new idea, is an indicator of the activity of inhibition of *growth-stimulating objects* and, therefore, that an envious link in the analysis requires investigation.

Contemporary scientific thinking and aesthetics notions such as complexity, uncertainty, incompleteness, non-linearity, negativity, undecidability, indetermination, etc., complement and integrate Bion's thinking. The concept of caesura would be unthinkable without these developments.

The causal theory is omnipotent "and is only valid in the domain of morality and only morality can *cause* anything. Meaning has no influence outside the psyche and causes nothing" (Bion, 1965, p. 59). It is an expression of the superego activity, an organization that is not influenced by meaning.

The discovery of a cause is more related to the tranquility of the discoverer than to the object of inquiry (Bion, 1967). Sandler (1997) tells us that the Enlightenment era was dominated by the idea that everything had a cause: only our unknowing would prevent us from reaching it. The unconscious then started to be seen as a deposit of such hidden causes.

Meltzer (1986) says that one of the fundamental benefits of analysis is a movement from a causal/explanatory attitude, which attributes guilt, to an attitude that seeks to understand and accept the uncertainty that is inherent in the infinite complexity of the human development and personal relations.

With this, conditions were established in psychoanalysis for the abolition of the notion of causality and its counterpart, results in favor of the concept of undecidability of the origin and of an infinite universe of significant discourse. The undecidability of the origin proposes that in each link there is a point ("O", for Bion) in which we cannot decide what belongs to the subject and what to the object, to the mother or to the baby, to the analyst or to the analysand.

Instead of the notion of causality, Bion's model works with the notion of undecidability in a spectrum. The concept of undecidability implies a tolerance of the aleatory and a sense of the infinite. As a consequence, the psychoanalyst is placed in a much more modest position, able only to express an "opinion" (Meltzer, 1986), very distant from an explanatory model (arrogance), intolerant to the no-meaning, supported by a causal hypothesis.

According to Meltzer:

> [M]uch of chapter 5 of *Transformations* is devoted by Bion to attacking the concept of causality in the realm of mental functions, a problem which Freud had skirted around by positing "overdetermination" in place of determinism.
>
> *(Meltzer, 1978, p. 76)*

Actually, Bion considers that:

> [t]he question implies the validity of a theory of causation which I consider misleading and liable to give rise to constructions that are basically false; if it is fallacious we may discard it for one as fallacious – which may be true of the formulation, by Heisenberg, of the problem of multiple causation. Both views [causation and multiple causation] have proved of value in the development of science, but developments of physics by the Copenhagen school appear to have made the theory irrelevant. If so, the logical step would be to bother no longer with causation or its counterpart – results. In psycho-analysis it is difficult to avoid feeling that a gap is left by its disappearance and that the gap should be filled. Over a wide range of our problems no difficulty is caused by regarding the theory of causation as fallacious, but useful. When it comes to problems presented by disturbances in thought the difficulty cannot be met in this way.
>
> *(Bion, 1965, p. 57)*

In this context, Bion categorizes the idea of cause as D2 in the Grid, that is, a relatively primitive preconception used to prevent the emergence of something else. In his opinion, the patient's communication in so far as it is to be described as logical, is a circular argument, supposedly based on a theory of causation, employed to destroy contact with reality, not to further it.

For Bion, invariant to beta elements and bizarre objects, to the extent to which they share the characteristics of beta elements, is the moral component of such objects. The moral component is inseparable from feelings of guilt and responsibility and from a sense that the link between one such object and another, and between these objects and the personality, is moral causation. The theory of causation, in a scientific sense in so far as it has one, is therefore an instance of carrying over a moral domain in which its original penumbra of moral association is inappropriate.

The consequences of the obstruction of the PS ↔ D interaction in this connection between morality and causation are highlighted by Bion:

> The observation of constant conjunction of phenomena whose conjunction or coherence has not been previously observed, and therefore the whole process of PS ↔ D interaction, definition and search for meaning that is to be attached to the conjunction, can be destroyed by the strength of a sense of causation and its moral implications. Patients show that the resolution of a problem appears to present less difficulty if it can be regarded as belonging to a moral domain; causation, responsibility and therefore a controlling force (as opposed to helplessness) provides a framework within which

omnipotence reigns. . . . The significance for the individual lies in its part in obstructing the PS ↔ D interaction.

(Bion, 1965, pp. 64–65)

For Bion, following Kant, we say "because" when expressing only a temporal sequence of phenomena. The difference between cause and "selected fact" helps us understand the notion of cause from a distinct vertex. The selected facts are related to the synthesis of the objects that felt like contemporary or without any temporal component. The selected facts differ, thus, from causes, which are associated to the synthesis of objects that are dispersed in time and, as a consequence, with a temporal component. Bion proposes that for patients the solution to a problem seems to present less difficulty if it can be considered as belonging to a causal realm. Causes are tools whose objective is to free the personality of the sense of responsibility (Sandler, 2005).

As noted by Sandler, Bion did not used the term "selected fact" after 1965. The concept of a tool that detects underlying realities in the midst of apparently disconnected material, that is, the theory of the selected fact, seems to have been substituted by a more developed concept, that of invariance.

Reasoning based on a cause-effect scheme hinders the psychoanalytical view. Chains of relations, meanings and functions cannot be obtained by a mind that thinks in terms of causality:

Some patients repeatedly state that they have some particular experience and then give the reason why – making it part and parcel of their formulation. This continued repetition suggests a state of mind that is proper to a person who only lives in a causal world. But the only world in which causes can be said to be a prominent feature is the world of things – not the world of people, or characters, or personalities. The patient who is always telling us that he feels such-and-such "because . . ." is avoiding [a] particular relationship which exists between one character and another.

(Bion, 1977, p. 51)

As Meltzer said, Bion "helped us by slaying the dragon of causality and opened the cosmos of the mind in its infinitude of possibility for the generating of meaning" (Meltzer, 1978, p. 85).

As described by Bion, morality corresponds to an aspect of the psychotic part of the personality and expresses the activity of a "super"-ego that installs itself prematurely due to flaws in the alpha function, and performs activities that would otherwise belong to the ego, for instance, discriminating true from false. The moral criterion considers the matters in terms of superiority/inferiority, or in the sense of something being morally right or morally wrong.

In *Transformations*, Bion wrote:

The usurpation by the super-ego of the position that should be occupied by the ego involves imperfect development of the reality principle, exaltation of a 'moral' outlook and lack of respect for the truth. The result is starvation of the psyche and stunted growth.

(Bion, 1965, p. 38)

It is also important to remember that for many authors there is no difference whatsoever between morality and ethics. I think the differences are fundamental for us to consider in order to understand why the notion of ethics works with the idea of a complex object, and morality, with the idea of a simple object.

Morality follows a binary code of good/evil, fair/unfair. The moral logic is that of right/wrong. It is exclusive: either yes or no. It is a binary logic, without any space for other logics that include a third possibility (complex logics, bi-modal, triadic, etc.). Under the vertex of morality, doubts, uncertainties, singularities, etc. will gain meaning as malicious maneuvers with the objective of confounding the parameters that define what is right or wrong. The question "which side are you on?" or the affirmation "if you are not with me, then you are against me" are expressions or attempts to eliminate the "confusion" created by the logics of complexity.

Dr. B and his "impressive" caesuras

Dr. B, a young doctor, came to analysis because of a generalized feeling of emptiness and futility, and significant inhibitions in his relationship with women. He wore his mother's clothes and masturbated looking into the mirror, as his fantasies oscillated between heterosexual and homosexual scenes in which he was penetrated by an older man. Afterwards, as he undressed, he looked at himself in the mirror and castigated himself, as if speaking to another person: "You are pathetic, you disgust me". Once dressed in his own clothes, he looked in the mirror again to confirm that it was he, himself, recovering his "true identity". He recalled as a very important moment in his life the birth of a brother when he was 18 months old. In the last months of her pregnancy, his mother had sent him to his grandparents' home, and when he came back he met the new baby. He now intended to report that it was the possibility of pregnancy that stopped him from having intercourse, but he said instead: "It is the fear I have during a pregnancy". This slip of the tongue, which we can link with the transvestite act (wish/fear of being penetrated by an older man/the father and the wish/fear to kill all of mother's internal babies as if he were the only and eternal baby inside her), was very meaningful in his analysis. At the same time, he had constant doubts about his fertility, which he rationalized as being due to a post-mumps orchitis he had suffered in puberty.

In his work life, Dr. B's performance as a physician was very much affected by his fantasies, as he feared inducing severe hemorrhages every time he performed a bronchoscopy (connected with the conflicts around penetration and the mother's babies). He referred to such medical procedures as "manoeuvres on people's selves".

His unconscious use of the fiber-bronchoscope as a physical device to allow contact with the inner self of the other was very pronounced, and linked to his voyeuristic fantasies (intrusive curiosity) and his transvestite activity. After we had explored some meanings of his acts and fantasies, he brought the following dream:

> I was bathing two tiny babies, ten to twelve centimeters long, they were only head and body, they had no limbs. One was normal, but the other was made of some kind of fabric, something flaccid without any consistency, that folded all the time. The face separated from the skull as if it were a mask. With much anguish, I think "the link between the eyes and the brain will get lost and he will go blind". Suddenly, one of the eyes escapes from my hands and flies up like a moth.

There are a lot of "impressive" caesuras in the internal world of Dr. B. We can observe the impossibility of continuity between life and death, dream and hallucination, imagination and delusion, psychotic and non-psychotic, his father and mother identifications, his adult and infantile states of mind, his heterosexual and homosexual sides, the two babies/penis (normal and abnormal) in his dream, the brain and the eyes of the damaged baby/penis, etc. Envy and a strong sense of morality and causality were a pronounced characteristic of Dr. B. The analytic work with him was a constant exercise in linking these different sides, aspects or states of mind. The terrible splitting used by him makes me consider it a psychotic way to avoid the caesuras' experience, to avoid suffering the pain (and the pleasure, pointed to by Bion) and to avoid the sense of paradox and complexity.

Final (?) words

For Bion, the concept of caesura indicates that the psychoanalyst with his patient, in the analytic consulting room, is in a transient state of "becoming a psychoanalyst". In this sense, becoming an analyst is an indicator that the caesura is happening, like the caesura of birth, which does not allow us to claim "when" a person is born or how much of a person has not been born yet.

The analyst should bear a transitory identity in each session, like a mental state, which is lost and found all the time. The caesura implies the coexistence of multiple mental states, in a situation of emotional turbulence, and without an evolutionary meaning from one to another (for instance, the idea of an evolution from the psychotic part to the non-psychotic part of the personality), almost always a sign of the presence of moral judgment. Thus, development means an increase in the possibilities of this coexistence, with the emergence of new forms of links among the mental states. The coexistence and the way they bond, transit and "negotiate" is what we call the uniqueness of the subject. It is what differentiates us and what unites us. A higher tolerance to such possibility, without a significant need for exclusions/projections, is my concept of a successful analysis: an analysis of achievement.

In *Cogitations*, Bion, using a double vertex, observes that:

> [o]ne of the weaknesses of articulate speech is shown in the use of a term like "omnipotence" to describe a situation that in fact cannot be described at all accurately with a language that is of one kind only. "Omnipotence" must always also mean "helplessness"; there can be no single word that describes one thing without also describing its reciprocal.
>
> *(Bion, 1992, p. 370)*

Every word includes its other side. According to Bion:

> [Martin Buber] came much closer to recognizing the realities of the situation when human speech is resorted to; [*I and Thou*: "The attitude of man is twofold in accordance with the two basic words he can speak. The basic words are not single words but words pairs. One basic word is the word pair I-You (. . .)".]; When one talks about "I-You", the significant thing is not the two objects related, but the *relationship* – that is, an open-ended reality in which there is no termination.
>
> *(Bion, 1992, p. 371, italics in original)*

Thus, every word is a coupling of words. It is a complex couple, like any couple. The human being is a multiple being. No isolated word can describe or define anyone. Starting from the vertex of complexity and from the spectrum model, there are no psychotic, envious or any other reductionist definitions. The question is how they are linked, how the caesura between the different mental states works, and how the intolerable states can be restrained for each subject. Different mental states may work or not, as adequate continents for other mental states, emotions or thoughts charged with violence, loving violence included. The moral system, cradle of all fanaticism, does not tolerate the idea of another side, but the system itself belongs to us as another side. And it is this complexity that helps us, to a certain point, to welcome it, hold it, tolerate it, within our possibilities.

There is a side of the moon that we never see. The hidden side of the moon is hidden to a certain focus; hidden and not dark, as we now know thanks to Apollo 16. The light on the other side is even more intense than the one we can see. In order to see what is not visible, we have to blind ourselves artificially, as Socrates, Freud, Bion and many others have said. Every focus demands defocusing to see the other side, the one that is hidden, but is still there, on the other side of the other, and on my own other side.

References

Bergstein, A. (2013). Transcending the caesura: Reverie, dreaming and counter-dreaming. *International Journal of Psychoanalysis* 94: 621–644.

Bion, W.R. (1948). *Experiencias en Grupos*. Buenos Aires: Paidos.

Bion, W.R. (1959). Attacks on linking. In W.R. Bion (Ed.), *Second Thoughts*. Northvale: Jason Aronson.

Bion, W.R. (1962). *Learning from Experience*. Northvale: Jason Aronson.

Bion, W.R. (1965). *Transformations*. London: Heinemann.

Bion, W.R. (1967). *Second Thoughts*. Northvale: Jason Aronson.

Bion, W.R. (1970). *Attention and Interpretation*. Northvale: Jason Aronson.

Bion, W.R. (1976a). On a quotation from Freud. In W.R. Bion (Eds.), *Clinical Seminars and Other Works*. London: Karnac, 2000.

Bion, W.R. (1976b). Four discussions. In W.R. Bion (Ed.), *Clinical Seminars and Other Works*. London: Karnac, 2000.

Bion, W.R. (1977). Caesura. In W.R. Bion (Ed.), *Two Papers: The Grid and Caesura*. Rio de Janeiro: Imago Editora. Reprinted: (1989) London: Karnac, 1984.

Bion, W.R. (1992). *Cogitations*. Ed. F. Bion. London: Karnac.

Bion, W.R. (2005). *The Tavistock Seminars*. London: Karnac.

Chuster, A. (1997). *O ensino de Bion*. Revista do Instituto Bion, 1.

Chuster, A. (2001). Comentários sobre a supervisão de Bion em Paris. *Revista de psicanálise da SPPA* VIII/1: 103–106.

Chuster, A. (2002). *W. R. Bion: Novas Leituras. A Psicanálise dos Princípios Ético-Estéticos à Clínica (Volume II)*. Rio de Janeiro: Companhia de Freud.

Chuster, A. (2012). [Personal communication].

Chuster, A. and R. Trachtenberg (2009). *As Sete Invejas Capitais*. Porto Alegre: Artmed.

Civitarese, G. (2008). "Caesura" as Bion's discourse on method. *International Journal of Psychoanalysis* 89: 1123–1143.

Freud, S. (1926). Inhibitions, symptoms and anxiety. *S.E.* 20: 138. London: Hogarth Press.

Meltzer, D. (1978). *The Kleinian Development. Part 3: The Clinical Significance of the Work of Bion*. Perthshire: Clunie Press.

Meltzer, D. (1986). *Studies in Extended Metapsychology: Clinical Applications of Bion's Ideas*. Perthshire: Clunie Press.

Morin, E. (2005). *O Método 6: Ética*. Porto Alegre: Sulina.

Oelsner, R. (2010). The multiple faces of envy. *Paper Presented at Evolving British Object Relations Conference*, Seattle.

Sandler, P.C. (1997). *A Apreensão da Realidade Psíquica*. Rio de Janeiro: Imago.

Sandler, P.C. (2005). *The Language of Bion*. London: Karnac.

Trachtenberg, R. (1998). A gangorra. *Revista do CEPdePA* 7: 137–154.

Trachtenberg, R. (2008). As fronteiras: uma proposta para pensar diferenças entre ética e moral. *Revista do Instituto de Psicologia (IPSI)* 2: 26–32.

Trachtenberg, R. (2013). Caesura, denial and envy. In H. Levine and L. Brown (Eds.), *Growth and Turbulence in the Container/Contained: Bion's Continuing Legacy*. London: Routledge.

17

CONJECTURES ABOUT DREAMS, MEMORIES AND CAESURAS

Carmen C. Mion

Introduction

I intend to address some conjectures arising from clinical situations with patients who present a peculiar psychic suffering. To illustrate I will utilize excerpts from the analysis of two patients I will call Penelope and Achilles in reference to my associations, at certain moments of their respective analyses, with the mythological characters Penelope and Achilles as described by Homer (800 B.C. b). Intelligent and professionally successful young adults, they came to analysis complaining of feelings of emptiness and/or absence of meaning in their lives, having achieved the professional development and position for which they had longed.

Penelope and Achilles

Penelope, with whom I have an analytical experience of twelve years, presented as her main motivation for seeking analysis a split between her successful professional life and her personal life, where she perceived significant inhibitions. Slowly, over a period of about two years, as analysis progressed, and Penelope began to get in touch with herself, an interesting process occurred. The successful, elegant and "tough" professional I met at the beginning of analysis gave way to the personification of a terrified little girl, who kept herself curled upon on the armchair in my office, hiding all the way up to her nose under a coat, unable to lie on the couch. From this day on, a coat became for some time a constant item in her wardrobe during the few sessions she happened to attend. Sometimes she would come to my office only for the final 15 minutes of the session, remaining verbally silent.

After months without any perceptible changes in the situation described above, I pondered some questions: What is the viability of analytical work within the context of persistent absences and silences? Which instruments can the analyst resort to when interpretations, brief interventions or even her/his own presence are experienced by the patient as intensely threatening, as a trigger point for a disaster? Which instruments can we use when faced with a nameless dread which the slightest mention may evoke a catastrophe? Would it be possible to penetrate the caesura of birth and differentiate it from the caesura of death, that is, to promote a creative change instead of a catastrophic change?

Achilles, who I had been working with for over nine years, was a young man, very success-ful professionally, but whose life had suddenly lost meaning. He felt nothing but emptiness inside his strong, athletic body, spartanly sculpted at the gyms. A life story centered on hard battles stoically fought, the image of Achilles in his shining armor came to me right at our first encounter, appearing again over the years with different meanings. He would tell me stories of drug addiction, sexual compulsions and risky situations he experienced with detachment and associated them with some kind of search, even though he was unable to identify what he was searching for; maybe for any emotion that might let him know he was alive? He had no dreams or premonitions, asleep or awake. I felt as if I was in the presence of a façade of a successful ruin (Bion, 1962).

After a long period of silences and deep sleep during the sessions, he began to describe some images that he called dreams, about which we could begin a conversation. They were images of walls or concrete structures, without any human presence or living element, not even him. These images seemed to me the debris of a disaster buried in the sands of imme-morial times, resulting in a caesura in the continuity of his existence. As I heard him describ-ing these fragments of dreams, I visualized images of a bunker or a "casamatta" (Italian word meaning "false house") used in the Second World War to protect coastal artillery from air attacks. I intuited a terror of such magnitude that might have erased the traces of this disaster in time and in space, preventing him from re-cognition of himself. Only through the con-tinuity of existence may the sense of oneself, of feeling real, be established. Is it possible for someone to exist enough to know he/she does not exist?

My impression from the first meetings was confirmed over time by their continued inabil-ity to "dream" their sensations, emotions, affections, as well as the presence of the analyst along the sessions. I am referring here to a level of psychic functioning more closely associated with the un-represented, pre-verbal experiences of the primordial mind and/or precocious psychic trauma, with intense but no ideational content (Levine, 2012).

By addressing the dream as a royal road to the Unconscious, Freud ushered in a field of knowledge that has the dream as its paradigm. Accordingly, the field where the clinical psy-choanalytical practice was to be established and developed is the territory of the repressed, the one we analysts are familiar with; we know its paths and passages through which we navigate with our neurotic patients. Here, the emotional and somatic turbulences that the psychoana-lyst and the patient experience in the office may be dreamed from elements of the patient's psychic life and certainly, from the psychoanalyst himself. But what happens to patients and the psychoanalytical function when the passages between the different psychological dimen-sions and their interfaces are obstructed or even non-existent?

Over time, it became clear to me that there was nothing to do or to say about Penelope's enclosures and restraints or about Achilles' drug addiction, compulsion and risky life situa-tions. Be it manifestations of desperate attempts for a cure or remnants of a catastrophe from immemorial times, these symptoms functioned as false clues that easily lead us to situations of abduction, as Penelope's eternal hopeful grooms waiting for a wedding that would never happen; or Achilles' companions in his hallucinated battles prophesied as a pathway to venge-ance and glory, even if at the price of collusions that may end up in murder/suicide. As Bion (1973–1978) pointed out in some of his supervisions, when faced with such situations, there is nothing we can do about the obvious and dramatic external event.

With time and patience, I began to identify another common factor in my relationship with these patients from the vertex I intend to use here: subtle yet powerful emotional experiences, difficult to convey to someone else. Feelings apparently not related to what they were saying at the moment, for which there were no words, only approximations through models, myths, images that would came to my mind during the sessions. I believe that the fact that they were not lying on the couch by that time could be related to these "sensations" and "emotions" experienced physically, and far beyond their ability to tolerate it and therefore beyond imagining, dreaming and verbalizing. What they could not express signals what needs and seeks expression, what has no name, *what is*, the thing-in-itself, "O" (Bion, 1965).

The absence of free associations for the impossibility of symbolization meant waiting for "signaling" that, arising from the intersubjective field (Baranger and Baranger, 2009), eventually would take us to approximations of psychic dimensions not accessible to the patients ("O"). As Bion (1975, p. 222) pointed out in *Myself*'s words, "in so far as communication takes place between the 'unconscious' levels the prevalent methods of communication . . . conform to rules which are very different from those 'articulate' communication". I realized that I would have to make way, open passages, cross the caesuras between different psychic dimensions, all the while knowing they are infinite. Hence the idea of a psychoanalyst with a "*mind in transit*" that occurred to me once, one who is able to navigate back and forth without cartography from the deepness of rough seas and dark caves to the surface of the calm waters and sunny plains. That is, a psychoanalyst able to receive, contain and dream the patient's sensations and emotions which have no psychic representation other than feelings of emptiness, unthinkable terrors and agonies, and thus, through her/his capacity for reverie (Bion, 1962), promoting and building an atmosphere for the constitution of a room for dreaming.

Dreams

Dreams are some of the most creative and unknowable human creations (Grotstein, 2000). We are more ourselves dreaming the dreams that dream us. Sometimes imagination and dream imagery are related to attempts to reach meaning as a private mythology, not necessarily desire. Through dreams and dreaming we get closer to ourselves: guided through hidden passages, we cross the Psycho-Somatic↔Somato-Psychotic, Conscious↔Unconscious, Finite↔Infinite, Internal↔External, PS↔D, Past↔Present↔Future psychic caesuras (Bion, 1975a). However, the defenses that line up against unthinkable agonies and terrors steal from the individual the possibility of dream-work-alpha and awake dream-thoughts, eliminating the precondition for creative impulse and living (Bion, 1962; Barros, 2000; Ogden, 2005).

Both the unthinkable agony described by Winnicott (1962) and the thalamic and sub-thalamic terrors mentioned by Bion (1978) refer to primordial somatic-psychotic experiences that, in so far as they do not reach psychic representation, are associated with the infinite, with no references to time or space and therefore, the impossibility of living an experience as transient, leading to a suffering without a glimpse towards the ending. There is no way of making a baby understand that "mummy is coming"; a delay is immeasurable and infinite. By proposing that the conscious/unconscious polarity be replaced by the finite/infinite, and by introducing the negative as an active part of the psychoanalytic elements, Bion allows us to approach the unknowable, the void, the nameless dreads and unthinkable agonies in our clinical practice.

Even though this ground was envisioned by Freud (1920), as the very foundation of psychic life, these are not realms in which he believed the psychoanalyst could venture. Freud's hypothesis that there is something very primitive in the human mind which precedes and is hidden by the impressive clinical picture of psychotic symptoms presented to the analyst was already considered in the Schreber case (Freud, 1911). According to Freud, psychotic symptoms would come later in the course of the disease as a "cure attempt" by the patient: movements towards the reestablishment of links and meanings in reality. In other words, the symptoms some patients show us are remains and consequences of a disaster, which conceal more than reveal the route that the analyst could follow up to the primordial pain. Clinical experience continually presents us with evidence of something remaining from states of mind that we could possibly locate in the prehistory of some adult patients (Cassorla, 2008; Korbivcher, 2005; Mattos and Braga, 2009; Sapienza, 2008).

Memories and memoirs

Trauma appears here as an emotional intensity that cannot gain meaning and/or exceeds one's capability of experiencing it. In other words, sensations or emotions that cannot happen in the context of a human relationship, cannot be experienced as shared reality and/or be dreamt, tend to be placed in the realm of the inhuman, become unthinkable and arouse nameless terrors and agonies. Paradoxically, this "disaster" that took place in the past is felt by the subject as if it has not happened yet, since it cannot be "experienced" consciously. Therefore, we may see a defensive organization developed unconsciously by the patient to avoid a dreaded future catastrophe which actually has already happened (Winnicott, 1963).

Bion (1975a) suggests that events contained in the womb of time may present themselves to the conscious life of a person who, nevertheless, will have to act and to exist in the present. Memoirs of the future buried in a past that cannot be (re)presented? He adds that in certain situations, looking at the patient as an adult can be so obtrusive that it blinds us to feelings that are not evident to the senses. Rephrasing Bion (1975b, p. 45): Can there be any communication capable of penetrating an impermeable caesura, from the postnatal/post-traumatic consciousness, and mirror back to the prenatal/pre-traumatic unconscious? Is it possible to find the sensations or emotions that had never reached consciousness?

The analyst's state of mind in sessions makes us sensitive to what "*is-not*", what "*does not fit*", to discomforts or pre-sentiments associated with psychic dimensions not mentioned or even perceived by the patient, but once captured by the analyst, may present themselves as intuitions, images, dream-memories, myths and other elements. Depending on the condition of the dream-work-alpha of the analyst, these elements could be classified as belonging to Row A (beta-elements), Row B (alpha-elements), Row C (dreams, myths, dreamlike thoughts) or even D (pre-conception) on Bion's Grid (1963). A state of mind necessary for the analyst to dream the dreams that cannot be dreamed by the patients in order to find the sensations or emotions that had never reached consciousness (Ogden, 2005).

I am referring here to the state of mind of the psychoanalyst in the office in the here-and-now of the session, to the being-with-oneself in order to be with the patient, *at-one-ment*, with no memory or desire; forgetting the characterization of thoughts that belongs to the usual awakened state; relying more on one's own alpha-function, $\female\male$, negative capability and PS↔D movements than on eventual "knowledgement" and meanings attribution. An analyst who is lively present in the session capable of turning the unrepresented absence into presence, of transiting between his/her own caesuras without becoming scared or immobilized, and of transcending his/her own vertices without losing sight of them.

Bion asked in one of his conferences in São Paulo: "How easily can you mentally change your position, your vertex, so that you can almost see both sides?" (1978, p. 110). He also suggested that we may understand these transformations in the same way we, for example, understand music, utilizing the discipline and the rules, so to speak, that govern hallucinations. This would be the domain in which the transformations to and from "O" belong.

Caesuras

There are many different caesuras. The caesura of a psychic birth can occur at any space-time.[1] The caesura of one state of mind to another, the difficulty of moving through different psychic dimensions, does not seem less dramatic to me, as Bion pointed out (1975b). According to him, humans owe their health to their ability to protect themselves while growing up, as an individual repeating the history of mankind in his personal life, for self-protection against truths that their minds are not prepared to receive without disaster (Bion, 1992). If the central nervous system stemmed from the ectoderm and the cortex is a modification of the primitive surface, we may assume, according to Freud (1920), that it has inherited some of the fundamental characteristics of that surface. Psychic layers, hardened as traumatized skin that loses the quality of living organism, become to some extent inorganic, acting as a protective shield for neighboring layers. The deeper psychic layers, therefore, continue to be vital, protected from the excessively traumatic stimuli from events as dramatic as birth, chance of success, breakdowns and death. Several skins that have been epidermis or consciousness, and now are traces appearing in day or night dreaming (Bion, 1975a, p. 47).

On the last page of "Caesura", rephrasing the original statement by Freud, Bion says: "There is much more continuity between autonomically appropriate quanta and the waves of conscious thought and feeling than the impressive caesura of transference and counter-transference would have us believe. So ...?" He then proposes to investigate the caesura: "Not the analyst, not the analysand, not the unconscious, not the conscious, not sanity, not insanity; but the caesura, the link, the synapse, the (counter- trans)-ference, the transitive-intransitive mood" (1975a, p. 56).

At a conference in São Paulo, Bion also suggested a very strong image: "*the caesura is a transparent mirror*" (1978, p. 108). On that occasion, he was addressing the issue of penetration of caesuras, which paradoxically separate and unite states of mind/irradiations of "O" in the infinite space-time (Sandler, 2000). Bion considers the possibility of a primordial thought of the fetus, projected in the caesura, reflecting itself from the child to his/her primordial levels of thoughts and feelings. From this model, I conjectured a spectrum of reflections and refractions in the different and simultaneous psychic dimensions and their caesuras. A spectrum ranging from transparency to complete opacity, from trans-ferences and inter-ferences to the impermeability of mirrors that reflect or reveal nothing, made opaque by bilateral layers of tin; Achilles' shields/armor? Penelope's drawings/weavings?

Stemming from Grotstein's (2000) formulation to conjecture impacts of "O" as the infinite, ultimate reality in the oscillations Conscious↔Unconscious, Sapienza (2008) presented a diagram adding to the proposal the concomitance of the irradiations of "O" in Ps↔D oscillations.

While attempting to change the approaching vertex to the irradiations of "O" for the investigation of the caesuras between the different psychic dimensions, as transparent mirrors presenting different "ferences", I was visited by some sort of dream-memory image. Therefore, I found myself troubled by the difficult task of building a diagram based on that image.

The utilization of Bion's theory of Transformations (1965) conveying a meaning of "*becoming*", or perhaps the movements of the couple analyst/analysand (Tp, Ta) shifting cyclically in the domains $\infty \leftrightarrow \beta \leftrightarrow \beta\alpha \leftrightarrow \alpha\beta \leftrightarrow \alpha \leftrightarrow K \leftrightarrow O \leftrightarrow \infty$, seemed to me a necessary and probably sufficient common-ground for discussing the irradiation of "O" in a multidimensional mind and its caesuras. From this viewpoint, I suggest that the analyst's function in the construction of a psychic space for dreaming involves not only the use of transitive ideas or ideas in transit as Bion proposes (1975a, p. 44), but also an analyst with a *mind in transit*, a "*becoming*" in terms of being able to transcend his/her vertices without losing sight of them, of "*being*" in both sides of the numerous mirrors/caesuras with which, like "Alice" (Carroll, 1865), we are faced every day in our offices; an analyst able to move within the multiple psychic dimensions, to cross through transparent mirrors/caesuras without paralyzing or drowning, qua Narcissus bewildered by his own reflection.

Nevertheless, a diagram to be presented was still pending.

Dream-memory images

The dream-memory images that associatively came to my mind and that I will present next are from an exhibition I attended in Quebec in 1990, "The Dance of the Universe" (Detouef, 1986). The French "Liaison Group for the Scientific Cultural Action" challenged the scientists

Ralph Steadman, in "*Moi, Léonard de Vinci*". Ralph Steadman, in "I Leonardo"

FIGURE 17.1 Ralph Steadman, in "*Moi, Leonard de Vinci*".

"Deprived of a tangible approach, physicists had to forge new tools, a new way of thinking, a different intuition . . . a language based on mathematics".

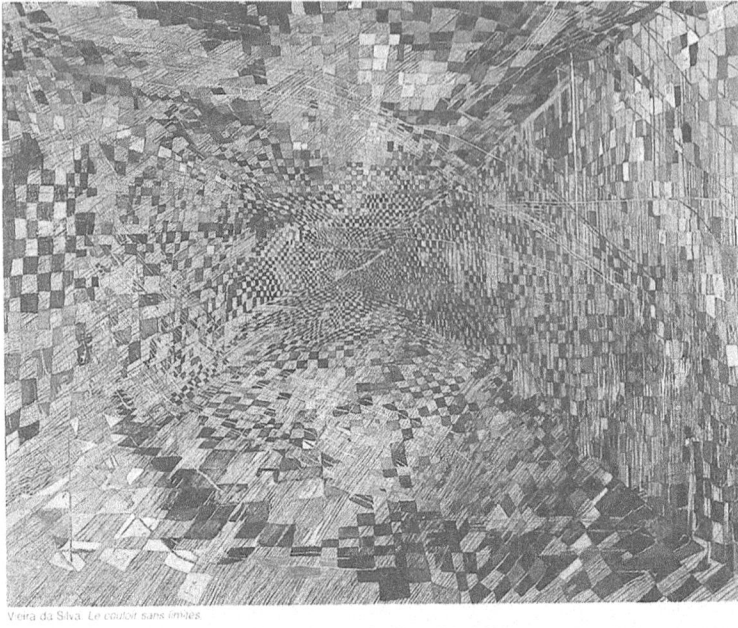

FIGURE 17.2 Vieira da Silva, "*Le couloir sans limites*". Private collection, photographer unknown.

"Alice walked through the looking glass and entered Wonderland, where the laws are different from those in our everyday lives". "How to express the fact that an electron can be (. . .) at the same time, a dot and an invisible cloud filling up the space?"

Grotstein-Sapienza Diagram

Irradiation from "O"

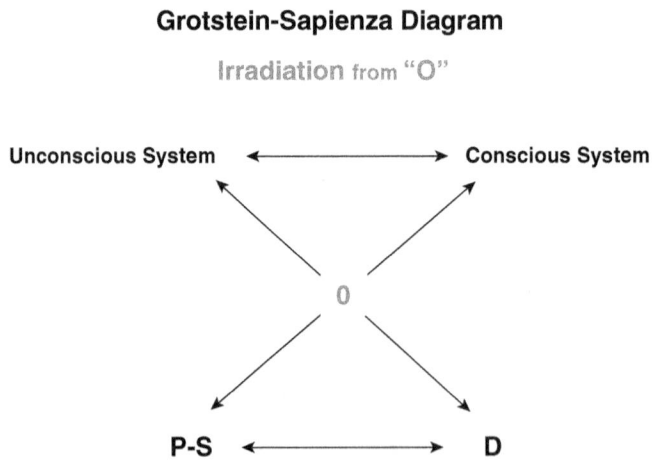

FIGURE 17.3 The Grotstein-Sapienza Diagram.

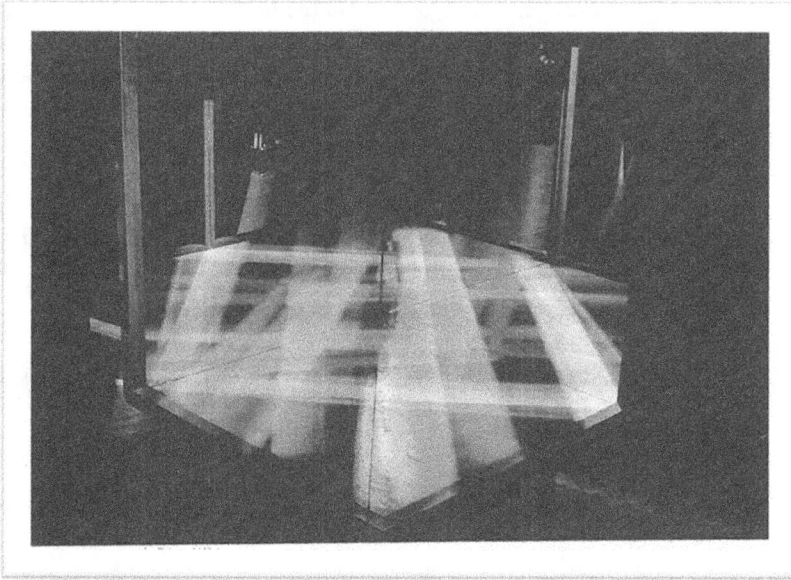

FIGURE 17.4   Memory-dream image: computer drawing based on the image obtained from reflecting/ detecting mirrors through a Heliostat.

who were working at that time on the "infinitely small", the wave-particle paradox, and the infinite in space-time in the field of quantum physics with a proposal: "Would it be possible to provide all persons an insight regarding the current research about the smaller elements that constitute our universe?" Detoeuf wrote: "With its poetry and mobilization power, art helps us evoke the invisible world".

I will utilize this dream-memory as a model of approximation or a metaphor for what I would like to convey. The captions of the paintings from the exhibition are shown below in italics.

Postscript

The selected fact that originated these conjectures was an emotional experience I had with my grandson when we were watching together a carp koi pond:

GRANDMOTHER: Look at the little red fish!
BOY: Does it not have a bottom, Grandma?
GRANDMOTHER: Yes, it does, my dear. Look, it's very shallow!
BOY: Can I dive in, Grandma?
GRANDMOTHER: No, you can't. . . . This is the little fish's home . . .
BOY: But if I do, am I going up to heaven?

I felt baffled for a few seconds, not knowing what to think or to say. At that moment, I raised my eyes up to the sky: it was a beautiful sunny morning, with a blue sky and white clouds overhead. When I looked back to the pond, I could see the sky reflected on the pond!

I had not seen it before because my attention was on the fish. Then I was able to tell to my grandson the way water reflects like a mirror, showing him his little face and mine reflected on the pond as does the sky above us over the water. Later that day, with benevolent incredulity, his parents heard the amazing story of the fish that hid themselves behind the sky ...

Note

1 Space-Time: concept used as the foundation for the study of special relativity. "Zavisa John. HowStuff-Works – How Special Relativity Works". December 2007.

References

Baranger, M. and W. Baranger (2009). *The Work of Confluence: Listening and Interpreting in the Psychoanalytic Field*. London: Karnac.

Barros, E.R. (2000). Affect and pictographic image: The constitution of meaning in mental life. *International Journal of Psychoanalysis* 81: 1087–1099.

Bion, W.R. (1962). *Learning from Experience*. London: Heinemann.

Bion, W.R. (1963). *Elements of Psycho-Analysis*. London: Heinemann.

Bion, W.R. (1965). *Transformations*. New York: Jason Aronson, 1983.

Bion, W.R. (1973–1978). Bion's supervisions in São Paulo. *Recorded, Transcribed and Presented by Dr José Américo Junqueira de Mattos at Scientific Meetings at SBPSP*.

Bion, W.R. (1975). *A Memoir of the Future, Book One: The Dream*, p. 222. Rio de Janeiro: Imago.

Bion, W.R. (1975a). Caesura. In F. Bion and M. Paterson (Eds.), *Two Papers – The Grid and Caesura*, pp. 37–56. London: Karnac, 1989.

Bion, W.R. (1975b). The grid. In F. Bion and M. Paterson (Eds.), *Two Papers – The Grid and Caesura*, pp. 3–33. London: Karnac, 1989.

Bion, W.R. (1978). *Four Discussions with W.R. Bion & Bion in New York and São Paulo*. London: The Roland Harris Educational Trust, 1980.

Bion, W.R. (1992). *Cogitations*. London: Karnac.

Carroll, L. (1865). *Alice in Wonderland*. Los Angeles: Empire Books, 2011.

Cassorla, R.M. (2008). The analyst's implicit alpha-function, trauma and enactment in the analysis of borderline patients. *International Journal of Psychoanalysis* 89(1): 161–180.

Detouef, M.-S. (1986). *The Dance of the Universe*. Paris: Group de Liaison pour l'Action Culturelle Scientifique.

Freud, S. (1911). Psycho-analytic notes on an autobiographical account of a case of paranoia (Dementia Paranoides). *S.E.* 12: 3–82. London: Hogarth.

Freud, S. (1920). Beyond the pleasure principle. *S.E.* 18: 7–64. London: Hogarth.

Grotstein, J.S. (2000). *Who is the Dreamer Who Dreams the Dream? A Study of Psychic Presences*. Hillsdale: Analytic Press.

Homer (800 B.C.a). *The Odyssey*. Trans. Robert Fagles. Deckle Edge: New York, 1997.

Homer (800 B.C.b). *The Iliad*. Trans. Robert Fagles. Deckle Edge: New York, 1998.

Korbivcher, C.F. (2005). The theory of transformations and autistic states: Autistic transformations: A proposal. *International Journal of Psychoanalysis* 86(6): 1595–1610.

Levine, H.B. (2012). The colorless canvas: Representation, therapeutic action, and the creation of mind. *International Journal of Psychoanalysis* 93: 606–629.

Mattos, J.A.J. and J.C. Braga (2009). Consciência moral primitiva: um vislumbre da mente primordial. *Presented in Scientific Meeting, SBPSP*, São Paulo.

Ogden, T. (2005). *This Art of Psychoanalysis: Dreaming Undreamt Dreams and Interrupted Cries*. Hove: Routledge.

Sandler, P.C. (2000). *The Language of Bion*. London: Karnac.

Sapienza, A. (2008). Alfa-Function: Catastrophic Anxiety – Panic – Continent with Reverie. *Presented in Roma: Bion Conference 2008.*

Winnicott, D.W. (1962). The aims of psycho-analytical treatment. In *The Maturational Processes and the Facilitating Environment.* Madison: International Universities Press.

Winnicott, D.W. (1963). Fear of breakdown. In C. Winnicott, R. Shepherd and M. Davis (Eds.), *Psycho-analytic Explorations.* London: Karnac, 1989.

Zavisa, J. (April 1, 2000). How special relativity works. *How Stuff Works.* http://science.howstuffworks.com/science-vs-myth/everyday-myths/relativity.htm (Last Updated December 5, 2007).

SECTION VII

Creativity and O

18

ON THE VERGE OF "MADNESS"

Creativity and the fear of insanity

Claudio Castelo Filho

I

I am in my office with an analysand. We have been working together for quite some time now. He is saying a lot of things in a rather moaning and complaining tone. I don't know what to say. No idea crosses my mind. I perceive myself as sterile for several minutes. I let it flow despite realizing that the analysand is going through an uncomfortable and somewhat hurtful situation. I would like to do something to help him, but I am convinced, out of my own experience, that submitting myself to the desire of helping the analysand is obstructive. Moreover, I know that every effort towards finding something, forcefully, to relieve his pain or explain what is happening may end up as a hindrance and may be an obstacle for reaching something more substantial and actually helpful that may eventually manifest. So, I remain silent.

I observe the space in the room. I see the analysand lying on the couch in front of me. I hear him speaking and I find myself somewhat dismayed, without perspective. I jot down that feeling I am experiencing. Maybe it can help me understand something, consider what it might indicate. I watch the analysand speak, and suddenly something frightens me, though I manage not to show it. I see a thin man, with curly blond hair and a red T-shirt, crossing the space in front of me, between my feet and the couch. He looks at me scornfully, making faces and grimacing, and gesturing as if despising the analysand, me and the situation taking place in the office.

When I say that I see him, I literally mean it: not only did I really see him with my very eyes, I felt the concrete presence of this man passing between us. It was not something that I imagined, as I perceived it in the exact moment it happened. It wasn't something produced by my imagination either, but rather it was a factual presence, real, before my eyes, that lasted for a few seconds and disappeared as if it had instantly walked out the door. I am bewildered for a few seconds. Have I completely lost my mind? I decide to take the apparition as a dream-image, a dream-thought, which would reveal something essential for what was going on. I could have taken it, if I were of a mystical-religious nature, as an otherworldly apparition, but I prefer to believe that it was something actually produced in the session taking place with the analysand.

I point out to the analysand that we were not alone, that there was someone else in the room besides us. The analysand says that he feels this perception is real and asks me, intrigued, how I knew about it. I answer that the reason I knew about it was because I had seen someone crossing the space between us. "You did?" asks the analysand, somewhat scared. I answer affirmatively, that I have indeed seen someone, in flesh and bone, and so I describe the person I had seen to him. I add that it could have been a moment of madness of mine, but that I didn't consider that to be the case – he, however, did not have to disregard the hypothesis of me having lost my mind and, if he believed so, he should take the appropriate measures. But I didn't think that was the case. The analysand says he cannot understand, but he feels that what I was saying was true.

After a silent moment, in which the analysand seems to be astounded for having confirmed my perception, I ask him: "Who do you think it might have been?" He answers that in his youth he would have said that it was '*the Other*'. "And who is the Other?" He replies: "*The Devil!*"

I don't know what to say for a while, and then suddenly, unexpectedly, an idea comes to me and I promptly let him know of it, considering the previous sensations of the session, of dismay and hopelessness.

> There is in fact an envious devil here, who seeks to demotivate us and treat everything we do as disdainful, useless and irrelevant, leaving us hopeless (in Hell). He endeavors to prove our efforts worthless and aims at intriguing and ruining your relationship with me. Above all, he wants to ruin a loving and creative relationship between you and yourself, besides the one you can have with me.

★★★

What happened in our work afterwards was evidence that this manifestation/perception opened an enormous space and insight for rather important things for both of us. It opened a path for the analysand to visualize and make contact with certain dimensions of his that he considered hellish, scary and unacceptable, but without which all his creativity was severely impaired. It seems that my possibility of seeing the devil, and not running away from it, nor losing my mind over having seen it, would have permitted the analysand to be willing to face it, to talk to it, to assimilate those primordial powers, of which he cannot either dispense.

II

I have mentioned in my book (Castelo Filho, 2015) the article "Beyond aggression in the theory of neuroses", by José Longman (1989a/2008). In the article, Longman describes an image, which he visualizes as a videotape unfolding before him, of a series of people walking in his direction and afterwards moving away, as if out of him. This **vision** later helps him to get an insight of what he was going through with the birth of his first granddaughter. In this situation, he perceived his transitoriness in this world, how unimportant he was in the whole scope of humanity and history, and the use which nature made of him to perpetuate something which had nothing to do with him or his ancestors and offspring represented by the people seen walking towards him and away from him. Longman states:

> One may object that the episode represents much more an imagined picturization of a theory, motivated by the will to explain the unspeakable, than the observation of an

individual, not a primitive one, but rather one who is sophisticated and psychoanalytically prepared. It just so happens that its unexpected appearing, unthought-of and not considered beforehand, its quality of being totally present, involving all the personality with the power of the certainty of reality that I would not dare affirm, does not speak for such an assumption. It is set in-between the dream and wake state, the experience transformed into a visualized image.

To my eyes, what I saw was an "evolution" (Bion, 1967), of the complex emotional experience taking place at that moment and which transpires through another reality, which makes it visible and communicable.

(Longman, 1989a/2008, p. 49)

In a different article, "The Psychoanalytic Object: an approximation from experience", Longman adds:

Once the psychoanalytic object is considered different from the sensuous object, it is clear that it cannot be observed in the same way. The science of its observation must be different. The capacity to observe it will not depend, therefore, on a wider acuity of the organs of the senses, but of a negative capacity in this sense. The "capacity to artificially blind itself in work, with the purpose of concentrating all the light in the single obscure passage", as Freud (1916/1980) wrote to a colleague and friend. We will be able to perceive it like poets, dreamers, artists, delusional and hallucinated, though conceiving it as a psychoanalyst.

(Longman, 1989b/2008, p. 69)

III

On the Globo News TV show *Starte*, on May 31, 2011, interviewer Bianca Ramoneda mentions to actress and Oscar nominee Fernanda Montenegro that in her biography by journalist Lúcia Rito, her daughter Fernanda Torres (winner of the Palm d'Or in Cannes as best actress) declared she had never seen a more insane actress on stage than her mother. She said her mother worked in an extremely dangerous and mad zone, on top of a very dangerous wall, and that astonished her.

The interviewer comments that there seems to be a large duality between Arlete – Montenegro's given name which seems to exist only inside her dwelling practically unknown and inaccessible to the public – and Fernanda, her stage name and that of her public figure. They seem to be two different people. The actress answers that they are indeed two, that she is a schizophrenic and that (I suppose she is referring to schizophrenia) had not developed because the theater had permitted her to "be". Fernanda was an "invention" of hers, which jumped right out of Arlete. Fernanda belongs to the spotlight while Arlete is an internal woman, within doors, of whom she speaks little and is intensely used in private, not as conflicted to the realistic side, as opposed to the other, who is the flying side ("it is this entity which, by chance, playfully, I named Fernanda Montenegro").

IV

Luiz Carlos U. Junqueira Filho (2004), in his paper "Alterpoiesis: on the genesis of ideogram in dreamwork-alpha", refers to Robert Louis Stevenson's work, who was known to say he did not write anything, he simply transcribed whatever, during the night, a group of little men produced and "delivered" to him.

Stevenson in a later essay called *A Chapter on Dreams*[1] writes that the little people

> are but just my Brownies, God bless them! who do one-half my work for me while I am fast asleep, and in all human likelihood, do the rest for me as well, when I am wide awake and fondly suppose I do it for myself. That part which is done while I am sleeping is the Brownies' part beyond contention; but that which is done when I am up and about is by no means necessarily mine, since all goes to show the Brownies have a hand in it even then.

V

In an interview to *Caros Amigos* (July 1999), writer Zélia Gattai said that her husband, the famous author Jorge Amado, participated in her books solely as a character. He would never interfere while they were being written, except once while she was writing *Crônica de uma namorada* (1994/2001). She started feeling afflicted, walking back and forth. Jorge wanted to know what was happening. Zélia decided to tell him:

> Look, Jorge, I cannot take this novel any further. I lost control over the characters. One of them wants to abuse a much younger cousin. He has already taken advantage of her, touched her. And the worst thing is that the girl is enjoying it. I don't know what to do with him.
>
> Jorge Amado looked Zélia head to toe and made a single comment, which was also a sentence: *Zélia, don't mind other people's businesses!*

VI

In *A Memoir of the Future* (Bion, 1991), there was an explanation of why we need to face ourselves with the Alices, Rosemarys, Rolands, Robins, Toms, Moriartys, Sherlock Holmeses, Priests, Germplasms, Doctors, Tyranossauruses, P.A.s (Psychoanalysts), Somites, Eighteen Years, Bions, Seventy-five years, Myselves, etc., who are nothing but ourselves and of whom we will never be free. How can one think with all that noise? The idea in this book is the meeting and feasibility of a talk between all those aspects. What is fundamental is the development of wisdom – the counterpart *would be the war and forgetfulness* (among those different dimensions). Analysis would permit the gathering of the mental dimensions: from the most primordial and archaic (somite), violent, cruel, instinctive, intuitive, creative (as are volcanoes, which not only devastate but also build islands and continents, and produce extremely fertile lands), up to the most "experienced" ones, in a way that they can talk among themselves, and eventually negotiate with each other, reaching some sort of term which is of mutual interest to those different parts.

In "Making the best of a bad job", he proposes:

> Freud described Two Principles of Mental Functioning; I suggest the Three Principles of Living. First, feeling; second, anticipatory thinking; third, feeling plus thinking plus Thinking. The latter is synonymous with prudence or foresight → action.
>
> *(Bion, 1987 [1979], p. 255)*

VII

A young adult came to me for analysis, complaining of several emotional disturbances and life experiences, which could be seen as hallucinations or delusions. He alternated between rather confused stages, in which I could barely understand what he said, and others where he described with great lucidity those instances he was deep in moments before, immensely contrasting the prior senseless speech, thus evidencing the possibility of us finding a crack from that point on (Rezze, 1997).

He was desperate to get rid of visions or commands that he received from "internal" figures (father, uncles, cousins, etc., whom he saw as authorities), who always oriented his conduct, or at least tried to reduce them to a single figure for him to be able to take a stand. These, however, disputed primacy, and he couldn't think for himself.

Seeing as useless his efforts to "heal" or get rid of the visions and contradictory commands, which made him even more desperate, I proposed that we did the opposite, that we looked at them closely and tried to understand what they were, instead of treating them as wrongful things that should not exist.

With time, despite the terror with which he made such an approximation (and to my eyes, being able to gradually do it by counting on me), we could see that among those "madnesses" there were several sexual fantasies which he judged unacceptable, as well as several perceptions which were apparently insightful, though potentially troublesome for the people around him, due to what they actually revealed. I saw him as someone extremely sensitive and capable of grasping important things "in the air".

The analysand began to feel more comfortable and started assimilating those feelings he tried to eject before. His newly acquired comfort, however, seems to have disturbed his family, who pressed him to stop his analysis. The way I see it, the family would rather have him mad than astute (Manoni, 1964).

VIII

An analysand, who had a successful corporate profession, manifests the desire to learn to sing. She can't take the initiative to begin, though.

During our conversation, I propose that what was stopping her from going after her desire was probably the fear of listening to her own voice, and what she would realize upon hearing it. She answers that she really does fear listening to her own voice. I go on to say that she fears that if she actually takes it up, the gap that opens will break some sort of protective dike, and that whatever it opened up, it would take everything with it like a flood, leaving her without a chance of survival. What would emerge, according to her expectations, would be unacceptable and would crush everything on the way. She confirms that to be her feeling. The counterpart she was going through (she complains that she doesn't know if what she does for a living is what she would really like to do) was that she couldn't listen to herself and she fears ending her days without having properly lived her life, according to something that was truly hers, and never attending to her true needs. On the one hand, a structured and severe framework permitted her to survive, but not actually live. On the other hand, listening to the life within her and the terror that such life, could be heard in her voice, was like an explosion that would devastate everything around it. She mentions it made sense.

I present the idea that she resents not taking her dreams forward, and that at the same time, she fears that if she takes that dimension into account, she would see herself as the girl in *Poltergeist*, who approaches some interference on the TV and is swallowed by that dimension/thing inside the image, sucked inside of it, not being able to escape again. She claims to feel that way. She sees herself at an impasse.

I offer to accompany her to approach that dimension that she sees as fearful, and if she's willing, to let me help her come into contact with that dimension, without losing judgment, being able to think, so that it can be perceived, considered and even used creatively.

IX

In "Attention and Interpretation", Bion (1977, pp. 35–36) writes:

> Receptiveness achieved by denudation of memory and desire (which is essential to the operation of 'acts of faith') is essential to the operation of psycho-analysis and other scientific proceedings. It is essential for experiencing hallucination or the state of hallucinosis.
>
>   This state I do not regard as an exaggeration of a pathological or even natural condition: I consider it rather to be a state that is always present, but overlaid by other phenomena, which screen it. If these other elements can be moderated or suspended hallucinosis becomes demonstrable; its full depth and richness are accessible only to 'acts of faith'. Elements of hallucinosis of which it is possible to be sensible are the grosser manifestations and are of secondary importance; to appreciate hallucination the analyst must participate in the state of hallucinosis. . . . Before interpretations of hallucination can be given, which are themselves transformations O → K, it is necessary that the analyst undergoes in his own personality the transformation O → K. By eschewing memories, desires, and the operations of memory he can approach the domain of hallucinosis and of the 'acts of faith' by which alone he can become at one with his patients' hallucinations and so effect transformations O → K.

Thus, the importance of the unknown is highlighted in psychoanalysis (and all the other sciences and creative activities). Setting aside memories and desires opens a crack for the outburst of the unknown, whose evolution can be grasped by means of the capacity of "visualizing" which is attributed by keeping that discipline and by the focus on what one doesn't know. The prior theories and knowledge which may "explain", in a situation of cause and effect, the event, or narrative of the present must be forgotten during the sessions, as they would stop the transformations in O and the perceptions of what may evolve. The *forgotten* prior theories and knowledge may, if as much, work as preconceptions, and in case they come across a realization in the experience they can also "evolve", and their own meanings will have been altered by that evolution once it occurs. It is another way of considering the adage that goes "in practice, theory is completely different". For that to actually be observed, only by stepping away from them and forgetting them during practice. In any way, the important point is not to hold on to theories. If they are preconceptions (unconscious) waiting for realizations, they may be important probing and investigation instruments to whatever is not known and which may end up pointing out incongruence or uselessness of themselves; if not, they are just clutter to the eyes of the observer.

Upon a later reflection regarding the aforementioned session of the first clinical situation, I realized that the image I saw condensed the ideas of **"Corisco, the blond devil", "Saci Pererê" (historical folk characters)**, and others from the sociological text "A aparição do demônio na fábrica, no meio da produção" (*Devil's apparition in the factory, in the middle of the production line*) (Martins, 1994), of the cartoon character "Louco" (*Mad*) of the "Turma da Monica" comics, by Mauricio de Souza, who has tangled blond hair, and that of the apparition of the revealing ghost in *Hamlet*. In the text by Martins, the modification of the production process from manmade to industrial in a ceramics factory in the 1950s, the workers were not aware anymore of the full process of producing the pieces, but rather only knew the process of the specific stage they now worked on. Working with the number of broken pieces while adapting from one process to another along with the police-like surveillance on the production line would have led that population to see the devil lurking around the halls of the factory, which only disappeared once a priest came to the factory to bless it. The devil, the way I see it, materialized from the mental situation of the workers. My prior knowledge of these characters and of the theoretical text, completely forgotten and unconscious during the session, served as a preconception to the situation that took place in the session; it evolved and showed itself in the apparition I saw. In a way, they correspond to Freud's remains of the day which organize plastically in a dream or a dream-image equivalent to a selected fact to permitting visualization of an insight that was reached, according to the update Bion made on this particular theory of Freud's (Bion, 1992, p. 233). Without that visualization and its binding by means of nominating the constant conjunction it expresses, the *insight* would be lost. The dream does not have a latent unconscious content. It is the act of dreaming itself that reveals what is latent and manifest, the unconscious and the conscious. The rational latent speech deformed by the dream work would, in fact, be created subsequently to the dream itself (to visualize), and would seek to attach, by nomination, the constant conjunction perceived (image(s)) and expressed through rational means − transformation of O to K.

On the other hand, opening to the unknown and to the perception of evolutions is a situation which mobilizes intense emotional experiences. Besides the terror before the unknown, common to every human being, there is the fear that whatever arises out of it may break all known parameters, revealing dimensions and unseen universes. This makes the supposedly known universe also strange due to the twists and turns that the new perceptions may bring. Just like the Earth that moves and is round as opposed to the still and plain view of it in Middle Age; the floor beneath mankind's feet was not the same anymore after those realizations (one can perfectly understand the terror and hatred experienced by the contemporaries of Copernicus, Galileo and Columbus about what they proposed). These perceptions are emotional and not rational experiences, made through the observation of the phenomena which present themselves to the senses and demand a container capable of expanding when in contact with them. If the container (or mind) is not resilient enough or is under-developed, it may break into pieces with the experiences. The analyst needs to be someone with a capacity of tolerating emotional experiences for which the analysand does not feel capable. The contact with the unknown and with the experience of hallucinosis affects the analyst with intense emotional shocks, which he needs to be able to assimilate and transform into knowledge he can communicate (O → K). For that to happen, the analyst needs a well-developed mental resilience and the possibility of fostering and assimilating the intense emotional mobilizations that such an activity instigates. This would only be possible through a long and thorough analysis of the analyst himself. According to Bion's idea of *rêverie*, that would be the condition which would permit the analysand, when realizing it in the analyst (or the baby in the mother), to expand his mental container, permitting him to make contact with what he doesn't know and haunts him. The contact with reality is always dreadful, and those who cannot feel haunted cannot be in contact with life as it is and with all the amazing things it has to offer. As the Bard said: "there are more things in heaven and Earth . . ."

X

Bion, in his third conference in São Paulo, in 1973, refers to a situation in which Freud thought his patient had a phobia of socks, which made it impossible for him to wear them. Bion suggests:

> that the patient did not have a phobia of socks, but could see that what Freud thought were socks, were a lot of holes knitted together. If this is correct, terms like 'phobia' in classical analysis do not do justice to the facts, and in particular do not do justice to the extreme capacity for observation which is natural to some patients. Just as it is natural for me in my gross, macroscopic way classically to see a pair of socks, this kind of patient has a visual capacity which is different, making him able to see what I cannot see. What I think, with the light of my intelligence, brains, knowledge, experience, is a pair of socks, **he** can see is not.
>
> *(Bion, 1974, p. 38)*

The work of the analyst would include the task of being able to see what the analysand sees, is capable of seeing while he, the analyst, is not.

In "Making the best of a bad job" (Bion, 1987 [1979]), Bion goes back to the famous reference of Hannah Segal's analysand, who could not play the violin because he thought he would be masturbating in public. The analysand could not see the "so-called" superior view that playing the violin is not masturbating. Bion considers this also a misleading vision. If the problem of the analysand is that he cannot recognize a man playing a violin in public, the problem of the other people is that they cannot perceive a person masturbating in public. I see this as a way of considering a binocular vision. The attempt to try to extirpate one vertex or the other would develop a mental disturbance and an impossibility of the development and creative growth, just like the account of actress Fernanda Montenegro puts in evidence.

Quoting him in the same text:

> If the S-state is regarded as being worthy of respect equally with the W-state – the arbitrium being impartial – then where one went, what one saw and experienced, must be regarded as having a value which is equally valid. This is implicit when Freud, like many predecessors, regards dreams as worthy of respect. So we can say that the wake-work should be considered equally worthy of respect as the dream-work. But why is the state of mind of being awake, conscious, logical, regarded as having 'our wits about us', but only if it is half our wits? How awful when you find a maggot in your apple! Not so awful as finding half a maggot in your apple. So we find that only having half our wits about us is a discovery that is most disturbing.
>
> *(Bion, 1987, p. 254)*

XI

To permit oneself to contact that binocular vision is usually a frightening experience (but which, paradoxically, may be equally pleasant and stimulating – the pleasure being associated to the expansion and reach that new perceptions may bring. This could make it extremely attractive, just like acting must be for some people, as actress Fernanda Torres mentioned when referring to the zone in which her mother works when on stage.

Without a long and extensive analysis by the analyst, which enables him to familiarize with that work zone that is also his, what he may end up doing is an imitation of psychoanalysis, restricting himself to one or another perception which would harm the development of "Thought", a situation in which he would not be prudent, capable of anticipating situations, or acting in accordance to what only this complementary vision could enable.

Note

1 Junqueira thanks Antonino Ferro for the reference to this essay.

References

Bion, W.R. (1967). Notes on memory and desire. In *Cogitations*, pp. 380–385. London: Karnac.

Bion, W.R. (1974). *Brazilian Lectures 1 – São Paulo, 1973*, p. 38. Rio de Janeiro: Imago.

Bion, W.R. (1977). Attention and interpretation. In W.R. Bion (Ed.), *Seven Servants: Four Works by Wilfred R. Bion*. New York: Jason Aronson. (First publication in 1970).

Bion, W.R. (1987). Making the best of a bad job. In *Clinical Seminars and four Papers*. Abingdon: Fleetwood Press. (First publication in 1979).

Bion, W.R. (1991). *A Memoir of the Future*. London: Karnac.

Bion, W.R. (1992). Tower of Babel: Possibility of using a racial myth. In W.R. Bion (Ed.), *Cogitations*, pp. 226–241. London: Karnac.

Castelo Filho, C. (2015). *O processo criativo: transformação e ruptura*, 2nd ed. São Paulo: Blucher.

Freud, S. (1980). *Sigmund Freud – Lou Andreas Salomé: BriedWechsel*, p. 50. Frankfurt, AM: Fischer Verlag. (First publication in 1916).

Gattai, Z. (2001). *Crônica de uma namorada: e de uma família paulista nos anos cinquenta*. Rio de Janeiro: Record. (First publication in 1994).

Junqueira Filho, L.C.U. (2004). Alteropoese: sobre a gênese da ideogramaticização no trabalho-onírico-alfa. *Revista Brasileira de Psicanálise* 38(4): 785–801.

Longman, J. (2008a). Além da agressividade das neuroses. In J. Signorini, A.M.S. Ziskind and E. Longman (Orgs.), *José Longman: psicanálise viva*, pp. 42–53. Rio de Janeiro: Corifeu. (First publication in 1989a).

Longman, J. (2008b). O objeto psicanalítico: uma aproximação a partir da experiência. In J. Signorini, A.M.S. Ziskind and E. Longman (Orgs.), *José Longman: psicanálise viva*, pp. 68–74. Rio de Janeiro: Corifeu. (First publication in 1989b).

Manoni, M. (1964). *L'enfant arrieré et sa mère*. Paris: Seuil.

Martins, J.S. (1994). A aparição do demônio na fábrica, no meio da produção. *Tempo Social: Revista de Sociologia da USP* 5(1–2): 1–29.

Rezze, C.J. (1997). A fresta. In SBPSP (Ed.), *Panorama*. São Paulo: SBPSP.

Stevenson, R.L. (1892). A chapter on dreams. In *Across the Plains*. New York: Charles Scribner's Sons.

19

SELECTIVE PRECISE INDUCTION OF NUMBING DEADENING NARCOSIS BY PRIMITIVE SUPEREGO SOURCES

A method of attacking links by severe compromise of attention

Michael Ian Paul

A peculiar experience began to become more frequent as I became capable of nearing accuracy in my analysis of a patient who had been quite frustrating to me. The frustration was understandable. When I interpreted, he blocked my interpretations and changed the subject. However, his diversion was close enough so that it was not obvious at first, just a hair off the point. I found this pattern significant and as I gained courage I noticed that his rejoinders became more intimidating. Because of his facility with language and high intelligence, it was clear that he was capable of recognizing what I had said and moving the meaning just off the point. If I got closer, he would split in time using so-called free associations, moving either in time, yesterday, or suddenly locate himself elsewhere, often France (see footnote),[1] where there were frequent memories of fine restaurants and pleasant interchanges with his parents. I was always tempted to linger in the restaurant fantasies offering the experience of a pleasant time and mutual admiration being included as a person of taste and education. However, as I gradually recovered my ability, I found a means of confrontation about his diversions. He became critically harsh, raising his voice to collimated threats, sat up, and glared menacingly. When I interpreted that he felt terribly threatened and menaced, he simply shut up and lay back. As this pattern continued, I noticed that I felt distracted by a sudden experience of my face, teeth, and nose being dulled as though injected with a local anesthetic. At first these phenomena were barely within my ability to observe them, but as I became more familiar, I gradually began to form interpretations that had bearing to his projections of numbness, anesthesia, and deadness that he was communicating to me. He thought that these interpretations were patently ridiculous and would simply remain silent. His associations picked up with frequent recipes for how to behave while being deposed during a criminal investigation. The phrase, he advised, was "I have no *specific* recollections." Then he could not be simply accused of being incompetent or simply having a bad memory. This phrase was a hint that he had no specific recollection of our interactions and that while he could 'parry' my interpretations, it became clear that he could not remember what I had said and therefore my interpretations were useless. However, when I realized that during these interactions I was having trouble remembering what I said precisely, I noticed that during these events I was struggling to stay awake against a force that was so powerful that I sometimes became completely numb but not 'comfortably.' As I became more and more able to predict these phenomena, I became aware of references of massive evasion of his wife and children, over working until the middle of the night, and absolute evasion of any contact with those few people who had tried to be friends or at least somewhat social. At this point he informed me that for the past few months he had been seeing another analyst who had been referred to him through a friend. He had been seeing both of us. Without any further explanation, the analyst agreed to stop seeing him. I drew the patient's attention to this and interpreted that he probably assumed that I had never known the emotion of jealousy and/or betrayal and that he was giving me the opportunity to know what that was like so that I might have a semblance of empathy. I began to show him that the splitting between us by evasion was an attack on the parental intercourse, leaving both of us out since our work was experienced as worthless and impractical, especially since he had very little, if any, memory of what was occurring verbally between us. Verbal interchanges were usually experienced as abusive, which I struggled to avoid by carefully attending to my intonation and being careful to interpret precisely but always remaining respectful and polite. What became clear is that he hated both his parents with a terrifying passion. Both were academics and skillful writers who were preoccupied with the academic 'high life' while he languished ignored in his crib only attended by nannies throughout his childhood.

An important clinical finding was illustrated by his entrance to the consulting room. There were numerous times when he would push by me as I opened the door, rush in and push me out and then slam the door with me left in the waiting room and he in the consulting room. While this was amusing, at first like a child's game, it became repetitively frustrating, and our relationship was like that of the character of Inspector Clouseau and Kato (his valet), who was constantly instructed to try to attack and get the better of him even while he was sleeping ("The Pink Panther," 1963). This was not only his characterization of our relationship but was highlighting his fear of being misused, attacked, and having no trust in anyone. This pattern continued so that the analytic relationship moved between apparent cooperation as long as the personal experience that could put him in touch with his mental pain occurring was blocked. Whenever he could not "control" these emergent feelings by directing an attack between us, he did feel severe mental pain. He was a master of cat and mouse, victor and victim, infliction of pain and revenge and retribution which were constant features of the analysis. All the while these processes were analyzed, he became increasingly capable of bearing emotional pain but deeply resented this as a function of our work. Even though his business relations and friendships flourished and he became wealthy, this was used for power purposes without a trace of gratitude or any pleasure – it was only his due and I, his servant.

I want to refocus on the drugging responses that I have been able to analyze now in a variety of patients and have noticed that others have recognized this including a popular rock group called Pink Floyd in an album called "The Wall." These are lyrics from that particular album:

> Hello, is anybody in there?
> Is there anyone at home?
> Come on now, I hear you're feeling down.
> Well, I can ease the pain.
> . . .
> There is no pain. You are receding.
> A distant ship smoke on the horizon.

You are only coming through in waves.
Your lips move but I can't hear what you are saying.
. . .
I have become comfortably numb.
OK. Just a little pinprick.
There'll be no more Aaaaaaah!
. . .
I do believe it's working. . . . Good.
. . .
When I was a child I caught a fleeting glimpse out of the corner of my eye.
I turned to look but it was gone.
The child had grown.
The dream is gone.
I have become comfortably numb. (Floyd, P. 1984)

The next set of lyrics are called "In the Flesh."

If you should go skating on the thin ice of modern life
Dragging behind you the silent reproach
Of a million tearstained eyes
Don't be surprised when a crack in the ice appears under your feet.
You slip out of your depth and out of your mind
With your fear flowing out behind you as you claw the thin ice.

Daddy's flown across the ocean leaving just a memory.
Snapshot in the family album.
Daddy, what else did you leave for me?
All in all, it was just another brick in the wall. (Floyd, P. 1984)

Although I am extensively quoting from this poetic approach to modern life, I found it intelligible and remarkably similar to my patient's experience and that of others. I also found it reminding me of Bion's reference to the death of Palinurus in Virgil's Aeneid with which when I first became familiar I had linked the story to prenatal life and the drug exposure. While I was familiar with the similarities to anesthesia and the drug experience, I found it remarkable that there were similarities to the primitive superego's handling of the process of the reception of psychic pain and the blockade by the induction of a drugging response which is rapid, anticipatory, and can be complete, so that one is not only "comfortably numb" but knocked out and returned to the watery environment. In a paper delivered to the Los Angeles Psychoanalytic Society in 1975, Bion (1975) referred to the death of Palinurus as an example of visual fantasy. I have quoted the section from Dryden's translation of Virgil's Aeneid (Dryden, J. 1887) which is relevant and have divided the section into its main elements as the form of the story seemed to be useful as a model to illuminate a series of mechanisms including sensory phenomena, takeover by the cruel superego or psychotic part of the personality, projective identification, the experience of drug narcosis, demonic possession, delusion formation, the entry into the mother's body representing the transformation from the air to a watery environment, and has been noted in the material of the above-mentioned patient.

Now smiling hope, with sweet vicissitude, within the hero's mind his joys renewed. He calls to raise the masts, the sheets display; the cheerful crew with diligence obey; they scud before the winds and sail in open sea ahead of all the master pilot steers; and, as he leads, the following navy veers.

The steeds of night had traveled half the sky, the drowsy rowers on their benches lay, when the soft God of sleep with easy flight descends, and draws behind a trail of light. Thou Palinurus art his destined prey to thee alone he takes his fatal way. Dire dreams to thee in iron sleep he bears, and lighting on thy prow, the form of Phorbas wears.

Thus the traitor god began his tale: "The winds my friend inspire a pleasing gale; the ships without they care, securely sail. Now steal an hour of sweet repose and I will take the rudder and they room supply." To whom the yawning pilot half asleep, "Me dost thou bid to trust the treacherous deep, the harlot-smiles of race? Shall I believe the siren south again and oft betrayed not know the monster main?" He said: His fastened hands the rudder keep, and fix'd on heaven, his eyes repel invading sleep. The god was wroth and at his temples threw a branch in Lethe dipped and drunk with Stygian dew: The pilot vanquished by the power divine soon closed swimming eyes and lay supine. Scarce were his limbs extended at their length, the god assaulting with superior strength felt heavy on him plunged him in the sea and with the stern, the rudder tore away. Headlong he fell and struggling in the main, cried out for helping hands but cried in vain. The victor daemon mounts, obscure in air while the ship sails on without the pilot's care.

(Dryden, J. 1887)

The elements of this story which these patients demonstrate in common include: 1) hope, bliss, and clear weather; 2) the falling of night, descent of sleep; 3) dire dreams; 4) the deception of Palinurus through the wiles of the traitor god; 5) recognition of Somnus' lie and the fight; 6) overpowering of Palinurus by Lethe and Stygian dew; 7) the ocean as smiling harlot monster; 8) the wakening before drowning; 9) the daemon mounts obscure in air; and 10) the ship sails on without the pilot. In the analytic work, there is evidence of the dread of falling asleep because of the fear of nightmares. The ubiquitous experience of numbness and sleepy deadness can be mimicked with a drug (Stygian dew) or Lethe (forgetfulness) which often involves an attempt to fight against the temptation to use a drug, leading to "giving in" to the siren south, a voice-like temptress promising bliss and relief from pain. The feminine nature of the smiling harlot monster is shown by a powerful infantile maternal transference with penetration in phantasy into the mother's body, giving rise to feelings of drowning, choking, and, in addition, to painful respiratory sensations and edema. There is always a powerful negative maternal relationship in which a dread fear of dependency upon an individual is frequently replaced by drug dependency. After the takeover phenomenon, the ship does sail on without a pilot, noted by disorientation in space, loss of judgment, mindlessness, and loss of perception. The story above describes a movement from air to water in terms of the maternal prenatal state and may be a clearer representation of what is meant by the "death instinct."

There are clear similarities in the descriptions given by Pink Floyd in 1984 and by Virgil 2000 plus years ago. The annihilation of psychic pain, the reentry into the water, mental death, the blunting or abolition of feeling when struck by Lethe (Stygian dew) forgetfulness, mental drugging, anesthesia, loss of steering as a result of the rudder breaking away, and death as a way of avoiding the need for helping hands, and an attitude of heroic omnipotence. Even what the recent generations have described as "cool" represent the numbing of feelings and thus steering. What appears as a form of sleepiness is more like the effect of being drugged and left without the experience of meaning and only the capacity to build a wall. Is this our increasing recognition and concern with a spectrum of autism writ large in our society and the helplessness which devolves?

The experience of numbness brought to consciousness by the recognition of a state of mind not apprehensible by the senses is an example of a transformation of O to K. That one has to be one with O is evident to allow the "recognition of the experience of something sent from that domain to reception by our minds of an experience which has not reached the level of recognizable emotion." In this way, numbness cannot be sensed but must be joined in order to be received. This transformation I believe to be necessary to recognize experiences which may be as Bion states to be psychosomatic or, in this case, somapsychotic. Operations at this level must occur in order to bring these experiences to the patient's awareness or they would remain meaningless and unusable. What lies beneath 'the ice' are emotions which can never be recognized without these investigations and may only be ignored at our peril.

The results of these states involve the inability to recognize another person. There is exceptional relevance to the inability to utilize effective communication through speech. The experience of reception of the spoken word can be so painful that a dreading response is immediately induced. Without the analysis of this somapsychotic phenomenon, the analytic process is rendered useless.

The consequences of this form of drugging intentional numbness of which I speak constitutes a form of 'sleep' which the patient is desperate to maintain. For ordinary intents and purposes, the patient appears to be awake and responsive and quite capable of what appears to be verbal interaction. Forces of projective evacuation of emotion are thrust unconsciously into the analyst so that after a time, one can formulate an interpretation which has precise relevance. The snag occurs when the patient hears the interpretation. These patients do not listen, nor do they register, the interpretation. Upon the awareness of the interpretation, they divert their attention and often pick up a semblance or gist of what is being said and evacuate the interpretation proper. Although their responses are close, they very rarely connect and are often just off the mark. As long as this 'inaccuracy' is maintained, there is no disturbance, and the session can seem to go along swimmingly. The trouble starts when this process is confronted, which then evokes the drugging and profound distancing. If this state of affairs is allowed to continue, there is no essential change or growth in the patient, who continues to deny and avoid the awareness of time. Their expectations include infinite time, interchangeable objects for use in substitution and to have no limitations which are experienced as beneath them. Time and limits are experienced as instigators of immense pain leading to death and must be avoided in order to 'function.' The patient feels that to experience pain is to have an attack inflicted upon him. Therefore, verbal direct contact is the culprit, and the words must be deflected and avoided. It can be very difficult to note these deflections, as often they are quite clever. The analyst is encouraged to allow these substitutions to stand or else. Eventually, if one is persistent, the pain will emerge along with the results of the avoidance. The anesthesia can be induced by drugs (relatively easy to detect), but also by internal drugging. Without this analysis and the projection of the pain into the analyst, no growth can occur except intellectually in the domain of 'knowing about' something without having any emotional meaning. Object relations, as Bion has noted, are thin and tenacious as well as studiously superficial. These patients can be preoccupied with money (must be an infinite amount) and are never satisfied, nor do they have any gratitude. Since there is no satisfaction, this preoccupation appearing as greed is boundless. And in this regard, they are utilizing a quantitative method to solve a qualitative problem, which never works. The qualitative problem includes the pain they feel and the difficulty of their object relations, but the solution is to get more and more and more of something quantitative that can be counted, like money or objects that are inorganic. They cannot distinguish their objects, and their relations are malignantly narcissistic. There is no recognition of real danger except for their feelings, which are experienced as immensely dangerous. They are often very unaware of danger and cannot distinguish good from bad. They retain the presence of the object which is experienced as bad but must be kept at a distance and controlled. Curiosity is virtually absent as they behave as though they were omniscient.

This 'sleep' is very like the sleep induced by the stick dipped in Lethe or Stygian dew. The experience of "his eyes repel invading sleep" is a remarkably accurate description by Virgil. The return to the water and the loss of the stern and rudder describe the consequences of this 'sleep of death.' The word lethal comes from Lethe. The victor demon mounts in air. The ship sails on without the pilot's care.

Are any of these people in leadership positions politically?

Technically, without this form of analysis and with the patient's toleration of emotional contact, they cannot verify an interpretation made in the here and now. Until they can maintain enough contact to verify the interpretation, that is to say, whether they think it is correct or not by virtue of comparing it to what they know they think or feel and be able to pay enough attention so that that is possible. When they are not in a position to agree or disagree, they are unable to use evidence. They then cannot make accurate observations of what the analyst has shown them verified. Therefore, when they are alone, their chance of making use of the practical value of the observation of the process shown to the patient cannot be accurately used. This results in continued misunderstanding and inaccuracy, which renders the analytic work impractical. The analysand must become able to hold in mind and compare what the analyst states by interpretation the analysand thinks or feels with that which the analysand knows he thinks or feels. If the analysand wishes to keep the analyst off the point, he can agree to an interpretation he knows is inaccurate or disagree with an interpretation that he knows is accurate. To be able to recognize these excursions from the truth is often very difficult to detect and depends on the precision awareness of what both members of the pair have said. This process requires practice and requires an intense degree of attention. Otherwise, the interpretation does not penetrate.

Note

1 These "free" associations have a polymorphous quality. Often, they are used for splitting in time or geographic space.

References

Bion, W.R. (1975). "Discussion in Reference to the Death of Palinurus." *Lecture to the Los Angeles Psychoanalytic Institute.*

Pink Floyd (1984). Recording of *The Wall.* Drama Music.

"The Pink Panther" (1963). Comedy-Drama film released 1964. Directed by Blake Edwards.

Virgil (1887). *The Aeneid.* Trans. John Dryden, 3rd ed. London and New York.

20

BEING IN THE THOUGHT-FLOW

Authentic Movement and Bion's "O"

Deborah Sherman

When I was in high school, my mother commented that if I pursued my dream of being a professional dancer, I would be "wasting my mind." Back then I understood her to mean that dancers do not think and that dancing, even as an art, neither requires nor gives evidence of thought. The notion that I would stop thinking or that my mind would cease to work through disuse terrified me. So, although I knew that thinking and dancing were equal parts of my being in the world, I stopped dancing and went to college to "use my mind." In college I studied writing and became interested in language and thinking. I also pursued various forms of dance/movement as I continued to experience dance as giving me a "home" in the world. My interest in thinking brought me to therapeutic work: I trained in counseling, yoga, dance/movement therapy, and finally, psychoanalysis.

I had been practicing psychoanalysis for 12 years and Authentic Movement for 20, when I encountered Bion's *Attention and Interpretation* (1983). Bion writes that it is an "act of faith" to think, that forming a thought is like making a piece of art, that "an 'act of faith' becomes apprehensible when it is represented in and by thought . . . and it is apprehended when it is a thought just as the artist's O is apprehensible when it has been transformed into a work of art" (Bion, 1983). Bion's attention here to thinking as an evolving creative vehicle for experiencing life and "O" brought my attention to my mind in the practice of Authentic Movement. Suddenly I saw that my mind was in the movements and my thoughts were movements of my mind. I found I could sometimes apprehend, and track in writing, my processing of analytic sessions emerging in Authentic Movement. Tracking my thought process while moving allowed me to experience myself as someone whose thinking and movement processes were intertwined and "fed" each other. The opposite of the fear that drove me away from dance and into college, I could now feel myself as a thinking mover and a moving thinker! Though I had been aware of clinical experiences being evoked in Authentic Movement before, Bion's perspective enabled me to conceptualize my explorations of these moments as a form of self-supervision, connecting my thinking/experiencing as a psychoanalyst to my thinking/experiencing in the Authentic Movement process.

Bion's containment and Authentic Movement

Bion described containment as an intersubjective process which provides a boundaried mental space in which thoughts can be born. One might say that in the process of containment mental space is also created (Ogilvie, Personal Communication). The psychoanalytic process offers patients containment for being-states, dream communications, kinesthetic data, and pieces of mind that have not been embodied meaningfully, realized, represented, or thought. In the containing process the analyst witnesses, metabolizes, digests, and dreams communications from the patient, attempting to recognize bits and pieces of sensory data as they emerge in forms which may be realized and possibly then represented in interpretive statements. The object of this witnessing, forming, realizing, and representing is to have and to bear our emotional experiences as well as to apprehend the truth or the "O" of these experiences.

Just as there are "thoughts without a thinker" (Bion, 1965) there are sensations, movement impulses and bodily energies without recognizable form. Movement impulses, organized by images, rhythm, spatial patterns/dimensions, and energy qualities, give form to inchoate sensory arisings – the flotsam and jetsam of data passing continuously through our systems.

Authentic Movement is a practice of structured movement and witnessing which enables participants to explore this sensory data, discovering forms that emerge in that process. This forming of movement impulses, through being expressed and witnessed, therefore supports metabolization and containing capacities in the psychoanalyst. In clinical sessions analysts receive communications and transmissions of patients' beings – some more fragmentary than others. Analysts listen for and associatively process their own and their patients' images, words, emotions, thoughts, and body/sensory data. At times one encounters patients who have no concept of a container into which they can project and the analyst must then pick up their patient's communications in sensory channels attempting to be with that patient's states, working to create mental space which can contain both patient and analyst.

Case example

M was a 38-year-old woman who came to see me because she felt depressed and was worried that her "dark moods" were getting worse. M told me she had broken up with a lover two years before and didn't understand why she was unable to "get over it and move on." She had a history of depression with a brief hospitalization 10 years earlier for a suicide attempt, but I did not know this until later in treatment. I experienced something with M almost immediately which was hard to describe and to which it was hard to ascribe meaning. When we spoke – we faced each other – her look, her gaze, carried something to which I could not put a feeling to or even a sensation. There was an "it" in her gaze and whatever it was, I found it impossible to receive head on – something between a glare and a stare; her eyes were penetrating but impenetrable. Her eyes pierced mine but when I sought her eyes for contact, they were flat, opaque surfaces which my eyes slid away from – no way in, no traction, nothing to hold on to. In those moments, I felt like a deer caught in headlights – I couldn't look and I couldn't look away. I was frozen in this bright light, unable to move or to respond, not knowing, unable to find anything I could respond to. Uncomfortable and afraid, I wanted to know what was happening in these moments between us. Eventually, I got the idea that M was communicating something to me that I was unable to receive, to bear or to process.

Maybe she was sticking with me hoping I'd find a way to process what she was sending me. Such moments repeated often between us, and in them I continued to feel frozen – unmoving, fixed in space as well as in my inability to feel or think or "be" in them. One day in an Authentic Movement peer group this repeated experience came to mind and I channeled that frozen feeling, being fixed in the beam of her eyes. I found I could not stay there but out of that frozenness came a fierce, snapping, growling sound and movement. As I followed the movement impulse and let it grow, I became a vicious creature, a combined wild dog and bird. I moved sharply this way and that, biting into the space, warning others with my growls not to come near. I was looking for something to attack and kill. As I felt the powerful urge to kill, I moved back into the person frozen in the headlights – now I realized that this person faced something that could kill her. I thought, "I'm going to die!" and felt the restriction of the one-dimensional channel between me and this vicious force. There was only the sagittal, forward-back dimension between us – I could neither run away, nor back up, and certainly I would not move forward toward her. As I stayed on the spot, right there with my terror of being killed, my body suddenly shifted side to side, my feet doing little shuffling steps. I moved with this impulse and found myself (absurdly) doing a side-to-side tap dance. I smiled to myself – a widening movement of my mouth – I had found the horizontal dimension! Here was some space to move and be in without being killed.

From this Authentic Movement experience, I took the following back to my work with M: when these moments of glare came, I would shift slightly sideways in my chair or think about breathing "widely" into the sides of my rib cage or attend to the periphery at the sides of my personal space – all ways of embodying subtly, and being able to think into, the horizontal dimension that had been missing in our interaction previously. With the horizontal dimension came the mental space to contain what had felt previously uncontainable. In addition, I found that the words "I am afraid I will be killed" and "I want to kill" gave voice (and representation) to the murderous aggression I now realized was in the room at such moments – inside her, inside me, being lived and re-lived between us. Thus, I was able to begin to receive what she was sending: an experience of murdering and being murdered for which there had been no containment previously; an experience I had been unable to witness, bear, or name until it emerged in the form of Authentic Movement.

Authentic Movement and Bion's "O"

Authentic Movement is a simple, meditative practice in which there are witnesses and movers.

Movers close their eyes and focus internally, waiting to be moved by a bodily impulse. Once an impulse comes, the mover follows it, allowing it to unfold. The movement gesture may be as small as an inhale of breath or as sudden as a run across the room. Allowing movement impulses to emerge and embodying them is similar to Freud's streaming of the unconscious through verbal impulses. Movers who are analysts exploring a clinical experience are asked to bring to mind a clinical moment in which they registered something which puzzled, frustrated, or alarmed them; perhaps an image, sensation, or fantasy that they did not know what to do with, or that did not seem to fit with the situation. The mover's exploration of these moments, taken together with the feedback of the witness often yields containing forms through which these bits of sensory data can become recognizable as realizations, thoughts, and emotional truths, allowing the "O" of the experience to emerge.

Witnesses keep their eyes open and remain physically still to see and receive the experience of the movement. Witnesses bring a receptive attention to the entire field, which is comprised of the mover moving, the witness attending to their experience of seeing the movement, and the larger space the mover moves through as well as sounds that may carry or vibrate through that space. The witness also holds other elements of the frame, such as calling an agreed upon beginning and end time to the movement and noticing if any movers are in physically unsafe situations that need intervention. Witnesses practice a particular kind of visual focus which is receptive, requiring a widening of the visual field to the periphery of one's vision. Focusing in this way one "steps back" behind the eyes, creating a slight distance in order to take in a larger field of space. Bion describes this form of focus as "a penetrating beam of darkness; a reciprocal of the searchlight" (Bion, 1973/1974). In this type of vision one can receive a whole field, noticing what jumps out, a "selected fact" (Bion, 1992) and things that repeatedly occur together as patterns, as in "constant conjunctions" (Bion, 1992). As the witness turns a beam of darkness onto the mover's and their own experience, they are also taking the attitude that Bion suggests for psychoanalysts in session of "eschewing memory and desire" (Bion, 1983) to allow the unsaturated space of unknowing for the "O" of the experience to emerge.

In closing, I will elaborate on Bion's ideas of containment and my evolving experience with Authentic Movement and clinical work. In *Attention and Interpretation* (1983), Bion formulates his ideas about the relation between projection, projective identification as communication, and our capacity to realize mental space. He uses "the geometrical concepts of lines, points, and space (as derived originally not from a realisation of three-dimensional space but from the realisations of the emotional mental life)" (1983). In projection, the projected emotion or fragment is understood to originate with one person (a point) in three-dimensional space and move along a line to another person (or point) in space. When the other projectively identifies with the fragment that comes to them, the first person knows that their arrow has flown through space and found its mark; it's as if they can visually and mentally trace the line of their communicative arrow's flight. There is an experience for that person of specific feedback coming from the other which enables them to realize something about what they have projected. And there is the sense that the psychic/mental space between the two people, and inside of each person, is both described and bounded by the coordinates of the arrow's flight. Bion then goes on to consider his experience with patients who are unable to project parts of their personality "because there is no conception of containers into which the projection could take place" (ibid.). This lack of conception of containers creates difficulty in using projection to map mental/psychic space or projective identification to communicate with others. Literally, there is no conception of mental space within which one can think. "The mental realisation of space is therefore felt as an immensity so great that it cannot be represented even by astronomical space because it cannot be represented at all" (ibid.). In my work with M, for stretches of time, I experienced myself as frozen – unable to move. Without mental space and the wherewithal to feelingly respond, I was unable to think – there was a lack of psychic space between us and in each of us. I experienced this lack of space in Authentic Movement when I felt myself held in the beam of her eyes as on a one-dimensional sagittal line along which I could move neither forward nor backwards. As I remained frozen on one point, I suddenly began to move side-to-side – in my movement, I found the horizontal dimension, and with it the psychic space to consider the positions we were both in as well as what was between us. To bring the emotional realizations of both wanting to kill, and being killed, into my work with M, there had to be a concurrent creation of the space to contain that realization. As I wrote earlier in this paper, I had to "embody subtly and think into the horizontal dimension that had previously been missing in our interaction." My discovery of the missing dimension, which enabled me to create mental and psychic space with M, allowed me to witness the birth of a containment in our treatment.

References

Bion, W.R. (1965). *Transformations*. London: Heinemann.
Bion, W.R. (1970, 1983). *Attention and Interpretation*. New York: Basic Books [Reprinted: London: Rowman & Littlefield, 2004].
Bion, W.R. (1974). *Brazillian Lectures, 1973 Sao Paulo, 1974, Rio de Janeiro/Sao Paulo*. London: Karnac.
Bion, W.R. (1992). *Cogitations*. Ed. F. Bion. London: Karnac.
Ogilve, J. (date) Personal communication.

21

THE ANALYST IS PRESENT

Viewing the psychoanalytic process as performance art[1]

Alan Michael Karbelnig

In 1896, when Freud coined the term "psychoanalysis" (Gay, 1988, p. 103), he created a technique specifically applicable to patients with mental disorders. Consonant with this initial view of the process, the first psychoanalysts treated individuals suffering from such disorders as obsessional neurosis, hysteria, and melancholia. Yet, even in those early years, Freud and other practitioners struggled with the nature of their work. Some considered psychoanalysis treatment for symptoms like anxiety or depression; others used it to address patients' concerns about work, relationships, and life. By the mid-20th century, the burgeoning controversy regarding the precise aims of psychoanalysis flowed into two distinct streams.

Many psychoanalysts remained devoted to the exclusively medical vision. They applied techniques like confronting ego defenses – exposing painful unconscious deficits or conflicts patients were masking – and thereby reducing psychological symptoms. They focused on the transference. Such psychoanalysts typically sought scientifically based sources of information. They pursued observational studies of infants, researched cognition and emotion, conducted outcome studies, and otherwise leaned towards scientism. They sought a logical–positivistic basis for psychoanalysis. They believed psychoanalysis would become one intervention among many, alongside psychopharmacology and cognitive-behavioral therapy.

Other psychoanalysts applied their techniques with broader strokes. They helped those with difficulties that defied traditional medical categorization, such as persons who felt socially alienated, failed to achieve romantic intimacies, felt personally inadequate, or found their lives meaningless. While not hostile to science, these psychoanalysts worked, wrote, and researched in these more humanistic realms. They sought information outside of their field – in literature, philosophy, and history – to support for their work. They believed these disciplines offered greater insights into human subjectivity. They viewed their work as hermeneutical and exploratory rather than as a process solely intended to cure illnesses. Orange (2011) notes that because of Freud's "stronger insistence on the status of psychoanalysis as a natural science, our awareness of psychoanalysis as hermeneutics has arrived only recently" (p. 2).

Despite the scientism versus humanism controversy, and regardless of their particular theoretical orientation (Freudian, Jungian, Kleinian, etc.), psychoanalysts have relied on four foundational tenets: the idea that an unconscious mind exists, that some kind of force or drive motivates human beings, that individuals tend to form repetitive psycho-behavioral patterns (the repetition compulsion), and that these patterns, as well as the contents of the unconscious, map onto the psychoanalytic relationship in the form of the transference. The four foundational themes were originally delineated by Freud (1914), and later elaborated upon by others including Lacan (1978), Rangell (2006), and Harari (2004). Psychoanalysts also attend to other signs of the unconscious, such as dreams or parapraxes, but these four elements have provided steady points of reference. Psychoanalysts bring no interventional technologies to the processes they facilitate. They offer reverie, containment, interpretation, confrontation, empathy, and more – to promote transformation. Whereas artistry certainly comprises a component of what other healing professionals provide, psychoanalysts work *entirely* within the inter-personal relationship, rendering the artful element of their services central. Inarguably distinct from each other, art and psychoanalysis nonetheless share critical features, by definition and by practice.

Previous views of psychoanalysis as art

Freud (1905) compared suggestion to painting and analysis to sculpture. He wrote that sculpture "proceeds per *via di levare*, since it takes away from the block of stone all that hides the surface of the statue contained in it" (p. 260). Loewald (1980), who considered his psychoanalytic work as artistic in nature, explicitly compared psychoanalysis to drama. He wrote, "In the mutual interaction of the good analytic hour, patient and analyst – each in his own way, and on his own mental level – become both artist and medium for each other" (Loewald, 1980, p. 369). Winnicott (1955) referred to "psychoanalysis as an art" (p. 24). Of him, Orange (2011) writes, "Both process and spirit embodied a two-person creative aliveness" (p. 162).

Bion (1965) described psychoanalytic work as a "transformation, analogous to the artist's painting that is a product of the particular artist's approach" (pp. 8–9). According to Jacobus (2005), Bion viewed the psychoanalytic encounter as "a site of turbulence, 'a mental space for further ideas which may yet be developed'" (p. 258). Years before Hoffman (1998) was writing, Bion (1991) had already noted the coparticipant nature of psychoanalysis. Szasz (1988) believed that psychoanalysts' "activities would constitute, and be classified as, art rather than science" (p. 208).

Bollas (1987) describes the psychoanalytic process as a performance in the sense that, to find their patients, psychoanalysts "must look for him within ourselves" (p. 202), adding "we are being taken into the patient's environmental idiom, and for considerable stretches of time we do not know who we are, what function we are meant to fulfill, or our fate as his object" (p. 202–203). Symington (2002), describing how patients engaged in psychoanalysis mourn, writing, "if the death is photographed, it does not become emotionally real; if it is painted, it does" (p. 68). More recently, Ringstrom (2001, 2007, 2008, 2012) emphasizes the role of improvization in the psychoanalytic process. He contends, as do I, that psychoanalysts must be emotionally present, prepared to respond to a variety of personalities.

Scholars from outside of psychoanalysis have similarly commented on the artistic, even theatrical, elements of the field. Burke (1966) writes, "The difference between a thing and a person is that the one merely *moves* whereas the other *acts*" (italics in original) (p. 53). In discussing psychoanalysis specifically, he offers a "dramatistic terminology (built around a definition of man as the symbol-using, symbol-misusing, symbol-making, and symbol-made animal)" (p. 63). Burke (1945) coined the phrase "dramatistic pentad" (p. 67), describing human motivation as presenting through act, scene, agent, agency, and purpose. He believed that, in understanding the unconscious, "dramatistic concepts of 'symbolic action'" (Burke, 1966, p. 73) must also be considered. Butler (1997, 2005) suggests that humans, on some level, perform their actions, their feelings, and their speech. Similarly, Orange (2011) observes how psychotherapies are, in general, focused on language. Psychoanalysts utilize elements of literary criticism as they illuminate the ideologies and narratives of their patients.

The artistic nature of the psychoanalytic process

Hoffman's (1998) dialectical-constructivist model of the psychoanalytic process offers a descriptive view without adhering to a specific psychoanalytic theory. It concisely defines the nature of the inter-personal, contractual service called psychoanalysis while highlighting its intensely creative, artistic nature. The dialectical component of the phrase refers to the manner in which psychoanalysts become engaged in *relationship* with their patients in dichotomous and paradoxical ways.

On the one hand, psychoanalysts become invited into any number of enactments propelled by their unconscious schemata, those of their patients, and the combination of the two – a concept captured by Ogden's (1994) idea of "the analytic third" (p. 4). Essentially all psychoanalytic theorists agree that the *unconscious inner world* or *the internal object world* – which I prefer to call *the internal drama* – becomes projected onto the psychoanalytic relationship itself. On the other hand, psychoanalysts pull away from their relationships with their patients – immersed with unconscious, dramatic themes – and reflect upon the interaction. They might construct models of what motivates patients, of the unconscious drama, of the repetition compulsion, or of the transference. They then intervene spontaneously, with interpretations, confrontations, reverie, or other methods – yet another example of psychoanalysis' creativity.

This innovative feature of psychoanalytic processes resides within the constructivist component of Hoffman's (1998) model. Psychoanalysis did not arise, as if by magic, from Freud's early writings. Its roots lie in millennia of writings in philosophy, history, political science, literature, and more. Psychoanalysts use the hand of human history – its humanism – in offering ideas about what motivates patients, how their unconscious internal dramas were forged, the nature of the repetition compulsion, and the "third" element (Ogden, 1994, p. 4). They behave like actors who similarly manage their emotional experiences while performing. They act differently on stage. Further, they adjust their theatrical work in reaction to the varied states or styles of different audiences. Thus, they occupy a distinct professional role and, regardless of their style of practice, modify their professional behavior to comport with patients' unique styles.

Psychoanalysis as performance art

The term "performance art," related to postmodernist traditions in Western culture, emerged during the 1960s and 1970s out of concepts of visual art. Its precursors include work by Antonin Artaud, Dada, the Situationists, Fluxus, Installation Art, and Conceptual Art (Parr, 2010; Goldberg, 2001; Goldberg and Anderson, 2004, McEvilley, 2012; Pena and Sifentes, 2011). Considered the antithesis of theater, performance art nonetheless features a relationship between performer and audience. It features "an event that cannot be repeated, captured, or purchased" (Parr, 2010, p. 25). Similarly, psychoanalytic encounters create an ephemeral encounter each session, one that cannot be repeated or captured. Pena and Sifentes (2011) would likely consider a psychoanalytic session a performance "exercise" (p. 35).

Performance artist Marina Abramovic (Cotter, 2010), in her performance art piece entitled *The Artist Is Present*, asked visitors to choose between walking around the two naked persons or walking between them – a decision intended to provoke an emotional experience. Like performance artists, psychoanalysts offer *experiences*. Even more classically oriented psychoanalysts provoke and disrupt; they at least interpret, or interfere with, the repetition compulsion in some way.

Psychoanalysts practice performance art in at least three distinct ways. First, psychoanalysts give with their actual *beings* Lacan (1960, 1978, 1979, 2002). In addition to offering patients their words (as in interpretations) and their desire (in their pursuit of unconscious themes), psychoanalysts lend their bodies, or their "psyche-somas" (Winnicott, 1992, p. 185), to their patients. They allow their patients to project onto them, using them as receptors, screens, or containers (Bion, 1965). The psychoanalysts' art form parallels that of actors whose cliché about their work – my body is my instrument – equally applies. Unsurprisingly, psychoanalysts often refer to, and write about, en-*act*-ments.

Describing working through transference processes, Butler (2005) explains how psychoanalysts create different ways of relating to others. Phillips (2012) similarly describes how psychoanalysts affect the transference by interfering with "our culturally inherited roles or parts or options" (p. 183). Bollas (2013) privileges the psychoanalysts' actual physical presence, their existence, as a transformational vehicle. These authors unite in their vision of psychoanalysts as giving of their *being*.

Second, much like the way painters describe the apprehension of the blank canvas, psychoanalysts encounter sessions with fear of the unknown. Of course, excessive anxiety early in an analytic process may be understood in terms of possible projective identification, but any sense of certitude – particularly based on theoretical conceptions – risks objectifying patients. As noted earlier, some patients speak of intense competition with their fathers, others present dream material, others feel the envy and rage described so poignantly by Klein and her followers, and still others experience hungry deficits of the type described by such theorists as Winnicott (1965, 1992), Balint (1979), Kohut (1977), and Brandchaft (2002). Psychoanalysts may be the *most* artistic in their openness in receiving the wide variation of patient presentations.

Finally, psychoanalysts and their patients choose from an infinite number of possible ways of understanding the phenomena they explore together. Psychoanalyst-patient dyads discover widely divergent ways of viewing unconscious internal dramas, motivations, the meaning of compulsively repeated themes and of the transference. Grotstein (1990) recommends psychoanalysts "become immersed in the language of the patient" (p. 182). What could be more spontaneous, intimate, and artistic than developing a shared language with patients unique to each psychoanalytic relationship?

Psychoanalysts' freedom to select from such a broad palette – consistent with Hoffman's (1998) model – provides further support for the foundational artistic foundation of their endeavors. They are tasked with helping patients animate models of self that are varied, mobile, and capable of continuous revision, especially beyond the consulting room. The transformational *experiences* in the consulting room allow patients to become persons, enacting an authentic self that exercises its right to be, and to be anew, across various social contexts.

Two performance pieces

These two psychoanalytic scenes exemplify how psychoanalysts work to achieve transformation through the performance art called psychoanalysis. Psychoanalysts enter their sessions "refraining from memory and desire" (Bion, 1970, p. 31), utilize the four basic tenets, and ready themselves for spontaneity and improvization. Depending on an essentially infinite number of variables, psychoanalysts might interrupt their patients' speech or they might not; they attune to patients' emotional states at some points and distract them at others; they ask questions at times and avoid doing so at others; sometimes they comment on a transference theme but other times they will wait; exploration of motivational forces will be relevant at some points but not at others. In accordance with the dialectical-constructivist model, psychoanalysts *perform* in a certain unique fashion. These case examples are fictionalized to protect the identity of the patients:

First Scene*:* A particularly startling point of urgency occurred after treating Mr. A, a young man age 17, towards the end of the first year of psychoanalytic psychotherapy. He consulted me, at his parents' request, on a twice-weekly basis for two years. I felt I made no progress in helping him during the first year. He behaved aggressively in school. He refused to do homework assignments. He challenged the authority of teachers. The most obvious feature of his personal history surrounded his having two likely sources of rage, both of which he consciously denied: he had an autistic younger brother, his only sibling, and he felt that this brother had taken much of his parents' attention away from him. He adamantly opposed any suggestion that these situations had injured him, saying, "My parents love us both equally." He yearned to seek employment in law enforcement. His parents were physicians. Mr. A believed that his career choice would either demean him, his family, or both. When I interviewed his parents right after the treatment started, I found no evidence of their judging him for what appeared to be his authentic interest. On the contrary, they seemed to be supportive of him. His mother behaved in a particularly loving fashion towards her sons.

Towards the end of that first year of the analysis, I began to feel anxious that his parents would feel frustrated by his slow progress. That image entered my psyche-soma at that point, creating tension, conflict, and irritation. The acting out that had brought him to my attention continued with little change. Mr. A and I had discussed, repeatedly, the potential meanings of his anger, the way his behavior at school impacted others, the underlying need to for him to be in control (and therefore not vulnerable), and his general lack of empathy. He entertained these theories intellectually, but quickly rejected them. He regularly distracted me from the analytic process by asking about my work; he particularly enjoyed asking me pointedly about other individuals he would see in my waiting room.

One day, and without warning, Mr. A was speaking about his future when he made this simple slip, "I'm not sure that I'll ever have money because I'll *just* be working as a cop." I heard that slip of the tongue like a clap of thunder. Here is our exchange:

ANALYST: Did you hear what you just said?

MR. A: I don't think so. I only said that I wouldn't make that much money.

ANALYST: You qualified your statement with a '*just.*' That was the first time I've ever heard you describe your plans for your life in a devalued way.

MR. A: What do you mean? (He seemed defensive.)

ANALYST: Mr. A, you know what I mean. You said it. (I felt irritated.) You put yourself down.
   I just realized that it's not your parents you need to worry about. It is *you*.

MR. A: Holy shit. (A long silence ensued.)

ANALYST: Yes . . . you see that now.

MR. A: (Another long silence occurred). Oh my god, oh shit. . . . I've never felt it like that, like
   I'm bad in some way. I could never get your point because I expected that it came from
   my parents, but it doesn't. It comes from me. It's the way I feel about *me*.

ANALYST: Yes, exactly that, you feel as if you are bad in some way. And sadly that has become
   your creation.

This unique moment represented a turning point in this young man's life. The ensuing year
was markedly different from the first. Mr. A's defenses became more pliable. He became emotionally vulnerable. He was intrigued about the type of relationship he had with himself. He
felt the pain of his own self-attack. These developments led to an ensuing year characterized
by his working through his self-judgment and his pain at that internal assault. Gradually, he
retracted his projections onto his teachers back into himself, lessening his anger. He became
more engaged in his work with me, i.e. the distracting commentary regarding other patients
abruptly stopped. The process ended with his enjoying a newfound self-respect. He understood how he felt inadequate living in a world with two highly academically achieving parents. He developed a greater appreciation for his parents' positive qualities. He terminated the
treatment with greater self-respect.

Second Scene: This example also highlights an urgency point that similarly altered the
course of the analytic process and the patient's life. In stark contrast to Mr. A, Dr. B – an
African-American professor of anthropology – had an extremely negative experience with
her parents, particularly her mother, during her childhood years. A highly intelligent, attractive 40-year-old woman, Dr. B sought psychoanalysis due to chronic depressive symptoms.
She was the second of three children, the only daughter. Her father, an attorney often away
at work, was critical and self-centered. Her mother, a surgeon, seemed to compete with her
from infancy. Dr. B has many early memories of her mother calling her "stupid" or "ugly."

Dr. B's mother practiced with another surgeon. He molested Dr. B first at ages 4 and 5, and
then again at age 14 when he sexually assaulted her. The mother, who was having an affair
with this same medical colleague, defended him. When Dr. B told her mother, she insisted
Dr. B had fabricated the events. The evolution of the chronic mental pain in Dr. B – the
extreme feelings of emptiness, emotional insecurity, and phobia of intimacy – was unusually
obvious. Equally so was her terribly negative image of herself, a self-valuation that contributed to her compulsion to repetitively choose abusive romantic partners.

This particular interchange occurred about two years into the psychoanalysis, after many
layers of defense had been penetrated, and while we together intensely scrutinized the
transference.

DR. B: If you continue to move that close to me, to follow me so well, to know me, I will
   hurt you.

ANALYST: How?

DR. B: Remember that dream I had, of the glass window with the wooden frame around it?
   And I am on a grass field, lying down, covered by it?

ANALYST: Yes.

DR. B: I'm now imagining nothing but the glass. The frame is gone. As I try to stand, the glass shatters. You are there, trying to help me up, but the shards of glass are pointing towards you. (She began sobbing intensely.)

ANALYST: And you fear I will be hurt.

DR. B: More than just hurt, bloodied and killed.

ANALYST: You feel fury to the point of violence towards me. You believe you could kill me.

DR. B: (She entered a semi-psychotic state and appearing agitated.) It is real. I'm stabbing you right now. (She sobbed again.) The glass is cutting you up.

ANALYST: (I kept silent for a minute or two.) You feel your *being* itself is dangerous.

DR. B: Because it is. I will poison you for sure, and you won't see me anymore. You will vanish. You will not have me as a patient.

ANALYST: (I remained quiet for another minute or two.) Dr. B, we are here, together, at the core of your open wound. I'm sitting right here, listening to you, listening to your fury.

This exemplifies a transformational encounter, to use my phrase, or a "transformation" (Bion, 1965). According to Jacobus (2005), Bion would have viewed the scene just described as occurring at the "site of turbulence" (p. 258). The relationship between Dr. B and I had fallen into an extremely regressed state: Dr. B experienced herself, in the anguished present, as the enraged infant experiencing homicidal affect towards caretakers projected onto me. I contained her painful and aggressive state. I interpreted how her childhood trauma had understandably elicited rage and how it was also accompanied by the conviction that she was the unworthy child deserving of criticism and neglect. In time, I competed with Dr. B's attachment to her internal objects (referring here to Fairbairn's [1952] idea that all psychoanalysts compete with their patients' relationships with their internal families). Inter-subjectivists or Relationalists may well have not stayed with the patient's aggression for as long as I did. Perhaps they would have offered the interpretations – which I only introduced later – during that session itself.

Dr. B's depression lifted for several weeks immediately following this intense encounter. In the subsequent months, we re-visited these encounters with depth and intensity – "shattering" describes them best. The chronic depression subsided for longer periods of time, revealing that, to use Fairbairn's (1952) own words, the "bad" (p. 66) self was being "exorcised" (p. 70) by the then-deepened process. The alteration in Mr. B's identity relates to Butler's (2005) ideas regarding the performative elements of self-concept. She describes how individuals "make a sequence and link one event to another, offering motivations to illuminate the bridge, making patterns clear, identifying certain events or moments of recognition as pivotal, even making certain recurring patterns as fundamental" (Butler, 2005, p. 66).

Again, patients and psychoanalysts are both performing. Butler's conception, as applied to identity, differs substantially from my conception of the performative aspects of the clinical psychoanalyst. Burke's dramatistic pentad comes closer to illuminating the psychoanalytic process in which, to use his five words – act, scene, agent, agency, and purpose – dynamically unfold throughout each psychoanalytic encounter. In the course of the psychoanalytic process, both psychoanalysts and patients perform, but how they act, their purposes, their responsibilities, their roles, and their objectives diverge. Each psychoanalytic encounter is unique. Psychoanalysts' performances can be neither duplicated nor mechanized.

Although psychoanalysts may ascribe to formal theories, no theory will be performed the same way because their "singularities" (Ruti, 2012) vary with their personalities. Thus, a single analyst's subscribed theory combined with that same analyst's personality renders every performance unique. (Even carefully written theatrical scripts are never performed the same way twice.) Using their means of engaging like brushes, or like choreography, and utilizing their creative interpretation of the work of analysts past, psychoanalysts perform their transformational work.

Conclusion

Psychoanalysts are neither research scientists objectively observing inter-personal processes, nor are they medical practitioners applying procedures. They are, instead, vulnerable human beings engaged in a profession – one most rare in an era when all that cannot be measured, weighed, or quantified in some fashion tends to be viewed as lacking legitimacy. Their aid primarily takes the form of exploring unconscious schemata, personal motivation, and repetitive psycho-behavioral themes. They explore how these map onto the psychoanalytic relationship. Their work or, more accurately, their performances with their patients are nonlinear, dynamic, and unpredictable.

From its earliest formation, psychoanalysis rebelled against the profession to which it was bound. It would not be strictly medicine; it differed from education. It became a field of its own. It continued to evolve away from other traditional definitions of most professions, certainly far from the typical services provided by industrialized health care. Psychoanalytic practice resides firmly in the realm of humanities, specifically art, and more specifically performance art. It is no accident that Freud pulled Oedipus from a staging of Sophocles's *Oedipus the King*. First performed in Greece, c. 429 BCE, and highly popular with Western European audiences in Paris and Vienna in the early 20th century, these theatrical productions led many philosophers and psychoanalysts – not just Freud – to develop fundamental ideas concerning the transformative power of art and performance.

This more artistic vision of psychoanalysis will likely require further cultural accommodation. By definition, art brings something new into being. The English word "create" derives from the Indo-European root, "ker," kere, which means to grow, to make, to create (Weiner, 2000, p. 41). Typically, new ideas in psychoanalysis encounter, at least initially, skepticism and resistance to change. Perhaps Toynbee (1962) put it best when he wrote, "A fatuous passivity towards the present springs from an infatuation with the past" (p. 261). Psychoanalysts may struggle to embrace primarily artistic nature of their clinical work. They creatively work to help patients to grow, to create, and to come into being. The psychoanalytic project would benefit by relinquishing its *infatuation with the past* and breaking its reductionist comparisons to science. In truth, psychoanalysts, in conjunction with their patients, practice performance art, bringing relief to suffering that defies description through language alone.

Note

1 This chapter consists of a shortened and revised version of the paper of the same title printed in an online edition of *Psychoanalytic Psychology* in 2014, doi: dx.doi.org/10.1037/a0037332.

References

Balint, M. (1979). *The Basic Fault*. London/New York: Tavistock Publications.
Bion, W.R. (1965). *Transformations*. London: Tavistock.

Bion, W.R. (1970). *Attention and Interpretation*. London: Tavistock.

Bion, W.R. (1991). *A Memoir of the Future*. New York: Karnac.

Bollas, C. (1987). *The Shadow of the Object: Psychoanalysis of the Unthought Known*. New York: Columbia University Press.

Bollas, C. (2013). *China on the Mind*. New York: Routledge.

Brandchaft, B. (2002). Reflections on the intersubjective foundations of the sense of self. *Psychoanalytic Dialogues* 12(5): 727–745.

Burke, K. (1945). *Grammar of Motives*. Berkeley: University of California Press.

Burke, K. (1966). *Language as Symbolic Action: Essays on Life, Literature, and Method*. Berkeley: University of California Press.

Butler, J. (1997). *Excitable Speech: The Politics of Performance*. New York: Routledge.

Butler, J. (2005). *Giving an Account of Oneself*. New York: Fordham University Press.

Cotter, H. (2010, March 12). Performance art preserved, in the flesh. *The New York Times*, p. C25.

Fairbairn, W.R.D. (1952). *Psychoanalytic Studies of the Personality*. New York, NY: Routledge.

Freud, S. (1953). On psychotherapy. In J. Strachey (Ed. & Trans.), *The Standard Edition of the Complete Psychological Works of Sigmund Freud (Vol. 7)*. (Original work published 1905 [1904]).

Freud, S. (1958). Remembering, repeating, and working-through: Further recommendations on the technique of psycho-analysis II. In J. Strachey (Ed. & Trans.), *The Standard Edition of the Complete Psychological Works of Sigmund Freud (Vol. 12)*. (Original work published 1914).

Gay, P. (1988). *Freud: A Life for Our Time*. New York: W.W. Norton & Company.

Goldberg, R. (2001). *Performance Art: From Futurism to the Present*, 3rd ed. New York, NY: Thames & Hudson.

Goldberg, R. and L. Anderson (2004). *Performance: Live art since the 60s*. New York, NY: Thames & Hudson.

Grotstein, J.S. (1990). The contribution of attachment theory and self-regulation theory to the therapeutic alliance. *Modern Psychoanalysis* 15: 169–184.

Harari, R. (2004). *Lacan's Four Fundamental Concepts of Psychoanalysis: An Introduction*. New York: Other Press.

Hoffman, I. (1998). *Ritual and Spontaneity in the Psychoanalytic Process: A Dialectical-Constructivist View*. New York, NY: Routledge.

Jacobus, M. (2005). *The Poetics of Psychoanalysis: In the Wake of Klein*. London: Oxford University Press.

Kohut, H. (1977). *The Restoration of the Self*. Madison, CT: International Universities Press.

Lacan, J. (1960). *The Seminar of Jacques Lacan, Book IV: The Ethics of Psychoanalysis*. Trans. D. Porter. Ed. J. A. Miller. New York, NY: W.W. Norton & Company.

Lacan, J. (1978). *The Seminar of Jacques Lacan, Book XI: The Four Fundamental Concepts of Psychoanalysis*. Trans. A. Sheriden. Ed. J. Miller. New York: W.W. Norton & Company.

Lacan, J. (1979). The neurotic's individual myth. *Psychoanalytic Quarterly* 48: 405–425.

Lacan, J. (2002). *Ecrits*. Trans. B. Fink. New York, NY: W. W. Norton & Company.

Loewald, H.W. (1980). Psychoanalysis as art and the fantasy character of the psychoanalytic situation. In *Papers on Psychoanalysis*, pp. 352–371. New Haven, CT: Yale University Press.

McEvilley, T. (2012). *The Triumph of Anti-art: Conceptual and Performance Art in the Formation of Postmodernism*. Kingston, NY: McPherson & Company.

Ogden, T. (1994). The analytic third: Working with intersubjective clinical facts. *International Journal of Psychoanalysis* 75: 3–19.

Orange, D. (2011). *The Suffering Stranger*. New York: Routledge.

Parr, A. (2010). *The Deleuze Dictionary*. Edinburgh: Edinburgh University Press.

Pena, G. and R. Sifentes (2011). *Exercises for Rebel Artists: Radical Performance Pedagogy*. New York, NY: Routledge.

Phillips, A. (2012). *Missing Out: In Praise of the Unlived Life*. New York: Farrar, Straus, and Giroux.

Rangell, L. (2006). An analysis of the course of psychoanalysis. *Psychoanalytic Psychology* 23(2): 217–238.

Ringstrom, P. (2001). Cultivating the improvisational in psychoanalytic treatment. *Psychoanalytic Dialogues* 11(5): 727–754.

Ringstrom, P. (2007). Scenes that write themselves: Improvisational moments in relational psychoanalysis. *Psychoanalytic Dialogues* 17(1): 69–99.

Ringstrom, P. (2008). Improvisational moments in self-psychological relational psychoanalysis. In P. Buirski and A. Kottler (Eds.), *New Developments in Self Psychology Practice*. Lanham, MS: Jason Aronson.

Ringstrom, P. (2012). Principles of improvisation: A model of therapeutic play in relational psychoanalysis. In L. Aron and A. Harris (Eds.), *Relational Psychoanalysis*, pp. 447–478. Harris, NY: Taylor & Francis.

Ruti, M. (2012). *The Singularity of Being: Lacan and the Immortal Within*. New York: Fordham University Press.

Symington, N. (2002). *A Pattern of Madness*. London: Karnac.

Szasz, T. (1988). *The Myth of Psychotherapy*. Syracuse: Syracuse University Press.

Toynbee, A. (1962). *A Study of History* (Vol. 4). London: Oxford University Press.

Weiner, R. (2000). *Creativity and Beyond*. Albany: State University of New York Press.

Winnicott, D.W. (1955). Metapsychological and clinical aspects of regression within the psycho-analytical set-up. *The International Journal of Psychoanalysis* 36: 16–26.

Winnicott, D.W. (1965). *The Maturational Processes and the Facilitating Environment: Studies in the Theory of Emotional Development*. London: Hogarth.

Winnicott, D.W. (1992). *Through Paediatrics to Psycho-analysis*. New York, NY: Brunner-Routledge.

22

"A MEMOIR OF THE FUTURE"

Reading proof and enactment

Guelfo Margherita

Introduction

Bringing this paper to the 8th International Bion Conference, *Psych'O'analysis: explorations in truth*, in Los Angeles in 2014, I play the role of the presenter because it was a work written not only by me but by the whole group.

The author of this work was the *T.I.R.A.M.I.S.U. – Study-group – Naples, Italy (Team Italiano di Ricerca sulle Attività Mentali degli Insiemi Sistemici Umani)* of which I am coordinator. The participants and writers of the paper are: Pasquale Alborino, Guelfo Margherita, Orietta Occhiuzzi, Giuseppe Palladino, Renato Pizzuti, Salvatore Rotondi, Raffaele Russo, Eva Trifuoggi, Monica Vanni and Licia Vetere.

An amateur video of the paper is also available on YouTube at the link: https://m.youtube.com/watch?v=lfJir0w8UAk. It is acted in Italian with English subtitles. The editing and direction of the video are by Salvatore Rotondi. Part of the video was shown during the "*Juegos Bionianos*" in Bariloche (Argentina) 2–5 May 2013.

★★★

The aim of this presentation is to relate an original approach to the study of *A Memoir of the future* consisting in grasping, through a group experience of reading, re-writing and reciting, depth and chiaroscuro otherwise precluded to linear understanding through the individual reading.

The produced paper and related video are an attempt to export it, from our group to a wider auditorium trying to involve you too, by immersion, in our attempt to align as much as possible our group mind with the mind of Bion, to investigate his creative excitement and awe, to become parts of the atmosphere of a Bion-ic matrioska.

The group did not try to understand the text, but tried to grasp it participating in the visceral experience to cross the context-scenery that the text was creating alongside the fantasy of the group brain.

The reading group that gathered one evening a month for one year in my office for four hours, has shared, on the stage of a "Bionian Symposium", taken food, mouthfuls of reading

Bion and bodies, emotions and minds of the participants themselves; it devours, with similar voracity, the all, everything, homogenizing and dreaming the free associations suggested by the text (α-function) in order to rewrite a new script, to act and film, using the language of achievement and enactment.

The convivial field, as a dynamic scenery, oriented group, dream, bodies, emotions, languages, thought, expression and institution; as if they were tools of a common attractor that asymptotically tended to the "O" that the mind of Bion had alchemically disguised in the text to induce us to look for it within ourselves. So we studied Bion in the transformations of the group mind involved in receiving it.

The circulating questions were: What does learning mean? Or grabbing? Or feeling?

Should the orientation of K → O be done by reasoning? Or feeling? Or intuition?

The group, searching for its own Bion, invented the ludic provocation to rewrite the text transforming roles and scenery but leaving unchanged the dynamic entanglement of desire, awe, confusion, fantasy.

The complexity of the hidden "non-sense" could be grasped with a group reading that frays the perspective binocularity in a poli-ocularity; as a mirror room reflecting a multiple reality; so a dreaming atmosphere was created (vision of the eye of the fly). Bion therefore must be read in a group.

The capacity of the negative taught us to wait for Godot accepting the "absolute non-understanding of anything" as a mental state of incommunicability that becomes paradox and even language to communicate itself.

★★★

Prologue – decalogue

1 "A Memoir of the Future" is a play for the theater.
2 The scene (container) in which it takes place is an invaded nation, my body, my group of friends, different moments of my growth, the borders of my mind, all rolled into one.
3 The actors (contents) play as invaders and invaded, as real or virtual characters, as my organs, as my ways of development, as my thoughts and emotions. Their interaction is similar to the psychoanalytic operation that constructed parts of my mind, as well as yours and ours.
4 Every scene (especially those regarding my mind) is painstakingly constructed by actors using the language of achievement.
5 The individual study can bring one only to a linear and academic understanding. The sense, given without chiaroscuro, appears thus to be necessarily a false one.
6 The complexity of the hidden nonsense could be only understood through a group reading, using that particular collective vertex that I call "the eye of the fly". *Bion must be read in a group.*
7 To exercise to the end our right of non-understanding (suspension of memory and desire), the vertex of "the eye of fly" must be conjugated with the language of

achievement and with the enactment; space and body will be so involved. *Bion must be recited in a group.*

8   The psychoanalytic research between illusion and reality, between objects and representations, can be carried out only through the exploration of the caesura that divides them and by filling it with the concrete production of a language. In our workshop we tried to use group, bodies and minds to read, rewrite and act "A Memoir of the future".

9   The capacity of the negative taught us to wait for Godot, tolerating the fact of understanding absolutely nothing as a mental state of uncommunicability that becomes a paradox and a language.

10   The Za-zen is the sudden lightning that, coming from the depth of improbability, lights up, from a new vertex, a restructured system. It is often produced by the beating that the master inflicts to our "Ego".

★★★

Scene I – *Waiting for God- "O"* (Beckett, 1952)

VLADIMIR AND ESTRAGON (*dressed as tramps stand under a tree on a country road*) (Bion, 1975)

ESTRAGON: Can you give me an idea what this is about?

VLADIMIR: Psycho-analysis, I believe.

ESTRAGON: Are you sure? It looks a queer affair.

VLADIMIR: It is a queer affair – like psycho-analysis. You'd have to read it.

ESTRAGON: How much does it cost?

VLADIMIR: It says it on the book. You would have to read it as well though, or maybe to write it.

ESTRAGON: Of course. But I don't think I can afford the time or money.

VLADIMIR: Nor do I.

ESTRAGON: But haven't you read it? Or maybe written it?

VLADIMIR: Yes, in a way.

ESTRAGON: You're a queer salesman. I'm only waiting to know . . .

VLADIMIR: I'm not the salesman, I cannot sell something unsaleable. I only wrote it. Maybe haven't read it. No one wants to read it, it's too absurd. It is still waiting for an understanding that will never come.

ESTRAGON: You have a strange way of answering, I just want to know. . . .

VLADIMIR: Well, I will tell you about *Salvatore*, opening a page by chance and suddenly vomiting. It wasn't a beautiful sight; pieces of soul were floating on vomited. *Pino* then remembered how the courtiers followed in the cemetery the death King of Ur.

I wanted to run away. But the sneaky and youthful look of *Anfitruo* held me back. So I looked at that vomit, and touched it, breathed it and hated it. I closed my eyes for a long while. My mind was stubborn. How to get to the truth? *Orietta* questioned the oracle, but the oracle, as expected, answered with an enigma. In that moment *Derrida* said: "Do not think about the content of this text but about the idea that generated it". Magically clots assembled the two hemispheres of a unique brain. The right hemisphere was *Licia as a* sweet and spiral-like narrator; the left one was Derrida speaking through the mouth of Eva. In the middle my corpus callosum was trying to produce sense to the formless infinite. My corpus callosum met many others, everyone bearing their own sense. *Renato*, who loves to complicate things, showed us many other senses: the sixth sense; the double sense; the reverse sense. I was stunned! *Pasquale* was speaking about pulsating sun. Was it an hallucination or a natural phenomenon that linear logic could explain? None of this. The calm voice of *Anfitruo* said: "It's a myth that, like the dream interprets and orders reality as images and not as logical concepts". Reopening my eyes and looking at the same vomit without memory or desire, it appears now to me as a gift that the Providence brought from my "act of faith".

ESTRAGON: Do you feel any wiser now than you were at the beginning?

VLADIMIR: Well, I do not know. Surely older by one year.

ESTRAGON: Oh, I beg your pardon! I quite thought . . .

VLADIMIR: I'm flattered, but I'm only the author.

ESTRAGON: May I have your autograph?

VLADIMIR: No, I cannot write. As a matter of fact the book is mine and it is not for sale anymore.

★★★

Scene II – *The Banquet*

The scene is the previous one. The tree is now full of leaves and on every leaf is written a name, for example: Anzieu, Beckett, Borges, Derrida, Brecht, Calvino, Shakespeare, Plato, Keats, Osho, Matte Blanco, Eco, Freud, Stanislawski, Artaud, Pirandello, Jung, Moreno, Corrao, Kafka, Sofocles.

The Characters enter the stage slowly, someone carrying cushions that will be put in a circle, someone will carry a lamp, or books, recording tools, leaflets, food (bread, taralli, salame, cheese, wine).

The voices of the characters speaking to each other, mix up creating a buzz; everyone speaks as he begins to eat; someone laughs, someone keeps silent (seems absorbed). Also participate One liver o more (in angry silence because they do not understand anything), Perhaps a group, Everyone of us and any part of us.

NARRATOR WHO LOSES HIS TRAIN OF THOUGHT *(moving from a corner of the scene with the task to narrate what's going on)*: I'll tell you the story of the six characters, or more, looking for an author, trying to animate, re-animate, Bion in their own heads.

PROPHET WHO SPEAKS THROUGH SENTENCES OF BION *(with an emphatic tone)*: "Reject your memory, reject the future time of your desire; forget them both to leave space for the new idea. May be it is hovering in the room seeking an abode for a thought. An idea that nobody claims".

(Every guest holds still the position in which he was before while listening. Someone is staring to the prophet with a skeptical air and someone joins hands in prayer.)

MEMORY *(in a conversational tone)*: An unknown thought is the meeting between the reader and the writer; between the speaker and the listener; and as I cannot understand who I really am, (reader or writer, speaker or the one who keeps silent) I go back to seeking who I was, the one I fear to find later, at the end.

PROPHET *(emphatic)*: I could even find that I was better and different than the one I am now. Until I will exist.

(Desire enters the scene covered with a veil.)

DESIRE *(slyly)*: The meaning to fulfill an empty "signifier" could be incomprehensible, inexhaustible.

NARRATOR: Desire is carrying books, takes off the veil and puts the books on the floor in the middle of the room, near the food.

(The group sits around the books and the food. Then everyone greedily feeds themselves with both.)

PROPHET: Let's try to put ourselves in that dialogue between Wilfred and Francesca that we could call: "I hate to examine my own vomit".

Dialogue (Bion, 1979a)

FRANCESCA: Are you there?

WILFRED: You have woke me too soon, I must –

FRANCESCA: Oh, do get a move on – we shall never finish this index at this rate – three pages an hour! It's endless –

WILFRED: It's very hard work – and whenever am I going to get any writing done?

GROUP: We are asking instead, When can we finally get any reading of yours?

FRANCESCA: This is writing – and a necessary part of the trilogy.

GROUP: This way of writing about ourselves is perhaps the most important part of our reading.

WILFRED: I hate having to examine my own vomit.

GROUP: So do we and to mix to it our own vomit.

FRANCESCA: All right – let me know when you have a free hour and the inclination –

GROUP: Never!!! What's up? Is it my time now?

WILFRED: I never have. Let's get on with it –

FRANCESCA: I can arrange my schedule to suit you –

WILFRED: For Christ's sake let's get the ruddy thing done now!

GROUP: Oh yeah, lest he doesn't want anymore.

FRANCESCA: It's no good trying to do it if you are in a bad temper. I shall do some gardening.

GROUP: We are fed up too; we will open the window of our imagination and walk, by ourselves, in your garden!

NARRATOR *(goes to the tree, pulls up a leaf and reads)*: Beckett.

SAMUEL BECKETT *(who just finished his analysis with Bion)*:

What is the word (Beckett, 1988)

> folly –
> folly for to – for to –
> what is the word –
> folly from this – all this –

. . . (and is goes on reading his poem to the end) . . .
what is the word

Ah! And, at least, this is the end.

MEMORY: In spite of Bion it seems that this analysis did not work so good. *(Then she goes up to the tree and pulls out a leaf and reads:)* Borges.

BORGES AND HIS EGO: I am Borges; now I will tell you about Borges and me (Borges, 1960). "It's up to the other, to Borges that things happen. It doesn't cost me anything to confess that he obtained some good pages, but those pages cannot save me, perhaps because the good they do doesn't belong to anyone, not even to the other, but they belong to the language or the tradition. Some years ago I tried to get rid of him, going from the mythologies of the suburbs to the games with time and the infinite; but those games now belong to Borges and I have to invent something else. So my life is an escape and I lose everything and everything belongs to oblivion, or it belongs to the other. I don't know, between us, who is writing this page".

MEMORY *(goes to the tree and pulls out a leaf and reads on it)*: Brecht. As taught to us by this fellow (Brecht, 1957): now is the moment of the didactic poster. Damn, I'm looking forward to the time this tree becomes useless: then we will call it the tree of the senseless sense.

First didactic board

Staging for a deconstruction

- *Setting the scene*: **The mind as a theater and as an actor allows thoughts to be experienced in order to be thought about. This happens through the loss of the sense, the orgiastic chaos, the muddling up of plans, or in other words, through madness.**
- **The theater brings one back to the origin (zero, the <O>, the full stop).**
- **Deconstruction (the one in which children pull toys apart) is not purely negative, it is a prelude to understanding. It is not just an irresponsible game.**
- **It can show connections and reveal frames.**
- **A Dervish dance that puts us in the right brain, such as the setting of Allan Schore (2012); at its center a binocular corpus callosum for giving depth and stability to the formless universe.**

★★★

Scene III – *The Spiral of Crono-tope*

NARRATOR: The group is a circle, a ring that, once dynamized, will get involved. Confused in the time, it will become the spiral of space-time. In the center there is Thought that, spreading out on to the ground, waits for the voice of desire.

GROUP: I am the ring waiting for the illumination to become a spiral!

DESIRE: I would like a focusing that would burn the moment in which I began to think to measure where the beginning and where the end are.

NARRATOR: From the center of the group thought begins to change position: He sits, then slowly he stands up and says

THOUGHT: I don't feel I am practicable right now.

(Thinker departs from the group and says to Thought)

THINKER USED FOR CATALOGUING THOUGHTS: You were in the formless infinite, why did you choose to bore just me?

THOUGHT: I am suspended in this scene, waiting for ideas to come.

THINKER *(looks and points at the group)*: You can find there a different idea for any of those heads.

NARRATOR: A "We" with many "You", rescued in the atmosphere, looks at himself in the mirror, doubles itself, copies itself, pretends not to be; becomes true and then false, till it becomes a bright beam towards the oblivion. Then there is the one who remains and settles, but staying still falls asleep and risks to die, to sleep, perchance to dream?

INK FLOWING AS BLOOD TO FILL WORDS WITH LIGHTS AND COLORS *(takes the line of partici-pants by their hands and leads them to move around and exchange their places)*: The participants mingle and change their places, while the present hides itself in the page where I'm liv-ing. The participants, as they were words, mix themselves and change their places as in kaleidoscope. They create new sentences, ideas, colored with my blood, that are pulled in the books of BION by a vortex. The books on the center of the stage are piled one over the other as if building an altar.

Dialogue (Bion, 1979b)

WILFRED: Are you there?

FRANCESCA: Don't interrupt me – I'm trying to finish this index.

WILFRED: I wondered what you had been doing these last few months.

GROUP: An index, a glossary, perhaps, a beam of intense darkness.

FRANCESCA: Well, since you went off on an extended trip I thought I'd better have a go at completing the job we started so long ago.

WILFRED: We were aiming high, weren't we? An index, glossary, notes, a book in itself, the definitive volume that would illuminate the obscurities –

GROUP: It closed us several openings, instead.

FRANCESCA: I only hope it can stand up to scrutiny in its final form. By the way, I'm going to call it 'A Key'.

WILFRED: What is it supposed to open?

FRANCESCA: A few small chinks perhaps. Anyway, it's refreshingly short. Have you any suggestions?

WILFRED: How about 'The Long Week-end'?

GROUP: Waiting for whom? Godot? We can't stand him anymore!

FRANCESCA: Have you forgotten? That's supposed to be the title of your autobiography.

WILFRED: More words, words, words – how can you stand it? Excuse me, I must get back to my cubby-hole.

GROUP: We want to sleep too; especially when we run into bloodless words.

FRANCESCA: Sweet dreams.

Second didactic board

The difference

- Deconstruction displays the interdependence between the oppositional terms and brings out a third: the difference.
- The difference indicates that two things are different and it also indicates the act of differing in the sense of temporally postponing.
- How can it be shown on stage, though? Do brightness and emptiness do the trick? Do they reveal the difference between the continuous and the discrete and the softening of the chiaroscuro upon the chronological differences?
- The light of a candle in the center of the group to conjure up in the mind intense effects of light and dark shades. The hyper-abstract falls thus onto the real in a firecracker fashion.
- The difference becomes overwhelming when the mind is unable to tolerate the splendor of the Mystic.
- There is always a tendency towards making new gods (BION -> DION) when things cannot be grasped by the mind.

$\star\star\star$

Scene IV – *The Ritual of the Burial*

NARRATOR: The group is waiting for the airplane of ideas that lands on the "tabula rasa" airport. In the room the group keeps a deafening-noise like of silence, all the participants protect themselves with their arms on their head as if they were frightened by the ideas. The sacred word of Bion is about to land.

(Some leaflets are falling from the ceiling scattering all around the room)

THINKER: Vomited words that do not belong to anyone, neither the writer nor the reader.

GROUP: A funeral is necessary to recover the vitality of a thought.

MEMORY: Everyone keeps an uptight silence; in the coffin, beside the death body, there are the pages of books. The dead writer buried inside "A memoire of the future"; it is there that he will meet the soul that will narrate him.

NARRATOR: The airplane of the ideas left the "Guelfo" airport empty after the funeral of the emperor of Ur. All the participants kept silent, moved in front of the coffin where the dead body of the emperor was lying among many written pages, floating on his own vomit, mixed to the one of the searchers. The oddity is that everyone, as the emperor of Ur himself, seemed to smile at his own funeral.

DESIRE: The ideas need to land before they are looked at. As long as they are suspended they can provoke a quake on the immense plain. The ideas have no destination and it will be necessary to sacrifice a waited time and a vacuum of sense to be sure that everything will be good. The centrifugal force of reality could cause a loss of altitude and, if besides the stratum of clouds the skies are clear, there will be no escape.

MEMORY: The plane will fly in the stratosphere for the whole night before landing. Then all, passengers and crew, will be on the "Island of the Castle", ruled by the moods of the surveyor of Kafka. The bodies become lighter, defying the force of gravity. After an intense brightness, the tiredness will bring us into a deep sleep. An unstable ground will not support us.

GROUP: Maybe it will! The desire for senselessness helps the search for knowledge.

THOUGHT: To know our own identity?

MEMORY: *(goes up to the tree, pulls out a leaf, and reads)*: Calvino

*(Under the suggestion of Calvino, Marco Polo tells Kublai Khan: "**Elsewhere**" the city of Bion)*

MARCO POLO: Elsewhere is a city made of dreams. Reality loses concreteness and becomes fluid. It becomes purely mental. It is realized in the imagination. Elsewhere is like a negative mirror. The traveler recognizes how poor he is, while he discovers the treasures he didn't have and will not have. By now, he feels excluded from the slums of his real or hypothetical past; he cannot stop, he must go on to another town where another past is expecting him. Something that could be one of his possible futures and now is the present of someone else. In this city, the unachieved futures are only branches of the past: dead branches.

(The soul of Bion comes out from the darkest corner of the room; it wears a white dress with words written on it and carries in its hands leaflets that, without any logic, it flings them at everybody in the room.)

NARRATOR *(speaking as a hostess)*: The landing travelers will meet the soul of Bion. Our task will be studying it or eating it; or maybe both!

SOUL: Where are you from?

GROUP: We come from the funeral.

SOUL: Are you dead or alive?

GROUP: We're just confused.

SOUL: You look like pieces of brain!

GROUP: I feel sick, I'm going to vomit.

SOUL: Is there anyone who wants to write?

GROUP: Yes, but we don't know where to start.

SOUL: If you try to move freely in the space, something will come out as a gift.

GROUP: We are hungry!

SOUL: The island is very poor, however it is possible to find something on the trees or in some hole.

GROUP: In some hole?

SOUL: Yes in the voids you can find things never seen before; just do not stumble. And if you find something dead just light a big fire to burn the corpses.

(The participants stand up and start to move around the room.)

DESIRE: Time is short and uncertain, not even a minute should be missed.

MEMORY: The soul had to tell what he wrote before he died, before he thought, before he returned.

DESIRE: No one is telling us the truth?

GROUP: We are exhausted, broken, frightened, and here's vomit on the floor.

SOUL: I hate to look at my vomit, I feel disgusted. Is there a doctor among you? Please come and examine it, he could see, eventually, pieces of himself or of me.

NARRATOR: The group is struck dumb, while the breeze splits the clouds.

SOUL: You are reading now exactly what is happening now!

NARRATOR: The point of experiment has been to make the thought of the soul of Bion coincide with the thought of our whole group. A magic operation in a dreaming dimension. But the soul didn't give any truth but the gift was only an enigma to be solved in a still suspended time.

★★★

Scene V – *The Dawn of the α Function* (Bion, 1967)

NARRATOR: The group tries to find the sense within the mouth of Renato.

RENATO: I feel like little Beckett who just finished his analysis with Bion.

Looking for sense

Sense, – The gift of receiving sensations from inside and outside stimuli; – Feelings, – The gift to distinguish Inside and Outside sensations; – Dichotomy, – Trichotomy, – Outside, Where, – Appendage of sense, how, – Sensation, what, – When Sense of oppression: Now, – Inside who, – Sense of frustration, guilt, death – Death of sense, – Illusion of senses, – Sixth sense, – Sense of life, sense of dream, – Dream of sign, – More or less, less or more, – Recapitulate, – Evade, – Liberation, – Nonsense, – Double sense – Inside-Outside direction – Forbidden sense – Parking sensor – Senseless, – Essence, – and without it? Sense, – The gift to distinguish Inside and outside sensations.

On the wall appears a pulsating sun (use a red intermittent lamp)

PASQUALE: A shining sun was fading – it becomes greater, and then slowly contracts itself. – The phenomenon repeats. – Like the miracle of Medjougorje with the apparition of Our Lady. – Should it be a boreal dawn? An hallucination that appears on the way to the group's dream? – But for sure, I am awake.

NARRATOR: The sun loosens and tightens because of its pulsations in order to focus and to blur the thought.

THOUGHT: I will explode the brain in a thousand pieces before the sunset.

GROUP: Some pieces in the spaces will be lost.

THOUGHT: We will have time to pick them up.

GROUP: Is it necessary to have an hourglass to measure it?

THOUGHT: Look into my eyes, set to infinite to watch the whole field.

NARRATOR: In the room mess and confusion all over; will a sense ever exist?

(on the floor books, scattered objects, circles, spirals, boxes; the lights are slowly switched off)

ANFITRUO: The Martian invaders will arrive from space to bring us the real sense; the Martians, superior beings, masked as "Strange Attractors".

Third didactic board

The vision of the supra-system

- Time and Space in a dream-like manner converge in the Eye of the Fly (Margherita, 2011).
- The temporality: the alchemy of the opposites: the living dies and the dead rises to new life everything is in time, in the delaying that establishes the differences.
- In the opposing pairs of tradition there is nothing stable or given; they are arrhythmias, mere time lags. The space of the unconscious is not a compact structure. It is made up of fragments that create a difference with respect to the unity of consciousness. The composite view of all the fragments is that of the Eye of the Fly.
- The space is therefore understood as a kind of funerary urn that contains the fertilized earth: the ashes and the seeds. The aim is that once you're dead you slot in the seed of the plant that you loved the most in life. Love makes it come out of the urn and challenge the senselessness in order to know his own new identity.

★★★

Scene VI – *Symmetry*

(The room is in darkness for some minutes. Then a candle lights up. Upon the white wall only shadows.)

ANFITRUO: The quantum mechanics says that the universe has been generated from a discontinuity of the symmetry.

Memory and Desire draw on the wall, converging together from opposite sides:

BioN $\longleftrightarrow$ *Noiβ*

NARRATOR: The intent will be to make the lifeless book explode. Everyone is focusing on a silent thought. The power of the silence and of the glances, after all that darkness reanimated a text that nobody had read. What an odd formula: maybe it means that only recovering us as beta elements we can experience contact with the true Bion.

Fourth didactic board

Circularity

- A fossil from the future. A probe which is retrograde in time. Our topic could be defined as "limitrofia": that is, what draws the limits closer but also what nourishes, feeds itself, sustains itself, grows, takes shape, comes to fruition in the dialectic of the "I" versus "the other" on the rim of the membrane's edge.

- The membrane is the key of dissipative structures, i.e. of Life. "*What I mean to say is not at all intended to remove the limit but to multiply its patterns, to complicate it, to thicken it, to outline it, to bend it, dividing its line so as to actually make it grow and multiply*" (Derrida, 1967). Who knows, perhaps Derrida too is setting up a multi-layer.
- There emerges a circularity: the deconstruction brings to light the difference that is at the heart of being but, in turn, it energizes the difference and liquefies everything that is stable by turning it into a dialect by means of precariousness.
- Man comes after the animal. But he is not perhaps at the same time ahead of it. For a long time the animal has been looking at us. But the time of the coming together is the same for both.
- "*In front of the cat looking at me naked should I not feel ashamed like a beast that no longer has the sense of its own nakedness? Or rather like a man who maintains his sense of nakedness? But then who am I? Who is it that I am if I am both? Who shall I ask if not the other? I might actually ask the cat*". It appears that Derrida (2006) has borrowed from Bion on projective identification.

***

Epilogue

LELLO: I didn't want to come over this evening.

EVA: Neither did I, I hate to argue after 8 p.m.

LICIA: Ok, now I will provoke you by reading you a story.

ORIETTA: Here we need diagrams to bring us back to life.

GUELFO: But what kind of mushrooms did you eat tonight? We all seem to be full of envy and gratitude.

GROUP: Something indigestible weighs on our stomach and, at the same time, makes us fly.

(In the room a participant begins to prowl like a cat, slow and mysterious, she will glance around staring everybody in the eyes, then she looks at the books in the center of the room)

DERRIDA'S CAT: I want to provoke you and leave smells and sensual traces of my fast crossing over the edge of the limit!

(The soul in front of the cat, stares back at her eyes.)

SOUL: Why do I feel so ashamed of being so naked in front of you? Am I a beast or a book that is not aware of his own nakedness or, an exposed flesh that harbors the risk of its own shame. Who am I? To whom could I ask this but you?

CAT: Maybe you're a book that finally becomes flesh.

MONICA: The time creates the alchemy of opposites.

RENATO: None of us has understood anything, but together we understood a little!

PINO: When the sun was pulsating before to exploded, we were getting nearer to the truth.

NARRATOR: Here we need a bifocal lens to read the pages of a book where life and death are fighting. Everyone has to read with similar glasses and to try to see double. The binocular vision of the same concept stimulates different points of view, originating the construction of different images.

GROUP: A kaleidoscope! To see ever changing figures, that never repeat themselves.

GUELFO: Are we awake or are we dreaming? Ultimately it could be the quantum bi-location of the same thing!

(The room becomes dark again, then a strong shining light; a participant stands up, out of the circle, and draws on the wall an enormous question mark!

Everyone remains still, everyone holds their own different position and expression.)

GROUP: ?

***

Monologue (Bion, 1979c)

SOUL OF BION: *"All my life I have been imprisoned, frustrated, dogged by common-sense, reason, memories, desires and – greatest bug-bear of all – understanding and being understood. This is an attempt to express my rebellion, to say 'Good-bye' to all that. It is my wish, I now realize doomed to failure, to write a book unspoiled by any tincture of common-sense, reason, etc. (see above). So although I would write, 'Abandon Hope all ye who expect to find any facts – scientific, aesthetic or religious – in this book', I cannot claim to have succeeded. All these will, I fear, be seen to have left their traces, vestiges, ghosts hidden within these words; even sanity, like 'cheerfulness', will creep in. However successful my attempt, there would always be the risk that the book 'became' acceptable, respectable, honoured and unread. 'Why write then?' you may ask. To prevent someone who KNOWS from filling the empty space – but I fear I am being 'reasonable', that great Ape. Wishing you all a Happy Lunacy and a Relativistic Fission . . .".*

References

Beckett, S. (1952). *Waiting for Godot.* London: Faber and Faber, 1956.

Beckett, S. (1988). Comment dire. In *Poèmes, suivi de mirlitonnades.* Paris: Les Éditions de Minuit, 1992, from: *Grand Street* 9(2), Winter 1990: 17–18, New York. ISSN 0734–5496.

Bion W.R. (1967). *Second Thoughts.* London: William Heinemann.

Bion, W.R. (1975). The dream. In *A Memoir of the Future,* Vol. 1, p. 5. London: Karnac, 1990.

Bion, W.R. (1979a). The dawn of oblivion. In *A Memoir of the Future,* Vol. 3, p. 2. London: Karnac, 1990.

Bion, W.R. (1979b). The dawn of oblivion. In *A Memoir of the Future,* Vol. 3, pp. 151–153. London: Karnac, 1990.

Bion, W.R. (1979c). The dawn of oblivion. In *A Memoir of the Future,* Vol. 3, p. 251. London: Karnac, 1990.

Borges, J.L. (1960). *Borges y Yo en El Hacedor.* Emecé, Buenos Aires, www.cs.northwestern.edu/~fabianb/borgesandi.html.

Brecht, B. (1957). *Schriften zum Theater.* Berlin: Suhrkamp.

Derrida, J. (1967). *De la Grammatologie.* Paris: Éditions de Minuit.

Derrida, J. (2006). *L'Animal quedonc Je Suis.* Paris: Galilée.

Margherita, G. (2011). The eye of the fly: Psychoanalytic gestalten and chaotic attractors in large groups and institutions. *Chaos and Complexity Letters* 4: 3.

Schore, A. (2012). *The Science of the Art of Psychotherapy.* New York: W. W. Norton & Company.

SECTION VIII

Freud, Klein, Winnicott, Lacan and O

23

THE NAVEL OF THE TRUTH[1]

Andrea Bocchiola

In *Transformations*, Bion introduces the concept of O as the unknowable matter-of-fact of the session. Let me quote Bion's words: "Something happened during the session the facts 'in themselves' of the session. What the facts in themselves are we shall never know; thus, I shall indicate them with the mark O" (Bion, 1965, 12).

I must thank Avner Bergstein for an even more precise description of how O makes its appearance on the analytic scene:

> When I'm with a patient, there is sometimes a moment, perhaps a fraction of a second, when I feel something that I will never be able to fully grasp or communicate, even to myself. This happens every time we come out of a session, and can never find the words to describe our emotional experience to an other.[2]

These are the cobblestones that pave the clinical situation, where O is the "source of any emotional turbulence" as well as "the authentic object of psychoanalytic listening". As Sandler specifies, O is "a quasi-mathematical symbol created to denote the numinous realm of the unconscious, where the human and the individual truth resides. Ultimate reality, absolute truth" (Sandler, 2005, p. 527).

Thus, the matter-of-fact of the session is the place of the truth, and the truth is something we cannot fully grasp, that produces all turbulence and that we must listen to.

The unspeakable – and its turbulence – defines psychoanalytical experience and listening right from its founding myth: Oedipus. The Sphinx's question in fact does not require an answer, that would be invariably destined to a misinterpretation of the enigma, rather, it requires an exercise that will inevitably lead to turbulence. The Sphinx's question is not something we respond to but that we correspond to. And this should suggest that psychoanalysis, far from being a scientific discipline, has more to do with ethics than it does with neuroscience. It is a practice of truth, revealed through the practice itself.

So let us for a moment dwell upon the way we experience truth in O and the nature of O itself in psychoanalysis, from the Freudian navel of the dream to Bion's alpha function.

The navel of the dream

As we know from *The Interpretation of Dreams*, whilst analyzing Irma's dream, Freud is faced with the image of her throat and notes:

> I have a feeling that the interpretation of this part of the dream was not carried far enough to make it possible to follow the whole of its concealed meaning. [. . .] There is at least one spot in every dream at which it is unplumbable – a navel, as it were, that it is its point of contact with the unknown.
>
> *(Freud, 1900, p. 111)*

Pages later he will return to this delicate point:

> There is often a passage in even the most thoroughly interpreted dream which has to be left obscure; this is because we become aware during the work of interpretation that at that point there is a tangle of dream-thoughts which cannot be unraveled and which moreover adds nothing to our knowledge of the content of the dream. This is the dream's navel, the spot where it reaches down into the unknown. The dream-thoughts to which we are led by interpretation cannot, from the nature of things, have any definite endings; they are bound to branch out in every direction into the intricate network of our world of thought. It is at some point where this meshwork is particularly close that the dream-wish grows up, like a mushroom out of its mycelium.
>
> *(Ibid., 525)*

The navel of the dream marks the point in which the thinking of both analyst and analysand comes to a standstill. Free associations, rêverie and dreaming-together cannot grasp it. For Lacan, this is the Real: a concept that can partly be over-lapped with O as it defines the moment in which the process of thinking falls into a void (Lacan, 1973). In this sense the navel of the dream is the point in which all stories evaporate.

Moreover, the navel of the dream is shown to be the point from which the patient's desire emerges, "where the mushroom explodes from its mycelium", its deep origin. It is where the truth of the dream (and of the dreamer) is incarnated, inaccessible and traumatic. We cannot grasp this truth, but every time we intuit it, it produces turbulence. Freud will state it clearly in *Constructions of Analysis*: "If the construction is wrong, there is no change in the patient; but if it is right or gives an approximation to the truth, he reacts to it with an unmistakable aggravation of his symptoms and of his general condition" (Freud, 1938, p. 265), which goes so far as to produce memories and dreams that are almost hallucinations, if not real delusional formations. The truth, like the sun, burns our eyes and the dream is one of the screens through which we can bear this light.

I think it is difficult to find a more precise example of the experience of O than we do in Freud's annotations and taking a closer look is well worthwhile as it allows a deeper understanding. What is this black stain on the surface of the dream if not what prevents the thought of the dream from being the whole of the dreamer's experience? What is it, if not the specific internal resistance, the line of fracture, the caesura of the dream that allows it to make sense?

Because only if something resists thought, may thought have meaning and make sense. The navel of the dream hence defines the conditions of "thinkability" of the dream itself. If we took away the dream, we wouldn't have the sight of its navel and vice-versa. The navel belongs to the surface of the dream and cannot be separated from it. The dream's masks are the point in which truth takes place and shape. This can be considered the radical outcome in *Constructions of Analysis*: we see the patient's truth thanks to the masks of the unconscious formations, not despite them. In other words, the truth is in its masks and their movements, and nowhere else, without thereby reducing it or making it coincide with its figures.

On the same note, if we look at the image of the navel directly, we see that we are looking at a sign. The navel is a hole or "button-hole". The hole is sign: sign of something that was there and is no longer there. Something we were and no longer are: the umbilical cord and the uterus that were once connected and that were each other's end. The image of the "belly button" reminds us that this is the place where there once was and still is a latch. The navel of the dream, for however opaque to meaning it may be, is sign of the origin that "we are". The navel of the dream sends us back to an origin that is singular as it is "mine and only mine", plural – because it is made of something else. It is made of the Other – determined – because it is that shape and no other, and that shape lacks nothing to be what it is: our pre-egologic and pre-subjective knot to the world.

Naturally this may raise all sorts of questions. Having accepted the analogy between O and the navel of the dream, one might rightly wonder how the "real, anonymous, undetermined and infinite" (as O is often defined) can be singular/plural, determined and finite at the same time? How can what seems unthinkable have the nature of sign, if not of symbol even? How can what seems located in the space of an undefined transcendence (as the Kantian noumenon or Platonic idea) find its place and take place on the surface?

To understand things better we can attempt a small experiment. Bion used the mother-child encounter to reflect upon the alpha function. We shall do something similar to reflect upon O, looking at the mouth-breast encounter and trying to remain as close as possible to the experience of that encounter and to its concreteness.

The mouth-breast encounter

At the origin of the first mouth-breast encounter we have a mouth that ignores itself as such; nor is it somebody's mouth. It will become all this but in origin it knows not of itself and of the breast that awaits it. At the same time, there is a breast that knows not of itself in the encounter with the specific mouth that awaits it. Neither breast nor mouth pre-exist as figures of their encounter until the breast is touched by the mouth and vice-versa making the world explode somewhat in the form of that mouth for that breast, and vice-versa.

It is fundamental to keep in mind that we are speaking of the first encounter of that mouth and that breast. The intentionality of the mother and the instinctiveness of the child are not at play here because the level of our reflection concerns the encounter of the breast with the mouth, and before this happens, each of them is something, but not a figure of their encounter. Thus, we should say that the intentionality is of the encounter, not of the subjects involved. The intentionality is of the nature of the event, of the affective and sensorial way in which the two touch. This way is the original interpreter that defines the meaning of what that mouth will be for that breast and vice-versa and their destinies from that moment on.

This amounts to saying two things. First, that the experience of the world is always an experience of the Two. The event that gives origin to that mouth for that breast, is nowhere else if not in the encounter that makes them explode. It is explosion of the world in its two folds. It is the caesura that institutes, differentiates and therefore unites and contains the facets of experience. It is the experience itself that safeguards the intimate and singular meaning and truth of the encounter.

Thus, we could define O in Sandler's words: "the numinous realm of the unconscious, where the human and the individual truth resides" (Sandler, 2005, p. 527), however we should be cautious before placing it in some type of transcendence. That is assigning the nature of a fundament to O, as if it could precede the Two. Instead, we must reflect further upon considering its nature as that of an "original", in perennial explosion, the center of which is – as the navel of the dream – on the surface of experience. Only if we are able to think of a Truth that is not an a-priori, but as something that happens, of an original that is not fundament, will we be able to grasp the nature of O. The reference here to Kant's thing-in-itself or Plato's Ideal forms could not be more misleading; if we really must find interlocutors, we will have to look to the rise and fall of metaphysics: at the ἄπειρον (apeiron) the pre-Socratics or at Merleau-Ponty's idea of Flesh (M. Merleau-Ponty, 1964).

From sign to symbol: the alpha function

Starting from the caesura that "institutes" this encounter, breast and mouth act as a sign of each other and as object of each other. The way they correspond as sign and meaning is in no way arbitrary or abstract. On the contrary, it is utterly concrete and "sensible". In experience, even at its primordial level, there is never an encounter of a "sensitive" or psychic apparatus with raw matter, with the thing-in-itself devoid of meaning. Every event of the world occurs within a sign relation that is not arbitrary but interpreted and interpretant.

Secondly, if in the beginning breast and mouth are the sign and object of one another, even more so, they are the two faces of the same event. In other words, they are symbolon (Sini, 1998, pp. 165–171). Each of them refers to the other as to the other face of itself, of one's self, of one's being. And what holds the two parts of the symbol together, what makes symballein, is precisely the crack, the caesura which, in separating and thus instituting them, destines them to one another in their being "the same thing" (Ibid.).

The symbol is an original, as it refers to nothing more than itself and thus does not require any pre-existing reality, which means that the symbolon is the necessary condition for any relation between sign and object. And here lies the transcendental condition of thought which is of course important for our reflections regarding the alpha function, alpha beta elements and so forth. The most important of these is that the alpha function is contained within the logic of experience. In other words we are always immersed in a symbolic and interpretative relationship that precedes and produces the mother and the child as an evolution of the mouth-breast encounter. It follows that neither the mother nor the child are the persona of the alpha function. The alpha function lies within their encounter and precedes their being as mother and child. As a consequence of this, we could say that there are no beta elements as things in themselves either, nor can there be a raw element that is without meaning.

Hallucination

Every time a mouth encounters a breast, we can be sure it will begin to hallucinate it. At the tip of the mouth, the breast is hallucinated – but also, at the tip of the breast, the mouth is hallucinated. A mind is not needed to do this. All that is needed is a mouth, that, so to speak, will be given birth by the nipple that has urged it and touched upon its surface. In our lexicon, the mouth can hallucinate the breast because it is sign of the breast and object of the breast as a sign.

Through this hallucination, we move from the experience of Two – the mouth for the breast, the epistemological register which is that of the truth – to Three: the mouth, the breast and the mouth-breast as "hallucination" of their identity – the epistemological register which is that of knowledge and thinking, which by definition separates truth from knowledge and thinking.

Absolute truth

From the moment in which the mouth hallucinates the encounter with the breast, the hallucinated identity of the two-in-one produces the idea of an origin, a lost origin that strives to be recomposed. This hallucination coincides with the idea of a whole that is founding, undifferentiated in its founding parts, symbiotic and in no way symbolic.

There is, so to speak, the risk of a backward projection, a retrojection, that would entail going back from the experience of Three to the experience of One, of a whole. As if the caesura, the painful and necessary line of fracture and separation could be canceled in this recomposition.

This is what happens in any form of delusion where the idea of an idyllic union represents the lost origin and is taken for the absolute truth.

I propose to identify the idea of "O as final truth", and its ontological misunderstanding as "Absolute truth" in this retrojection as it alludes to the whole as the origin and attempts the cancelation of the caesura, and leave the privilege of transcendence to this "Absolute" alone, whatever it maybe.

Notes

1 This paper would not have been possible without the invaluable dialogue with Sonia de Cristofaro, Psy.D. To her goes my utmost gratitude for the years of joy of which this paper is testimony. For the complexity in output of the English translation of these pages, the help of Olivia Marchese, Psy.D. has been more than precious.
2 Private conversation with A. Bergstein.

References

Bion, W. (1965). *Transformations: Change from Learning to Growth*. London: Maresfield Reprints, 1984.
Freud, S. (1900). The interpretation of dreams. *S.E.* 4 & 5. London: The Hogarth Press, 1964.
Freud, S. (1938). Construction of analysis. *S.E.* 23. London: The Hogarth Press, 1964.
Lacan, J. (1973). *The Four Fundamental Concepts of Psycho-Analysis*. London: Karnac. [Séminaire XI. Les quatre concepts fondamentaux de la psychanalyse. Paris : Ed. de Seuil, 1973]
Merleau-Ponty, M. (1964). *The Visible and the Invisible*. Chicago, MA: Northwestern University. [Le Visible et l'invisible. Paris: Gallimard, 1964]
Sandler, P. (2005). *The Language of Bion: A Dictionary of Concepts*. London: Karnac.
Sini, C. (1998). *Segni dell'anima*. Bari: Laterza.

24

THE PRIMITIVE SOMATOPSYCHIC ROOTS OF GENDER FORMATION, INTIMACY AND THE DEVELOPMENT OF PSYCHE WITH IMPLICATIONS FOR PSYCHOANALYTIC TECHNIQUE[1]

James Gooch

... Blessed the infant babe –
For with my best conjectures I would trace
The progress of our being – blest the babe
Nursed in his mother's arms, the babe who sleeps
Upon his mother's breast, who, when his soul
Claims manifest kindred with an earthly soul,
Doth gather passion from his mother's eye.
Such feelings pass into his torpid life
Like an awakening breeze, and hence his mind,
Even in the first trial of its powers,
Is prompt and watchful, eager to combine
In one appearance all the elements
And parts of the same object, else detached
And loth to coalesce. Thus day by day,
Subjected to the discipline of love,
His organs and recipient faculties
Are quickened, are more vigorous; his mind spreads,
Tenacious of the forms which it receives.
In one beloved presence – nay and more,
In that most apprehensive habitude
And those sensations which have been derived
From this beloved presence – there exists
A virtue which irradiates and exalts
All objects through all intercourse of sense.
No outcast he, bewildered and depressed;
Along his infant veins are interfused
The gravitation and the filial bond
Of Nature that connect him with the world.
Emphatically such a being lives,
An inmate of this active universe.

From Nature largely he receives, nor so
Is satisfied, but largely gives again;
For feeling has to him imparted strength,
And – powerful in all sentiments of grief,
Of exultation, fear and joy – his mind,
Even as an agent of the one great mind,
Creates, creator and receiver both,
Working but in alliance with the works
Which it beholds. Such, verily, is the first
Poetic spirit of our human life –
By uniform control of after years,
In most abated and suppressed, – in some-
Through every change of growth or of decay
Preeminent till death.
From early days,
Beginning not long after that first time
In which, a babe, by intercourse of touch
I held mute dialogues with my mother's heart,
I have endeavoured to display the means
Whereby this infant sensibility,
Great birthright of our being, was in me
Augmented and sustained . . .
. . . in this time
Of dereliction and dismay, I yet
Despair not of our nature, but retain
A more than Roman confidence, a faith
That fails not, in all sorrow my support,
The blessing of my life, the gift is yours
Ye mountains, thine O Nature. Thou hast fed
My lofty speculations, and in thee
For this uneasy heart of ours, I find
A never-failing principle of joy
And purest passion.
    From *The Prelude*, 1799 – William Wordsworth

Intimacy and passion

I shall briefly outline a model of mind, of psychical development, of interpersonal and of intrapsychic relationships of an intimate, passionate nature.

In a healthy parental relationship, the mother and father maintain their individual identities, yet, have become integrally involved in a complementary sexual, passionate fashion. If you will, imagine the couple represented by two equal ovoids, one designated "W-M" for wife-mother and the other "H-F" for husband-father, maturely and passionately interpenetrating one another (Figure 24.1).

Note the emphasis on mature passion. It is the intense emotion which compels the action of creating an in-depth relationship. It serves as the mental equivalent of a chemical, or catalyst, which dissolves or makes semipermeable, the psychical and emotional boundaries of two

Normal P.I. & Parental Function

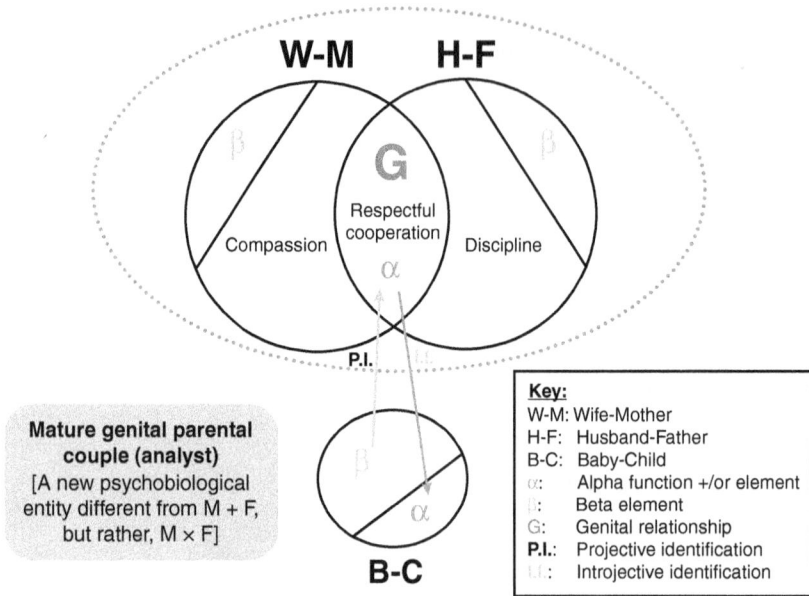

FIGURE 24.1   Normal projective identification and parental function diagram.

people, so that interpenetration can occur. Without passion, there would be no bonding, no reverie, no sustained compassionate empathy and no psychoanalytic alliance. Interpenetration creates the blended intermediary space occupied by both the wife-mother and the husband-father which can be thought of as the genital bonding of the sexual couple, a development from Freud's aim-dominated instinct theory. The two parents' psychical and physical mature, passionate interpenetration or bonding creates an enhanced and augmented third party, different from the sum of "M" plus "F" (M + F), but more their product "M" times "F" (M × F).

This interpenetrating relationship first begins to develop during the courtship, continues and has a progressive development into marriage, the honeymoon, pregnancy and the birth and rearing of their children. As a genitally bonded, new psychophysiological unit, the parental couple attains a particular suitability to perform vital functions for the baby. One such basic function will now be discussed on an interpersonal level and later, on an intrapsychic level. The child's optimal psychical and physical survival and development depend on the availability of such a function.

This vital process has been widely recognized and described by psychoanalytic theorists, though utilizing different vocabulary.

A   Bion: alpha function, containment, reverie, digestion, detoxification
B   Klein: good breast functions
C   Meltzer: toilet breast receptacle functions and feeding breast functions
D   Winnicott: handling and holding by a good enough mother capable of primary maternal preoccupation, and the transitional space facilitating personalization and the formation of the "true self"

E   Mahler: normal symbiosis
F   Ego Psychologists: parents' (and analysts') ego functions
G   Kohut: empathy used for mirroring – by narcissistic self-object functions
H   Freud: insight and working through
I   Sullivan: the tenderness theorem (the first analyst to describe this process)
J   Balint: the harmonious interpenetrating mix–up
K   Grotstein: regulating functions of background and foreground objects

I find Bion's terminology particularly useful because, to me, it is most experience-near. There is a heuristically useful dialectic tension amongst the vertices, or points-of-view, of the various other schools of psychoanalysis regarding this basic function (vertices in the sense that Bion uses the term).

The baby's unbearable, unfeelable, unthinkable, unmentalized somatopsychic experiences – beta elements, to use Bion's term – are tropistically evacuated, similar to a model conceptualized by Freud (1911) as the discharge of instinctual energy under the aegis of the pleasure principle, or by Melanie Klein (1946) as the phantasy of projective identification. Bion named this process normal projective identification. In health, the beta elements are received by the mother's receptive psyche – or more accurately the maternal-part of the parental person's psyche. By this not-yet-sufficiently understood process of reverie, or alpha function, as Bion (1959) called it, the mother-part or function understands (makes meaning, producing alpha elements) the baby's experience (Figure 24.2).

Bion called the transformed beta elements, alpha elements – where the meaningless somatopsychic experience now becomes meaningful. Discharged psychic energy from the baby gains psychic representation by the maternal alpha function. The baby's primary process becomes secondary process in the mind of the mother. This understanding process (alpha function) may be unconscious, preconscious or conscious. The understanding is conveyed to the

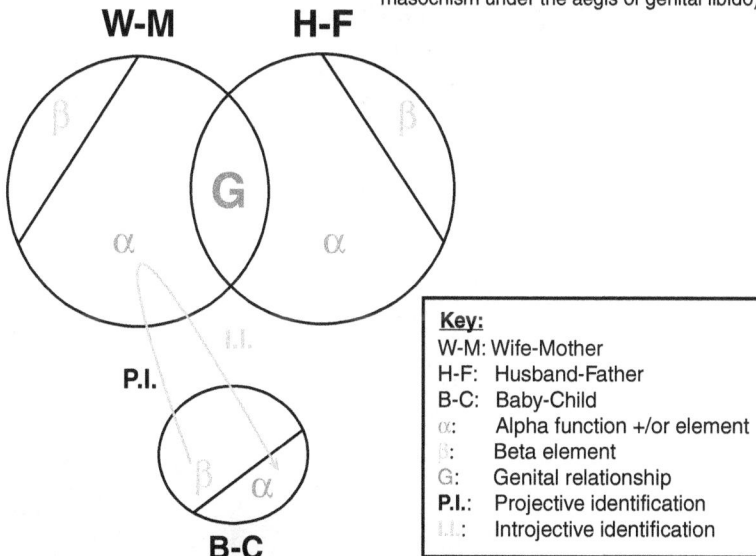

FIGURE 24.2   Mother function diagram.

baby by the mother's (mother-part) mindful ministrations to the baby. The proper (meaning adaptive or good enough) ministrations of the mother-part return to the baby's psyche, which now receives the transformed meaningless beta elements, transformed to meaningful alpha elements. Psychoanalysts have variously referred to this process as introjection, incorporation, identification, introjective identification, transmuting internalization, etc. For simplicity, let us assume that this introjective phase goes well, which is not necessarily always true in real life. This projective process of evacuation by the baby-part, maternal alpha function and ministration, introjection by the baby goes on – or fails to go on – with all the ordinary details of the baby's life. Additionally, in reality, each parent will have their own sectors of undeveloped parts of their personalities – their beta elements – the activation and discharge of which will depend upon the exigencies of adaptational demands from inside and out. Furthermore, each baby will have their own sector of nascent alpha function. Additionally, immature and undeveloped sectors of the parents and of the children will be discharging beta elements into the family system and its members, who will also be receiving beta elements from the extra-familial surround as well.

Coincident to the development of the alpha function in the baby is the beginning of mentalization, of psyche, of symbol formation, signal affect-formation, i.e. secondary process, be it ever so nascent. An internal world begins to develop – based on a projective-introjective feedback loop. Earliest developments tend to be the most fantastic and extreme – a pantheon of internal objects evolving and only gradually, if ever, becoming integrated. Parts of John Cage's 1947 symphony about Native American Indians is an evocatively descriptive musical version of nascent integration (Cage, 1947).

The model presented here emphasizes the role of the husband-father (or fathering-part) from pre-conception on (Figure 24.3). The model in this sense stands apart from the more usual mother-baby dyad models. In health, the parental couple is an alpha function-maker at a geometric (M × F) rate rather than an arithmetic (M + F) rate. The father, or father-part,

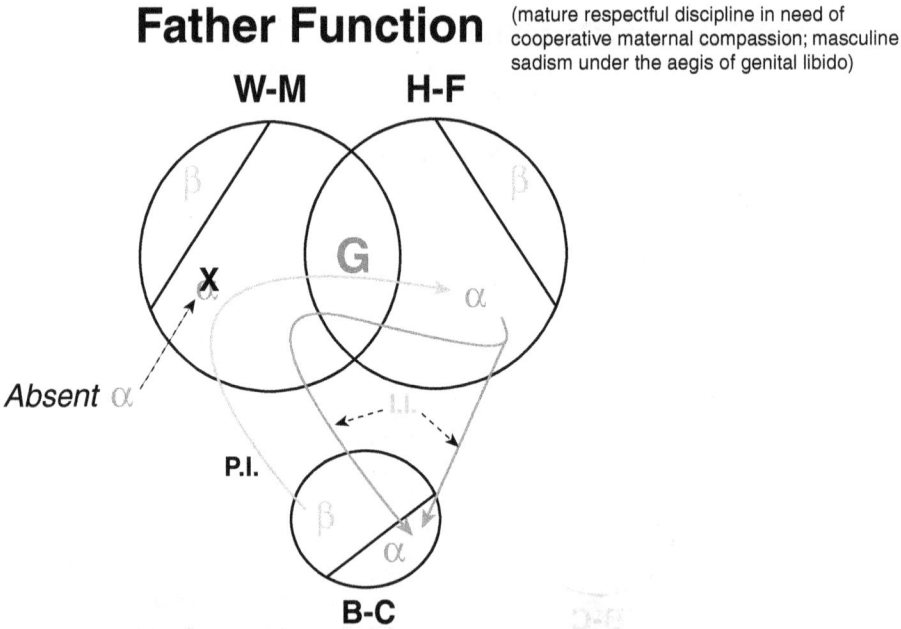

FIGURE 24.3 Father function diagram.

with its functions will tropistically (unconsciously, preconsciously and consciously) be receptive to, and seek for, the failed alpha function in the mother-part in the interest of providing it to the mother and/or baby by husbandly and fatherly ministrations. The father function also includes mature discipline – to be discussed in the following section.

Donald Meltzer (1973) has described a basic phantasy in which the father is seen as the mother's servant, benefactor and rescuer, providing relief via his good intercourse, for all the bad and painful projections into her by the children, and filling her breasts with milk. In health, there seems to be a genetic readiness for the development of these wifely-motherly and husbandly-fatherly parts, and functions, in each individual regardless of, but not unrelated to, their sexual anatomy and physiology – Freud's universal bisexuality. Clearly, environmental factors will have a crucial bearing on the outcome of the development of these inborn potentials.

In single-parent families, both the maternal functions and the paternal functions will have to be carried by one person. Actually, any caretaking person who has the necessary alpha function can provide it, if there is a proper bonding and attachment to the baby or baby-parts of the personality.

Mature sado-masochism and mature bisexuality[2]

I would like to extend Freud's ideas described in "The Economic Problems of Masochism" (1924), wherein he postulates the Death Instinct. He distinguishes between erotogenic, moral and feminine masochism when the Death Instinct is turned toward the self. When turned toward other persons or things it is called sadism. Libido and the Death Instinct are Freud's imaginative conjectures, serving his purposes, inferred from concrete facts.

Let us now add an additional imaginative conjecture of erotogenic, moral and masculine sadism. Imagine feminine masochism and masculine sadism under the aegis of genital libido, intrapsychically and interpersonally. Imagine this feminine masochism and masculine sadism in a mature conjugation whose aim is to be growthful, creative and nurturing toward the self, children and community.

These imaginative conjectures are powerfully and beautifully exemplified in the movie "The Miracle Worker" (1962), in the relationship between Ann Sullivan and Helen Keller where immature, erotogenic, moral and feminine masochism and immature erotogenic, moral and masculine sadism are contained by the discovery and evolution of the conjugation of mature femininity and mature masculinity, which are creative and nurturing. Only loving compassion and discipline lead to growth in both Ann Sullivan and Helen Keller. The growth of this mature conjugation of femininity and masculinity is essential for authentic growth and creativity. This mature conjugation constrains unnecessary, abusive suffering and unnecessary, abusive cruelty and violence. This mature conjugation is essential for growth in both parties as well as in workgroups. Growth cannot occur without mature suffering, and mature violence and cruelty, within minimum, but necessary, limits. Since none of us is omniscient, these processes are discovered by experimental guessing, and learning from experience, as portrayed in "The Miracle Worker."

Psychoanalytic interpretation

The theoretical understanding of psychoanalytic technique that I shall now describe has grown mostly out of my experience as an analysand of Bion, a reader of Bion and others, and my experiences as an analyst over decades (Gooch, 2001).[3]

Psychical objects (and elements), as they are available to both the analysand and the analyst in bison's Grid (Figure 24.4), have dimensions in the domains of sense (Row B), myth (Row C) and passion (Row G). Sense refers to noticeable sensorial manifestations, myth to signal affects and symbolic manifestations and passion to the empathic link. In *Elements of Psychoanalysis*, Bion writes:

> By 'passion' . . . I mean the component derived from L, H and K . . . an emotion experienced with intensity and warmth, though without any suggestion of violence . . . unless it is associated with the term 'greed'. . . . Awareness of passion is not dependent on sense. . . . Passion is evidence that two minds are linked, and there cannot possibly be fewer than two if passion is present.
>
> *(Bion 1963, pp. 12–13)*

Symbols are formed by transforming memories of sensorial experience into analogs, for example, ideographs such as a dream or myth.

A psychoanalytic interpretation, in my view, is a mature, respectful, compassionate, disciplined educated guess, an hypothesis, a description in words, accompanied by the appropriate music and dance, that addresses the analysand's emotional experience in the moment. Stated theoretically, the analysand's psychoanalytic (psychic) objects, intuited by the analyst to be happening, but unnoticed by the analysand in the moment, are described by the interpretation. Psychic objects are ephemeral, evanescent and only able to be observed privately by the individual. In fashioning an interpretation, the analyst uses his or her own psychoanalytic objects, also ephemeral, evanescent and only observable by the analyst, as these are evoked and provoked by the analysand's communication and behavior.

The analyst intuits the analysand's experience because similar psychical objects have been experienced by analysand and analyst, and these are communicated by the former to the latter.

The Grid

	Definitory Hypotheses	Ψ	Notation	Attention	Inquiry	Action	
	1	2	3	4	5	6	...n
A: β - elements	A1	A2				A6	
B: α - elements	B1	B2	B3	B4	B5	B6	...Bn
C: Dream thoughts, Dreams, Myths	C1	C2	C3	C4	C5	C6	...Cn
D: Pre-conception	D1	D2	D3	D4	D5	D6	...Dn
E: Conception	E1	E2	E3	E4	E5	E6	...En
F: Concept	F1	F2	F3	F4	F5	F6	...Fn
G: Scientific Deductive System		G2					...Gn
H: Algebraic Calculus							

FIGURE 24.4 Bion's Grid.

This is very similar, if not equivalent, to the baby's conveying to the mother by way of normal projective identification its incomprehensible experiences (beta elements).

These beta elements are acted upon by maternal reverie (alpha function), thereby creating alpha elements which are returned via maternal (parental) ministrations, often including the spoken, but incomprehensible word; the accompanying music and dance that convey the comprehensible understanding to the baby of any age. I would modify maternal reverie to parental reverie, including paternal reverie and maternal reverie in mature, cooperative, respectful, genital union, ministering to the baby. In Freudian terms, compassion is feminine masochism under the aegis of genital libido, and discipline is masculine sadism under the aegis of genital libido. Mature, respectful compassion and discipline cooperate to form dream function alpha (alpha function).

When psychoanalysts' accurate verbal interpretations are made from the heart, utilizing our own psychic objects, our words like the lyrics of the song help us get the music and dance right. I am increasingly convinced that it is the music and dance of our interpretations that are transformative to the infantile aspects of our analysands of any age.

Being without memory and desire greatly facilitates the observation of psychical objects by both analyst and analysand, as nightfall facilitates seeing the stars. The analyst needs to be under the aegis of this mature internal couple – mother and father – in generative communion with one another in relationship to the psychoanalytic objects being experienced (by the parental alpha function in the analyst and immature consciousness in the analysand). Such attuned, empathic experience in turn allows for psychical growth (+Y) in both analyst and analysand. In *Learning from Experience*, Bion proposes that, aside from physical ministrations to the baby, the mother shows her love through reverie, psychically (Bion, 1962, p. 36). I am suggesting that the analyst's main work is to make this internal mother and father in genital communion available to the analysand.

I BELIEVE THE INTERNAL MATURE PARENTAL COUPLE IN THE ANALYST IS THE PSYCHOANALYST'S INSTRUMENT IN TENDING TO AND ANALYZING THE UNBORN, IMMATURE, SOMATIZED, PSYCHOTIC, CRIMINAL, PERVERSE, AUTISTIC, AND OTHERWISE PATHOLOGIC AND PATHOGENIC ASPECTS OF OUR ANALYSANDS. Such in vivo parental alpha function shows the analysand how the intolerable, toxic, undigested experiences (beta elements) can be withstood (detoxified, digested). Through the mysterious process of introjective identification in a mature K → O link between analyst and analysand. The analysand develops a capacity that he or she did not previously possess. Under proper conditions of genitality; that is, mature, cooperative, respectful, compassion and discipline, the capacity for meaningful emotional experience is acquired. The analyst also needs to use their mature internal couple to interpret the analysand's healthy growth, strengths and psychic accomplishments.

Next, psychical exercise, analogous to physical exercise and athletic conditioning in the learning of a physical skill, develops psychical skills. I sometimes refer to this as the development of "mental muscle." In particular, this psychical exercise develops dream function alpha, and the alpha membrane. Bion, in *Learning From Experience*, uses the example of learning the skill of walking to illustrate the growth of alpha elements, alpha function and alpha membrane, which allow the thinking used in walking to be done unconsciously (Bion, 1962, p. 8).

The alpha membrane allows for selective repression, not only in doing physical tasks, but psychical tasks as well. Consciousness is then not over-encumbered because the needed thinking and feeling is being done unconsciously by dream function alpha, thereby freeing consciousness to attend to other tasks (Bion's normal Unconscious).

This sophisticated unconscious, as I call it, probably equivalent to Freud's preconscious, is to be contrasted with unconsciousness due to primary repression, and perhaps much of Freud's secondary repression, used to avoid psychic pain. The psychic growth made possible by the mature parental alpha function, including in psychoanalysis, allows for the development of psychic skills. Previously unbearable emotional experience can then not only be borne – but be borne by sophisticated unconscious thinking and feeling after such psychic skills are developed by working through – that is, through psychical exercise. This task is done by the analyst "showing" the analysand how to perform the necessary alpha function, by the analyst having the essentially needed emotional experiences in the presence of the analysand. The analyst must perform this function as long as necessary, until he/she has managed to success-fully communicate his/her understanding and until the analysand has grown the capacity to bear psychic experience for him/herself. This can happen on a conscious, preconscious or unconscious level for both analyst and analysand, hence the efficacy of different therapeutic modalities and of different theoretical models.

Psychoanalytic technique traditionally provides this by the analyst giving well-timed and well-dosed empathic interpretations which include verbal and non-verbal elements. Explicit self-disclosure is not what is meant here. An interpretation, formulated from the empathic understanding by the analyst, is an attempt to describe the analysand's, as yet, intolerable baby or immature experience. My experience leads me to conclude that analysis cannot exorcise, or get rid of, any of these pathogenic internal objects. It probably cannot even directly modify them. What it can do is allow the analysand to grow new ones, particularly the wife-mother and husband-father with the genital bond, able to tend to one another and the babies, that is, the growing parts of one's self, as well as giving birth to new parts of the self. Ideally, in health, this continually maturing internal parental couple presides over all of the internal objects, including those which were previously pathogenic, even turning them to good account – the ascendancy of genital Libido over pregenital Libido and Thanatos, to link it to Freud's eco-nomic point-of-view. Such generative and creative internal object relationships will allow for interpersonal intimacy with adults and children, friends and friendly enemies. It is the stuff of guts, heart and soul. It comes as no surprise that our good internal object relationships need tending and care, no less than our object relationships in the external world.

The incremental, ongoing growth of this mature internal mother and father into a mature generative internal couple is an optimal resolution of the Oedipus complex with the resultant potential for psychic growth and "becoming," throughout the entire life cycle.

This model of mind can be very useful for family therapy as well as psychoanalysis. The therapeutic task becomes one of helping the family or analysand identify the needed alpha functions and, if not already developed by the family and the individual patient, to provide conditions where it can be grown.

Function of culture and/or analyst to interpersonal family system or to internal objects "system"

In most cultures, extended family members, friends and institutions within the community have been available to come to the aid of individuals or families needing help to deal with uncontained, disruptive and pathogenic beta elements. There seems to be an instinctive aware-ness in many, if not most, people and cultures for this basic need of individuals and families. In fact, since prehistoric times, various people (oracles, shaman, medicine men, etc.) have been given the role within their social group or culture of performing alpha function for the needy members, and of continually regenerating the mythology, art, religion and healing professions to fulfill these needs. Psychotherapists and psychoanalysts are examples of such individuals. Winnicott (1967) described culture as the ultimate transitional space providing the imagery, myths, music, etc. – in short, the symbols necessary, as the working mental tools allowing the individual to make meaning of their ever-changing adaptational tasks. Psychoanalysis is an attempt to apply the scientific method to this age-old function. Psychoanalysts may do well to listen with more respect, not to minimize the value of skepticism, to those who have worked at this area of human endeavor far longer than we.

Notes

1 This paper was assembled for the 2014 Bion Conference, originally written in 1989 and was revised January 10, 2016.
2 See Figure 24.1.
3 Presented at the IPA Conference Nice, 2001.

References

Bion, W. (1959). Attacks on linking. *International Journal of Psychoanalysis* 40, part 4–5.
Bion, W. (1962a). A theory of thinking. *International Journal of Psychoanalysis* 43, parts 4–5.
Bion, W. (1962b). *Learning from Experience.* New York: Basic Books, Inc.
Bion, W. (1963). *Elements of Psychoanalysis.* London: Wm. Heinemann Medical Books Limited.
Cage, J. (1947). *The Seasons (For Orchestra).* Premiered in New York, May 18, 1947. Peters Edition EP 6744.
Coe, Fred and Arthur Penn. (1962). *The Miracle Worker.* United States: United Artists.
Freud, S. (1911). Formulations on the two principles of mental functioning. *S.E.* XII: 213–226, London: Hogarth Press, [1964].
Freud, S. (1924). The economic problems of Masochism. *S.E.* XIX: 157–179, London: Hogarth Press.
Gooch, J. (2001). Bion's perspectives on psychoanalytic technique (unpublished).
Klein, M. (1946). *Notes on Some Schizoid Mechanisms. Envy and Gratitude and Other Works.* New York: Adel Publishing Co. Inc., 1977.
Meltzer, D. (1973). *Sexual States of Mind.* Scotland: Clunie Press, Perthshire.
Winnicott, D. (1967). The location of cultural experience. *International Journal of Psychoanalysis* 48, part 3.
Wordsworth, W. (1799). The prelude. In *The Complete Poetical Works.* London: Macmillan, 1888.

25

LOST TO REPETITION

Hysteria from the perspectives of Bion, Lacan, and Green

Avedis Panajian

In the past several decades, the incidence of the diagnosis of hysteria has significantly decreased in the United States. One major reason has been the incompleteness of the oedipal level organization and fragmentation of the psychic structures in the patients we are now seeing leading to an increase in the diagnosis of borderline personality. Therefore, according to Green (1997), there has been a de-sexualization of psychoanalysis. Through a case presentation, I hope to demonstrate that pre-oedipal dyadic levels of personality organization can be integrated with oedipal struggles, and hysteria can be placed within the context of sexuality and gender identity. I hope to illustrate how the passions or madness of a patient must be invited in the transference to help treat the hysterical character. Furthermore, I hope to demonstrate how the models proposed by Bion, Lacan, and Green helped me in working with this patient.

S., a 30-year-old single female, is the oldest and the only female of three siblings. She has been in analysis with me for seven years. Her father abandoned the family when S. was 3 years old. Father and daughter had a very close, sensual, and mutually "adoring" relationship. They would whisper in each other's ears and tell how much they loved each other. Father called her "my angel" and always stroked her hair. They were physically very demonstrative of their love for each other and would repeat certain songs and develop a rhythm and a pattern together. Her siblings were very envious and S. remembers being rather angry at them, and at times biting them out of anger. When the father left the family for another woman, S. kept waiting for his return. It is very probable that her father was excessively exciting and over-stimulated S. to a point that ruptured her ego. Excessive excitation is destabilizing to a child and does not allow the child to experience her body in a potentially proto-thinking and binding manner. Without an internal sense of registering one's bodily experience, repression of the sexual unconscious would not be possible.

She shut down emotionally and did not tell anyone of her fantasies of his return. The father wrote to her constantly and called her my "special star" in his letters. Even though S. described her father and their relationship in terms of an idealized mirroring of each other, she knew from the beginning of her treatment that her father did not "lay down the law." He was unable to plan, organize, or set limits in the family. When I first looked at S. closely, I was reminded of a teenage boy behind the appearance of a well-dressed female. I always wondered to whom was I speaking: a boy, a little girl behind a dressed-up woman, or a 30-year-old female?

S. often described her mother as highly efficient and in constant work mode. Even though her mother left the children in utter chaos, she always made sure that they had food and all the material things they needed. S.'s need for comfort was fully satisfied by her mother. However, she described her mother as emotionally distant, removed, mechanical, and unable to be emotional or sensual with her children. Mother gave the children total freedom without tending to their emotional needs. She never told S. about her father; she was quite effective in evading anxiety and pain in life. Her mother married twice more, and each time, the men left her. According to S., her mother only needed a male body in the house. She would not give these men any power, nor did she care to have a real relationship with them.

S.'s brothers turned to drugs; one of them overdosed and killed himself two years ago. S.'s physical appearance became a preoccupation for the mother. When S. was 17 years old, her mother recommended, and found, a surgeon to do a butt lift for her. S. worked as a model and made a great deal of money. She became a very angry teenager and somewhat of a tomboy. S. joined her mother's empty life of compulsive shopping, eating, and going out together to the different malls. She was perfectly and completely there for her mother. They gave each other a pseudo sense of completion. S. has internalized her mother as a removed but omnipotent woman. The mother tells S. to marry a wealthy man – a man who would do anything for her. The mother shows little curiosity about her daughter and has little insight into her daughter's internal contradictory mental states. She wants the daughter to be satisfied, and not be interested in loving or learning, or to have the ability for emotional connections. S. has lived a life of unconsciously competing with her mother, harboring unconscious feelings of hostility and guilt. S. uses her anxiety to falsify herself. She is dominated by fantasies of complete satisfaction that actually lead her to disillusionment and dissatisfaction. Throughout her life, S. has been compulsively driven to have sex with men; be desired; not listen to herself; know exactly how to seduce, please, satisfy men sexually, and then abandon them. S. falsifies herself by self-induced auto-stimulation that leads to accelerated "thoughts" and ends up convincing herself that the encounter is going to be exciting. This way, she is ready to coerce herself and the other as if it is going to be a novel experience. Of course, this is nothing but repetitive masturbatory activity and not an emotional experience. This is organ and sensual pleasure that she has experienced countless times, leaving her rather deadened. She repeats creating a deformed container/contained relationship. Underneath her anxiety, satisfaction, and disillusionment, there is a removed coldness that allows her to keep identifying with her mother. She establishes auto-erotic excitation by an ongoing fixation to physical exercise, performed to a point of utter exhaustion; and by exact food intake, while strictly watching her weight. Seeking pleasure with "cute" men, S. is focused on organ pleasure and sensual stimulation. She has felt little remorse about her manipulative and seductive skills.

When a baby is not properly contained, the baby lacks the experiences of being gathered, held, and given some form by a containing person. It is natural for babies to actively search for sensuous objects in order to organize their experiences. Such objects, including one's mental capacities, act as substitute containers. S. has been living with two different identities. From early life, she got full satisfaction at home. She continued to nurse from her mother until the age of 3 without feeling any emotional connection or loving feelings toward her mother. She loved the satisfaction and the safety of sucking. When she was not nursing, she felt persecuted and attached herself sensually to her father in the narcissistic mirroring of an ideal self and an ideal object.

Bion (1962) described the above in the following way:

> The need for love, understanding and mental development is now deflected, since it cannot be satisfied, into the search for material comforts. Since the desires for material comforts are reinforced, the craving for love remains unsatisfied and turns into over-weening and misdirected greed. . . . Since this state originates in a need to be rid of the emotional complications of awareness of life, and a relationship with live objects, the patient appears to be incapable of gratitude or concern either for himself or others. This state involves destruction of his concern for truth. Since these mechanisms fail to rid the patient of his pains, which he feels to be due to lack of something, his pursuit of a cure takes the form of a search for a lost object and ends in increased dependence on material comfort; quantity must be the governing consideration not quality.
>
> (p. 11)

S. holds on to this reality unconsciously and experiences it as the only reality that governs life and living relations. She is stuck in wanting to prove that she is loved on the one hand, and sexually desired on another hand. She confuses craving, desiring, and love all together. She uses her anxiety in the service of overstimulation and is fully confident on how to give a man an orgasm. Her fantasy life is based on material possessions and the illusion that drives her to crave and search for the "cute" man whom she can sexually conquer by being desired, and whom she can devalue and abandon without the slightest disappointment. She will always leave the man and feel fully comfortable with satisfaction and retaliation. In her relation-ship with men, nothing is kept unknown. She ensures that the future feels just like the past: triumph, satisfaction, and retaliation. The demands to satisfy her cravings, desires, and being adored transform the reality of the unknown other – and the unknown herself – into predict-able, repetitive, and masturbatory activities. Her cravings destroy awareness of time and space. She uses her erotic manipulative skills to induce excitement for the purpose of annihilation of psychic reality, and prevents herself from learning from experience. She operates as she calls it on "autopilot." Through projective identification she annihilates differences. She satisfies the man sexually and receives the "proof" that she is loved by having a man treat her exactly the way she plans it. Shortly after, she is unsatisfied, bored, and leaves the man. Her cravings are satisfying for her. She transgresses taboos and feels satisfied during the sexual craving. After-wards, she finds herself at times in a paralyzing depression with conversion symptoms. She becomes very tired and cannot leave her bed – the bed which she equates with her father. Suffering the guilt and tolerating the ability to be conscious of guilt are very difficult for her. Mourning the emptiness of her mother as well as her own emptiness lead to labile feelings of anger, sadness, and defeat. One way she evades facing anxiety around her psychic reality is by using crying in a quiet and grudging way. She tries to pressure me through non-verbal, confusing communication by transforming herself from a childlike, despairing, worthless per-son to a silent, angry, and bitter one. All these are aimed at diverting my focus away from helping her to pause and tend to herself and her disillusionment. Her craving for reassurance and intense need for repetitive proof that I desire her become very powerful. The madness or the passion in the transference becomes quite powerful and very erotically charged when she transforms herself into a young girl or boy. During these moments, there is no concern for self-respect or for respecting the truth of the moment. She appears pained and defeated in failing to actualize her imaginary predetermined and familiar plan. The Real and the Imaginary dominate the session. Paternal symbolic functions are at their minimal. The question that occurs to me is what does she want from me? Does she want me to take in her dramatic, passionate display of herself? Is it all one big repetition? Soon, she gets a severe neck pain and headache in the session. They seem to come as a defense against understanding herself. Perhaps the key is not to understand but to receive her madness without retaliating or abandoning her. Then, angrily, she avoids eye contact with me and wets her lips with her tongue. After a few minutes everything disappears. I am erased. By not looking at me, she uses her negative perception to erase my presence. This is what is called negative hallucination. Every attempt is made to deny my presence once she is not given the feelings of being desired or adored. The only reality is the reality of her cravings and illusions to be desired and satisfied. External reality of others is negated. Rapid shifts of identifications become quite confusing since her internal state is characterized by contradictory identities. At times, simultaneously, while she is denying my presence, she exhibits erotic and seductive moves to induce me to go along with her reality. She covers her love of ignorance by asking me questions. I am seen as the "subject who is supposed to know." I am not sure that she wants to learn from experience. I experience such demands for knowledge as a seductive attack on my mind. They are directed to distort and confuse me, hoping that she could discover that I too misuse knowledge, and I too am unworthy to be listened to and trusted. The genuine and tolerant analyst is experienced as a threat to her difficulty in dealing with the truth of the moment.

Kohon (1986), influenced by the French school on hysteria, describes it this way:

> The question the hysteric poses is: 'Am I a man or a woman?' (Leclair, 1971, p. 376). She cannot decide whom to finally choose between her father and her mother. She will remain in the middle without getting too intimate with either. Her desires will stay unsatisfied. She cannot determine the object of her desires. She stays dependent on another's desire. The hysteric is able to detect what is really missing in the other and what is really vulnerable in the other. That way, she ignores her desires and avoids her dread of dependency by controlling the other's desires.
>
> *(p. 376)*

Kohon is not trying to describe a developmental phase but a moment, when after the full recognition of sexual differences, a woman has to make a change from mother to father. This is the place where a drama develops. She tries to win the father as an early triangular object. The maternal and paternal relationship makes it difficult for the woman to develop healthy triangulation. Pseudo-triangulations lead to a pseudo-separated identity for the woman. As Bion (1962, p. 11) stated, "The craving for love remains unsatisfied and turns into overweening and misdirected greed."

S. met R., an extremely wealthy man who had his own plane and was married with two children. R. is also on autopilot, buying her countless shoes, clothes, furniture, cars, travel tickets, and volunteering to buy her a house in an exclusive neighborhood in California. This idealized figure is supplying her with non-stop adoration, desire, and admiration. S.'s defense of disavowal is very effective. On one hand, she knows something significant is lacking in the man and in herself; on the other hand, she sees him as a powerful, ideal figure. At times, she has spoken about him as "heartless, cold, and spineless." S. is not aware that the man is rather identical to her mother – and to herself – in his coldness, emptiness, and heartlessness. She is always excited about his endless supplies. She does not desire him. However, there seems to be a hidden rivalry around who excites the other and who controls the excitement. S. frequently regresses to anality, such as controlling, cleaning, turning vitality into deadness, and planning in order to control her oral regression that will take her right back to her cold and removed mother. She denied the truth for a long time that she lacked the ability to love, and whatever ability of loving she had, was hostage to her cold and emotionally removed mother. With R., she becomes the *absolute* jouissance of the fantasy father who possesses all the women. She promotes the myth of infinite jouissance and devalues the finite jouissance. She said,

> I need to say no, but he gives and gives without stop. That really excites me, I crave it, but I have no feelings for him. All I do is be nice and give him sex. I can get him to do anything that I want.

With R., she lives "in the Real," in immediacy. She experiences no gaps or lacks, and lives in utter absence of signification. Lacan (1977) reminds us that a word is "a presence made of absence" (p. 65). In the Real, there is an absence of relations with herself or the other. In the Real, she totally loses herself in endless quantity. Muller (1983) states "the term jouissance catches the ecstatic quality of it but not the horror. Unburied corpse is stuck in the Real. Only the symbolic order can carry appropriate funeral rites" (p. 28, 29). In the session, when she becomes aware of not desiring R., she becomes disillusioned about the loss of her craving. The "pleasure that is beyond the pleasure already implies the existence of other people and that impedes the satisfaction" (Fink, 1997, p. 226).

Fink (1997) describes how interpreting the unconscious can go on forever. Questioning in a way that invites the patient to talk about her excitement, questioning in a way that shows the analyst's desires and interests, and the importance of the analyst staying an enigma, all these will help the patient to become aware that she is "that person that is craving."

S. has met another man whom I shall call B. B. is a waiter, a recovered alcoholic, who is in rather poor medical condition. He is recovering from an accident and is hardly making it financially. S. states that B. is the only man who does not put up with her. He is the only man who turns her down sexually. He is kind, loving, and very funny. To her shock, he does not crave to touch her all the time. Her feelings of rejection, anger, and hurt are very intense. When she is with B., she craves the material comfort through constant touching and craving "to be fucked and fuck him." B. finds her very beautiful; he is kind to her, but also has told her that she is a very "confused child/woman." What has been so striking to her is that B. loves to tell stories and loves to read. She is realizing that she does not know how to talk. B. talks to her and listens to her. However, she does not know how to communicate without sensuous craving and "fucking the guy." At one point, I recognized that our communication was too smooth and suspected that she had sensed that our communication was somewhat pleasing me. Therefore, she was going on pleasing me while there was utter absence of emotions and disturbance between us. There was no dynamic communication – only static. I said to her, "This communication lacks back and forth; this you find very painful and it provokes you. Indeed, I wonder if you are covering your resentment and keeping yourself silent to hide your pain by keeping me pleased with this empty speech." She covered her face and began to cry. It felt genuine. She was covering her face while crying. I asked her if she was "ashamed, discovered." She said, "Yes." I said, "an imperfection without anger and hurt by me but turned against yourself." She said, "It is all my fault." I asked her, "What is so frightening about displaying your feelings without knowing the outcome?" She did not explore it.

The above static communication is an example of what Bion (1963) called "reversible perspective." He said,

> Reversible perspective is evidence of pain; the patient reverses perspective to make a dynamic situation static. The work of the analyst is to restore dynamic to a static situation and so make development possible. The patient maneuvers so that the analyst's interpretations are agreed; they thus become the outward sign of a static situation.... It is the dynamic quality of the interpretation that evokes evasive reactions.

> *(pp. 60–61)*

S. frequently resorts to the "superiority of Un-Learning" as a way of preventing the search for truth. She has a difficult time freeing herself from a life that is based in the prison of the concreteness of her senses. Tolerating a no-thing in her and between us is very difficult for her.

One day, she made dinner for B. for taking care of her dog. Then, she asked him if he could help her at the farmer's market setting up certain items for sale. B. responded by saying that he had to work and that he needed the time to rest. She went back and forth trying to persuade him in her seductive and erotic ways. B. told her "why don't you get your crazy rich guy to fly his plane and help you?" She said, "I am planning to break up with him. He only gives and gives but has no heart." Later, she called R. and R. said that he would be there next day. R. came the next day after flying for five hours in his private plane. He bought her a $200,000 car and helped her set up the tent at the farmer's market. S. was beside herself with excitement. In telling me, I wondered if her entire body was a phallus that was in endless orgasm. However, slowly, the phallic jouissance tied to the symbolic led her to feel a lack. I had asked her if their bodies were present in their sexual excitement. She said no, she does not feel her body or his. She finds herself somewhere else. I said, with a question, "Somewhere beyond pleasure?" She said, "How did you know?" in an erotic way. The more she asked, the more she was getting shy and blushing. S. is not connected and present with her own body. In fact, as Lacan would say, she rejects her body. Her somatic symptoms are reminders that she has rejected her body. Although she offers her body to the delight and to the excitement of the other, she is not really present. Desire does not enter in her experience. R. made a comment during the farmer's market visit, which S. experienced as empty and heartless; he was already devalued and dismissed in her mind. She then called B. and asked him if there is a problem between them sexually. B. said, "I don't know who you are. You have problems and something about your chemistry. You are a machine that does not stop." S. asked a girlfriend about what B. told her. The friend said, "He is probably disgusted by you." She said, "Nobody has ever turned me down sexually. I will drive him crazy if I want to. I will wear and act in such a way that he cannot turn me down." She continued, "R. is like my mother, non-stop in giving, but no feelings, no sensitivity."

She started the next session by saying that if she slows down, she becomes really angry at her mother. S. said she needs to be touched all the time. She cannot be with a man without the two touching each other. B. was reading a story to her but read the story from a distance. She said that she had never listened to a story. He was not next to her touching her while reading. R. tells only facts. He gives facts without elaborations. S. finds it is very difficult to listen without being touched. I told her "that even though you try to touch me through her movements, gestures, sounds, it must be difficult for you to be with me for the entire session." She recognized how little she was able to carry our work outside the sessions. She started to cry, and it seemed genuine. I noticed that her tongue was wetting her lips, and it did not strike me as a seductive move. By having her tongue and saliva touch her lips, there was a comfort that was allowing her to be present with me.

S.'s hostile feelings toward her mother instantly turns into crying. Unconscious feelings of guilt instantly turn against herself. It is difficult for her to suffer the guilt around erotic and hostile feelings without turning them against herself. In one of the sessions, she had a dream of two women having sex with each other. She had a difficult time elaborating or expanding on my questions. She could only hear the dread of separation from her mother but not the erotic wishes and phallic wishes to triumph over her. Her mother calls her and tells her to marry R. R. will take care of her and B. has no money. S. said: "How does she [mother] think that I know how to be in a relationship?" She continued, "She lives in a separate room with her third husband who is leaving her and she does not care. She married a much younger man who looks good and they never talk to each other." Unlike her mother, S.'s body is always in distress. Her body's distress is due to her conversion reactions and her confused sexuality. She always looks fragile physically. S. finds herself viewing others as too fragile to receive her projections. Her identifications with the fragility of others are in part to deny her own sensitivity, hurt, and sadness. Splitting, denial, and projective identification are among other defenses that she uses to disconnect from her own fragility.

S. is curious about B.'s symbolic ability which she lacks. Recently, she woke up in the morning in the same bed with B. Unlike other times, when she gets up from bed very quickly and plans her day, she stayed in bed with B. until 10 a.m. B. was being very loving and sensitive to her about the stress that she was under due to selling her house and looking for a new place. It was the first time that she recognized he was being loving from a few feet away from her. In describing the distance, she pointed to the straight line between us and said, "Just like this," showing the distance between us. She began to cry, and I was very touched. I felt that I was with a very wounded girl and had the conscious fantasy of holding her and stroking her beautiful hair. I recognized the paternal transference was also at work. Her father always stroked her hair. S. recognized that it was the first time that a man was talking to her from a distance and that she was listening without the man touching her. Listening to B. was making up the loss of maternal touching, the loss of the sensuous. She said to me, "There is distance between us but you are always here for me." She said: "Is it my fault that I never learned this?" I said: "You are now having two feelings about the same thing. Sadness for the distance, but you are moved by the closeness that you feel." This is an example of what Bion called "binocular vision" – the ability to have two different feelings about the same thing. It is a must for the development of confidence in oneself. She said, "Mother had no friendship with her husbands." They were just bodies in the house. B. had told S. that she has lived like a "princess" and that he would not put up with that.

S. totally negates her primal scene fantasies. She uses the emptiness and the coldness of her mother to annihilate the primal scene. In the previous session, when she was describing the distance between her and B., and between her and myself, her sadness was hiding a great deal of hate. The sadness and the hate had to do with her awareness that none of the sensual excitement and touching had awakened her cold mother and herself. Only by reviving traces of memory of her mother, such as how little her mother helped the children, including the brother who had recently died due to an overdose; and only by reviving the memory traces of her overexciting father, S's novel fantasies can come forth and get projected onto me, allowing her a new and unique experience that has the potential to heal her narcissistic wounds and feel alive – not cold and deadened. Facing such traumatic feelings in the present and in a dramatic way gives her a chance to feel transformed through an alive analyst who is in an emotional relationship with her – not a cold and deadened, mother analyst. This provides her a renewed freedom to have a deeply felt experience.

R. has been telling her that she needs a house in an exclusive area where she could relax and be away from all the pressures. She has been tempted to let him buy her a house. But, she is becoming aware that to be an object of desire for him is to keep denying her desires, body, and sexuality. It only keeps her more confused and lost. She is slowly learning that R. does not really represent "the law of the father." He dreads castration just like her dread around being castrated. S. has to negate "the name of the father" by being with R. The imaginary function of the symbolic prevails over the unknown of the Real. Father was the imaginary symbolic for her. He left and she had to suffer by becoming the phallus for the mother. She stays anxious and unsatisfied. Anxiety leads her to be in an ongoing phallic state ready to fill up the fantasy of a castrated mother and men with ongoing castration anxiety like R. When she becomes aware of my limitations such as during a pause or a gap, she becomes disillusioned, anxious. Then the erotic and dramatic theatrical display takes over. Or, she shuts down and becomes numb. She is unable to oscillate between omnipotence and helplessness. The numbness is often a communication of how often she lived in such a pressured mental state.

S. has been a very frightened person all her life. The only one with whom she felt safe was her father. She looked after her siblings, and she hated it. S. sold her house and asked B. if she could stay with him for a month before she finds a place to live. B. said that changes the nature of their relationship into more boyfriend and girlfriend. S. was instantly disillusioned and said, what about as friends? B. was hesitant but sensitive to her feelings. S. felt intensely that she wanted to fuck him very badly. However, she did not try and left to go to her home. The next day, R. called her and asked if he could come by and help her pack. S. agreed and R. came to help her the next day. He helped her by showing her how to make boxes for packing, rented a truck for her to move, and got her tickets to have her father come and visit her. According to S., he did everything for her. S. called B. and told him that she missed him. B. asked if R. was there. After learning that R. was with S., B. was really frustrated. She asked him "Why are you upset? You said that you wanted to be friends." I asked her whether that was a way to exact revenge for not fucking him the night before and for B. being hesitant to invite her to live with him. She agreed and started to cry. She said, "He told me that there was something wrong with our chemistry." I asked her if she understood chemistry only in terms of sex and craving for each other. She said "Yes, what else could it be?" I told her, "If I too do not instantly satisfy you and adore you, but I'm interested to help you transform and find your own truth, then, you might be feeling that I don't desire you." She was crying more, and the nature of her psychic pain was expanding into different dimensions. There was more interest in staying with the truth of her transformation. She said,

> I create such a mess; I get so disconnected from myself. I am not even present. R. gives and gives, it's for himself. He has no spine. I repeat the same things. B. respects me, how could I do this to him? I really hurt him. How could there be any chemistry? There is something about my father in this. I have been missing him.

She was unconsciously connecting the rage at her father and her wish to destroy and castrate him for abandoning her and perhaps for choosing her mother over her. S. was having some ability to feel her guilt.

Bion (1963) said, "For the analytic experience to increase the patient's capacity for suffering even though patient and analyst may hope to decrease pain itself" (p. 62). He also said,

> The patients come for treatment, of whom I wish to formulate theories, experience pain, but not suffering . . . the intensity of the patient's pain contributes to his fear of suffering pain . . . pain is inflicted or accepted but is not suffered, except in the view of the analyst or other observer.
>
> *(1970, p. 19)*

The next session, S. looked drained and it was obvious that she had been really suffering. She was slowed down and the gaps helped her come up with more and new transformative feelings and thoughts. While crying non-stop she said, "I don't connect with myself." I was very quiet, respecting the not craving. There was no internal Pac-Man chewing her feelings and thoughts and creating nothingness. She said, "I don't hear myself; it is not my father or mother. It is me." She said again, "I don't hear myself." She was suffering her psychic pain. She was finally tolerant and able to have some inner containment. I said, "You don't hear the things that take you from your truth." She cried and was slowed down and contained. She repeated, "My own truth." Eventually, she said, "She feels like going away somewhere, just under the sun, with a glass of water." Clearly, she was hoping that she would not disappear in craving, but would continue to stay connected with herself. The sun, the water, and the aloneness act as a warm and loving relationship with herself. She said, "It helps her that she has been swimming in the pool at night when no one was there." Again, water and aloneness act to hold her together without the stimulation of people, enabling her to feel her body and become aware of her body. I asked her if the water was warm. She said, "A little, but, I am always cold." I had noticed after I said that, she had been shivering in the session and I had not noticed it. It was only after I asked her, I recognized that I had seen her shivering. This is an example of the analyst dreaming the patient in the session. I was unaware that I was so connected with her reality of the moment, I felt my mental state was matching her mental state. I noticed that there was a sense of at-one-ment between us. I asked her if she wanted a blanket. She said, "Yes, do you have one?" I gave her the blanket and she wrapped it all around her and was resting her head. At this point, as if she was dreaming also, she said, "I feel like a woman." I said, "Pausing, not running to mother or father, not getting lost whether you are a male or a female, you feel as a woman from within and not from outside." She was crying without much noise. I found her very attractive and erotically desirable. I said, "You are the priority, your center, your presence." She cried more and seemed very moved by what I said. When S. said that she "felt always cold," I was reminded of Green (1986) stating how people who suffered from the "dead mother complex" always felt cold. She said something that I did not remember even in the session. I ended up telling her, "You don't owe anyone anything." That statement really touched her. As if tons of weight was lifted from herself. She said that her father being present also helps her to slow down. Was she talking about the father who was visiting her or the father in the session? She said that she does not let herself feel that she has a choice. I said, "The choices are pretty clear – craving, autopilot, sexualizing living or tolerance." I posed the question, "What helps you to be true to yourself?" She said, "Between what I know and keep doing it or being in a battle." I said, "Self-respect, respecting others and noticing your inner movements do involve being in a battle."

When hate, envy, greed, minus K, hallucinatory states, and reversible perspectives attack the alpha function, transformation is not possible. With S., it has been important to know the functions and differences between anxiety, pleasure/displeasure, mental pain, and psychic suffering. Seeking and craving satisfaction through sensuous means has led her to ongoing displeasure and to mental pain due to the repeated destruction of transformative emotional connections with the self and others. Her ability to suffer mental pain has been seriously damaged. In the past few weeks her capacity to suffer mental pain and contain mental elaboration has enabled her to place some value on the paternal symbolic function. She has been able to communicate her mental pain in verbal ways. As she is able to tolerate psychic suffering, she is able to find words to tell me about it.

One year after termination, the patient sent me the following letter:

> Dear Dr. P. You rectify the wrongs done by loving me and showing me that way. A father from a different time and place. All in reverse but better late than never. And how you heal the world so – fighting for the truth and a better world. You were born straight as an arrow and with an ancient wisdom. Your gifts are my miracle. Constant reminder that I must wake up and find my own inner voice. A faint murmur is slowly becoming more pronounced. Finding my way with your light shining above. I see the picture more clearly now – superimposed images connected by some powerful magnetism that transcends this dimension I know. We say good-bye but I never really do leave your office.

In conclusion, I discuss how the models proposed by Bion, Lacan, and Green helped me in my work with this patient.

Bion's Grid was a great help in understanding how the analyst needed the patience to detect the patient's stuckness on the proto-mental level of operating. She was stuck in repeating a cycle of beta elements in the service of action. She was using verbal and non-verbal communications in the service of lies, falsities, and hallucinatory superior ways. Her functioning on the Grid was rigid and not dynamic. She was often unable to move from beta to alpha functioning. She was rigidly stuck in the middle of the two and oscillating from beta to alpha and from alpha to beta. Too often, the container/contained relationship was characterized by minus container/contained. Therefore, it was difficult to allow the evolution of a third that was beneficial to both of us. Her sensory functioning spoiled the containers, or she was able to find rigid containers. As a result, she became more frantic and greedy.

Bion's model of projective identification and the importance of being patient, undisturbed, and flexible were of major significance. Projective identifications were rapidly shifting, and it was important to stay as a feeling analyst who was able to receive them. The patient needed to show me her emotional and mental difficulties, and it was important to remember how Bion had valued Wittgenstein's teachings on looking and not thinking. One has to look at how a word is used and learn from that and not think about how a word is supposed to be used. For Bion and Wittgenstein, it was crucial to observe how one was acting, and for what use the act was being carried out. Bion's reminding us to have imaginative minds was significant in understanding the internal clashes that were going on within this patient. I was reminded of the significance of being able to experience the meaning of a word. The patient only within the last two weeks has been able to understand the difference between using words she does not mean and taking the time to experience the words that she does mean. The consideration of intolerance of no-thing and having a greedy mind that devours time and space was very helpful in showing the patient her terror, rage, and envy of loving connections. The concept of enforced splitting, between material and psychical satisfaction, was essential in understanding the entire treatment of this patient.

Lacan's concepts of the Real, the Imaginary, and the Symbolic were very valuable. The patient's illusions in living in the completeness of the Real and foreclosing the paternal symbolic function were equally useful. The differences between need, desire, demand, and jouissance played a major role and were a major confusion with this patient. The notion that desire has no object was an important contribution. The movement from desire to jouissance and how jouissance led to guilt and dissatisfaction became clearer for this patient. Lacan's focus on the analytic attitude had a great deal of similarity with Bion's advice to analysts. The importance of not inducing guilt and judgments, and not acting as all-knowing were good reminders in working with this patient. What has been helpful is questioning the area of knots in the patient in order to welcome the repressed and the taboos that had caused so many symptoms. The notion that psychosexuality and the unconscious have a complex relationship was something to which I held on. Incestuous desires that had generated repression and other defenses needed to be welcomed. The relationship between lack and desire and the symbolic father were useful in working with this patient. The role of castration anxiety, primal fantasies, and masculinity and femininity were all helpful and complex in exploring with S.

Andre Green's focus that analysis has been desexualized by focusing on representations and the accuracy of such representation has deprived analysis of being a place of welcoming passion and madness in the working relationship. Green's focus on the hysteric's relationship between love, desire, and sexuality was a reminder of this patient's confusions. Green comments on the nature of desire, object choice, the role of fantasy, and the patient's relationship to her body. The hysteric is more concerned to get proof that she is loved and desired rather than the quality of the love she is offered. She interprets the analyst's respect for her as his finding her undesirable. If she is told the truth, she feels she is undesirable. The hysteric suffers from repeated narcissistic injury and depression. She feels guilty about her incestuous and aggressive feelings, and may have anal fixations, which are used to try to control her oral needs. The hysteric has a very difficult time suffering guilt due to her difficulties in facing separateness from the primary object. She cannot choose between the mother and the father, and as a result, she questions whether she is a male or a female. She has a hard time bringing the two parents together in her fantasies. I found Green's work on the "dead mother complex" to further help me with this patient. Her overexcitement and overstimulation often were not only a sense of feeling alive, but also a defense against being her cold and emotionally removed mother. They were a defense against aliveness and separation from her mother.

References

Bion, W.R. (1962). *Learning from Experience*. London: William Heinmann. [Reprinted London: Karnac, 1984 and *Seven Servants*. New York: Aronson, 1977].

Bion, W.R. (1963). *Elements of Psychoanalysis*. London: Tavistock. [Reprinted in *Seven Servants*. New York: Aronson, 1977].

Bion, W.R. (1970). *Attention and Interpretation*. London: Tavistock. [Reprinted in *Seven Servants*. New York: Aronson, 1977.

Fink, B. (1997). *A Clinical Introduction to Lacanian Psychoanalysis: Theory and Practice*. Cambridge, MA: Harvard University Press.

Green, A. (1986). *On Private Madness*. London: Hogarth.

Green, A. (1997). Chiasmus: Prospective-borderline viewed after hysteria; retrospective-hysteria viewed after borderlines (Part II). *Bulletin* 49, pp. 28–45, European Psychoanalytic Federation.

Kohon, G. (Ed.) (1986). *The British School of Psychoanalysis: The Independent Tradition*. New Haven: Yale University Press.

Lacan, J. (1977). *Ecrits: A Selection*. Trans. A. Sheridan. New York: W.W. Norton & Company.

Leclair, S. (1971). Jerome, or death in the life of the obsessional. In Schneiderman (Ed.), *Returning to Freud: Clinical Psychoanalysis in the School of Lacan*. New Haven: Yale University Press, 1980.

Muller, P.J. (1983). Language, psychosis, and the subject in Lacan. In H.J. Smith and W. Kerrigan (Eds.), *Interpreting Lacan*. New Haven: Yale University Press.

26

TRUTH, BEAUTY, REALITY

Paulo Cesar Sandler

> And finally, we must not forget that the analytic relationship is based on a love of truth – that is, on a recognition of reality – and that it precludes any kind of sham or deceit.
>
> *(Freud, 1937, p. 248)*

> When one **fabricates** an ideal ideal world, one deprives Reality from its value, its sense, its truth. . . . *The 'real world' and an 'apparent' world . . . in plain terms: reality and a **fabricated** world. . . . One curses on reality when one propagates the lie of an ideal world; through such lie mankind itself has been mendacious and utterly false down to its deepest instincts.* It worships the inverse values to those which alone could assure its prosperity; its future and the noble **right** to a real future.
>
> *(Nietzsche, 1888, p. 4; bold by Nietzsche, in italics, by myself)*

Is the principle of uncertainty, a principle of ignorance?

Are there any facts that at least partially justify the spending of time, life, and money when going to see an analyst for treatment? If they exist, they include the empirical substratum of psychoanalysis: the double tracked (Grotstein, 1981, 1986) situation of being submitted to analysis coupled with attempts to analyze other people (Sandler, 2013). **One subjects oneself to truthfully *listen* to what another has to say about his or her suffering, or lack thereof.** I define *to listen* as the act of paying the fullest possible *attention and care*, that includes an affective emotional experience of giving in which there are two constantly conjoined factors: (i) self-surrender and (ii) an absence of psychopathic profiteering. *To listen* must be differentiated from *to hear*, which is limited by our sensuous apparatus. Therefore one may listen to "the brave smell of a stone" (Chesterton, 1914; Melville, 1851). Clinical practice is the pursuit of "truth-O" (Bion, 1970, p. 9), which confers *the* scientific status to psychoanalysis, its truth-value. Bion's quasi-mathematical notation to "Origin", "O" represents an absolute, immaterialized truth (Bion, 1965; Sandler, 2005), ultimately unreachable – but "intuitable", usable, albeit transiently and in glimpses. Such a pursuit can be made through a trained "sensible intuition" as adumbrated by Kant: an apprehension of reality as it is, without resorting to rationalistic, explanative powers of deductive and inductive methods of "pure reason".

Rationalization is a term borrowed from primitive mathematics, meaning, to extract implicit "ratios". It corresponds to a typical mode of functioning of narcissistic, paranoid psychosis – hallucination and delusion are the climax of denial of Truth (Freud, 1911, 1912). Freud tried to unearth an approximation of "O" tooled by verbal formulations; initially, he used the German word *unbewusst*, translated to *unconscious* or *unknown*. Yet later he defined it as the quasi-Nietzschean "*das Es*", translated by Strachey's as *Id*. Hate of Truth, the mythical prohibition toward knowledge (Thorner, 1981), unfortunately also existent in the psychoanalytic movement as it is in the social milieu (including related disciplines, as psychology, sociology, literature, philosophy), debased those un-materializable terms into materialized, concretized jargon. In consequence, a matter of fact (unknown, das Es) turned out to be facts of the matter: their *sense* was lost, replaced by chaotic, idealistic *meanings*. Science was replaced by hermeneutics. There are those who hallucinate that they can grab the "unconscious", "O" as if it is a concrete thing, denying the ethos of "no-thing" appertaining to "O". Unable to tolerate "no-thing", one is unwittingly the prey of nothingness; one falls into the self-righteous delusion of "owning O". An added complication is that this first "victim" in a war against truth is the name of the discoverer: as soon as he dies, he or she is turned into gilded idol or hero. Crowned with the superiority ring and buried by fame (Bion, 1975; Thorner, 1981), its work leaves no trace of truth.

There are people within the psychoanalytic movement, who think that psychoanalysis is just a clever manipulation of symbols (Bion, 1962, p. 38; 1967, p. 148; and specially, 1975, p. 92) to concoct a "vast par amnesia to fill the void of our ignorance" (Bion, 1974, 1976, 1977b). Bion's warnings, according to him, were not heard:

> When I tried to employ meaningless terms – alpha and beta were typical – I found that "concepts without intuition which are empty and intuitions without concepts which are blind" rapidly became 'black holes' into which turbulence had seeped and empty concepts flooded with riotous meaning.
>
> *(Bion, 1977a, p. 229)*

In the year of his death, he renewed this warning:

> Much the same sort of thing happened when I transferred my activities – for a short space of time, I thought, perhaps five years – to the United States. It took a long time to get used again to the fact that nobody had ever heard of me, except one or two people who seemed to feel for some reason that they wanted further assistance. At the same time there were attributed to my qualities or abilities that seemed to be very wide of the mark: if I had had the qualifications or the addiction, I could have found myself thrust into the role of a sort of messiah or deity. All of this ran parallel with its being made crystal clear to me that I was a mere human being, that psycho-analysis was, after all, only a form of verbal communication, and that there were limits to what could be done with it – especially as one was dependent on having somebody who would listen to what one had to say.
>
> *(Bion, 1979, p. 377)*

Thirty years after his death, I witness vast, cunning clever paramnesias built with a rearrangement of his words, duly excised from the context in which they were written. There remains a persistent failure in apprehending that verbal formulations in psychoanalysis are just approximate models that keep correspondence in reality – *truth*, however they are not *truth-in-themselves*. A fleeting insight about the correspondence depends on the reader, the onlooker, or the audience.

Clinical experience demands "participant observation" of real facts, as they are, quite independently of the idealized, delusional idea of reaching them exclusively. Real facts, *Reality, Truth, Truthfulness*: quite independent of the name, it must be apprehended as what it is . . . *and* is not. *It* is anything that exists, *materialized and immaterializable*. But not *material or immaterial*. Freud elicited the existence of two forms of the *same* existence: material reality *and* psychic reality, *not* material *or* psychic. Contemporaneously to Freud, Einstein made a foray into apprehending reality with his intuition to describe the precise relationship between energy and matter, that of the square of the speed of light. Bion, in *Reality Sensuous and Psychic* (1970, p. 27), tried to unbury Freud's clarity, denied and suppressed by little learning.

The view that follows serves the practical tasks but not the rhetoric "manipulations of symbols" destined to rationally prove or disprove statements. For only lies require a thinker (Bion, 1970, p. 97). One must dispense with the established criteria of "oughtism" (Bion, 1977a, p. 277), applicable to the realm of external enforcement – as religion, politics, law, police, ideology, and pedagogy. My aim is to reach authoritative, but not authoritarian and false psychoanalysis (Sandler, 2015a):

> When this happens you feel the change deserves to be recorded and the dialogue between me and me might just as well be conducted between me and a fictitious character. The fiction can be so rhetorical as to be incomprehensible; or so realistic that the dialogue becomes audible to others. There is thus a double fear; that of the conversation being so theoretical that the thoughts might be taken for meaningless jargon; and that of the seeming reality. Having two sets of feelings about the same facts is felt as madness and disliked accordingly. This is one reason why it is felt necessary to have an analyst; another reason is the wish for me to be available to be regarded as mad and used to being regarded as mad. There is a fear that you might be called an analysand, or reciprocally, that you may be accused of insanity. Should I then be tough and resilient enough to be regarded and treated as insane while being sane?
>
> *(Bion, 1975, p. 124)*

Either the individual is engulfed by the herd, or the herd risks to be destroyed by the individual. To pursue the Truth-O, or "becoming O" or not to pursue, that is the question posed since Shakespeare, but rarely heard.

MYSELF: . . . the O which you represent seems to be itself a part of O which is sensuously apprehended. It is a part of an O of morality which is itself part of a sensuous domain of "ownership", sensuously perceived. There may be, and it would be impossible to believe that there is not, a domain which is infra-and ultra-sensuous. It is for this reason that I doubt the importance of "significant" ownership and all the accompanying apparatus of debt and morality as we usually conceive it. This assumption throws one back into a mental domain which is a source of endless confusion and difficulty and in which unending confusion is an essential (not accidental) feature. I do not suppose I shall ever know escape, but I think the character of the "sensuous" domain has not been exhausted.

BION: I don't understand.

MYSELF: Perhaps I can illustrate by an example from something you do know. Imagine a piece of sculpture which is easier to comprehend if the structure is intended to act as a trap for light. The meaning is revealed by the pattern formed by the light thus trapped – not by the structure, the carved work itself I suggest that if I could learn how to talk to you in such a way that my words "trapped" the meaning which they neither do nor could express, I could communicate to you in a way that is not at present possible.

BION: Like the "rests" in a musical composition?

MYSELF: A musician would certainly not deny the importance of those parts of a composition in which no notes were sounding but more has to be done than can be achieved in existent art and its well-established procedure of silences, pauses, blank spaces, rests. The "art" of conversation, as carried on as part of the conversational intercourse of psychoanalysis, requires and demands an extension in the realm of non-conversation.

BION: Is there anything new in this? You must often have heard, as I have, people say they don't know what you are talking about and that you are being deliberately obscure.

MYSELF: They are flattering me. I am suggesting an aim, an ambition, which, if I could achieve, would enable me to be deliberately and precisely obscure: in which I could use certain words which could activate precisely and instantaneously, in the "mind" of the listener, a thought or train of thought that came between him and the thoughts and ideas already accessible and available to him. (Bion, 1975, p. 189–189)

I try to differentiate typographically, "Truth" – appertaining to the Platonic realm – from "The truth", a phantasy of knowing and owning absolute truth. How to measure one's ability to apprehend Truth without disaster? (Bion, circa 1960a, published in 1992, p. 192). This demands a range of insensibilities and trained sensible intuition achieved only with experience. It is barred, in inverse proportion, to those who fear "catastrophic change", which always includes facing "Truth". Some cannot cope with their own endogenous aggression and lack of capacity to love. Tolerance *and* intolerance to pain can be expressed either by its narcissistic variation, homicide, or by its social-istic variation – suicide, and sometimes, by both.

To feel encompasses: (i) **sensations**, almost wholly materialized; they can be measured, as Helmholtz, who greatly influenced Freud, did; (ii) **feelings**, which has a predominant immaterialized existence. In the future, may be measured in quanta, if and when a method would be discovered to do it. Electro-biochemical data currently available are too gross to measure it. Feelings belong to the realm of "becoming", first proposed by Bion (1965). He earlier expressed it under an observational theory: "alpha-function" (Bion, 1962). That takes raw external and internal sensuous apprehended stimuli,[1] "beta-elements", a quasi-mathematical sign to denote the ultimate, unknowable reality, and transforms them in memory storable "alpha-elements" useful to make myths, to think and to dream (Bion, 1961, 1962, 1965, 1970). I suggested elsewhere that alpha-function "de-sensorializes" ultimate reality – or beta-elements, or "O" – in order to apprehend it (Sandler, 2011). This is sorted out in the space-time that "abides" the ultimately indivisible energy and matter, once formulated by Plato as "Ideal Forms". Our human sensuous apparatus may grasp, albeit imperfectly, mere appearances – which may dazzle the inattentive one. In contrast, real psychoanalysis is a method to intuit and then formulate verbally insights, made of materialized and immaterializable invariances, underlying and overlying the external "sensational" appearances. It is a living, first-hand, empiric, ever-renewed, and transient process, made from successive cycles of saturations followed by de-saturations followed by renewed saturations/de-saturations, or cycles of transformations. Doing this, Freud discovered dream-work, in a conjoint labor with his patients: the couple transformed the manifest content into a latent content; doing this Freud, as any scientist, a researcher into the unknown, spotted free-associations floating "in the air", or thoughts without a thinker, which, by their turn, allowed him to make constructions in analysis (Freud, 1937). There are people who endure pain, but do not suffer it (Bion, 1970); they feel the burden of the Truth, but do not suffer it; they go to see an analyst, but do not suffer the experience of analysis. Nietzsche's '*fundamental insight*' previewed it:

> There is no pre-established harmony between the furthering of approximations to truth and the well-being of humanity.
>
> *(Nietzsche, 1878–1880)*

Nietzschean's "well-being" corresponds to slavery to the Principle of Pleasure-Displeasure and abhorrence of the Principle of Reality (Freud, 1920). We analysts have at our disposal a compacted myth, in the form of a good humored, subtle quasi-parable elaborated by Bion, about liars'

> courage and resolution in their opposition to the scientists who with their pernicious doctrines bid fair to strip every shred of self-deception from their dupes leaving them without any of the natural protection necessary for the preservation of their mental health against the impact of truth.
>
> *(Bion, 1970, p. 100)*

Bion follows up: liars "laid down their lives in affirmations of lies so that the weak and doubtful would be convinced by the ardor of their conviction of the truth of even the most preposterous statements" (Bion, 1970). Those with enough experience in dealing with the so-called psychotics in hospitals are used to this; some are shielded from it. Not so the population, increasingly pray of Trumpian demagogues and its latest brand of defenders, that infected even the once serious editors of Oxford Dictionaries, the riders in the "post-truth" bandwagon. Let us follow with Bion:

> It is not too much to say that the human race owes its salvation to that small band of gifted liars who were prepared even in the face of indubitable facts to maintain the truth of their falsehoods. Even death was denied and the most ingenious arguments were educed to support obviously ridiculous statements that the dead lived on in bliss. . . . Their lives and the lives of their followers were devoted to the elaboration of systems of great intricacy and beauty in which the logical structure was preserved by the exercise of a powerful intellect and faultless reasoning. By contrast the feeble processes by which the scientists again and again attempted to support their hypotheses made it easy for the liars to show the hollowness of the pretensions of the upstarts and thus to delay, if not to prevent, the spread of doctrines whose effect could only have been to induce a sense of helplessness and unimportance in the liars and their beneficiaries.
>
> *(all quotes, from Bion, 1970, pp. 100–101)*

Turbinated by a tendency to favor pseudo-theatrical, cathartic manifestations in groups, I witness that members in the psychoanalytic movement interested in Bion's writings, unwittingly or not, deny the usefulness of an "underlying loyalty to the K link" and thus deny

> that the personality of the analyst and analysand can survive the loss of its protective coat of lies, subterfuge, evasion and hallucination and **may even be fortified and enriched by the loss**. It is an assumption strongly disputed by the psychotic and **a fortiori by the group, which relies on psychotic mechanisms for its coherence and sense of well-being**.
>
> *(Bion, 1965, p. 129; my bold)*

There are those who try to grasp "O", as they already have made before with other theories; those who promote cults of personalities, duly deceased. There are those who behave as if they "own" the truth, and as if they were apostles of the idol erected by themselves, with the approval of the group.

Previously, Bion's warnings were contained in scientific models: column 2 of the grid and transformations in hallucinosis that warranted feelings of emotional security to those who were clung to it. A man who, according to Freud, knew himself more than anyone who lived before and after him, questioned: *"To what extent can truth stand to be included in us, human beings"*? (Nietzsche, 1778–1880, 1881), Bion's inspiration from the work of Nietzsche – who may be seen as an intellectual, albeit the unknown "uncle" of Freud is (until now) rarely, or probably, never emphasized.[2] Deniers of truth, adept of novelties, fashionable today as they ever have been, prefer to eliminate the unabashed final admiration displayed by Nietzsche, Freud, Klein, Bion, and Italo Calvino towards the ancient world; they profited from the old Hebrew and Greeks' – especially from Socrates and Plato – discovery of *"an incomparable art: that of reading well. This is the prerequisite for all systematic knowledge. . . . the **sense for facts**, the last-developed and also the most valuable of all human senses"* (*The Antichrist*; my bold). Nietzsche, unlike many members of the political meritocracy of psychoanalytic, scientific, and artistic movements, questioned if truth could be just "a movable host of metaphors, metonymies, and anthropomorphisms" if "human relations" could be "poetically and rhetorically intensified, transferred and embellished, and which, after long usage, seem to people to be fixed, canonical and binding"; if "Truths: forgotten illusions to us . . . worn out metaphors drained of their former sensuous force; truths are coins which have lost their embossing: coins now considered as just metal, no longer can be considered as real coins" (Nietzsche, 1873). Bion used the same metaphor (1977b). His warnings received no wide audience: debasement by uncaring users who abhorred their own ignorance and loved their own vanity had been the winning side.

Two misconcepted habits of "mind"

Despite popular theorems from Descartes and his followers in the next centuries that claimed to own The Truth, up to now, no rationalized rules and explanations have been proven helpful to reach Truth. The latter requires no proof. It just *is*, waiting for an intuitive person to transiently intuit and use it – but not own it. It does not demand a thinker. There are thinkers and Thinkers; probably it would be better not to call some of them as such: those who perform ingenious manipulation of symbols, using parts of a former Truth, split by rationalizations, justifications, and explanations in order to disguise lies; clothed with the colors of Truth, they are presented as The Truth. There is no respect for Truth, nor to compassion and consideration to life. Truth is used just as a furnisher of parts to be used in those disguises – that seem seductive to some onlookers. They are used to prove a priori, or ad hoc theorization, which I suggest to call, "pseudo-theorization".

> Once psychologically necessary meaning has been achieved reason, as the slave of passions, transforms psycho-logically necessary meaning into logically necessary meaning.
> *(Bion, 1965, p. 73)*

> The lie and its thinker are inseparable. The thinker is of no consequence to the truth, but the truth is logically necessary to the thinker . . . the lie gains existence by virtue of the epistemologically prior existence of the liar. . . . Descartes' tacit assumption that thoughts presuppose a thinker is valid only for the lie.
> *(Bion, 1970, pp. 102–103)*

One may investigate the ever-rationalized rules invented by man to delay or preclude the cognition of Truth made through the action of wishful thinking – slavery to the Principle of Pleasure/ Displeasure principle, function as a means to avoid the pursue truth-O. Prevailing of Memory is a pleasure-ridden activity devoted to the past; desire is a pleasure-ridden activity devoted to the future; understanding is a pleasure-ridden activity to deny the unknown. Not only patients in the analytical setting, but also members of the psychoanalytic movement and related disciplines that

> proliferate endless stories, coherent, plausible, and apparently true. After some analysis it becomes evident that something is wrong: the associations vary from accounts of episodes alleged to have happened, to accounts that sound no less convincing but reveal flaws. From internal evidence it is clear that the event could not have happened. But for incongruities, the tone of assurance of the narrative would have lulled all suspicion.

If one challenges the narration, some of those people admit "the fault and at once begins to proliferate further fabrications": a forcing invitation to the onlooker "either to withdraw his comments and acknowledge the truth" of one's "assertion or to say openly that he is lying".[3]

There are real limits to human perception of reality that may or may not be intrinsic, *natural*, linked to our relative immaturity among the living species on Earth. The real limits escort our distorted, untruthful observations; they envelop Truth. Sheer need of survival from untruth may develop – under scientific and artistic apprehensions of Truth.

Among the mind's manipulative maneuvers one may quote the seemingly perpetual looking for meanings: a formation of constant conjunctions (Hume, 1748) as "a function of consciousness in the observer" (Bion, 1965, p. 73). My clinical observation suggests an expansion from Bion's emphasis about intolerance of "meaning or its lack". I observe the existence of an **excessive** tolerance of meaning, which is the "intolerance of **lack** of meaning". A posture that denies that there is a need to further searching, when one is involved in a pursuit of the truth-O. An alternative is the looking for the vector sense of any function considered; of any behavior or reaction that occurs, in the realm of phenomena. Conversely, when real psychoanalysis is replaced by hermeneutics, Truth is lost from one's sight. There will be as many "truths" as there are thinkers – the so called philosophical Idealism, or subjectivism, or solipsism. This deteriorates further, into relativism (Norris, 1997), in which there would be as many "truths" as the individual mind can invent. Apprehension of Truth and Reality are lost; to look for a *sense* (direction) is replaced by the finding of meanings – the "flights from fantasy" referred by Francis Bacon in *Novum Organon* (1620).

Outlined in Freud's complementary series (1915a, 1916–1917), one may realize that neuro-logic, historic, phylogenetic, ontogenetic, and ethologic studies indicate the limited range that can be grasped by our sensuous apparatus: sight, hearing, taste, smell, tactile, and the conscious system (Freud, 1900, pp. 620–626). Those limitations determine post-sensuous limitations, linked to intra-psychic distortions. The result of this complex situation is the realization that multiple factors are hampering a good enough apprehension of the many Invariants that char-acterize the original stimuli.[4] "Alpha-function" is a theory that attempts to study this mysteri-ous, but usable "processing path"; there are disturbances in our operation of alpha-function (Bion, 1962, p. 25).[5] Such a "processing path" proved not to be amenable to be studied by neurologic-endocrine (or electro-chemical) research: too macroscopic, too materialized ver-tex that leaves aside its ultimately immaterial, energetic ethos, already studied in the form of "functions" – as Freud did in his work about aphasia. Nevertheless, the sheer velocity in which this "processing track" occurs – since the observations of Helmholtz – and the currently dis-covered neuroplasticity indicate that its factors may well belong to the level of quanta. Those limitations distort a good enough apprehension of the basic invariances of the object observed.

Adding to those "natural" distortions one must consider those stemmed from the realm of affects, emotions, and emotional experiences. All of those distortions are both factors and functions of desire-ridden, hallucinated, and delusive activities of the mind. They may be seen as post-sensuous tendencies to distort perception, cognition, and realization of Truth. A good enough synthesis of all those distortions is furnished by Plato's metaphoric fable of the shadows in a cave. Those are, at least in part, the limitations of the participant observer, who interferes in the behavior of the object observed, a fact illuminated by Freud in his discovering of transference and projection; expanded by Klein, with her discovery of projective identifica-tion (1946); and, in physics, by Heisenberg (1958). I consider the existence of two syndromes that illuminate the origins of those distortions:

i   The "*sensuous-concretization syndrome*" (Sandler, 1988, p. 62; 1997a, 2015b, p. 284; 2015a, 2015c p. 277), a condition that in the face of the limited human perception "turns" what is neither entirely concretized nor sensuously apprehensible into a concrete entity. It is made through an obstructive belief, namely, that a neutral observer would not have any influence on the object observed. It is manifested by that which Immanuel Kant called "Naïve Realism" (Kant, 1781). The main consequence of this oversimplification reached its climax in the Positivist Religion, founded by Auguste Comte (1848).

ii The "*subjectivist idealization*" is the idea that there is no such thing as an external reality, an *out there* universe quite independent of us. It posits that truth does not exist at all: the universe would be what human beings think it is, because it would be entirely created in our minds: thoughts-with-a-thinker. I proposed elsewhere another broad designation to this posture, inspired by Kant, Naïve Idealism (Sandler, 1997b, 2001, 2013, p. 217). It hampers or precludes any kind of apprehension of Truth, overloading the capacities of mind with the prevalence of hallucination.

In both distortions, apprehension of Truth is replaced by feelings of owning The Truth.[6]

A basic, elemental misconception

Both habits of the mind, borne in misconceptions, are conducive to increasing mis-understand, under the prejudice that "an ability to mis-understand is superior to an ability to understand" (Bion, 1962, p. 95). This is an obstacle to the operation of the epistemophilic instincts (Freud, 1909), the begetter of the K-Link (Sandler, 2005, 2006).

A sense of truth?

A most unquoted contribution from Bion, "*Sense of Truth*" (Bion, 1961, p. 111) may be added to Freud's idea of conscience as a sense to apprehend psychic qualities: it is achieved when one realizes that the object that is loved and the object that is hated are the one and the same object. In the area of human thought, there seems to be an evolution from primitive paranoid states, the warmonger's *mind*, that phantasizes that he (or it) has the ownership of the absolute truth, as an attempt to win by force a situation when differences emerge. To wage wars against Truth is a hallmark of our still uncivilized civilization. It's inextricably linked to an immobilization in the Paranoid-Schizoid position, precluding a free movement toward the Depressive position: a severe submission to the pleasure/displeasure principle at the expenses of the inception of the reality principle. All of this depends on the paranoid, narcissistic endowments of a given individual, and the way it was dealt with by parents (Freud, 1915a, 1915b).

Roger Money-Kyrle (1978) offers us an historical illustration of a war against Truth, based on Alfred North Whitehead's (1925) scrutiny of the history of Galileo and the Inquisition's diatribe, under the vertex of Einstein's physics, which led to the conclusions that can be extended to all false discordances that characterize issues that were, in their beginnings, scientific, but later deteriorated into fashionable, ideological trends. As soon as Galileo, a representative of the scientific meritocracy, displayed the results of his telescope findings in astronomy, that the Sun was the center of the Universe, an outraged Roman Catholic establishment, representative of a political meritocracy, imposed, by sheer use of force, that the Earth was the center of the Universe (Sandler, 2012, 2015c).

Whitehead's conclusion differs from that of Bertolt Brecht's (1940) – the latter is an example of Naïve Idealism. Brecht phantasizes, ideologically, a tension between progressive science and a backward religion and puts forth an a priori rationalization: Galileo was "right" due to his anti-clerical posture and the Roman Catholics were wrong due to their obtuse authoritarianism – which he cannot see in his elected "party"; that can be put as "the left is always right".[7] Whitehead observes falsity in both Galileo and the Inquisition's statements: a real case of little learning, "a dangerous thing" according to an author dear to Bion, Pope (1711) – for the Universe "has not center". Under the psychoanalytic vertex, both of them, limited by the same *basic invariance*, that of nourishing phantasies of superiority, waged an hallucinated war against Truth, borne in paranoid-schizoid states of mind. To both, there was a belief: the Universe has a "center". Whitehead's insight proved to be much less popular – or immune to banality – than Berthold Brecht's ideological transformation. As the saying goes, "The first casualty of War is Truth"; its corollary is that any war is a conveyor of untruth.

There are more similarities between Naïve Idealism and Naïve Realism than what meets our eye through our rationalized, vain philosophy: both feel that they "*own*" the Truth. To the Realist, Truth resides in the concretely perceived things, in pure matter; it is immediately given to our senses; it can be wholly reached through the use of pure reason and depend of the application of morals: hell's gates are open to warmongers who claim to have a "positive", self-righteous view.[8] To the Idealist, Truth, reduced to personal opinions, is something relative to all opinions, having no importance whatsoever with the exception of indicating one's ideology. Both are the nest of "authoritarian personalities"[9] who claim to have dominion over The Truth: The Naïve Idealist feels that he is the only one who "really" *knows* the "ultimate truth": namely, that Truth does not exist. In its most recent guise: "post-modernism", a philosophy that states that Truth is not a philosophical issue. It embodies a "negative" view: hell's gates are open to rebellion and "revolution". The two naïvetés are expressions of the prevalence of the non-psychotic part of the personality, at the expenses of the psychotic part, sheltered from view through the former. Both Naïve Realist and Idealist display greed, or an ample and deep avoidance of displeasure. The capitalist and the communist ideologies may be an expression of this. Real historians of the twentieth century furnished descriptions about the invariants uniting the great defenders of bloody wars; or the greatest liars hitherto knew: Joseph Stalin's[10] and his still more famed plagiarist, Adolf Hitler's[11] hate toward truth and lack of consideration to life.

Even though the outward manifestations of the two naiveties admit discrimination, both are part of a common psychotic core. There is a social and psychiatric entity that phagocytes both Naïve Idealism and Realism: the psychopathic personalities with a destruction-bounded tendency. Those personalities, noticed by Bion in *Cogitations*, can be divided, according Jayme Sandler (1969) into Delinquency, which is mainly inward driven, and Psychopathy, genetically unconcerned with love (Bion, 1960a, p. 125), corresponding to Freud's primary narcissism and Klein's primary envy. Their acts are always acting-out, thanks to the abusing of projective identification. Both are endowed of a good sense of Reality but little or no regard for Truth. Their enhanced sense of reality enables them to avoid Truth at all costs. They may even stumble into Truth by accident or as a result of bad calculation. Evasion and lie are warranted by resistance as described by Freud; they postpone the apprehension of Truth *ad eternum* – life is so short. They gamble that their own life will run out before the moment that to face Truth becomes a real possibility. Chronic suicide usually replaces acute suicide; catastrophic change brought about by covert violence subdues its perception and facilitates the rationalized resistances (Sandler, 2009).

The Psychopathic Naïve Realist displays the acme of the feed-back cycle composed by greed and (self) envy: he cannot take into account that "the 'mind' is too heavy a load that the sensuous beast cannot carry" (Bion, 1975, p. 38). In his greedy search for complete satisfaction of his own desires, he appeals to enforced splitting (Bion, 1962, p. 10) to make an unending look for material goods. He over-values that which is materialized, at the expense of that which is immaterializable (or psychic). Concrete milk is seen as a good replacement for warmth and solace when the child deals with the breast. Because of this kind of splitting all Naïve Realists overvalue sensuously apprehensible facts: in brief, theatrical acting-out. Their acute sense of reality and acute disregard for truth makes him or her an indefatigable worker in some areas: politics, economics, entrepreneurial activities, robbery. All Naïve Realists display the prevalence of schizoid phenomena rather than paranoid phenomena. They were, historically, the main actors of the artificial separation (splitting) of matter from the mind. Under the social vertex, they are responsible for "wild" or "crony capitalism" that marked the inception of capitalism.

The Naïve Idealist believes that the universe and human beings are not what they are, but they are that which we desire them to be – since the nineteenth century, this was subsumed by a "new man", both by Marx and Engels and by Hitler and Himmler's "SS man". Both Naiveties deny the existence of "thoughts without a thinker" (Bion, 1963).

Naïve Idealism is expressed in the psychoanalytic movement by the belief that the analyst may focus just on the "inter-subjectivist" hermeneutics. In emphasizing just the analyst's reactions, feelings, and emotions, it phatastically "empowers" the analyst as if he or she would be the most important person in the analytic session, rather than the patient (Bion, 1957). Idealism had a few disguises in fashionable "theoretical" non-sense since 1950: the conscious "use of counter-transference", outside the analyst's own analysis; later, the claims about "enactment", full of confessions of "counter-transference", as if the unconscious would be the reservoir of the patient, but not of the analyst. Increasingly less value is attributed to the patient's state of mind, or his or her intra-psychic functioning, to the point of denying its existence. The conscious examination of the analyst's state outside the session replaced the analyst's own training or re-analysis. The analyst will be contended with his issuing of personal opinions. Transformations are overvalued; invariances are dismissed. Bion's attempts to pursue Truth-O are currently subjected to jargonification and other debasements: a fact acknowledged by him.[12]

Imagination and individual feelings are enthroned as methods of apprehension of reality. The 'individual' factor forcibly, quite independently of one's desire, makes its presence when one occupies different points of view in order to observe anything, or when one permits the existence of different versions of a fact. What remains is that a fact follows on, as it is – be it perceived or not, disregarding the many versions.[13] Many, in an omnipotent way, correspondent to philosophical idealism, 'replace' the fact for a product of their imagination. Are the members of the psychoanalytic movement who believe this aware that the phrase, "Imagination is the basis of knowledge" was authored by Adolf Hitler? He was deeply impressed by the false knowledge of a quack-novelist, Mr. Karl May (1875), who wrote a mélange made of imagined characters from the Wild West, Amazon, and Africa without setting a foot in those places and much less based in anthropological research. May and Hitler shared the condition of being non-travelers.

P.A.: I wouldn't waste my capacity for belief on facts – I only believe when there is no facts available. (Bion, 1977a, p. 294)

PRIEST: I believe in moral, religious death. Truth can be nourished; it can be allowed to die of neglect or be poisoned by seductions, cowardice too often repeated. But truth is robust; 'facts' cannot be killed even if we do not know what they are. The fragile human respect for the truth cannot be as easily disposed as often appears. (Bion, 1979, p. 498)

Note: this writer is not ignorant about the hypothesis of a "Truth Instinct", or "Truth Drive" by Dr. James S. Grotstein, first published in 2004. Our lasting and long friendship included mutual respect to our different views. Dr. Grotstein seemed to me to be the kindest member in the psychoanalytic movement of our time: a man open to constructive criticism. I owe to him many things, including the stimulus to publish books on controversial aspects of Bion's written heritage – a fact made clear by him in a preface to one of my books, as well as in his many acknowledgements in his books. We began to discuss this matter. But, life being what it is determined that the end of the discussion could not be.

Notes

1 Both Freud and Bion profited from Claude Bernard's (1865) seminal formulation about internal and internal environments, when one attempts to study human beings.
2 Bion quotes Nietzsche at least three times: (1970, p. 74; 1975, p. 118; 1979, p. 491).
3 All quotes, from Bion, 1970, p. 59, modified to encompass people other than patients, who equally have a prevailing non-psychotic personality, at the expenses of the psychotic personality: they passing as "normal". More accurate psychiatric and psychoanalytic diagnoses may display their manic, or hysterical, or psychopathic features. Most of times, all of those are mixed in various proportionalities.
4 I use the term "invariance", in the same sense that the mathematicians Sylvester and Cayley used it in the mathematical realm; that Paul Dirac used it in the realm of quanta phenomena, that Bion brought to the realm of human unconscious phenomena and much later, Nozik brought to philosophy (Dirac, 1930; Bion, 1965; Nozick, 2001; Sandler, 2006, 2009).
5 A complete review of Bion's reversal of alpha-function can be seen in Sandler, 2005, p. 646, which gave origin of a clinical based hypotheses of an anti alpha-function (Sandler, 1997, 2011, p. 189).
6 The measuring of interferences in the realm of the interacting micro-particles, analogical to the study of the relationships between two units, which, in themselves, are unknown. Einstein's equation may be quoted as a prototype of this situation, as Oedipus: they describe knowable relationships between ultimately unknown units.
7 Under the political vertex banalized since the French Revolution, the words "left" and "right lost their philological initial sense and turned to be political banners.
8 Hence the "Positivist Religion" from Auguste Comte (1848).
9 I.W. Adorno, E. Frenkel-Brunswlk, D. J. Levinson, and R.N. Sanford (1950) *The Authoritarian Personality*. New York: Harper & Row.
10 As robbers, politicians are known by fake names; his real name was Iossif Vissariónovitch Djugashvili; some historians say that Hitler's original surname was Shicklgrüber.
11 A.J.P. Taylor, Allan Bullock, Ian Kershaw, Anthony Beevor, Tony Judt, Thimoty Snyder.
12 Alas, some analysts regard Bion's contributions allowing and recommending in this tendency. A split and partial reading of some chapters in *Transformations*, excising the part from the whole of the text, where it refers to the self-sincerity demanded by a real psychoanalytic posture seems to be linked to this conclusion. It is outside the scope of this chapter to discuss this misunderstanding, which was dealt with elsewhere (Sandler, 2005).
13 The same issue was told by the parable of the seven blind men around an elephant – it was an elephant despite many different, conflicting, right or wrong ideas about it. The "whole" – rather than the parts perceived – elephant itself should be intuitively realized – and perhaps avoided by those who are next to any of the elephant's feet.

References

Bacon, F. (1620). Novum Organon. Aphorisms Concerning the Interpretation of Nature and the Kingdom of Man. In *The Great Books of the Western Hemisphere*. Chicago: Encyclopaedia Britannica Inc.
Bernard, C. (1865). *An Introduction to the Study of Experimental Medicine*. Mineola: Dover Publications, 1957.
Bion, W.R. (1957). On arrogance. In *Second Thoughts*. London: Heinemann Medical Books, 1967.
Bion, W.R. (c. 1960a). Mental health. In *Cogitations*, p. 125. Ed. Francesca Bion. London: Karnac, 1992.
Bion, W.R. (1960b). Compassion and truth. In *Cogitations*, p. 192. Ed. F. Bion. London: Karnac, 1992.
Bion, W.R. (1961). A Theory of Thinking. In *Second Thoughts*. London: Heinemann Medical Books.
Bion, W.R. (1962). *Learning from Experience*. London: Karnac.
Bion, W.R. (1963). *Elements of Psycho-Analysis*. London: Heinemann Medical Books.
Bion, W.R. (1965). *Transformations*. London: Heinemann Medical Books.
Bion, W.R. (1967). *Second Thoughts*. London: Heinemann Medical Books.
Bion, W.R. (1970). *Attention and Interpretation*. London: Tavistock Publications.
Bion, W.R. (1974). *Bion's Brazilian Lectures – 2*. Rio de Janeiro: Imago Editora Ltada.
Bion, W.R. (1975). *A Memoir of the Future: The Dream*. London: Karnac, 1991.
Bion, W.R. (1976). Evidence. In *Clinical Seminars and Four Papers*. Ed. Francesca Bion. Oxford: Fleetwood Press, 1987.

Bion, W.R. (1977a). *A Memoir of the Future: The Past Presented.* London: Karnac, 1991.

Bion, W.R. (1977b). Emotional turbulence. In *Clinical Seminars and Four Papers.* Ed. Francesca Bion. Oxford: Fleetwood Press, 1987.

Bion, W.R. (1979). *A Memoir of the Future: The Dawn of Oblivion.* London: Karnac, 1991.

Brecht, B. (1940). *Life of Galileo.* New York: Penguin Classic, 2008.

Chesterton, G.K. (1914). The Song of Quoodle, www.online-literature.com.

Comte, A. (1848). A General View of Positivism, www.archive.org.

Dirac, P. (1930). *The Principles of Quantum Mechanics.* Oxford: Clarendon Press.

Freud, S. (1900). *The Interpretation of Dreams.* The Standard Edition of the Complete Psychological Works of Sigmund Freud, Volume IV (1900): The Interpretation of Dreams (First Part), ix–627.

Freud, S. (1909). Notes upon a case of obsessional neurosis. *S.E.* 10. London: Hogarth.

Freud, S. (1911). Psycho-analytic notes on an autobiographical account of a case of paranoia. *S.E. 12.* London: Hogarth.

Freud, S. (1912). The dynamics of transference. *S.E.* 12. London: Hogarth.

Freud, S. (1915a). Instincts and their vicissitudes. *S.E.* 14. London: Hogarth.

Freud, S. (1915b). *A Phylogenetic Fantasy: Overview of the Transference Neuroses.* Cambridge: Belknap/ Harvard University Press.

Freud, S. (1916–17). Introductory lectures in psycho-analysis. *S.E.* 15. London: Hogarth.

Freud, S. (1920). Beyond the pleasure principle. *S.E.* 18. London: Hogarth.

Freud, S. (1937). Constructions in analysis. *S.E.* 23. London: Hogarth.

Grotstein, J. (1981). Wilfred R. Bion: The man, the psycho-analyst, the mystic. In J.J. Grotstein (Ed.), *Do I Dare Disturb the Universe?* Beverly Hills: Caesura Press, 1981.

Grotstein, J. (1986). The dual-track: A contribution toward a neurobehavioral model of cerebral processing. *Psychiatric Clinics of North America* 9: 353.

Heisenberg, W. (1958). Physics and philosophy. In *The Great Books of the Western World.* Chicago: Encyclopaedia Britannica Inc., 1994.

Hume, D. (1748). An enquiry concerning human understanding. In L.A. Selby-Biggs (Ed.), *The Great Books of the Western World*, pp. 468–478. Chicago: Encyclopaedia Britannica Inc., 1994.

Kant, I. (1781). Crítica da Razão Pura. Versão brasileira, por V. Rohden. In *Os Pensadores.* São Paulo: Abril Cultural, 1980.

Klein, M. (1946). Notes on some schizoid mechanisms. In M. Klein, P. Heimann, S. Isaacs and J. Riviere (Eds.), *Developments in psycho-analysis.* London: The Hogarth Press and the Institute of Psycho-Analysis, 1952.

May, K. (1875). *Winnetou, the Chief of the Apache: The Full Winnetou Trilogy in one Volume.* Merseyside: CTPDC Publishing Limited, 2014.

Melville, H. (1851). *Moby Dick: Or the Whale.* New York: Harper & Brothers.

Money-Kyrle, R. (1978). Belief and representation. In D. Meltzer (Ed.), *The Collected Papers of Roger Money-Kyrle.* London: Karnac, 2015.

Nietzsche, F. (1873). *On Truth and Lies in a Nonmoral Sense.*

Nietzsche, F. (1878–1880). *Human, All too Human.*

Nietzsche, F. (1881). *The Gay Science.*

Nietzsche, F. (1778–1888). *Will to Power.*

Nietzsche, F. (1888). *Ecce Homo: How One Becomes What One Is.* All quotations from Friedrich Nietzsche: Free translation of the author, from D'Iorio, P. (Ed.) (2006–2010). *Friedrich Nietzsche. Digital Kritische Gesamtausgabe Werke und Briefe.* Nietzsche Source, http://doc.nietzschesource.org/de/dfga.

Norris, C. (1997). *Against Relativism.* New Jersey: Wiley.

Nozick, R. (2001). *Invariances: The Structure of the Objective World.* Cambridge: Harvard University Press.

Pope, A. (1711). *An Essay on Criticism*, www.poemhunter.com/poem/an-essay-on-criticism.

Sandler, J. (1969). Delinqüentes, personalidades psicopáticas? *Rev. Bras. Psicanal.* I: 263.

Sandler, P.C. (1988). *Introdução a "Uma Memória do Futuro", de W. R. Bion.* Rio de Janeiro: Imago editora.

Sandler, P.C. (1997a). The apprehension of psychic reality: Extensions of Bion's theory of alpha-function. *International Journal of Psychoanalysis* 78: 43.

Sandler, P.C. (1997b). *A Apreensão da Realidade Psíquica*. Rio de Janeiro: Imago Editora.

Sandler, P.C. (2005). *The Language of Bion: A Dictionary of Concepts*. London: Karnac.

Sandler, P.C. (2006). The origin of Bion's work. *International Journal of Psychoanalysis* 87(1): 179–201.

Sandler, P.C. (2009). *Dreaming, Transformation, Containment and Change: Vol I of A Clinical Application of Bion's Concepts*. London: Karnac.

Sandler, P.C. (2011). *The Analytic Function and the Function of the Analyst: Vol. II of A Clinical Application of Bion's Concepts*. London: Karnac.

Sandler, P.C. (2012). Publicações, psicanálise e o movimento psicanalítico. In *Dimensões. Psicanálise. Brasil*. São Paulo: Sociedade Brasileira de Psicanalise de Sao Paulo.

Sandler, P.C. (2013). *Verbal and Visual Approaches to Reality: Vol III of A Clinical Application of Bion's Concepts*. London: Karnac.

Sandler, P.C. (2015a). *An Introduction to "A Memoir of the Future" by W.R. Bion: Volume I Authoritative, Not Authoritarian Psychoanalysis*. London: Karnac.

Sandler, P.C. (2015b). *An Introduction to "A Memoir of the Future" by W.R. Bion: Volume II Facts of Matter or a Matter of Fact?* London: Karnac.

Sandler, P.C. (2015c). Grupos: o vértice psicanalitico. *Jornal de Psicanálise* 48: 95.

Sandler, P.C. (2015d). Commentary on "Transformations in hallucinosis and the receptivity of the analyst" by Giuseppe Civitarese. *International Journal of Psychoanalysis* 1139.

Thorner, H.A. (1981). Notes on the desire of knowledge. *International Journal of Psychoanalysis* 62: 73.

Whitehead, A.N. (1925). *Science and the Modern World*. New York: Free Press, 1997.

27

REGRESSION IN THE WORK OF WINNICOTT AND BION

Rudi Vermote

Clinical material

Session

She says that there is mist, like a curtain, nothing is clear (the first time that she talks about that).

One or two sessions later

(a dream) It was not pleasant, a bit like a sexual excitation – frightening for me – it is dirty – anxiety that I try to tolerate – it makes me sick – I do not know what – I am there and I do nothing – then I see you at a short distance before me; you – I do not think that you say something – but there is something reassuring about you – no sharp angles – I want to move but it doesn't work – yesterday it was the same, but mostly, it is hidden – something that is there, no concrete memory – it is there – it becomes something that. . . – it is tiring, also shame – a dirty sensation – all the time – like everything is the same – I do not know – confusion – (the noise in *L'Avventura* (1960) of Antonioni or in *Mulholland Drive* (2001) of David Lynch).

   Dirty . . . also in your dream ??

   Maybe not – I do not know, maybe it did not start like that – it is not that . . . long silence . . .

   Maybe – I do not know – not that . . . I think that . . .

Silence

I know well that . . . often it is as everything is confused – I would like to come back to the first part of the dream, without this chaos – maybe it is not possible that it turned in the dream –

   It is dirty when it changes – the . . . the . . . the . . . it does not stop – it changes completely and is far from the first part – I don't think that you said something – like – like – it . . . it – like something that you have said.

Next session

Dream: It was like I was in your arms – it was warm and this gave me a good feeling – it was you and not you – then – it is somewhere in the beginning and it is vague – I am afraid that something will appear – what ?? – I do not know what it is – I see a swimming pool, but nobody is there – I have the feeling that somebody, but I see nobody – it is frightening – I hear something, like footsteps behind me – near the door – the door does not open – I do not know –

Next session (after a short break)

This night, I had a very dirty dream – I could not escape – but I did not feel anything – at once, it was before me – an enormous witch – I cannot escape – I look at that figure: scales, shit on it – I cannot move – it is even more dirty when I tell it here, now – it is even more dirty when I tell it now – it is paralyzing and the same time, it is appealing.

I say something comforting; that what happens in her dreams is actually important work and that I do not like to intervene much, not to break what happens now.

Session

It was a horrible night, I cannot explain what it was – there are no words – everything is confused – there was something undifferentiated about the night – at a given moment, I thought of you – he is there.

Session

Dream: I come to the session – I say nothing and you are there – a surgeon, cold and at a distance.

What I want to illustrate with these sessions, is that in a state of regression; something psychic appears; that we may call a "psychoanalytic object" (Bion, 1963), it takes form in the dreams, it is a pattern that is in itself a-sensuous. The attitude of waiting, not explaining, and certainly not thinking and breaking the spontaneous process; looks important to me.

It brings us to a point of view that both late Winnicott and late Bion shared in their work: the regression to undifferentiated states of mind.

Two kinds of selves

The psychoanalytic concept of the Self does not exist in the work of Freud. It finds its origin in the work of Hartmann in the '50s. Blatt (2008) and Balint (1968) and many others distinguish an objective self which is a differentiated mental representation (not an image but a kind of internal running program, working model) and a non-differentiated subjective self, rather a kind of feeling of being oneself. From the point of view of the subjective self, we can say that we are ourselves the most when we lose ourselves like in sports, orgasm and creativity. We cannot define this undifferentiated core of our being. It is this concept that Winnicott (1963) named the "incommunicado self" that I will try to develop. We can also apprehend it by the theories of Bion, Lacan and also by the arts and religion.

The incommunicado self in the work of Winnicott

Winnicott (1963) introduced his concept of the incommunicado self, when he noticed that while preparing for an invited lecture in the US, he actually felt no need to communicate something. Instead of seeing this as a resistance, he found it a sane splitting; not a Kleinian splitting by an internal aggressive source, but a splitting to protect something in him. He noticed that a part retreats from and another part communicates with and adapts to the environment.

Winnicott (1960) called this adaptive part the "false self", which Meltzer compared with a kind of social oil. The incommunicado part corresponds to the "true self". One cannot compare these two "parts" as the false self can be defined and known, while the true self is unknowable by thinking and senses and a-verbal. The words false and true do not seem well chosen as it is not that Winnicott finds one good and the other bad, both are necessary. And true and false do not imply a moral judgment here. To Winnicott the incommunicado true self is formless and originated in the primary interaction between a mother and a baby before they were differentiated and represented. Winnicott links it with the experience of the baby of breastfeeding, which he finds most adequate when it takes place in a nearly mechanical form (McDougall, 2003). In other words, in a way that the mother is nearly not present, so that the baby can keep the illusion that the world is not intrusive. Such "good enough mothering" is a typical English notion. It is a kind of understatement; good enough is actually more than perfect. Winnicott compares this primary world with the primary unconscious of Freud. This zone is for Winnicott not only a source of creativity but also a place to retreat and relax. The mother is a kind of buffer to protect this zone against an intrusive environmental reality. A nice example is Roberto Benigni's 1997 movie *La Vita E Bella* (Life Is Beautiful). In the movie, he spares his son the traumatic situation of being imprisoned in a concentration camp, by making it into a story in which they have to compete with others to win an army tank.

For Winnicott, the incommunicado self is a clinical reality that is present in everyone, a sacred zone that one must take care to not disturb. In his analyses, he facilitated a deep regression so that the patient could experience a contact with this zone. He was very careful in his interventions not to get the patient out of this zone. This is illustrated by *the Use of an Object* that Winnicott (1969) wrote for his conferences in the US. As Bion did, Winnicott distrusted words and preferred silence; he asked patients to remain silent, and he even said to a patient: "You are just a mouth" (Bollas, 2013). Often, he himself or his patients fell asleep, which he found a good thing. He let his interventions emerge from this world, as if they came from somewhere else, from the outside. Masud Khan (1983) elaborated this kind of intervening in the form of poetry. It shows the analyst in the role of midwife, as a transformational object (Bollas, 1979) facilitating the experience of this "created found world".

Winnicott did not rely on the death instinct in his theory, but his incommunicado self was however not an idealized nirvana. He did not deny aggression, but he saw it as a creative force. When McDougall's (2003) husband asked Winnicott what a little boy does when his gets a pencil and a paper to draw, Winnicott answered that the little boy makes first some holes in the paper and only then starts to draw.

Critics of Winnicott pointed at the danger of excesses in facilitating regression. His analyses were of very long term and some patients followed him during his holidays or stayed in his home after sessions; there was the danger of suicide. The question remains how far a regression should go.

Winnicott treated severe patients with deep psychic wounds. It is often difficult, in borderline patients for instance, to see whether it is a malignant regression that we must try to avoid or a regression that is necessary for a transformation. Winnicott believed that one could regress to a level of madness, and that this has a curing effect.

Winnicott based his interventions on the undifferentiated zone. He had a great respect for this world which he saw as an internal unknowable zone. He often understood pathology through an intuitive contact with this zone.

McDougall (2003, p. 20) recalls the story of a young Cockney mother, who came to see Winnicott at his consultation because "her boy, Bobbie, did not shit". Out of the blue, Winnicott asked the mother how many weeks she was pregnant. The mother is astonished because she even did not tell her husband yet; Winnicott replied: "Bobbie knows, and you do not have to tell your husband yet, but you need to tell Bobbie". In the next consultation, Bobbie seemed to be cured.

It can be argued (Vermote, 2014) that this zone as a source of life was developed by Lacan as well, in his notions of the "lamellae", and seeing the kernel of the Unconscious as "a cause béante", a causal gap.

The undifferentiated zone in the work of Bion

To Bion we do not need to facilitate a regression, we are already regressed. Although Bion's world was as romantic as Winnicott's – he was even reciting poems in the trenches – his model of the mind was less peaceful. The Kleinian world of Bion is a world of internal war; we need to evacuate the aggression with which we are loaded since birth and before. He saw the mind as a poor thing that is not equipped for its function at the actual evolutionary state. His theory of thinking started from the idea that the mind must protect itself and has two ways of doing this: evacuate painful experiences by splitting which happens in the psychotic part or take these experiences in and digest or process them which equals to thinking and happens in the non-psychotic part. A psychic skin of alpha function is the result of it. For Bion thinking is therefore intrinsically linked with frustration tolerance. In Alvarez (1992), it is by contrast the result of playing.

The largest part of Bion's theoretical work is a further elaboration of these transformations in Knowledge (TK); he defined the different categories, elements of the process in his Grid, and could formulate the transition between them in his alchemic formula (Bion, 1962): (Ps $\leftrightarrow$ D) (Container-Contained) (selected fact).

At the end of his book *Transformations*, Bion (1965) realized that the transformations in K and hence the categories of the Grid remain at the level of representations and that real change happens at another level. This other level cannot be known, it is non-verbal, undifferentiated and experiential. He uses religious, mathematical, poetic and philosophical notions, like infinity, and the Godhead to talk about it. They are the noumena of which the phenomena are only reflections (Kant, 1781) or the essences in Plato's cave of which the perceivable world is just a reflection. Because this zone cannot be represented, Bion gave it an abstract sign: O from origin. It is an a-sensuous world that is at the base of our representations and emotions. Anxiety for instance is there before it becomes anxiety with its symptoms at a sensorial level. Also representations and dreams originate at this a-sensuous level.

Later Bion (2005) compared it with a subterranean flow, like the Alpheus in Kubla Khan (Coleridge, 1816) with which we are in contact from time to time.

The great difference with Winnicott is6 that Bion takes another attitude towards this undifferentiated zone. While Winnicott tried not to disturb the analysand in this zone, Bion developed techniques to get in contact with this zone which was for him not a hidden zone within the self as for Winnicott, but a great Unknown in and outside the self (Grotstein (2007) called it the two arms of O). While looking for ways to facilitate a contact with O, he was aware that such a contact happens spontaneously and cannot be wanted. This contact is an experience that Bion called "becoming O", which is equivalent with a transformation in O. These "Transformations in O" only take place two or three times in an analysis but they make an analysis terminable. The analyst must have experienced an analysis, not so much to resolve his own inner conflicts and not to have a role model (which Bion sees as a form of defense), but for being able to recognize such transformations in O from his own experience.

The technique that Bion developed to get in contact with the zone or O is as follows: as it is an a-sensuous world, one must try not to use the senses (blinding oneself to see better – directing a shaft of darkness). He compares relying on the senses with a camera that leaks light and becomes useless (Bion, 1970). The pleasure principle does by definition not apply to the a-sensuous undifferentiated zone. Therefore, notions like the unconscious are not fit for it because it is rooted in the pleasure principle and also because getting in contact with the undifferentiated zone has conscious as well as unconscious aspects. Thinking and understanding are driven by the pleasure principle. To have less frustration and adapt to reality, man developed a categorizing logical thinking, but this part of our psychic functioning closes the possibility to be in contact with the basic undifferentiated zone O. So to enable the contact with the undifferentiated, a-sensuous zone, we have to renounce "the pleasure principle", hence Bion's motto: no desire, no memory (a desire directed towards the past), no understanding, no coherence. The analyst must train to develop this attitude during the sessions (like starting with not looking at one's watch, not taking notes) but also during daily life (being dispassionate and waiting). The aim is to function as close as possible to the a-sensuous, infinite zone of O and see with intuition, which happens from itself. To Bion the vertex unconscious-conscious is less important than the vector infinite-finite.

Bion, not unlike Winnicott and Lacan, supposes that this zone is formless, undifferentiated, but that there are a-sensuous patterns, i.e. conjunctions "in potentio" which are not expressed yet in forms that can be perceived by the senses. They are analytic objects, noumena that are the essence of who we are. These basic patterns like the personality are irreducible. The aim of analysis is to render these essential patterns, psychoanalytic objects (Bion, 1963) to the patient. They can take holographic forms like in the movie *The Abyss* (Hurd and Cameron, 1989), where water takes a shape within the water. Perceiving them, when being close to the infinite zone, happens spontaneously by intuition. Images that emerge from this undifferentiated, infinite zone take form on the infinite-finite vector. For Winnicott and Bion, it is as if these images come from the outside – like a Muse.

At the end of his work, Bion returns to its beginning of *Experiences in Groups* (1961): the hallucinatory matrix (without distinction between psyche and soma), full of awe for its unknown forces and it's a-sensuous patterns, the psychoanalytic objects.

Truth is defined in terms of distance and contact with this zone. With these new insights, Bion's ideas on psychosis changed (from transformation in K and alpha function). He now saw a psychotic as having no contact with this infinite zone because he is frightened by it, as he quotes Pascal (Bion, 1965, p. 171), "*ces espaces infinis m'effraie*". Without any references, the psychotic is lost in it and he retreats into a sterile world that he repeats. A delusion is a sterile protection. According to Bion, man invented geometry not because it reflects reality but to have a reference, a grip not to get lost in the infinite.

Conclusion

We find an undifferentiated, unknowable zone in Bion as well as in Winnicott's work. For Winnicott it is a life-giving area, a core within the self that has to be protected and that is related to creativity and relaxation. The contact with it is by intuition.

For Bion it is a great unknown, outside and inside – also related to life, creativity and change, but less peaceful than in Winnicott; one can get lost in it. The attitude towards it is different than in Winnicott, it is not a facilitation of regression but a facilitation of experiencing it by a special attitude in the analyst, that of waiting in Faith in a state of no memory, understanding, coherence and desire.

References

Alvarez, A. (1992). *Live Company: Psychoanalytic Psychotherapy with Autistic, Borderline, Deprived and Abused Children*. London: Routledge.

Antonioni, M. (Director) (1960). *L'Avventura*. Italy: Cinco Del Duca.

Balint, M. (1968). *The Basic Fault. Therapeutic Aspects of Regression*. London: Tavistock.

Benigni, R. (Director) (1997). *La Vita è Bella*. Italy: Miramax Films.

Bion, W.R. (1962). *Learning from Experience*. London: Karnac.

Bion, W.R. (1963). *Elements of Psychoanalysis*. London: Karnac, 1984.

Bion, W.R. (1961). *Experiences in Groups: And Other Papers*. London: Routledge (revised Edition, 1991).

Bion, W.R. (1965). *Transformations*. London: Karnac, 1984.

Bion, W.R. (1970). *Attention and Interpretation*. London: Karnac, 1986.

Bion, W.R. (2005). *The Tavistock Seminars*. Ed. F. Bion. London: Karnac.

Blatt, J.S. (2008). *Polarities of Experience: Relatedness and Self-Definition in Personality Development, Psychopathology, and the Therapeutic Process*. New York: American Psychological Association.

Bollas, C. (1979). The transformational object. *International Journal of Psychoanalysis* 60: 97–107.

Bollas, C.M. (2013). *China on the Mind*. East Susex: Routledge.

Coleridge, S.T. (1816). *Christabel, Kubla Khan and the Pains of Sleep*. London: John Murray.

Grotstein, J.S. (2007). *A Beam of Intense Darkness*. London: Karnac.

Hurd, G. (Producer) and Cameron, J. (Director). (1989). *The Abyss* (Motion Picture). US: Lightstorm Entertainment.

Kant, I. (1781). *Critique of Pure Reason* (The Cambridge Edition of the Works of Immanuel Kant) P. Guyer and A.W. Woods (Ed., Trans.), Cambridge: Cambridge University Press (1999)

Khan, M. (1983). *Hidden Selves: Between Theory and Practice in Psychoanalysis*. London: Hogarth Press.

McDougall, J. (2003). *Donald Winnicott the Man*. London: Karnac.

Lynch, D. (Director) (2001). *Mulholland Drive*. U.S.: Universal Pictures.

Vermote, R. (2014). Transformations and transmissions of psychic functioning: An integrative approach and clinical implications *Revue Française de Psychanalyse* 78: 389–404.

Winnicott, D.W. (1960). Ego distortion in terms of true and false self. In D.W. Winnicott (Ed.), *The Maturational Process and the Facilitating Environment: Studies in the Theory of Emotional Development*, pp. 140–152. New York: International Universities Press Inc., 1965.

Winnicott, D.W. (1963). Communicating and not-communicating leading to a study of certain opposites. In D.W. Winnicott (Ed.), *The Maturational Process and the Facilitating Environment: Studies in the Theory of Emotional Development*, pp. 179–193. New York: International Universities Press Inc., 1965.

Winnicott, D. (1969). The use of an object and relating through identifications. In D.W. Winnicott (Ed.), *Playing and Reality*, pp. 101–111. New York: Basic Books, 1971.

28

WAS FREUD A BIONIAN?

Perspectives from parent-infant psychoanalytic treatments

Björn Salomonsson

Was Freud a Bionian? This paradoxical question emerged when I was re-reading *The Project of a Scientific Psychology* (Freud, 1895/1950). Freud sought "a psychology that shall be a natural science . . . to represent psychical processes as quantitatively determinate states of specifiable material particles, thus making those processes perspicuous and free from contradiction" (p. 295). Today, *The Project* seems outdated, both to neuroscientists and to psychoanalysts. But my fascination with a creative conflict in Freud, between the natural scientist and the hermeneutic, suggested that under a "cloak of brain physiology", this text might reveal "a wealth of concrete psychological hypotheses, of general theoretical assumptions and of various suggestive hints", to quote from Strachey's preface (p. 350).

In this paper I will proceed to investigate how far I can integrate the Freud from my basic training with the Bion that I studied in my child and parent-infant analytic training programs. During the latter I re-discovered, in parallel, that Freud took the baby seriously – as a human being whom he observed carefully and as a linchpin in his theoretical enterprise. I was dissatisfied when colleagues threw him out with the bathwater to the advantage of an interest in, or veneration of, Bion. To make me even more disheartened, I found that much parent-infant therapy literature neglected Freud *and* Bion to the advantage of attachment and developmental theories. So, how was I to make a personal truth and a beacon out of all these sources when treating a distressed baby and an unhappy mother?

I found another beacon, in *A Beam of Intense Darkness*, Grotstein's (2008) expert work which also compares Freud, Klein, and Bion. In the following, I compare Freud's and Bion's descriptions of the baby and submit Freud's notion that the baby can regard a non-satisfying object as hostile, which elicits a defensive activity that may damage her relationship with mother. I then submit Bion's notion of the infant mind, the use of projective identification in the traffic of beta- and alpha-elements, and the role of the container-contained relationship. Some clinical material will illustrate our discussion.

Tina and her mother Nathalie

At the Child Health Centre where I work as a consultant I am asked to see Nathalie, a mother of three. Her 3-month-old daughter is yelling and she cannot decide on the girl's name, which torments her. Nathalie speaks of her mother's self-preoccupation, her father's demanding character, and an anorexia at the time of her parents' divorce when she was 17. We start working twice weekly in mother-infant therapy and this material comes from the fifth session.

The girl is asleep. Nathalie speaks of the recent christening:

> Finally she got her name, Christina Jennifer Martine! My father's great grandmother was called Christina. Martine comes from my husband's family and Jennifer from myself. I wanted her to have a name containing 'Na', to match my name. I even fantasized she'd carry my name, but that would be weird! Christina is good; it carries some of my own letters. At home, we call her Tina.

MOTHER: Tina starts screaming when I put on her sweater before we're going to take a walk. I don't understand why!
ANALYST: Something to do with how *you're* feeling about going out?
M: I don't feel anything special. Maybe I'm tense because she's tense.
A: Some kind of vicious circle between you. And who knows where a circle starts?
M: Her screaming is terrible. At my son's nursery, they call her "the Fire Alert".

The girl wakes up. Nathalie picks up Tina with a smile and puts her on her lap. Tina is sleepy and smiles briefly at me. After another minute, she starts yelling. The terrible sound pierces my marrow. I have a feeling that someone is drilling my head and my brain is swishing about. Nathalie gets tense.

ANALYST TO TINA: You are screaming terribly and we don't know why. This must be hard on you. How are things for Mum?
MOTHER: I feel sorry for her. I don't understand why she's screaming. Only the breast will do now. But it can't be right to breastfeed her all the time!
A: Tina, I note that you don't look Mum in the eyes. They wander about but when they return to Mum you close them. I wonder why you don't look into her eyes.
M: Yeah, I wonder . . .
A. TO THE SCREAMING BABY: Tina, maybe you've got two Mums? One when you smile at Mum and look into her eyes. The other one you don't dare looking at. You seem scared of her.
M: When you mention two Mums, I think of "Christina" and "Tina". Tina sounds nice and cosy while Christina is stern and old-fashioned. But it also contains "Stina", which has a gentle ring to it. I have made her confused by calling her Christina and Tina. I've been joking that she'll become schizophrenic one day.

The girl continues yelling until mother offers the breast. She takes it and calms down.

ANALYST: Perhaps there is a third Mum? I got this idea now that you, Tina, are looking drowsy. Is "Drowsy-Mum" the third Mum?
M: It's all my fault! After birth, she always looked into my eyes when breast-feeding. But I kept checking my cell-phone! I feel guilty that I rejected her and that's why she doesn't look into my eyes.

We have a beautiful, ambitious, loving, ambivalent, and formerly anorectic mother and her baby who screams and doesn't look in her eyes. The excruciating scene raises questions: Why doesn't Tina look at Mum? Why did Mum avoid deciding on a name? Let us first sketch how Freud might have answered our questions.

Freud on babies in *The Project*

In *The Project* (1895/1950) Freud links the baby's frustration and pain with her defensive activities and her view that the object is hostile. She will couple her unpleasure with a "mnemic image" (p. 320) of the object that she holds responsible. She then seeks to get rid of the unpleasure and, in parallel, regards the object as "hostile". The next time she thinks of or sees it, an unpleasant state arises. She tries to discharge both the unpleasure and the object: 'I see you again and I feel bad. Get away!' Repeated experiences will make this memory of the hostile object re-emerge more easily. Unfortunately, the baby cannot delete it. What remains is to change *internally* by initiating "a repulsion, a disinclination to keeping the hostile mnemic image cathected. Here we have primary wishful attraction (*primäre Wunschanziehung*) and primary defence [fending off, *primäre Abwehr*]" (p. 322). The mental apparatus seeks "to obviate, by means of side-cathexis, the consequent release of unpleasure" (p. 325). Unless this functions swiftly, "there will be immense unpleasure and excessive primary defence" (p. 325).

The baby's dilemma is that the first hostile object is also her "sole helping power". This results in a conflict of ambivalence. Freud concludes that she learns to cognize in relation to a "fellow human-being" (p. 331). The German word *Nebenmensch* (Vol. 18S., p. 426) is more evocative; by discovering the identity of the objects that the baby hates, loves, and is soothed by, she discovers that "they" are one *Nebenmensch* or "neighbour". Much intercourse with this *Nebenmensch* occurs when the baby is replete with negative affects. They will now link with her screaming and henceforward, "the information of [her] scream [*Schreinachricht*] serves to characterize the object" (p. 366): 'I scream because I feel bad. I scream to get rid of the bad. You don't and you didn't take away the bad. You're just like my scream'.

To dampen these internal demands the child needs a "specific action" (p. 297), at first supplied by the external world. "The attention of an experienced person is drawn to the child's state by discharge along the path of internal change" (p. 318). "I feel bad, I discharge the bad through my scream. You hear it and come to me. You're no longer bad, you're good". The screams are communicative, they bring about the specific action and also have a secondary, intersubjective, and ethical function; "The initial helplessness of human beings is the primal source of all moral motives" (p. 318). Freud thus links the baby's distress, hostile object representations, and defensive activities with her relationship with the mother, one that contains rage, disappointment, gratitude, solace, and hostility.

In my first encounter, I found *The Project* abstruse and not in touch with my budding analytic experience. The second encounter occurred when I started working with babies and mothers and studying the relevant literature. Many authors portrayed the baby in terms of interactions, attachment constellations, or as a respondent in a lab setting. But where were the intuitions about the baby as subject? Where were her sexuality and passions (Salomonsson, 2012)? Her specific relationship with the therapist (Salomonsson, 2013)? Why so much focus on a quartet of attachment categories and so little on the kaleidoscopic internal object relations? Why "implicit memories" and so little of "primal repression" (Salomonsson, 2014)?

I had learned from Norman (2001, 2004) to seek contact with the baby in therapy with her mother. I began wondering how such experiences linked with Freud's theories and observations. Re-reading him I discovered, or perhaps de-repressed, that he was an astute infant observer who based many concepts on speculations about the baby's internal world. His theories about the dream (1900), the formation of the unconscious (1915a, b), the mastery of trauma and the repetition compulsion (1920, 1925), primal repression and repression proper (1915b), the primary and secondary processes (1911), and sexuality (1905) sprang from intuitions about how the baby's mind is formed in interaction with his parent. The quoted passages from *The Project* triggered my imagination. How did Freud get this "Kleinian" idea about the frustrating and hostile object? How did he conceive that the information of the scream will characterize that object?

Bion on babies

I started investigating connections between Freud's portrait of the screaming baby and Bion's theories about thought as concrete matter waiting to be given a digestible, symbolic form by a containing *Nebenmensch*. So, what did Bion say about babies? Let me pick up the contributions that are most useful in parent-infant work. To quote Isaacs Elmhirst (1980), "Early infantile emotional states, pleasurable as well as painful, are experienced concretely and as such are not available for mental growth" (p. 161). This corresponds to what I could say to the baby: "Something terrible is running around inside you. It scares you and you don't know what it is". I might proceed with, "You want to get rid of that 'scare'. How can you get rid of it?" I would then be following another suggestion by Bion; the baby cannot long for the redeeming absent breast to relieve her panic. Instead, she experiences "a present persecuting [breast], which must be evacuated". "The taking in of milk, warmth, love, [we might add interpretations] may be felt as taking in a good breast. [But] under dominance of the, at first unopposed, bad breast, 'taking in' food may be felt as indistinguishable from evacuating a bad breast" (Bion, 1962, p. 34).

I might end up with saying: "You are scared about that thing inside you. You don't know what it is. Neither do I. But I wish to find out more about it". This would invoke Bion's idea that the baby seeks someone prepared to submit himself/herself to the bombardment of, and reflection on, the concrete experiential matter he called beta-elements. The baby needs – and here Bion suggested two contrasting terms – reverie and containment. Reverie, though not any romantic and cozy enterprise. Containment, though its aim is not to confine and annihilate an enemy at war but to help a suffering soul. This comes about by a *Nebenmensch* receiving and processing the affects and translating and communicating them to the baby. Beta- and alpha-elements are thus also semiotic concepts, and the container is a processor of signs. I note that Tina avoids her mother's eyes. I suggest she's got two Mums; one lovable and loved, one frightening and ousted. This is how I observe her bodily signs and process them in reverie, and then communicate my translation as a verbal, symbolic "libretto" along with my concomitant un-premeditated gestural "music and ballet", in brief, the opera of parent-infant therapy (Golse, 2006).

Bion and Freud on Tina and her mother

What, in my rendition of Bion's ideas about the "intersubjective dimension" (Grotstein, 2008) of the mother-infant relationship, corresponds to Tina and her mother? Tina is fed and well taken care of, but her screams and avoidant gaze point to her emotional dissatisfaction. What does she see in her mother's face? Winnicott (1971) says the ordinary baby sees herself. But many babies "have a long experience of not getting back what they are giving. They look and they do not see themselves" (p. 112) and seek other ways of "getting something of themselves back from the environment" (ibid.). Such a baby's mother "reflects her own mood or, worse still, the rigidity of her own defences" (ibid.).

Bion (1962) might have described Tina as a baby who is fed but feels unloved. He suggests that a mother who does not allow reverie or does not link it with "love for the child or its father" (p. 36) can only half-heartedly receive projective identifications, good or bad, from the baby. Mother's look at Tina reflects ambivalence, anxiety, shame, rejection, love, and guilt. Since her love is fickle, reverie becomes anguished and filled with negative projections on Tina, which blocks the formation of alpha-elements. "A split between material and psychical satisfaction develops" (p. 10). No wonder Nathalie exclaims, "I don't understand my baby!"

How would Bion have explained Tina's gaze avoidance? I would answer in a roundabout way: what Freud termed the baby's unpleasure, Bion (1962) described as feeling possessed by a bad breast that must be evacuated for the good breast to expand. But, "omnipotent mechanisms" (p. 36), notably projective identification, loom in the background. When the mother has a capacity for reverie they are salubrious and inspire thinking. Or, if the baby is "endowed with marked capacity for toleration of frustration [she] might survive the ordeal of a mother incapable of reverie and therefore incapable of supplying its mental needs" (p. 37). Furthermore, only if alpha-elements are "aesthetically arranged and configured into narrative images . . . [can] the indifference and impersonal-ness of Absolute Truth [be] trans-lated into a mercifully and personally tolerable and *meaningful* but *fictive truth*" (Grotstein, 2008, p. 161, see also Meltzer and Harris-Williams, 1988). Tina looks into her mother's eyes but cannot transform this into a meaningful emotional truth. Just like when we see a horror movie, she closes her eyes in front of mother's face since it does not reflect her unequivocal wish to contain her.

Freud (1895/1950) would have conceived of Tina's gaze avoidance as a primary defense by which Tina tried "to obviate, by means of side-cathexis" (p. 325), the release of unpleasure. But this effort derails and we observe an "excessive primary defence" (ibid.), that is, the gaze avoidance. Freud would also suggest that the defense was aimed at a non-satisfying and hostile object. Up to this point Bion and Freud would agree, though using different concepts. Freud's notion of dissatisfaction is linked more to biology, while Bion addressed its emotional aspect. He would have looked for the frustrating dimensions in mother's ways of handling her baby and her emotions vis-à-vis the girl.

Was Freud a Bionian?

Indeed, up to a certain point Freud was a Bionian. His view of the baby as passionate, unstable, defensive, distrustful, and love-seeking tallies with Bion's views. A passage in *The Project* points to another similarity, though Freud lacked the object relations conceptual framework to describe it more fully; the information of the baby's scream "serves to characterize the object" (p. 366). This sentence condenses Klein's and Bion's ideas about projective identification. The baby screams because she is in pain. Its secondary function is to draw Mum's attention to her. But the scream "is" the bad, and this "bad" will infect the object which, consequently, becomes "screamy" or bad. This is one reason for its being viewed as hostile. The other reason is, à la Klein and Bion, that the object will retaliate. Now we are in the realm of the present persecutory breast – as an internal object and as an external avenger one cannot look at.

Freud thus submitted well-founded intuitions about infant emotional life, later to be described in a more comprehensive and elaborate terminology by Klein, Winnicott, and Bion. Grotstein (2008) suggests Freud was closer to the scientific Establishment and to positivism – as indicated by his use of mechanistic and biological terms. He focused on infantile neurosis and sexuality, whereas Bion also sought to inspire the analysand to attain "the faith and discipline of 'negative capability'" (p. 38). Freud's conception of the relationship Ucs-Cs was, according to Grotstein, "linear and conflictual and therefore one-dimensional" (p. 47). Instead, Bion saw it as "one of binary (cooperative) opposition" (ibid.) and preferred not to differentiate between conscious and unconscious but between "finite and infinite" (Bion, 1965, p. 46).

I am, rather, taken by the similarities between Freud and Bion. First, the elements of style with terms from natural science, terse formulations about excruciating experiences, and an enigmatic density of the text. I think it reflects an element of restraint that these two geniuses felt was necessary when erecting and expanding their scientific constructions. Behind this restraint, their texts breathe of unbridled lust, torment, rage, curiosity, and contradiction. Consider the following passage (Freud, 1900):

> There is often a passage in even the most thoroughly interpreted dream which has to be left obscure . . . a tangle of dream-thoughts which cannot be unravelled and which moreover adds nothing to our knowledge of the content of the dream. This is the dream's navel, the spot where it reaches down into the unknown. The dream-thoughts . . . cannot, from the nature of things, have any definite endings; they are bound to branch out in every direction into the intricate network of our world of thought.
>
> (p. 525)

Freud states he will learn nothing at the navel, a finite perspective. Had Freud, as Grotstein suggests, "submissively identified" (p. 23) with the scientific Establishment he would have stopped there, as if standing in front of a worthless lab specimen. But the indefatigable hermeneutic proceeds that the dream-thoughts branch out everywhere; they are infinite.

I thus think Freud was more of a Bionian than we acknowledge. To discern this aspect we must read him, not only as a conveyor of nineteenth-century natural science – which he was – but also as a cabbalistic soothsayer of the infinite world of secret signs – which he also was. When Freud continues, "the dream-wish grows up, like a mushroom out of its mycelium" (p. 525), he is a scientist searching for *the* spot where the pathognomonic sign will visualize. But, he also says that this sign will emerge from a mycelium – a beautiful metaphor of infinity and connectivity. Freud also knew that a scientist does not believe he has found the one and only interpretation of an observation. Rather, his disclosure continues ad infinitum.

References

Bion, W.R. (1962). *Learning from Experience.* London: Karnac Books.
Bion, W.R. (1965). *Transformations.* London: Karnac Books.
Freud, S. (1895/1950). Project for a scientific psychology. *S.E.* I: 281–391. London: Hogarth.
Freud, S. (1900). The interpretation of dreams. *S.E.* 4–5. London: Hogarth.
Freud, S. (1905). Three essays on sexuality. *S.E.* 7: 123–246. London: Hogarth.
Freud, S. (1911). Formulations on the two principles of mental functioning. *S.E. 12*: 213–226. London: Hogarth.
Freud, S. (1915a). Instincts and their vicissitudes. *S.E. 14*: 109–140. London: Hogarth.

Freud, S. (1915b). The unconscious. *S.E. 14*: 159–216. London: Hogarth.

Freud, S. (1920). Beyond the pleasure principle. *S.E.* 18: 1–64. London: Hogarth.

Freud, S. (1925–1926). Inhibitions, symptoms and anxiety. *S.E. 20*: 87–178. London: Hogarth.

Golse, B. (2006). *L'être-bébé (The baby – a Being)*. Paris: Presses Universitaires de France.

Grotstein, J.S. (2008). *A Beam of Intense Darkness. Wilfred Bion's Legacy Psychoanalysis*. London: Karnac Books.

Isaacs Elmhirst, S. (1980). Bion and babies. *The Annual of Psychoanalysis* 8: 155–167.

Meltzer, D. and Harris-Williams, M. (1988). *The Apprehension of Beauty: The Role of Aesthetic Conflict in Development, Violence and Art*. Strath Tay: Clunie Press.

Norman, J. (2001). The psychoanalyst and the baby: A new look at work with infants. *International Journal of Psychoanalysis* 82: 83–100.

Norman, J. (2004). Transformations of early infantile experiences: A 6-month-old in psychoanalysis. *International Journal of Psychoanalysis* 85: 1103–1122.

Salomonsson, B. (2012). Has infantile sexuality anything to do with infants? *International Journal of Psychoanalysis* 93(3): 631–647.

Salomonsson, B. (2013). Transferences in parent-infant psychoanalytic treatments. *International Journal of Psychoanalysis* 94: 767–792.

Salomonsson, B. (2014). *Psychoanalytic Therapy with Infants and Parents: Practice, Theory and Results*. London: Routledge.

Strachey, J. Editor's Introduction to Sigmund Freud: Project for a scientific psychology (1895/1950). *S.E.* 1: 282–294. London: Hogarth Press.

Winnicott, D.W. (1971). *Playing and Reality*. London: Tavistock/Routledge.

SECTION IX

O in the consulting room

29

ON KNOWING AND BECOMING

From an informed mind to a nourished mind

Darcy Antonio Portolese

When I chose the title for this paper one question was already implicit for me and I would say that it is at the core of all scientific discussion. The question is: Can there be any level of observation with a degree of objectivity such that the qualities of the object (be they sensorial or mental) can be known or observed without interference from the observer? On the one hand, the nature of the emotional contact between analyst and patient requires the construction of a type of link that generates emotional nutrition able to fulfill the patient's needs. On the other hand, the contact must generate knowledge that will comply with requirements equivalent to those Bion (1976) found in Kant's formulation of the integration between intuition and theory.

The aim of science is to know the truth in the sense of coming closer to the "essence" and the reality that one intends to contact and know. Physicists, using their own specific methods, can cause nuclear fission in order to know the constituents of nuclear particles (today, neutrinos) and this movement seems to me to be a search for this specific truth.

Analogously, in psychoanalysis, we seek to detect and know the contents of the most archaic areas of the mind, such as fragments of the Oedipal configuration. Bion (1962) called the earliest elements of the mind beta elements. When transformed into alpha elements, they make up the basis of dreams and thoughts, allowing for the evolution of knowledge as it becomes increasingly complex and sophisticated. Each step in this is evolution was illustrated by Bion (1963) in the vertical axis of the Grid (beta elements – alpha elements – dream thoughts, dreams, myths – pre-conception – conception – concept – scientific deductive system – algebraic calculus).

In my opinion, the knowledge obtained during analytic work represents the essence of psychoanalysis and is part of a process that can be compared to tropism in plants. In *Experience in Groups* Bion (1961) compared human behavior to tropism and this comment led me to reflect on the following question: "Where do plants look?" The source of life for plants is in their search for the sun's rays in order to process photosynthesis. Along the same line we can infer that, like plants, the analytic link seeks to nurture the mind with emotional nutrients extracted from emotional contact. Let us reinforce this line of thinking with a quote from Bion (1965): "If narcissistic love is unsatisfied the development of love is disturbed and cannot extend to love of objects" (p. 73). In this passage, it is implicit that mental development necessarily takes place by supplying the mind with emotional food. For there to be growth, there must be a transition from centripetal (paranoid-schizoid position) to centrifugal movement (depressive position), in the sense of caring for objects.

On the methodological level of investigation, Bion (1962) discusses the need for equilibrium in the distance kept between the contact with the objects being investigated and abstractions resulting from the investigation. If, for physicists, the fission and splitting of atoms aims at understanding micro-particles, we analysts seek to establish, or re-establish, links of intimacy so that we can bring together and integrate split off fragments and generate meaning, such as when experiencing a selected fact (Bion, 1962).

I quote below two very meaningful statements Bion (1978a) once made at a seminar in Paris:

> The situation in the consulting room, the relationship between these two people, could be like the ashes of a fire. Is there any spark which could be blown into a flame? In this little bit I have described, we would have to examine, observe, devote care to mental debris – bits of what we have been taught, bits of what we have learnt, bits of what the patient has been taught. In analysis one is seeing the totality of debris.
>
> *(p. 204)*

> . . .

> I do not mean by calling it debris that it is not worthy of attention; I mean that it is something which has to be observed and scrutinized with very considerable care, otherwise you might throw away the necessary, vital spark. One cannot afford to cast aside imaginative conjectures on the grounds that they are not scientific – you might as well throw away the seed of a plant on the grounds that it is not an oak or a lily but just a piece of rubbish. This applies to all that goes on in your consulting room.
>
> *(p. 204)*

In these passages I see a validation of our profession: they show the possibility of generating life for human objects. This is similar to a puppet show, where an actor transforms inanimate objects into beings with life, which are able to interact with their counterparts.

Let us now take another formulation by Bion (1978b):

> [T]here is a continuity between the full-term foetus and the infant although the continuity is both maintained and broken by what appears to be a synapse, or diaphragm, or screen, so that the primordial thought of the foetus is projected onto this caesura and is reflected back from the infant to its primordial levels of thought and feeling. There is a contact through this permeable membrane in both directions; the caesura is a transparent mirror.
>
> *(p. 354)*

Bion contributed significantly to the development of psychoanalysis with a new way of seeing the method.

In Bion's late works the emphasis in analysis is toward making contact with areas referred to here as undifferentiated, incomprehensible, and ineffable, which represents the other side of caesura. The objective becomes to attain access to what Bion (1965) called "O" (the ultimate truth). "O" can only be attained through emotional experience and its transformations.

It might be worthwhile now to bring in a quote from Rudi Vermote (2011) where he describes the change that took place in Bion's work with the introduction of the notion of O and its transformation (T(O)), and how he came to see the oscillation between the paranoid-schizoid (PS) and the depressive position (D):

> As we have seen, Bion (1962, 1963) saw thinking . . . as a transition between elements, a transition that he could define as a PS-D oscillation. This entailed an attitude of tolerating insecurity and frustration until a container finds the contained and a coherence between dispersed elements is revealed, a 'selected fact'. In T(O) Bion (1970) recuperates this PS-D oscillation, but now as a movement between Patience-Security, which entails waiting and tolerating doubt and mystery until something finite emerges from infinity.
>
> *(Vermote, 2011, p. 1092)*

This quote reminds me of very similar experiences I had with two separate patients, which I would like to discuss here. I think this will help us observe the movement of emotional phenomena in situations of transformation of the infinite and formless unknown.

In my work of long years with these two patients I felt a certain "internal pressure" to generate new meanings, to the point that I thought it might be better to break off the analyses. In both cases, we had arrived at creative limits. But I gradually came to realize that this pressure was related to the pressure of thoughts seeking new mental representations and knowledge. It was a type of pressure from an undifferentiated zone seeking new representations. This might be described as the primitive and primordial mental zone showing new and unknown areas consisting of thoughts in search of a thinker.

Patient A (age 35): "The story of two bacteria, or the phenomenon of phagocytosis"

Patient A told me about two love relationships he had had at different moments in life and, despite their having involved different types of bonds, they came to the same point: he ended up alone. He described these bonds in an undifferentiated and confused way. In the first situation, it was he who had broken up with the girlfriend whereas, in the second, it was the girl who left him. He then continued his description in the first person, "I", and told about his experience with each girlfriend as "my experiences", and his own points of view. As he continued I began feeling somewhat "uncomfortable" and, little by little, I began realizing that I had been incorporated, or drawn up, into his way of thinking. An area of ambiguity emerged between us. The "I" became "we", or "us". His ideas and thoughts were also attributed to me. I associated this with the phenomenon of phagocytosis, a biological phenomenon whereby one bacteria approaches another, extends pseudopods, and engulfs it. The other side of the caesura indicated a primitive type of thinking equivalent to the nutrition of undifferentiated organisms, such as certain colonies of bacteria. It seemed to be characteristic of a parasitic type of link.

I chose to discuss this experience because it seems to represent a method of bonding that corresponds to a complaint of this patient of feeling alone, even when in the company of others. Some elements caught my attention here. For example, as things continued I noted a certain sadness and a complaint of not feeling satisfied with affective relationships, since he often complained of a certain emptiness. He also stated that, recently, he had been feeling a certain pain. I could see this pain and this emptiness as a feeling of loneliness where a type of separation takes place between him and the other, to the point that the object is no longer engulfed as an object of possession and domain. Other developments occurred in a direction where he seemed to take on a feeling of perception of the other.

In a way, I see that the patient's present feeling of loneliness is different from what he described in earlier periods. Before, there had been a possession of the object (phagocytosis) whereas now, there is a separation from the object creating emptiness and the consequent need to fill it. There seems to have been the deconstruction of a hallucinatory mental configuration that generated an emotional pseudo-fulfillment.

During this period a dream came up where the patient was in the clinical area of a hospital where he works and there was a group of children among the patients. In the next room there was a sign that read: "Pregnancy Tests". At the same time he noticed, in a recent encounter with friends, that they have children and that there is some closeness between the friends and their colleagues. One important recent fact is the patient's approximation to his father, with whom he has been having positive dialogue, including exchanges about personal experiences.

Patient B (age: 30): "The blackberry, the fertile egg, and the morula"

The patient arrived a few minutes late, cheerily said, "Good morning", and lay down on the couch. He then talked about his father with a tone of concern because the father was complaining that he was getting old and tired.

The patient too has been working very hard and feels tired, but he thought this should not be happening because he is young. I noted that he found it difficult to express needs coming from inside him. A moment of silence followed and then he talked about his need to rest, especially after lunch.

The patient spoke about the noise of voices coming from a nail salon on the floor above the office where he worked. This noise irritated him because the people there often left the door open and he could hear everything. He said that every day he would have lunch and then sit in an armchair in his office, often masturbate, and then take a snooze. With time, after listening to this patient regularly a dream image came to mind that took on the form of a *sprout* and then seemed to represent a blackberry in a cyst stuck to a tissue suggesting a fertile egg on the wall of a uterus. It later took on the shape of a morula (the first stage of development of animal embryos). I told him there seemed to be emerging between us the embryo of something alive, a bond of fertility.

The patient showed surprise at my observation and said he was impressed that something he mentioned gave rise to a reference to life. I saw him as surprised by the unexpected, by something indescribable that took place during this encounter.

The triad including a blackberry, a fertile egg, and a morula, seemed to represent very early stages in life that emerged from the "deep waters of emotional contact" and took on a representation and language that allowed the alphabet of a bond to be created.

One further fact I found interesting was the emergence of a similar emotional phenomenon in these two patients. Each one in his own way began to feel enormous loneliness and self-inflicted isolation. This feeling mobilized them both to seek new forms of emotional fulfillment.

For long periods in our work, we were able to delve into certain opaque areas and extract or create from them new possibilities for thoughts in an inclusive and bond-like direction. It became clear that the mind of Patient A produced dreams that gave us some intuition into meanings to life (particularly the room in the hospital with children and the sign saying "Pregnancy Tests"). With Patient B, we were able to dream and generate embryonic elements of life, the meaning of which came from a common bond, in this case, the morula as a seed or an embryo of life.

★★★

At the beginning of this article I brought up the question of the interference of an observer into what is being observed. We can consider that, in our work, we delve into the deep waters of the emotional climate created by the encounter and from there we emerge with hypotheses and thoughts that gradually reveal the meaning of the experience. This quality of interaction can give meaning to the experience, thus generating knowledge rather than theory.

The analyst's mind was fertilized and brought about fertilization through the emotional contact that generated the new meaning obtained during the long voyage of a faith in "O", starting off from the unknown.

A few months after the experience described, I read the following in Bion (1977):

> Physicists and chemists can draw this wonderful diagram of the DNA molecule but they have not defined the difference between the animate and the inanimate. We are sure that there is one. A table seems to be different from the things that we are. Defining it may be a matter of little importance but I am sure that there are feelings, embryonic ideas, primordial ideas which deserve to have a chance of development. I do not know whether they will turn out to be good or bad; somebody has to have the courage to say, "Even if the child I give birth to is a monster I'll risk it".
>
> (p. 299)

Signs of possibilities: the emerging of pre-conceptions

At the beginning of a recent session, Patient A asked me: "Can you miss something that doesn't exist?" In return, I asked him: "Doesn't exist where? Outside? Objectively? Because inside something exists that you want to know about, the experience of something unknown, that has an internal meaning to be examined". During the period that followed it was possible to note greater closeness to his father and to me, indications of recognition for our work and the perception that he had been benefited since the beginning. This loving link with his father and with me seems to have evolved from pre-conceptions related to a primary link with the breast, which, for different reasons, had been attacked and fragmented.

In these two experiences described above we can note the patients' contact with mental areas and levels from which centrifugal motion emerged, where both of them turned from narcissism toward aspects that in earlier times had been undifferentiated or non-existent. I feel that this experience corroborates Bion's formulation regarding the mind's need for nutrition in order to turn the vector away from narcissism and toward what Bion called "social-ism", thus generating development of the personality in the emotional and cognitive senses.

Trying to reflect on this paper, I believe I have brought up a question that was implicit regarding knowledge and theory in psychoanalysis. Knowledge results from the intimate connection with the emotional experience that is inherent to the psychoanalytic encounter. This encounter consists of an emotional experience that makes possible transformations in "O", where the nutrition of the mind takes place. The product of these transformations has an epistemologically understandable meaning that Bion (1965) called Transformations in K. This process, in turn, seems to me to correspond to integration in the construction of knowledge according to Kant, between theory and intuition.

References

Bion, W.R. (1961). *Experiences in Groups*. London: Tavistock, 2004.

Bion, W.R. (1962). *Learning from Experience*. London: Karnac, 1991.

Bion, W.R. (1963). *Elements of Psycho-Analysis*. London: Karnac, 1984.

Bion, W.R. (1965). *Transformations*. London: Karnac, 1991.

Bion, W.R. (1970). *Attention and Interpretation: A Scientific Approach to Insight in Psycho-Analysis and Groups*. London: Tavistock.

Bion, W.R. (1976). Evidence. In C. Mawson (Ed.), *The Complete Works of W. R. Bion. Vol. X*. London: Karnac, 2014.

Bion, W.R. (1977). New York. In C. Mawson (Ed.), *The Complete Works of W. R. Bion. Vol. VIII*. London: Karnac, 2014.

Bion, W.R. (1978a). A Paris seminar. In C. Mawson (Ed.), *The Complete Works of W. R. Bion. Vol. IX*. London: Karnac, 2014.

Bion, W.R. (1978b). São Paulo (Ten talks). In C. Mawson (Ed.), *The Complete Works of W. R. Bion. Vol. VIII*. London: Karnac, 2014.

Vermote, R. (2011). On the value of "late Bion" to analytic theory and practice. *International Journal of Psychoanalysis* 92: 1089–1098.

30

CATASTROPHE AND FAITH IN ANOREXIA NERVOSA

Tom Wooldridge

The first time I met Sara, I knew that something terrible had happened. In spite of her youth, her skin was pale and her hair gossamer. As we walked toward my office, the painful hollows of her cheeks and the spindly insubstantiality of her legs left me uncertain about whether she was appropriate for outpatient treatment or, in fact, about whether I wanted to work with her at all. Before we'd exchanged more than a few words, I was scrambling to digest the impact of her physical presence.

When working with anorexic patients, I've often thought, "Something terrible has happened." Their bodies are the canvas on which this catastrophe is rendered. One has the sense that we are far from the original catastrophe, yet the only aspects of the patient that can be contacted are residues from that event long past. The impact of the patient's physical collapse threatens to overwhelm and erase meaning altogether.

In these treatments, Bion's writing has been an invaluable lens. Michael Eigen (1998) has written, "A sense of catastrophe pervades Bion's work" (p. 184). In this paper I ask: What is the nature of the original catastrophe? How did the patient survive it and what drastic compromises had to be made for her to survive? And in the accompanying fallout, what is needed for something new to take root and grow?

I. Catastrophe

Anorexia nervosa results, at least in part, from failure in the caregiver's containing function. This failure in containment results in profound persecutory anxieties in the anorexic patient, as well as more primitive anxieties about falling apart. Williams (1997) has discussed the former in her work on "no-entry" systems of defense, which are a response to an intense fear of intrusion related to early persecutory experiences of being the recipient of projective identifications.

In the early months of treatment, Sara became angry and withdrawn when I suggested possible meanings to her associations. These interactions often culminated with Sara curling up in her chair, yelling while tears ran down her face that I was "cold and cruel." In our first iterations of this interaction, I found myself feeling defensive and embarrassed, searching myself for any sign of irritation with Sara. In time, I came to recognize a strong dissonance between Sara's description of me and my own experience of extending myself to understand her experience. In short, I recognized my desire to offer her nourishment and her need to reject it.

The experience of being heavily projected into in the countertransference often reflects the patient's experience of having received profoundly intrusive projections in early development (Grinberg, 1962). Sara remembered one incident that represents the intensity of her mother's projective identifications. Around age 8, Sara had been eating a pear in her family's kitchen. When her mother walked in and saw "the juice running down [Sara's] chin," she became distraught and insisted that her daughter explain her overt exhibition of sexuality. Sara's mother's need to divest herself of her own psychotic anxieties left Sara feeling "filled up" with toxic shame.

This "no-entry" system of defenses manifested itself throughout Sara's life. Sara was terrified of physical manifestations of penetration and had strenuously avoided sexual contact. She had also never received a gynecological exam and was terrified of injections. While Sara was on occasion able to tell me things that felt important, she described confiding in me as "giving you weapons that you can pierce me with." William's (1997) invaluable "no-entry" system of defenses against persecutory forms of anxiety was immensely helpful to me in this period.

As treatment unfolded, Sara and I encountered more primitive anxieties centering on the dissolution of the self. On one occasion, I was struck by the fact that she filled every moment with work, deploying a complex array of manic defenses to avoid the feelings lurking beneath the surface. In an early conversation, she mentioned the possibility of trying to slow down, and I remarked that I thought this would be difficult.

SARA: I tried walking here more slowly today. Without the music I usually listen to. You were right, it was hard.
THERAPIST: What came up for you?
SARA: It's hard to describe. I kept saying to myself, in my internal monologue, you know, "There's a pain that shatters." It's like I'm remembering, but I don't know what I'm remembering.
THERAPIST: That's something you've known before, shattering.
SARA: Yes, and that's what it feels like when I'm fighting with my mom, too, that I'm going to fall apart if she leaves, or even when she walks into the other room during a fight, leaving me by myself.
THERAPIST: That's the anxiety we've been talking about, that fear of falling apart in some way.

In this excerpt, Sara is beginning to symbolize, rather than enact (through her physical emaciation, for example), the early catastrophe. Although she can remember specific events associated with this feeling, there is also a sense that shattering has been an invariant aspect of Sara's personality throughout her life. Even as her experiences can be thought, worked into alpha elements, they retain the imprint of the shattering that was their origin.

The sense of catastrophe we find in Bion is enriched by including Winnicott's (1974) work on the fear of breakdown. Catastrophe pervades Bion's sense of psychic life; Winnicott, in contrast, locates the catastrophic in particular experiences. His thesis is simple: the patient's fear of breakdown is, in fact, a fear of a breakdown that has already happened. It is a fear of the original agony (anxiety, he notes, is not strong enough) that caused the defensive organization of the patient's character. Until the patient can gather into the present what happened in the past so that it can be experienced completely, the event will always recede into the future, experienced as a fear of breakdown.

Winnicott (1974) briefly lists a number of primitive agonies, along with their characteristic defenses. These include a return to an unintegrated state, falling forever, loss of psychosomatic collusion, loss of sense of the real, and loss of capacity to relate to objects. Consider the following excerpt:

SARA: The most I can remember from my elementary school years . . . I wouldn't eat at school. Nobody could figure out why. I remember feeling sick to my stomach a lot. I mean, that's the way I feel now, too. Like my stomach is going to drop out of my body or something.

THERAPIST: You wondered whether things were okay at home, whether your parents would be there for you at the end of the day.

SARA: Yeah, I mean, my mom and I would have terrible fights almost every evening. I remember thinking, "She's done with me," and that she wouldn't be there when I was done with school.

THERAPIST: That she would withdraw her love.

SARA: And she did – every day after school she went back to her room and didn't come out until dinner. She'd hold grudges for a long time.

If you've ever been on a rollercoaster, you have a sense of what falling feels like. The hands tighten into fists, the back arches, and the stomach falls. We come into the world hardwired with something like a fear of falling. The Moro reflex is an infantile reflex that's present in all newborns, a response to a sudden loss of support.

II. Management

The anorexic patient has made use of physical emaciation to manage his sense of catastrophe. He has said "No" to the growth and buildup of experience. It has become too dreadful to be thought and, somehow, has been imploded. Psychic life has been compressed into a single point, a "reverse big bang" (Bion, 1970, pp. 12–15). The space upon which meaning depends has been destroyed.

Without the capacity to tolerate her unfolding experience, Sara feared that she would fall apart and thus attempted to obliterate the meaning of her experience.

SARA: I was driving downtown the other day. When I was sitting at a stoplight, I noticed how thin my waist was. The seatbelt was tight around me and it was like I was empty. I thought, "I want to fucking shrink my waist to zero." Until there's nothing left, you know?

THERAPIST: You want to shrink yourself until there's nothing left, no feelings, no hungers, no wanting.

In this excerpt, we can see Sara's almost frenzied desire to destroy the import of her feelings, to stop the buildup of experience. Although Sara is unable to think about her experience – to make use of alpha function – she nonetheless must find a way to manage the impact of her experience, which is felt on a sensory level (as beta elements). Without the capacity for mental representation, experience is managed through its physicality.

Put differently, emaciation serves as a way of managing primitive anxieties about the dissolution of the self. In discussing the experience of skin in early object relations, Bick (1968) notes that the most primitive parts of the personality have no binding force amongst themselves. Needing a way to be held together, in optimal development a containing object must be introjected over time, which will be experienced concretely as a skin. Without this internal object, Sara experienced herself as always having the potential to fall apart. Consider the following excerpt:

SARA: I feel huge. I feel so goddamn fat and disgusting. I've only eaten a little more today than usual, a bagel. But I feel gross.

THERAPIST: If it feels okay, let's try to describe that feeling being fat and disgusting in as much detail as possible.

SARA: It's really hard to describe . . . this way I feel like my stomach is going to fall out of itself? I feel like a big blob lying on the couch.

THERAPIST: It's like there's nothing holding you together.

SARA: I told you about my stomach. It's humiliating. Every time I eat something, I look down and there are these huge red marks. It looks like a cat clawed me.[1] It feels like I'm overflowing.

In a brief aside, Winnicott (1974) comments that the fear of falling forever is defended against by "self-holding." To my knowledge, Bick (1968) was the first to describe one form that this self-holding might take in her notion of "second-skin" formations. The patient's attempts at self-holding, whether through physical and muscular formations or inappropriate use of certain mental functions, constitute this secondary skin, which is a best attempt at holding the personality together.

Bick (1968) notes that this phenomenon is most easily studied in problems of dependence and separation in the transference. In the following example, I think we can most clearly see the way that *being thin* actually served as a secondary skin for Sara. In this example, Sara increases her food restriction shortly before my upcoming vacation.

SARA: I haven't eaten much today or yesterday really, either. It feels good. You know, my stomach feels tight again.

THERAPIST: Tell me more about how it feels.

SARA: It's like my body feels compact, clean. You know? I mean, I can feel my arm muscles, there's no excess. I know where I begin and end.

THERAPIST: A few weeks ago you felt like a blob, spilling out of yourself, but now, everything is held together. Nothing's falling out.

SARA: Exactly.

THERAPIST: It seems worth noting that this is showing up right before we won't be meeting for a few days.

Here we must make an imaginative leap. How is it that the experience of being thin, of being intensely thin, might provide a kind of psychological holding at a primitive and physical level? Sara's fear that I would leave her, as her mother did, forced her to find a way to hold her profound anxiety without my help. These anxieties began to manifest as the fear and the *feeling* of becoming fat – of loose skin, a bulging stomach, of flabby arms. Sara's caloric restriction countered this experience, giving her the feeling of being lean and compact – in essence, held together.

The treatment of anorexia nervosa is complicated by the frequent necessity of inpatient hospitalization and enforced feeding. While often medically necessary, we must never forget that depriving the anorexic patient of his agency is often deeply traumatic and, furthermore, weight restoration without accompanying attention to patient's primitive anxieties is deeply terrifying. In our willingness to hospitalize patients, we must be prepared to be experienced as inflicting extreme emotional pain.

During our treatment, Sara had to be hospitalized twice when her weight became dangerously low. At times, I had to set aside the priority of meaning making in favor of concrete management of the catastrophic enactment between us. It was essential, though, that space for dreaming was maintained throughout the process and, in particular, after discharge. Consider the following excerpt:

SARA: I know that you think you were trying to help me. But actually you're just like my mother, and just like her you don't even know it. Intrusive and controlling.

THERAPIST: I put you through a terrifying experience. And it seems like I'm deluded, thinking I'm trying to help but actually being intrusive and controlling – something you've had too much of already.

SARA: Do you realize what that was like for me? Everybody wants me to be fattened up, but nobody actually gives a shit about how I'm feeling.

THERAPIST: Part of what felt intrusive and controlling is that your feelings were erased, their meaning wasn't taken up in any way.

SARA: It was like being shattered all over again.

In this excerpt, Sara has returned from a month-long inpatient treatment that was initiated by her treatment team. Sara's hospitalization was both a manifestation of my role as a "proper object" (Caper, 1999) and also a traumatic repetition of her earlier experience. That original catastrophe cannot be transcended – only lived through and managed together.

III. Faith

For Bion, faith is the only proper response to catastrophe. But how can we jettison desire (for the patient's survival, at its most extreme), even though it may prevent us from fully comprehending the patient's psychic experience? Though Bion urged analysts to focus upon the non-sensual, the patient's *physical* deprivation must be reckoned with.

In a sense, too, I think precisely what the anorexic patient has lost is faith. Consider the following excerpt:

THERAPIST: My sense is that you don't feel particularly alive.

SARA: No kidding. Not much seems worth doing to me. I guess I spend most of my time thinking about what I've eaten for today, and what I'm going to eat. How to keep the calories down.

THERAPIST: That makes sense, since you're so malnourished. At the same time, I have the feeling that you're not particularly curious about yourself, about what's happening inside.

SARA: That might be true. I don't know.

THERAPIST: It's hard to be curious about why you're not curious.
SARA: I just don't want to have these feelings. I'm so tired of them.

In this excerpt, the active link is -K, an absence of curiosity. At a deeper level, though, I think we can see Sara's orientation toward O – the emotional truth of the moment – is characterized by mistrust. She lacks the sense that living through and opening to ongoing impact and transformation will be fruitful. As Bion noted, the patient (and analyst's) orientations toward pleasure-pain regulation can work against the evolutions in O that might lead to the most profound moments of psychic change. We might say that the patient lacks another vertex from which to feel emotional opening might be worthwhile.

The anorexic patient's lack of faith also manifests as a devaluation of relationship. Indeed, insofar as we experience curiosity about our own emotional truth as fruitful we will tend to imagine that contact with other subjectivities will be worthwhile. For the anorexic patient, relationship with the maternal object entailed receiving intense and intrusive projective identifications. Over time, these breakdowns led the patient to lose the sense that communication moves things forward. A crucial aspect of successful treatment is slowly moving into and eventually reestablishing a sense that communicating with other minds can be an enlivening process.

How does faith develop? I believe we approach its realization together. Over time, but not as a linear progression, Sara and I developed more confidence that the impacts of her inner life could be borne, this was a fruitful process, and understanding would crystallize in its own time. This "basic trust," to borrow Erikson's phrase (1956), allowed us to continue to open to the unfolding of experience. Equally important, Sara came to feel that contact with me could offer comfort and our minds, together, could be generative.

Conclusion

What is the nature of the original catastrophe in patients with anorexia nervosa? I have argued that the patient suffered a terrible failure in early maternal containment leading to intense persecutory and primitive anxieties. How did the patient survive it and what drastic compromises had to be made for him to carry on? I have explored the psychological functions of emaciation, as well as how early trauma is repeated in the therapeutic situation. And in the accompanying fallout, what is needed for something new to take root and grow? I have argued that faith is one of the essential missing ingredients.

Note

1 In fact, as the skin loses its elasticity and flexibility, patients with anorexia nervosa often develop striae, or stretch marks on the skin, as they gain weight; often these occur on the stomach, legs, breasts and other areas with prominent fat deposits.

References

Bick, E. (1968). The experience of skin in early object-relations. *The International Journal of Psychoanalysis* 49: 484–486.
Bion, W.R. (1970). *Attention and Interpretation*. London: Tavistock [Reprinted London: Karnac, 1984].
Caper, R. (1999). *A Mind of One's Own: A Kleinian View of Self and Object*. London: Routledge.

Eigen, M. (1998). Wilfred R. Bion: Infinite surfaces, explosiveness, faith. In P. Marcus and A. Rosenberg (Eds.), *Psychoanalytic Versions of the Human Condition: Philosophies of Life and Their Impact on Practice*, pp. 183–205. New York: New York University Press.

Erikson, E.H. (1956). The problem of ego identity. *Journal of the American Psychoanalytic Association* 4: 56–121.

Grinberg, L. (1962). On a specific aspect of countertransference due to the patient's projective identification. *International Journal of Psychoanalysis* 43: 436–440.

Winnicott, D.W. (1974). Fear of breakdown. *International Review of Psycho-analysis* 1: 103–107.

Williams, G. (1997). Reflections on some dynamics of eating disorders: "no entry" defences and foreign bodies. *International Journal of Psychoanalysis* 78: 927–941.

31

FROM A TALKING HOLE TO A CONTAINER FOR GROWTH

Majlis Winberg Salomonsson

I've asked myself many times: As an analyst, what can I do when, on giving an interpretation, I get the feeling that there's no patient there to talk to? What makes an adequate interpretation not the slightest bit of help to the patient? One way to think about these questions is in terms of the depressive and paranoid-schizoid positions. When the patient finds himself in the depressive position, he is receptive to my interpretations. When the patient is totally in the paranoid-schizoid world, and in most need of my interpretations, there doesn't seem to be anyone there who hears what I have to say.

If I go ahead with my interpretation anyway, what happens? I have the feeling that the patient completely rebuffs my interpretation. Much later on in the analysis he/she may take up the interpretation and reflect on it or, for that matter, present it as if it was his/her own thoughts! One can say that these reflections are to a large degree concerned with myself as an analyst, and the frustration I feel in these situations. Many times the problem is more inclined to be that I don't, in fact, have any interpretations. In other words: my own thoughts have gone down the drain.

Eve

Eve is 15 when I meet her for the first time. During our first meeting she is visibly strained and expresses great doubt about this project – the idea that she should come to me for analysis. She immediately sits in the armchair in the farthest corner of the room, curls herself up, and talks non-stop. She looks around the room, asks about the pictures I have on the walls, the many books in the bookcases, and if a lot of people come here. She also says that she doesn't want to come here, but some boy has told her about analysis and he got better. She might need to go when she is grown up, and she has heard that that is expensive. She wonders if I receive flowers and presents when someone completes analysis here.

Eve expresses her doubtfulness with a flood of words, questions about me about my room and my other patients. What benefits will she get from an analyst, sitting there with her words and her books? She has grown up with a mother suffering from alcoholic problems and a father she has met only a few times in her life. She feels like a strange bird in my room. She is not used to expressing herself in words. It is actions that count. To her, I am like some kind of creature from another planet.

What do I see? I see a girl who interests me; her liveliness fascinates and bewilders me. She is an amazing mixture of curiosity and chatty openness, and someone who says, "Here I am and I can manage just fine by myself". But I also begin to feel a creeping unease. The feeling to defend myself grows stronger, and I feel closed in. She presses in on me; she makes comments about the room, about my appearance; and I get the feeling that she wants in everywhere.

At this point I comment on her thoughts and questions, so that she can learn what kind of person I am – if I am someone who can help her, and what I can help her with. This helps settle down the situation, and we can take a look at each other. Now I see the fear and inse-curity that uses the flow of words, not only to make contact and learn something about this new situation, but also as a shield, a wall, and a way to take control. As if she is saying "Don't get too close".

Analysis is very foreign to Eve. She doesn't really know how to behave. She calls it a "talk-ing hole". She thinks I should come to the foster home where she lives, so that I can see the people she is talking about and what it looks like there. "How can you understand anything otherwise?" she asks. The fact that she can tell me – that it is her version that counts here – is waved away as nonsense.

Several times during the initial period Eve repeats that there is something wrong with her nose – it has had a bump on it since a dog bit her. She demonstrates thoroughly for me. She is not the slightest bit interested in my attempts to talk about what is bothering her; it is the nose and nothing else. She cannot think symbolically about that which causes anxiety.

As the weeks go by, Eve becomes more and more critical about the analysis. She doesn't think I am doing anything – just sitting here in my talking hole making loads of money while, for example, her mother has to work and wear herself out for much less. It's too slow here in the talking hole. She is an active person – she seeks out action, and things have to be happen-ing all the time. She is afraid of what might come out if she quiets down and listens. She says, "This is the only damn place where you can hear the quietness". She also complains about getting so tired. "The air is so sleepy here", she says, and curls up in her armchair and quite simply falls asleep. There is a period when she sleeps through sessions.

Lack of space

I get the impression that Eve, the first time she comes into my room, is overwhelmed and throws herself into the situation. I need to help us both find the space. My interventions in the first meeting tried to make a space between us, so that we could take a look at each other. What "space" are we talking about? We might need to open up our original ideas about space for interpretation. Here it is more about space for thinking and for feeling. Eve is not used to reasoning or, for that matter, giving consideration to ideas and feelings. On the contrary, her activities seem to serve the purpose of keeping thoughts and feelings at bay.

When I offer her space for her thoughts and feelings, she defends herself in many ways. Also, the space between us is attacked. One minute Eve crowds me and I feel forced into a corner, the next she falls asleep and completely leaves the scene. I am often concerned with whether or not she will show up for her next appointment. Every time I think, "This was definitely the last time, she won't come tomorrow". Why am I then so concerned by this? This is no longer about room for interpretation; this is about room to breathe, to live.

When I look back on the first period of the analysis I can see how Eve evacuates her inner self by way of projective identifications on me. It gushes out of her, my inadequacy and use-lessness make her ill, and I truly feel more and more useless and bad. My container function is characterized by the fact that I identify myself with her projections – and feel useless. Or, I want to throw them out and get rid of this difficult girl. What I do not succeed in doing for myself, is to translate her tossed out comments, her attacks, and her somatic symptoms as an expression of unorganized demands, anxiety, and fear. My attempt to create space has been attacked, and I find it hard to think. And I find it hard to feel. I become cold and distant. In other words, I become the very object that she has a picture of in her inner world – a cold, dissociated person.

Eve's attacks on me and the analysis are strong. Her fear is expressed in different ways. In relationship to me, it comes in the form of a strong distrust – I'm not good enough, I can't help her who, by the way, doesn't need any help. Another channel for her fear is bodily phe-nomena. She has symptoms, bodily reactions, and a fear that the cracks she has on her skin will expand and everything will be torn apart.

On a conscious level Eve is against the analysis project, she expresses an open distrust and contempt for my talking hole. At the same time there is, to a large degree, an unconscious hope, a belief in me and in the analysis, that keeps her coming back. This level is most often unconscious for me also. Instead, I think that she has a sadistic desire to torment me. But I also realize something else, something that expresses itself in a wistful glance when she leaves at the end of the session or in a message left on the answering machine. "I'm not going to come today, I don't feel like it, it's not worth it. You can call me if you want". It could be that she realizes that there is a person here who is prepared to be interested in her and who wants to understand. On another level, there are fantasies that I am some kind of magician who can make her problems disappear. I often notice that she seems to have the conception that I would understand without her saying anything, without words.

Eve also tries to use me as protection against her inner world. She wants me to reassure her that the cracks in her skin are not going to expand, that they will heal. She is afraid she is going to be torn apart, and she questions if I am strong enough to hold her together.

The illness

After about six months of analysis, Eve becomes sick and is admitted to a hospital. Her blood count is unexplainably low. The hospital suspects leukemia. After a thorough investigation the conclusion is reached that there is no serious physical ailment.

In our first analytic session after her stay in the hospital Eve is pale and quiet. She starts to draw on her drawing pad. She draws a picture of the foster home where she lives and shows me what it looks like inside. She draws a cat and a mouse. The cat is chasing the mouse. Eve says that they have been running around there for many years with no success. Then she talks about the time of her illness. Her blood count was 54, and that's very low – you should really have 140 or 150 she tells me. She says, "I had blood up to my knees, after that it was only water". She remembers that when she was 3 years old she was in the hospital with croup. She says, "There was a load of tubes and things". She also remembers the cot. She didn't like it at all. She says that, of course, she was also in the hospital when she was born. Then she was cold and bloody and had to be put in an incubator.

I talk about her being in a crib and an incubator by herself, that she was cold and bloody. I talk about her feelings of loneliness. Eve takes the drawing pad and draws a couple, "a him and a her", she says. They are facing each other and holding each other. She sees the drawing she did of the house and comments, "They don't take care of that lovely house". I interpret this to mean that she thinks that she should also be taken care of, that I should take care of her, so that she won't get sick like this again.

What is Eve saying? What kind of picture is she painting? Blood up to her knees, and then only water! A pregnant picture which forms her primitive, concrete fear that there is not enough strength, a fantasy that things will flow away. That she will die! I think to myself, "This girl is sicker than I realised, and it's not physical!" I'm like a parent who has taken her child to the hospital and found out just how sick she really is. I understand that part of her functions in a very concrete manner and that fantasies exist where everything can just flow away. At this point I feel her fantasy myself, that she can just disappear, just flow away from me and die. I begin to understand that she needs me to survive, not just as a trash bin but as an active, sustaining person. A containing person.

Eve's dissociation now becomes stronger. During analysis she takes up a new theme. She says she wants to go to someone else. She thinks that this analysis business may be a good thing and adds that another analyst would be the solution. I reply by saying that it's difficult for her to think about coming to me at this moment because we are now getting closer to things that are important and difficult for her. But I can help her with this. She snorts. She says she will think about it. She thinks about it and comes to the conclusion that I can help her with one thing: I can convince those over there in the foster home that she should get another analyst.

At the next session Eve is disappointed. She has understood that I am not going to help her with her request. She looks out the window, looks at the clock, and is sulky and difficult. She also tells me that her mother is revolting when she's drunk. Mother gets exaggeratedly happy and exaggeratedly sad. I take up her reaction to me when she realized I wasn't going to help her the way she wanted. "Mm, yes", says Eve, and adds that by the way she doesn't think I care about her at all. I think only about myself and making money. She becomes more and more upset and really spits it all out. Mother, and me, yes, everyone – we are revolting, all of us.

The next day she tells me that she felt ill and threw up all night. She complains about the family, that they don't take care of the house properly, for example the big clock in the living room doesn't work. They've tried to mend it, "but", says Eve upset, "they surely must understand that a specialist is needed". I perceive that she is addressing me as her analytical specialist and make a remark to this effect. I also comment on our previous session when she was angry with me, and probably became anxious afterwards. She snorts at these interpretations at first, but after a while becomes serious and says that it was difficult to come here today, but she decided to do it.

When Eve became anemic and was admitted to the hospital, a change also began within me. The cat and mouse game we have been playing comes to an end. I begin to understand a more complex problem. When we commenced our work, I did not take into consideration the primitive feelings, the fear that existed in Eve – the fear that she would die. I thought mostly that she would break off the analysis. And I kept myself distanced and cold. I only begin to understand when she developed her anemia. I associate her anemia with lack of warmth, lack of life. Her fear reaches into me and awakens my warmth. My insight leads me into not answering her proposals about another analyst. When she feels that I understand her, she becomes more and more aggressive and wants to break off the analysis. I experience fantasies about the child who won't take the breast, and spits and sputters instead. I offer containment and thoughts, while she wants immediate gratification.

I see a significant connection between Eve's anemia and the analysis. The locked situation in the analysis leads Eve to her strong somatic reaction. This makes room for me to see the scope of her predicament. Eve then has the experience of feeling she has been given a chance that she so far has never had, to be understood at that level. My understanding and warmth awakens a pain that becomes impossible to endure. The experience of loss becomes more intensive, as well as the bitterness over this loss. Bion (1959) describes how this can lead to exaggerated projective identification, where the connecting link between the analyst and the patient become that projective identification mechanism, that which is attacked.

Another analyst

Eve wants another analyst, and she could be right about it! What she needed was someone who understood that her fear was something much more basic, more primitive than I had imagined. When Eve spoke about her body, the blood up to her knees, the cracks that could expand, everything flowing away, she wasn't talking in symbolic terms. It was concrete, direct, and she wanted an analyst who could immediately hold her and help her stay together, and not collapse or flow away. During this strain I switched between melancholy – yes, she's right, this isn't working (her projective identifications go straight to the point) – and anger – so what! It's just as well she doesn't come then (I want to throw the projections right back).

She gets another analyst – though not in the way she thought. This shift started as a change in me. I gradually let go of the picture that her trying to find me is a game, where she elusively runs away and I hunt in vain after her. My own inner work to meet Eve can be described in terms of not being set on doing something, but rather on seeing what was happening here and now in the room. I feel the fear; I understand the anemia as an expression of her horror at not surviving. When I succeed in understanding, when I can surrender and control my zeal – then that she can sense a new opportunity. And then her attacks intensify. My only chance is to seek to be an active container analyst and help us develop the talking hole into a container for growth. Outwardly, I don't do so much; no clever interpretations. I work with my injured feelings not to be defensive and, most importantly, to keep my warmth. And after a while her curiosity about me, and what this can mean for her, is aroused. I create a space in the analysis where something can take shape, it can be given an opportunity. My containing function is beginning to work.

This is a shift that opens up and allows us to leave the dyad that had bound us together in an eternal cat and mouse game. And to reach the triad that provides the space. From an intra psychic perspective, when her attacks intensified, I could see a girl who fights despairingly, rather than a patient who, in a sadistic manner, wants to attack me and throw me out. Interpersonally, the thought about another analyst becomes an opening for the triad.

Space in this way can be described from the inner world, inside the patient and inside the analyst, as well as from the outer world, and the relationships with each other. In Eve's case, we can see her difficulties with both the outer and inner world. The picture of an inner mental space, inside the body, did not exist for Eve. She had no access to this inner home, the good inner object; she thought it leaked. To listen meant to leave space for the other to speak and to allow the other to introduce their projections. Many times Eve could not hear what I said – she couldn't leave space for another person. And this resulted in me not hearing what she said!

In the outer world, we can understand the concrete, functional Eve and the fixation with her own exterior, outside the body, as an expression of this problem. Eve also clings on to the outer world in another way, by believing it is outer changes that will provide her with the complete solution: to get another analyst, to change school, to change foster home, and so on. When she returns to these thoughts, she is searching for a concrete outer space like: "I have to get out of here, it's too crowded in here", and I understand that she is warding off an inner space.

I look at our work in Bion's terms of the container and contained (1963). In the session after her stay in the hospital, Eve begins by drawing the house, she shows me where she finds herself. Then she continues by drawing the cat and mouse, someone is being hunted, and this continues into eternity. In this way she produces a significant picture of the paranoid terror at the thought of being hunted, imprisoned, and eaten up, locked in the container. Then she tells me about the stay in the hospital and comments on blood up to her knees. She talks about the cot and the incubator. I comment on this in terms of being alone, not being taken care of. Then she draws the picture of "a him and a her" – a picture that Bion often uses to create and describe the container-contained metaphor. Here, Eve gives a picture of mutuality and being taken care of without fear. Then she comments on her drawing of the house ("they don't look after . . ."), and I interpret this in terms of taking care of her, that I should take care of her.

Eve gives two pictures of her fear: one where containing is dangerous because you can be caught and eaten up, and another where containing is filled with terror because you can be shut out, thrown out, "They don't care, you don't care". The fear becomes so strong because you feel caught in the dyad, there are no alternatives – either you will be eaten up and lose your own individuality, or you will be thrown out and die from lack of nourishment. The symbiosis is, in the long run is, an impossible way to live.

Space for three

Freud writes in *An Outline of Psycho-analysis* (1938): "We assume that mental life is the function of an apparatus to which we ascribe the characteristics of being extended in space". He talks about space also in connection to dreams and dream interpretation. In this connection he describes the hungry child, who is satisfied and thereby develops a perception identity – Freud calls this a roundabout way to fulfilling wishes. He means that thoughts can be described as replacing hallucinatory wishing. The empty room that is consequently created when the object is not there leads to a hallucinatory wish, which in turn leads to the development of symbolization, to thinking and thought.

Klein (1930, 1940) has a somewhat different way to describe the space. She talks about the third and connects it to the father – the oedipal triangulation. She talks about the early Oedipus complex, which develops in relation to part objects – breast and penis. She includes the oedipal situation in what Freud calls the primal scene. She means that the continued development of the Oedipus complex goes hand in hand with the development of the depressive position. She emphasizes that cognition, thoughts, and language come out of and develop through the mourning process in the depressive position. It is consequently not easy to accept your own inner space when it contains memory and knowledge tied to a feeling of sorrow.

Bion continues this thought on space. He says that not only a thinker and thought is required, but also a thought machine. He describes a two-headed mechanism for the design of this thought machine. One is the relation between the paranoid-schizoid and depressive positions, or the pendulum between disintegration and integration (1962). The other is the dynamic relationship between something that projects, the contained, and an object that shelters it, the container. Bion's container refers to an inner psychic reality. Winnicott's concept of the holding environment seems, on the other hand, to refer more to the outer object (1971). If we were to say with Winnicott "there is no such thing as a baby" (1975, p. 37) I would like to add that there is never such a pair as mother-child, without a father figure. Even if the father is missing in the relationship, he has the potential presence.

Britton (1989) describes two types of difficulty in accepting the Oedipus complex. The first contains the inability to internalize the triangular situation resulting in the inability to integrate observations and experience. The other is what he calls the oedipal illusions, something he compares to Steiner's conception of "a blind eye" (1985), a defense that denies what has actually been seen. Britton emphasizes that the oedipal triangle provides a "triangular space". If not, this leads the patient to lack the ability to imagine the third position, being unable to accept that the analyst communicates with himself, and a feeling that space can only be created by increasing the distance on a line. In that situation, the analyst feels a desperate need for his/her own space.

Britton means that this condition is often connected with an inability of containment with the early mother. Technically, he means that first of all, you need your own thought space, to be able to articulate to yourself and then to be able to communicate an understanding for the other. Then the patient can start to think. When working with Eve, the situation became more complicated. What happened was what I described as Bion's attacks on linking (1959). My understanding of her inner situation did not lead to relief in the beginning, but rather it increased the power of the projective identifications (Bion, 1962).

The analyst – the patient – the analysis

Sometimes we speak about a field, in which the analyst and the patient move about. Winnicott's concept of the transitional phenomenon and transitional space (1953) deals with the subject. He seems to be interested in how the baby detaches itself from the mother, how the space between them is created. We even find the analyst's thoughts about this space in several places. Johan Norman (1993) talks about the psychoanalyst's instrument as "a mental space".

I think of three points, composed of the analyst, the patient, and the analysis. I would emphasize that this space is connected with the father in a transferred way. A geometric figure with three sides is built, and thereby a space is created. It is this space which is required for creativity and interpretation. The triangle provides sides, deep dimensions, and space. Already when the little child is at the breast, the child isn't looking at the breast but the mother's face. Through this perceived distance a space is created. Without separation in time and distance, there can be no conception of psychic space and thereby no perception or representation. It needs not only two, but three, to bring about an interaction between us. When there are two, there is no space to think in, to admit interpretation and reflection. This space exists in three-dimensional, not in the dyadic thought.

We can also think in terms of a prism. The prism, with its many sides and edges is a talking metaphor for the many faceted, for the space. The prism contains several aspects in relation to the outer world and to others. The prism can also be seen as the many sides of the personality. Some of them we may not want to know about and try to keep in the shadows, while others we want to illuminate. In the transference, movement from one surface to another exposes cracks that awaken fear.

Andre Green (1975, 1986), as well as Quinodoz (1992), write about the idea that even in the very beginning, the child finds itself in a triangular relationship through what the mother, consciously or unconsciously, represents about the father. The refusal to accept the space, to see its multi-dimensionality, to see the triangular situation, leads to the denial of the existence of the oedipal triangle, the primal scene, and the father's role in the scene – even if it is within the mother's inner self. The little child often defends itself against this knowledge by omnipotent defenses in an attempt to protect its self-esteem. For Eve, a teenage girl, the situation is more complicated. A continued omnipotent stance requires a split in relation to the fact that she is now sexually mature. She seems to "turn a blind eye" in relation to her knowledge about the oedipal scenario (Steiner 1985).

What is so threatening about looking at the triangle? It leads to the depressive position's entire spectrum of feelings of loss and sorrow, but also to symbol formation and a desire for repair, something which enables the oedipal couple to be established as symbolic forms in the inner world. The thought of space should in this way be connected directly to the ability to symbolize. The ability for symbolization is what is so terrifying for Eve. She is quick to take action instead of thinking. Moreover, I think this reaction functions as a source to sustain her conception of life, the activity being her rescue from the fear that she will die.

Andre Green talks about a situation where the object relations are not dyadic, but triadic, and mother and father are not distinctly separate, they are symmetrical (1975). In this instance it is impossible to constitute absence. The consequence is a closed psychotic system where projective mechanism is dominant. Furthermore, there is no opening for depression, where sorrow could take effect. The result is paralysis. One cannot think, cannot concentrate, and cannot remember. This is often most noticeable in the analyst. It creates a feeling of tension and inner stress for the analyst. In response to the patient's "empty space", the analyst makes a great effort to force herself to think that which the patient can't think. If the emptiness is filled too quickly with interpretations, the invasion from the evil object is only repeated. The analyst needs to reach a kind of inner tidiness and peace, long before a verbalization can take place. It is important that the analyst succeeds in binding and containing. The solution is to allow room for the patient to develop a potential space for possibilities and the ability to tolerate absence.

I started with a clinical question: Why do I feel that the patient doesn't seem to hear when I talk or give an interpretation? One way to think around this is that she shuns triangulation and the space it creates. For her there are two ways: to press herself in on me so that I feel crowded – or to run away. To shun triangulation also leads to even bigger problems, as she is thrown back into a relationship that imprisons and frightens. Eve's regressive attempts to find a solution lead, in their turn, me to respond in a similar manner to either want to protect myself and throw her out, or be aggressive and push myself onto her.

My original questions changed as I worked with Eve. Instead of wondering about a space for interpretation, my investigation led me to find a way for creating this space, this container for growth. My work became meaningful only when I was able to create a distance between us and find myself in a condition where "it is possible" or, in Bion's terms, in a state of reverie. Then I am able to think and go on to my theory, to thoughts about analysis. It is only now that I can find interpretations that are possible for her to accept.

So gradually Eve dares to see me as a separate person, who says and does things that are sometimes helpful and other times not. When her mistrust is strong, when the projective identifications are predominant, she seems to think: "You are stupid". When she is able to see me as a person, separate from her, she is more able to express thoughts about what I am saying, i.e. "That was good", or, "That was stupid". Now there are three on the scene; Eve, myself, and what she can now take in from my interpretations. We have created a space, where growth can take place.

References

Bion, W.R. (1959). Attacks on linking. In *Second Thoughts*. London: Karnac.

Bion W.R. (1962). A theory of thinking. In *Second Thoughts*. London: Karnac.

Bion W.R. (1963). *Elements of Psycho-Analysis*. London: Heinemann.

Britton, R. (1989). The missing link: Parental sexuality in the Oedipus complex. In *The Oedipus Complex Today: Clinical Implications*. London: Karnac.

Freud, S. (1938). An outline of psycho-analysis *S.E.* 23: 139–208. London: Hogarth.

Green, A. (1975). The analyst, symbolisation, and absence in the analytic setting. *International Journal of Psycho-Analysis* 56: 1–22.

Green, A. (1986). Negation and contradiction. In *On Private Madness*, pp. 254–276. London: Hogarth.

Klein, M. (1930). The importance of symbol-formation in the development of the ego. In *Love Guilt and Reparation*, pp. 219–232. London: Hogarth.

Klein, M. (1940). Mourning and its relation to manic-depressive states. *International Journal of Psychoanalysis* 16: 145–174.

Norman, J. (1993). The psychoanalyst's instrument: A mental space for impressions, affective resonance and thoughts. In *The Analyst's Mind: From Listening to Interpretation*. London: IPA Press.

Quinodos, D. (1992). The psychoanalytic setting as the instrument of the container function. *International Journal of Psychoanalysis* 73: 627–636.

Steiner, J. (1985). Turning a blind eye: The cover up for Oedipus. *International Review of Psychoanalysis* 12: 161–172.

Winnicott, D. (1953). Transitional objects and transitional phenomena. *International Journal of Psychoanalysis* 34: 89–97.

Winnicott, D. (1971). *Playing and Reality*. London: Tavistock.

Winnicott, D. (1975). *Through Paediatrics to Psycho-Analysis*. London: Hogarth Press and the Institute of Psycho-Analysis.

32

PENELOPE'S SUITORS[1]

Ester Hadassa Sandler

The shadow of the object

When I first met Penelope, she was almost 4 years old and came along without hesitation, holding my hand and stumbling by my side. Halfway to the analysis room she stopped and uttered my name, asking why I took so long to arrive. She pointed at the plants in the garden and said in a reproaching tone: "They are dying, they are dry". Lack of care and death would be mentioned several times along our work, the same flowerbeds carefully watched, session after session.

In the first months, she occupied herself obsessively with a roll of string and wooden blocks, tying, knotting and cutting strings, making presents, throwing them out and restarting the entire process. She stood either in silence or murmuring what sounded like a litany, sometimes gibberish; I tried to make contact, repeating her phrases. She giggled briefly and said, like a cartoon character: "Thank you, I liked that". The surrounding atmosphere seemed to have no continuity, only repetition, with an almost hypnotic effect upon me. One day she brought her face very close to mine and stared into my eyes. Her gaze was blurred, oscillating. Astonished, she said that she was seeing herself in my eyes. Immediately she got angry and stretched her fingers, trying to pierce the eyes in which she had prematurely mirrored herself, maybe feeling that she was captured inside me.

Many rolls of string went by until I remembered the boy of the wooden reel whom Freud (1920) described as trying to accomplish instinctual renouncement. But Penelope, unlike him, who considered himself responsible for the comings and goings of his mother, rendered her tributes to an object that she neither attracted nor dispelled like Ulysses' wife. Her uncertainties about whether he was alive and would return or not postponed the choice of a new husband amongst her suitors. She kept them waiting by un-weaving by night what she had woven during the day. Considered as the epitome of faithfulness, Penelope also displayed an ambivalent and unreliable relationship with her internal objects that could be glimpsed when she failed to recognize the aged and wrecked Ulysses as her beloved husband; the object of her loyalty was an idealized one, not the man who left her behind to follow his warrior duties.

One month into Penelope's analysis, her mother went away on a trip and during this time she brought to all sessions an old, worn pillow doll. Over her clothes she wore something of her mother's, a piece of some sheer and frilly evening wear, a ring and a necklace.

Her downcast and pale appearance made her look like a sleepwalking and strange figure, a sad and elegant rag doll. Whenever I tried to talk about the feelings aroused by her mother's absence, she interrupted me, screaming: "I don't want you to be my mother", showing that I began to take on for her the figure of a suitor.

My patient, as Ulysses' wife, could not overcome her grief and get on with her life, unable to trust her internal objects, keeping me in orbit around her, at a precise distance that made me feel that I could neither get closer to nor get away from her.

A mutiny in my setting

A few months later, it was my turn to be away for a short trip. When we met again, Penelope received me with grimaces, protests and cries. She hid in a corner of the waiting room, crouching behind a vase, talking to herself, anguished and unapproachable. After a few sessions, the mother decided to interrupt the analysis but considered that these events could be meaningful and important parts of the work and agreed to keep the analysis for a while. During a month or so, Mother failed to bring Penelope to some sessions or arrived very late, sometimes in the last five minutes. Impatiently, Mother decided to come into the analysis room with Penelope who closed the door in my face, leaving me outside. During this period, which lasted for six months, I could do little but patiently wait and reflect, trying to disentangle myself from intense feelings of anger and exclusion, a massive Projective Identification carried on by this sort of riot over the analytical setting. One day I was sitting outside so immersed in my doubts and sour feelings about this situation that a little thrush landed very close to me. I remained motionless, so I could watch the thrush at work, picking threads from my doormat and taking them to a tree branch, where I could see that a nest was being built. Watching this incessant work, back and forth from the ground to the tree, I unveiled not only the mystery of my disappearing doormat, but also the mystery of my own presence in that situation. I felt free to draw a sketch of me in this situation and put it under the door. This form of communication was accepted. In reply, Penelope passed me rough drawings indicating that I was forbidden to enter. In each of these sessions, at some point, quietly, she unlocked the door, allowing me into the room, where I kept silent, restrained to a receptive attitude.

I had to work through my emotions to be able to observe without intruding. Penelope's mother was overactive all the time – maybe imagining that in this way she could replace the analyst – telling Penelope what to do and how she should spend her time there, teaching her to copy letters and numbers, desperate to turn her daughter into a less weird girl, who would not fall behind in school. She used to point out: "It is ugly, it is wrong. A person should have two legs, not three!" Penelope made efforts to please, but eventually became disheartened, always failing to gain her mother's approval or arouse her interest, particularly when she insisted on painting the "black hole", a big spot of black paint spread over the paper.

The next step used to be Mother's loss of interest – reading a newspaper or talking on her cell phone, making professional and social arrangements – and Penelope withdrawing into her monologues. Occasionally Penelope protested by expressing her discontent aggressively, annoying Mother even more.

At some moment, in each of these strange sessions, Penelope turned to me with her finger on her lips as if to keep me from speaking, and with gestures asked me for some specific help: to hang the towel on the hanger, or to take off the lid that was stuck on an ink pot. She thanked me with a nod of her head.

Little by little, Mother gave us space to work, dozing off. Penelope left her sleeping on the couch of the playroom, inviting me to play in the "room of the books" where once she says, pointing at the couch: "Don't worry, one day I will lie down there", and "then I will let you work". Even when Penelope was clearly and willingly able to stay alone with me, Mother continued to come in with her. She pledged to stay around, because the waiting room was too cold and too far for her and she could not bear this. I believed that it was true for her.

Approximately one year into our work, Penelope was brought to my office during our holiday break. She did three small drawings and passed them under my office door. Under the raw figures, Mother wrote the respective subtitles: a "screaming whale", a "crying whale" and a "screaming dragon". Mother became very moved by Penelope's despair when she saw the door closed. From that moment on she cooperated as she could with our work. Confidently, Penelope re-established a routine of getting closer and withdrawing. She could spend a part of each session walking around the garden, aloof, mumbling her ruminations, examining the plants, hidden from my sight, indifferent to the cold or rain. Whenever I tried to approach her, she became angry. We re-started our correspondence in which I had to look for her only to be rebuffed, in a mixed atmosphere of acting-out and role-playing.

One day we created Puppy, performed by two fingers of my right hand, a transitional object that consolidated her capacity to play, think and dream about her life's events.

Puppy, a boy who had neither a home nor a mother, would have to travel a long and bumpy road; when he was close to reaching a shelter, some blown element forces him to restart the whole journey. Countless times this play had to be repeated. Whenever I did not resist to give an interpretation, the play was interrupted, Penelope withdrew, and the enchantment was broken. As a token of tolerance, she explained to me: "It is not fair to remember". This reversal of roles helped Penelope to cope with her pains and to bring out phantasies of rejection and aggression among other emotions.

Elaboration

Reparation of the Alpha-function

What I have just described above, a kind of passage from reality to playing, was achieved thanks to the reparation of Penelope's Alpha-function in tandem with an enhancement of my capacity for reverie. According to Bion (1959b), when Alpha-function is destroyed "the psyche gets deprived of its supply of reality. There is therefore nothing that can be opposed to phantasy. This is an additional reason for failure to wake up. There is not enough 'up' to wake up to". The repair of the Alpha-function entails recovering and reuniting the split-off fragments, "restoring also an extremely destructive super-ego, which restoration is unavoidable if any restoration at all is attempted".

The restoration of Alpha-function precedes the work of reparation of the ego and of the object, as classically described by Klein (1940), because Alpha-function mediates every step of the intervening processes, especially the free interplay between the Positions (Bion, 1959a) upon which the discovery of the selected fact depends, so fundamental for being in contact with reality without feeling lost or confused. Improving one's contact with inner and outer reality lessens persecutory anxieties and assists the taming of instinctual drives without annihilating its strength. Reciprocally the outcomes of the reparation processes help to constitute or consolidate the contact barrier, thus creating a virtuous cycle. I presume that when Penelope started her analysis she was already able to 'pour out' dream thoughts, but not to use them for thinking and dreaming, living in a sort of bare and raw reality, deprived of the mediating and modulating elements of dream and fantasy.

Phantasies of aggression and first attempts at reparation

Wisdom (1962) affirms that amongst some differences between Freud's (1917) and Klein's (1940) theories on melancholy, the concept of reparation is Klein's truly and original major contribution. According to him, in melancholy the awareness of destructive love interferes with the achievement of the depressive position. The reparation, which is the outcome of achieving the depressive position, starts with the projection of an amorous attitude sprung from the nucleus of the self towards the object for restoration purposes. It depends on the ability of the early ego to separate love and hate, building the good and bad objects separately. Thanks to primary splitting the amount of stress and anxiety over the rudimentary ego is lessened, furthering the development processes. Wisdom formulates hypotheses about inability for reparation, the main one being a sense of exhaustion and wastefulness of love in function of vain attempts to save the object.

Ogden (2002) observes that in "*Mourning and Melancholia*" Freud describes a different kind of ambivalence besides the unconscious conflict of love and hate, using the term to

> refer to a struggle between the wish to live with the living and the wish to be one with the dead . . . thus the melancholic experiences a conflict between, on the one hand, the wish to be alive with the pain of irreversible loss and the reality of death and, on the other hand, the wish to deaden himself to the pain of loss and knowledge of death.

To Penelope's still undeveloped mind, the strong ambivalence and consequent disappointment drove her to seclusion and to the freezing mechanism that I described as weaving and 'un-weaving'. Apparently, the primary splitting was never accomplished, leading to premature attempts at integration and reparation destined to fail and to be felt as useless. Her continuous and careful surveillance of the state of the object, and her sharpened sensibility and intelligence are some of the supporting evidences to the hypothesis above.

The inhibition of aggression for fear of overloading the object, whose capacity of survival she doubted, interfered with her spontaneity, as Winnicott (1950) described. One day Penelope made a few brushstrokes of paint on the wall, followed by imprinting the palms of her hands there. It was a very joyful experience, but it deflagrated a strong anxiety followed by phobic and obsessive mechanisms. For months Penelope avoided the playroom and dedicated at least one session a week to a thorough cleaning of the room.

Transitional objects and transitional phenomena were required for a long time. When she first tried to play without using my fingers and voice performance, strong feelings of frustration were aroused; whatever she did, it always fell under her standards, with harsh self-criticisms very like to her mother's former behavior towards her. By lending my voice and fingers to Puppy and other characters, some fun, softness and liveliness were introduced in our play – and, above all, we shared the responsibility.

Ruthless love, curiosity

Penelope became literate and able to get pleasure from cultural activities, reading books, visiting museums, experiences that she reproduced in our games. She became a great storyteller, curious and eager to learn, displaying wide-ranging interest in languages, sciences, history.

Although I was told by her parents that she had improved a lot in many ways, sleeping well and making friends at school, she did not feel well loved; they told me that even small failures or disappointments still aroused melancholic self-reproaches.

One time, she brought her dog to the session; after some time, she came with a rabbit; and then she introduced me successively to three female cats. The cats were very much alike, and Penelope was pleased with my incapacity to distinguish one from another. The cat of the day was wrapped in paper, hugged and kissed furiously, pursued, provoked, cornered and thrown from heights and at various distances. After all, according to Penelope, cats have seven lives, allowing her to display a ruthless love.

Again, I found myself having to witness and withstand a repetitive maltreatment, having to contain and work through deep emotions. Winnicott (1945) remarks:

> The depressed patient requires of his analyst the understanding that the analyst's work is to some extent his effort to cope with his own (the analyst's) depression, or shall I say guilt and grief resultant from the destructive elements in his own (the analyst's) love.

Suddenly, the pets vanished. Penelope appointed me as her assistant. "I think that when I grow up I will be a psychoanalyst. Let's play".

New attempts at reparation

Creating dialogues between patient and analyst, she asked the patients: "Tell me the story of your life". The patients had the most diverse complaints: a bruised finger, something lost. . . . She gave them advice, prescriptions and above all colored stones that were medicine sweets. Among the queue of clients, she chose a woman "who became ill because she got very sad and did nothing but cry. She became like that because her husband went away". Penelope gets up brusquely and says. "Enough! I'm going to be a doctor, and I will only treat tummy aches, sore throats and broken legs". But at the end of the session she stated: "What I really want to be is a mechanic", writing a series of dirty words on her box.

The sudden change of play, from the psychoanalyst who listens, to the mechanic who fixes things, made me consider the overload brought about by a sharp sensibility and premature attempts at reparation. We spent months playing a game of fixing all the toys in the box. Penelope also became a hairdresser.

In this period of approximately two years, there was intense, often obsessive reparation of some of her inner objects: father (cars); mother (balls); babies (animals); coitus and gestation (flowerbeds and balloons). I believe the restoration of the animals would also correspond to a return of her vitality.

Sometimes, the repetition of these games tired me. One day, Penelope got irritated because I was not able to formulate a proper complaint for one of her clients. "That's not it! You must say something else. Speak! Speak! You do not understand! You don't want to speak! If that's how things are, I will have to go away, I will have to leave". When she was about to leave the room, I realized that I had been less present in the play. I asked her whether she could give us a last chance. She agreed: "Just one minute!" I said she got desperate because she realized that I was distant and unwilling to play, and this was very painful to her, wishing to leave me in the same way I left her. She came back to the playroom and started playing again, ostensibly offended and sad.

The very fact that I could recognize and name my absent state of mind to her without feeling excessively guilty was extremely important. I apologized and asked her to give us an opportunity to repair.

Her reaction to my mood relates to what Green (1980, p. 149) called the dead mother complex, of which the essential feature is not "a depression caused by the real loss of an object . . . but a depression that '*takes place in the presence of the object which is itself absorbed by a bereavement*' [italics in original]. In any event the mother's sorrow and lessening of interest in her infant *are in the foreground*" [emphasis mine]. He describes also a defensive mechanism where there is a kind of primitive mirror identification with an object:

> This reactive symmetry is the only means by which to establish a reunion with the mother – perhaps by way of sympathy. In fact, there is no real reparation, but a mimicry, with the aim of continuing to possess the object (who one can no longer have) by becoming, not like it but, the object itself.
>
> *(p. 151)*

Final year of analysis

Penelope began to complain about feeling bored. The typical repression of latency seemed to have gotten a hold of us. Signals of shame and modesty appeared, giving us the opportunity to talk about the changes in her body. She comments: "How is it that you, an adult, can still remember these children's things?"

She tells me that she wants to stop the analysis at the end of the year. There followed a phase of feverish creations and building of things. She drew projects and proceeded to build them. When they were finished, she proudly took them home: a palace, a nightmare-hunter, a crumb-catcher, a tree-house. The only finished project she did not take home with her was a balloon in which one day she would travel around the world. Every so often she hung it on a tree branch, as a kind of sentinel. To preserve the setting, I used not to follow her on these excursions to the backyard. One day she returned to the room looking very strange, pale and sad. When she finally left, I noticed that she looked insistently at a certain point in the garden, avoiding it. Afterwards I found a dead bird there.

The following session we talked about the bird's death; she made an inventory of relatives of hers who had already passed away: grandfathers, a great-grandfather and her mother's brother. She picked up the puppets, play-acting and pretending to be a doctor. As before, all the 'cases' needed an operation to remove a thorn. One of the patients was a cloth baby doll, the old lady that she had so far left aside. She performed the role of this old lady as a hypochondriac who thought she was ill and worried all the time, fearing death, thinking exclusively about the day she would die. The treatment of this difficult patient required not only the removal of several thorns but also an electroshock. After a brain transplant the patient is cured, being able to laugh and to stop thinking about illness and death.

A few days later Penelope looked for a rough figure that she had attempted to make years ago. She spent a couple of sessions working to remake 'Mary Toothpick', apparently a premature attempt at "having a baby", amongst her first attempts at reparations. In the final period of analysis, even the smallest fragments of clay, paper or string were retaken by Penelope as meaningful.

Penelope then proceeded to make several cotton sheep that she said were clones, like Dolly, the sheep. They looked healthy, but as they were clones they died suddenly. This play was repeated several times. I relate this play to two achievements of Penelope's: managing to differentiate herself from her mother and no longer trying to be her mother's clone, and accepting the necessity of a creative couple, a father and a mother, to give birth to a healthy concept.

Separation and farewell

One afternoon, Penelope arrived in a serious and sullen state. I noticed that she was rather agitated, but she did not want much talk. When I tried to talk, she picked up something from the box and threw it on the floor fiercely. I told her she appeared to be angry. She said that she was not angry but ill, and that she did not wish to talk about it. Then, she took a pot of brown paint, dipped her finger in it and defiantly smeared the wall with paint. I thought for a little while and then, taking a second pot of paint, I also smeared some paint next to the blot she had made. She laughed, surprised, asking me what I thought the blot she had made looked like. I answered: "To be honest . . . poop". She replied with a cheerful voice: "You've got it right"! She then proposed a test. She painted the wall with shapes, numbers and letters. I had to guess what they meant or solve the problems she proposed. She gave me marks. Then she painted a series of lines and spots and asked: "And this, what is this?" I replied: "A girl who wishes to dirty the wall, pretending she is drawing something". She laughed a lot and continued to alternate real drawings with spots and stains until the whole room was painted, including the ceiling. Then she admitted that she was angry. Looking disconcerted she told me that she had such a terrible tummy ache at school that she had to go to the school nurse's office and to phone home for someone to come and fetch her. "But there is something that I will not tell". She became embarrassed. I asked if she could reach the bathroom in time. She inquired: "How do you know?" I said: "Who hasn't gone through things like that?" She continued: "But the worst is that there was . . . horrible". I ask: "Some little beast"? She replied: "a tapeworm and a roundworm, oh, how disgusting". The session came to an end and she became preoccupied with the mess she had made. She wanted to clean up, but we had no more time left. She asked if I could leave it like that until the next session. I said this was not possible. She seemed to feel guilty because of how much work it would be for me to clean the room, and frustrated by what I told her. But she asked me to photograph the wall.

The next session starts with the wall being painted again, and she explained that this was an art-attack. She informed me that she was going to tell me a frightening story, the story of Mr. Jenkins.

> Mr. Jenkins is a happy man, with a beautiful house at the end of a long-curved street, where people go for picnics and all neighbors have parties. One day, a heavy

thunderstorm puts an end to the picnic. Lightning hits a beautiful tree and burns it down. Some of the neighbors die, others manage to escape, Mr. Jenkins' wife and children die, his house is burnt down, the neighbors move away. And Mr. Jenkins becomes a sour, sad and mean man. From that day on, he has a secret room where he imprisons and tortures happy people.

For a few sessions Penelope continued painting on the wall and telling stories. She looked extremely happy. She hummed songs. Two months before the summer holidays, I informed her that I was going to move my office to a different location. She asked questions. She wanted to know whether she would be able to continue painting on the walls. She asked for the new address, but she did not know if she wanted to continue. "After all, I have known you since I was born, you have always been in my life". I said that I understood that she wanted to live through other things, to have other experiences, to feel that she could continue by herself. In the following sessions, she did not return to the subject.

Then, she arrives and points to the room with the books, saying: "Today it is there". She asked me to sit in the armchair. She could not decide where to sit and ended up sitting on the arm of the chair, next to me. She said: "Call Puppy. Today, we are going to need him".

She proceeded to organize what she called the graduation of Puppy and his tween Poppy. They had finally learned how to read. They would be released from the forest in which they had lived a hundred years of loneliness, ignorance and incapacity to grow up. Poppy received slightly better marks than Puppy, who only managed to succeed after nearly failing the exams.

I told her that she now felt that she too could go away. She was extremely moved, close to tears. She recalled the various things we had done together and she started to complain: the castle was a little damaged, the nightmare-hunter had been lost, Mary Toothpick was broken. I told her that what we had lived through together would remain inside her and inside me. She pondered on this for a while and then she agreed.

She then stretched a finger in the direction of my eye, now with a delicate gesture as if to dry a tear from my face, a tear that maybe was there. At the end of this session she gave me a photograph that she had taken of me sitting on the floor, outside the room. She was less than 5 years old when she took this photo, now she was almost 10.

Some years later we met again. Penelope, now almost 14 years old, asked to see me. She came with her mother. I felt surprised by her figure, tall and strong with a very trendy haircut. Before entering the analysis room, she hugged me tightly. She lied on the couch with no hesitation, as if she had been there the day before. Then she started to cry, and cried almost all the time. In the few words she spoke, I recognized that metallic and stereotyped tone of the beginning of our work. When I told her that our session had ended, she asked if she could see the playroom, where I kept a chair that she painted in one of her art-attacks. She was very moved and said: "You kept it!" Then she asked her mother if she could come another day. We met two more times, during which she told me about her life – she had never stopped writing and drawing, and was especially interested in Manga comics. She also took drama classes and had friends with whom she played Role-Playing Games, friends whom her mother does not approve. She tells me in detail about her mother's fierce depressions, and how her mother had ruined her affective life, the second marriage that had given Penelope a sense of a restored family, security and happiness. Her feeling was being the only person on whom her mother relied, responsible for keeping her alive, fearing all the time that she could end her life.

Then she decided to restart her analysis, but she never appeared again.

A few years later I found out, accidentally, that she was now an art student at the University.

Note

1 This paper is a significantly reworked version based on two previous articles published in 2002 and 2005.

References

Bion, W.R. (1959a). The dream. In *Cogitations*, pp. 44–46. London: Karnac, 1992.

Bion, W.R. (1959b). The dream. In *Cogitations*, pp. 95–98. London: Karnac, 1992.

Freud, S. (1917). Mourning and melancholia. *S.E.* 14. London: Hogarth.

Freud, S. (1920). Beyond the pleasure principle. *S.E.* 23. London: Hogarth.

Green, A. (1980). The dead mother. In *On Private Madness*, pp. 142–173. London: Karnac, 2005.

Klein, M. (1940). Mourning and its relation to manic depressive states. In *Writings of Melanie Klein vol. 1*, pp. 344–369. London: Karnac, 1992.

Ogden, T. (2002). A new reading of the origins of object relations theory. *International Journal of Psychoanalysis* 83, 767.

Winnicott, D.W. (1945). Primitive emotional development. In *Collected Papers: Through Paediatrics to Psychoanalysis*, pp. 145–156. London: Tavistock Publications, 1958.

Winnicott, D.W. (1950). Aggression in relation to emotional development. In *Collected Papers: Through Paediatrics to Psychoanalysis*, pp. 204–218. London: Tavistock Publications, 1958.

Wisdom, J.O. (1962). Comparison and development of the psycho-analytical theories of melancholia. *International Journal of Psycho-analysis* 43: 113–132.

33

UNDERSTANDING THE REVERSAL OF THE ALPHA FUNCTION THROUGH A CASE

Anie Stürmer

In "A Theory of Thinking" (Bion, 1967), Bion refers to the use of the concept of the alpha function (fα), a function initially exercised by the mother, who converts sensory data into alpha elements, allowing the psyche to differentiate between being awake and sleeping, being conscious or unconscious. He adds that the failure to compose a mother/baby relationship, where the normal projective identification is possible, will block the development of the alpha function and the posterior psycho-analytic function of the personality. The baby is not able to use the sensory data alone, therefore, he's left to "evacuate these elements into the mother" (Bion, 1967a, p. 116), so the mother is responsible to welcome these elements and transform them in a way that they can be used again by the baby as alpha elements. "The mother's capacity for reverie is the receptor organ for the infant's harvest of self-sensation gained by its conscious" (Bion, 1967, p. 116).

The development is normal when the relationship baby/breast allows depositing into the mother intolerable sensations, re-introjecting the modified sensations after being kept in the breast long enough for the sensation to become tolerable. The unaccepted feeling is modified by the mother's alpha function. However, if that projection is rejected by the mother, the child will never learn the meaning of this sensation and consequently will re-introject an undefined terror, "a nameless dread" (Bion, 1967, p. 116). This would correspond to the "minus container/contained" model (-♀♂), highlighting the failure of the maternal alpha function and capacity of developing a hypertrophied projective identification.

With the rupture of the mother's capacity for reverie, the tasks that cannot be concluded "are imposed on the rudimentary consciousness; they are all in different degrees related to the function of correlation. The rudimentary consciousness cannot carry the burden placed on it" (Bion, 1967, pp. 116–117).

Thus, instead of establishing an internal benevolent object, it establishes an object that rejects the projective identification and internalizes an object that is not understood and identifies itself with it.

Bion (1967, p. 117) suggests that the psyche apparatus could be formed of four parts:

1   Thinking, associated with modification and evasion
2   Projective Identification, associated with evasion by evacuation and not to be confused with normal projective identification

3   Omniscience
4   Communication

This apparatus would be destined to deal with thoughts, these being conceptions, oneiric thoughts, alpha and beta elements – as if these objects had to be confronted, because they would express a problem or because they would be seen as unnecessary and undesired to the psyche and somehow having to be eliminated.

If these objects are expressions of a problem, they need an apparatus that can distinguish a deprivation and the action to be used to modify this need, which is the same as the alpha function does. The tolerance to pain and frustration and the strengthened "apparatus for thinking" (through the successful functioning of the container/contained mechanism as well as the alternation of the paranoid-schizoid and depressive positions) allow actions to deal with the external and internal world in order to modify the state of need. Therefore we have two conditions where a suitable apparatus for thinking can develop: innate factors such as tolerance or intolerance to frustration and environment factors such as the mother's capacity for reverie. These aspects determine the development of the capacity for thinking, combine thoughts and create symbols, including the process of correlation, publication and communication.

But, what if this development is frustrated?

Let's analyze the case of Carlos:

Carlos is 31 years old, lives with his parents, works in the family business where he doesn't fit in and is bullied by the other employees, which is related to his clinical condition and his relationship difficulties.

Carlos comes to the first appointment on his own, showing some psychomotor difficulties, slow speech, slow reasoning but with the capacity for intellectual understanding above expectation. He says that he gets along only with his mother despite arguing sometimes, and that his father doesn't care about him and calls him "lazy".

It bothered him that he was discriminated at work. He's the director's son but has to work with low level employees who don't respect him. Because of his limitations, that was the only department where he could fit in, but he found it difficult to carry out his tasks. The colleagues would call him "lazy-bones", "tramp" and "daddy's boy". He suffers because he doesn't have a girlfriend, something people often ask him. At a previous job he had to carry heavy boxes, making him feel like a "dogs body" (sic).

Despite being upset Carlos was questioning about not having a girlfriend. He had been to a nightclub before but was shocked to see so many call girls. He was afraid and aware of the dangers related to sexual diseases and unwanted pregnancy, as a teenager would be. He had started college but said it "was a disaster". The dean had facilitated an "inclusion" but Carlos said that he didn't understand anything during the lessons.

At an appointment, the mother recalled it started when he was 5 months old. He was born a normal and healthy child. His brother was one year older and was born with a leg problem, with life threatening risks; he had surgery at a very young age. When she got pregnant again, the father was angry with her, because they already had one baby to care for. The mother didn't want to have an abortion as suggested by the husband, and her father, Carlos's grandfather, said that he would take care of the child and support her. At the time of the elder son's surgery, her husband was so worried about losing him that he even mentioned suicide. The mother felt very much alone and scared, but the operation was successful. Then one day while breastfeeding, Carlos regurgitated and choked on his vomit, almost dying. She called the ambulance and they managed to resuscitate him, but his brain was deprived of oxygen for a few minutes, which could have caused some damage, leaving him with some psychomotor and mental retardation (this was mentioned by the mother; there is no neurological proof).

I was supervising Solange Weber dos Reis,[1] Carlos' therapist. She reported the meetings as being about an annoying mother, who is unable to understand her son, disrespects him, complains about him and "degrades" him in front of her. The therapist, in turn, pictured herself getting up and going for the mother's throat, to make her stop talking and respect her patient. In private, the therapist pointed out to the mother that it wasn't therapeutic to talk that way about her son, especially in front of him, because it would only increase his sense of worthlessness and low self-esteem. After the session, the therapist felt unwell, with strong headache, followed by vomiting and diarrhea; she had to cancel all the following day's appointments.

Therapist's illness denotes a countertransferencial feeling, work of her alpha function: the therapist feels empathy and manages to put herself into her patient's shoes and feels attacked by the way the mother treats her son in front of her. Also she manages to have an idea of how he probably feels and his inability to react. Thus, she transforms what she felt in something that can be translated both to the mother and Carlos, carrying out the psycho-analytic task, and putting into words the feelings of both of them.

Understanding the story:

> His mother recalls that the boy wasn't wanted. He came at the wrong time, when the family was busy with the eldest son's surgery.

According to Bion (1963, p. 77), "The myth may be regarded as a primitive form of pre-conception and a stage in publication, that is, in communication of the individual's private knowledge to his group". Bion (1963, p. 77) states that "the processes by which private knowledge is communicated within the individual is obscure; elucidation waits on advances that psychoanalysts have yet to make". For him, the Oedipus material highlights the primitive apparatus of pre-conception, which would belong to the ego as part of the apparatus to keep contact with reality. Bion proposes a private oedipal myth, a version of the -α element, which would be the means, the pre-conception through which the child is able to establish contact with the parents as they exist in the real world. The correspondence of this oedipal-α-element pre-conception with the realization of the parents, originates the parents' conception.

We could think that Carlos has an incestuous private oedipal myth, where the grandfather is the one who authorizes his arrival in this world. It's the grandfather who "adopts" him, his mother's father, making him the oedipal/incestuous son. As a consequence, this is imprinted in his life: he's the "daddy's boy", target of jokes, not legitimated by the father. Carlos's oedipal configuration is made from repulsion of the bastard son who comes to the world.

Carlos doesn't really have a relationship with his father and it's with his mother that he shares most of his life, forming a couple. According to Bion, the myth would have a value or pre-conception and would be the work of the α function. I think Carlos lives his erotic feeling in an almost concrete way. To Bion (1963) the child can never set up the apparatus to develop a conception of the parental relationship and consequently to the solution of the oedipal problems. This would happen because there would be an emotional charge conducted by the oedipal pre-conception -α element where his own oedipal pre-conception is destroyed. Therefore, there is no pre-conception. We thus have the symbolic equation (Segal, 1957): any woman **is** the mother. Carlos desires women and for him it is dangerous to approach them.

Sex has an incestuous character since he's in a symbiotic and infantilized relationship with his mother. As there is a failure of the alpha function, he's unable to develop an apparatus to think thoughts; he's blocked from appropriately using the functions of discrimination, differentiation and correlation. He works with the predominance of the psychotic side of his personality.

The regurgitation and choking on his own vomit, nearly dying, caused consequences in his future life. This episode is told by his mother in detail, and the therapist realizes the mother's incapacity for containment toward her son. I think it's the simulation of the failure of the maternal alpha function, indicating the incapacity of reverie.

The capacity of reverie means that a mother can be in contact with the emotional experience of her baby, allowing him to be understood and calmed in his physical and psychic needs, allowing him to "dream", welcoming the evacuation of what couldn't be thought by the embryonic mind, returning it in a tolerable and conceptualized way. A mother with the capacity for reverie will sense the truth regarding her baby, and this contact will allow the emotional experiences to be felt accordingly. On the other hand, a mother without this capacity won't be able to get in contact with her child's mind, not allowing the baby's experience to be felt as true and consequently making it impossible to enter K, the knowledge about oneself and about the truth of the emotional experiences, which little by little develops the apparatus to think thoughts. In *Learning from Experience* (Bion, 1962, p. 96), Bion points out that if the infant feels fear that it is dying, it

> splits off and projects its feelings of fear into the breast together with envy and hate of the undisturbed breast. Envy precludes a commensal relationship. The breast in K would moderate the fear component and the fear of dying that had been projected into it and the infant, in due course, would re-introject a now tolerable and consequently growth-stimulation in part of its personality. In − K the breast is felt enviously to remove the good or valuable element in the fear of dying and force the worthless residue back into the infant. The infant who started with a fear he was dying ends up by containing a **nameless dread** (emphasis mine).

To Bion (1962), any emotional experience has a correlate in the digestive system. The mind or the apparatus to think thoughts corresponds to the digestive system and all its functions. The regurgitating and choking explain the incapacity of reverie and the hindrance of this mother in welcoming the anxieties of her son, resulting in the development of the reversal of the alpha function. The mother puts her own anxieties inside Carlos's mind. This is highlighted in the session where the therapist wanted to stop the mother from talking and make her swallow her words. As a confirmation of this emotional experience, the therapist felt unwell and vomited. This situation would be a projective transformation (Bion, 1965): the therapist "lives" what Carlos must have lived since he was a baby: a discharge of the emotional experiences not contained by the mother, which are evacuated inside his mind, and who, unable to stand such weight, regurgitates and chokes while being breastfed. The therapist lives his same emotional experience and imagines jumping on the mother's throat to make her swallow her words. Such words are felt like "things in themselves". In the case of the baby, these beta elements, things in themselves, would return to him as bizarre objects and due to his incapacity to contain them, almost caused his death. Since the baby doesn't have the capacity to contain, he had no option but to "swallow" these bizarre objects, products of the reversal of the alpha function, choking and almost dying, as if the baby had been the target and the recipient of the beta elements, discharged by the mother in Carlos's mind/stomach. The mother, on the other hand, didn't have containment for her anxieties, having her mind occupied by the anxiety caused by the operation of her elder son.

The alpha function of the therapist allows her to apprehend the psycho-analytic object of the session. Through her emotional experience she imagines and captures what is communicated by the failure of the maternal alpha function, allowing the understanding of Carlos's mental state and his mother's incapacity of reverie and reversal of the alpha function. The invariance of this emotional experience is the anxiety that permeates all of Carlos's relationships.

Bion, when referring to psychotic patients, says that "such patients don't have memories but only undigested facts" (Bion, 1965, p. 41). Therefore, "thinking, in the sense of manipulating words and thoughts to do work in the absence of the object, seems to be just what the patient cannot do" (Bion, 1965, p. 41).

Carlos died emotionally. He developed a mental retardation and works predominantly with his psychotic personality which is a refuge for him. He has split his mind, and has difficulties in symbolizing and getting in contact with his truths and origin: rejected by his father, unable to thrive as a being. Carlos works in the periphery of his own life, frightened of what he feels and thinks, because he wasn't allowed to develop the capacity of containment of his emotional experiences.

Note

1 Psychologist – IPSI – Novo Hamburgo, Brazil.

References

Bion, W.R. (1962). *Learning from Experience*. London: William Heinemann. [Reprinted London: Karnac, 1984].

Bion, W.R. (1963). *Elements of Psychoanalysis*. London: William Heinemann. [Reprinted London: Karnac, 1984].

Bion, W.R. (1965). *Transformations*. London: William Heinemann [Reprinted London: Karnac, 1984].

Bion, W.R. (1967a). A theory of thinking. In *Second Thoughts*. London: William Heinemann. [Reprinted London: Karnac, 1984].

Bion, W.R. (1967b). *Second Thoughts*. London: William Heinemann. [Reprinted London: Karnac, 1984].

Segal, H. (1957). Notes on symbol formation. *International Journal of Psychoanalysis* 38: 391–397.

SECTION X
Epilogue

AVNER BERGSTEIN

Panel discussion/group discussion

Chair/Facilitator: James Gooch; with Monica Horovitz, Nanci Carter, Gisèle de Mattos Brito and Avner Bergstein.

A lot has been said about Bion's so called mystical turn, perhaps even religious turn – a thread that seemed to run through many of the papers.

It seems to me that the question of Bion's mystical turn is related to his attempts to describe the ineffability of O and of emotional truth, with which we too are all struggling. I would like to address this point a little more if I may.

The urge to communicate, alongside the difficulty to communicate, is the Ariadne's thread running throughout Bion's work and seems to be a very powerful driving force in Bion's need to write. In his writings, it often seems he is going out of his way in order to describe the frustration and suffering he feels in the face of the inability to communicate the emotional experience (Bergstein, 2015).

It is there that Bion turned to the mystics.

Mystical thinking maintains that truth is hidden from the senses, from language, and from thought. It is concerned with the unknown, concealed, and zero-ness. Bion began to be interested in mystics when he realized that many of them had found it very difficult to put their experiences of revelations into words and communicate it to others who had not had this personal and unique experience. He also realized that as analysts, we are close to the mystics in this sense, since, when we have an intuition about what is happening in the link with a patient, we can, perhaps, try to communicate it *to him or to her*, but it is almost impossible to communicate it as it is, to someone else who was not present (de Bianchedi, 2005).

Moreover, Bion says he wanted to bring in the word 'mystic' into the psychoanalytic discourse as a synonym for 'a scientist' or 'an artist'. He chose to use the word mystic, which does have a religious connotation, because he had wanted to push psychoanalysis into realms that were up until then occupied too much by religion and philosophy (Bion, 1967).

I would like to stress that to my mind, Bion did not try to equate the analytic experience with a religious one. All he tried to do was to describe the unbearable inability to express verbally the emotional experience, and for that he turned to the writings of theologians and mystics, where he found an echo for the experience he tried to describe.

Several papers have dealt with this link to mysticism and Christian mystics. Bion mentions only a few of the Jewish Kabbalists and Jewish philosophers, namely Isaac Luria (a sixteenth century mystic), Martin Buber, and Gershom Scholem (a scholar of Kabbalah and Jewish mysticism, who seems to have made a big impression on Bion's thinking).[1] I would like to refer to some notions in Jewish philosophy and in homiletic interpretations of the Bible, which reverberate Bion's thinking, and which poetically describe the experience of the weariless pursuit of emotional truth and the limited capacity of verbal language to facilitate its communication.

Jewish philosophy tries to address the ineffability of emotional truth and of ultimate reality through the issue of God. The name of God (similarly to the sign O) is merely a *symbolic representation* of an ultimate reality which is forever unformed and amorphous (Scholem, 1960). Inasmuch as one cannot describe in words the ultimate reality of the emotional experience, any attempt to describe God undermines its very essence. Moses Maimonides, one of the most acclaimed Jewish philosophers and author of *A Guide to the Perplexed*, a radical book written at the beginning of the twelfth century, claims that the deity is not amenable to linguistic representation. One cannot ascribe any adjective to God, and one cannot say a single word about him. All one can say is what God is *not*.

The writings of Maimonides are often reminiscent of Bion's descriptions of the elusiveness of truth. For example, he writes:

> [S]ometimes Truth flashes up before us with daylight brightness, but soon it is obscured by the limitations of our material nature and social habits, and we fall back into darkness almost as black as that in which we were before. We are thus like a person whose surroundings are from time to time lit up by lightning, while in the intervals he is plunged into pitch-dark night.
>
> *(Maimonides, 1191)*

As Bion writes, the fact that different disciplines at different times and from different vertices, describe the same experience, gives this experience greater validity, and one might say provide a 'multi-ocular' vision of truth. I would like to illustrate this with two interpretations of the Bible.

The first, described by Mayer (2016), relates to a story from the Book of Exodus, when the Israelites fled from Egypt, after crossing the Red Sea. As you might remember, the sea opened up miraculously allowing them to flee from slavery, after which it closed back, drowning the Egyptian army who was chasing them. The Israelites sung a song to God and in it they say: "This is my God, and I will praise Him" (Exodus, 15:2).

From the words of the song "*This* is my God", Chazal, the sages who were the Jewish spiritual leaders, concluded that the singers actually saw God, hence they could just point to it and say "this". 'This', in the Bible, denotes something that one can point to. The Israelites do not seem to need many words to describe God. It seems they are not anxious, nor in wonder or awe. For them, the presence of God is as simple as that of a person standing next to them.

From the language of the song it seems that they simply do not need a detailed description. God is actually there. They see God and so they only need to point at him. This is different than *an image, a vision*, or *a metaphor*; it is an actual sight that does not require verbalization.

This is in contrast to the prophets who describe God with many, many words. In the Book of Hosea, it is written that the prophets all saw *an image* of God, but not God himself. Even Ezekiel, who describes God in detail, writes "I saw *visions* of God", not the thing in itself.

So, it is concluded that the Israelites saw what the prophets did not. Hence it is asked, why should the simple Israelites coming out of Egypt see what the prophets themselves could not see?

One might say that language mediates the religious experience. However, language is required only for those who are in the *outskirts*, in the *periphery*. The Israelites who are standing right before the deity, denuded from metaphors and images, do not need language but simply the index finger alone. The prophets, Isaiah, or the exiled Ezekiel, are far away and do not expect such a revelation, hence they need language to describe to themselves and to their disciples the enormity of the experience. Language is nullified as we come closer to the intimate, burning center of the religious experience, and in the face of God it disappears altogether.

The limitations of verbal communication to describe emotional truth can be seen again in another interpretation of the Book of Exodus. It is said that when God was revealed on Mt. Sinai, when the Torah was handed down to the people of Israel, all handicaps were cured. Moses, who had been stammering since he was an infant, refused to be cured. When asked why, he said that his stammer is the way he communicates with God.

It seems that it is precisely his stammer that enables him to approach the emotional experience in the encounter with the deity, or ultimate reality. The stammer, as we know, for Bion too, designates a paradigm for the breakdown of the verbal container in the face of the intensity of the emotional experience.

For me, it is amazing and very moving to find these counterparts in mysticism, and I dare to think that for Bion too. But that does not make psychoanalysis mystical, and certainly not religious. The fact that different facets of the emotional experience can be 'observed' from different vertices, feels truthful, and seems to afford *a sense of truth*.

Note

1 Bion cites only seven authors apart from himself, in his book *Attention and Interpretation*, Scholem being one of them.

References

Bergstein, A. (2015). Attacks on linking or a drive to communicate? Tolerating the paradox. *Psychoanalytic Quarterly* 84: 921–942.

de Bianchedi, E.T. (2005). Whose Bion? Who is Bion? *International Journal of Psycho-Analysis* 86: 1529–1534.

Bion, W.R. (1967). Third seminar. In J. Aguayo and B. Malin (Eds.) *Wilfred Bion: Los Angeles Seminars and Supervision*, pp. 55–79. London: Karnac, 2013.

Maimonides, M. (1191). Introduction. In *The Guide of the Perplexed*. Trans. C. Rabin. Indianapolis: Hackett, 1995.

Mayer, Y.Z. (2016). Language belongs to the periphery. In *Readings*, pp. 103–105. Tel Aviv: Yedioth Ahoronoth Books.

Scholem, G. (1960). *On the Kabbalah and Its Symbolism*. Trans. R. Manheim. New York: Schocken, 1969.

GISÈLE DE MATTOS BRITO

Panel discussion/group discussion

Chair/Facilitator: James Gooch; with Monica Horovitz, Nanci Carter, Gisèle de Mattos Brito and Avner Bergstein.

I am very pleased with the invitation to participate in this panel. I feel very touched by it. I have the feeling that I am representing the Brazilian Group, that as you know, is deeply influenced by Bion's contributions. His time in Brazil had a profound impact on our psycho-analytical thinking. He is a landmark, especially for me, because he was my father's analyst. I'd like to share with you the great excitement I feel in this moment. To be in Los Angeles at a Conference on the Work of Bion, after so many years, is of great value to me.

I was here, accompanying my parents and siblings during my father's analysis with Bion, in 1979. At that time I was 17 years old and with great curiosity I tried to understand what a person like my father was searching for. He sold everything he owned and with five children and a wife he moved to have an analysis with an Englishman who was living in the United States. That was something amazing! At that time, my dad had six sessions a week. Sometimes I accompanied him to his analysis and from the waiting room I could see Dr. Bion. I was impressed by his athletic, tall build. My impression today is that he was not afraid of feeling. He looked at us in a very profound and penetrating way. His presence and importance in my father's life, and in our family's life, are invaluable. I once asked my father: "Are you aware that if something happened to you we will be in a real trouble?" He laughed and said: "Don't worry my dear, I've made a good life insurance." I was very impacted by this experience. I realized the necessity to find a person to help you, as much as possible, to be yourself, even if you have to cross an ocean! It is for this reason I became a psychoanalyst.

Well, many years have gone by, my father widely spread Bion's ideas in Brazil espe-cially in the Sao Paulo and Ribeirão Preto Psychoanalytic Society of which he is one of its founders. His passion for psychoanalysis and for Bion's ideas led him to collect around

130 audio tapes of supervisions Bion gave in Brazil during his visits in 1973, 1975 and 1978. The content of these tapes was transcribed and translated from English to Portuguese and since 2005 we have had a study group on Bion's Supervisions. Each month a colleague comments on one of the Supervisions and we discuss it in the group. Initially my father coordinated this group and I have taken over his role since 2009. The feedback that we have shows how important these discussions have been to the development of analytical thinking among our colleagues.

Our intention is to publish these Supervisions with comments. We are aware that we hold in our hands a very important technical treasure. Many years were dedicated to the transcriptions of those tapes. You can get an idea of this work through Howard Levine's and Giuseppe Civitarese's book (2016).

I would now like to say a few words about our Conference.

First of all, I was impressed with the way that the Organizing Committee planned the events, from the beginning until the end of the encounter: starting and ending with gratitude and recognition for the work of two great analysts Jim Gooch and James S. Grotstein. Most of all it revealed a spirit of loving gratitude capable of overcoming differences and gave to all of us the opportunity to live this experience. It was beautiful and deeply touching. We felt ourselves as part of it. Congratulations!

As analysts we know that there is no present without a past, neither a future without a present. In a certain way, Melanie Klein climbed on Freud's shoulders, as Bion did on Klein's and Freud's. Jim and James climbed on Bion's shoulders. So, we too are part of this legacy as we are building together this history. We are grateful for having you Jim and James with us so much alive.

As a second point I would like to highlight the aesthetic dimension that the Organizing Committee was able to offer to us. I think that the play so movingly acted and the poems became the background for many of our discussions: life and death intertwined.

On the one hand, this experience pushed us to the working through of our losses. Beckett's play, *First Love* (Premier Amour, 1946), takes place in a cemetery. While the leading character was trying to elaborate the death of his father, he meets a beautiful lady and they have a baby. The writing of this play occurred while Beckett was dealing with his own father's death. This coincides with the beginning of Beckett's analysis with Bion. He opens the play with the following line: "I associate, rightly or wrongly, my marriage with the death of my father, in time" (1946). On the other hand, there is gratitude and acknowledgement for life. At the same time Los Angeles was the last place where Bion was welcomed and was able to develop his most disconcerting, audacious and creative work, *A Memoir of the Future* (1979). In Los Angeles Bion found freedom to think and to feel.

In the beginning of the second day through the Soul Motion Dance we could experience a little bit of the search for that freedom. As a friend of mine said while watching the dance experience: "Perhaps that was why Bion chose California to live." And then I said: "Yes! Freedom!" Bion, in *A Memoir of the Future*, did a deep critical examination of psychoanalytic theories. In this work, in particular, he created a unique freedom of writing and roominess for the emergence of the new, the unknown, O. More than that he found a way to give birth to "what does not exist."

In the volume *The Dawn of Oblivion*, Bion said:

Physicists and chemists can draw those beautiful diagrams of the AND molecule, but so far have not been able to define the difference between what is animate and inanimate.

We are certain of one thing: the difference exists. A table appears different from what we are. Defining that can be of little importance, but I am sure there are embryonic ideas and feelings, primordial ideas that deserve the chance of development. I do not know if they will be good or bad, someone will need to have the courage to say: "Even if a monster is born, I will risk giving birth to the child."

(1979, p. 299)

What are we building? We cannot forget Bion's warning about the possibility that, in developing something embryonic, we may also be creating something monstrous. However, getting back to the play, I think we did not abort the baby. I was at different presentations during the conference and I observed that many embryonic ideas from Bion's legacy are being developed.

Bion lived here. And here, he gave birth to many babies.

Perhaps, we are the babies.

Thank you very much.

References

Bion, W.R. (1979). *The Dawn of Oblivion. A Memoir of the Future*, Vol. 3, p. 229. London: Karnac, 1990.
Beckett, S. (1946). *Premier Amour*. Paris: Editions de Minuit, 1970.
Levine, H. and Civitarese (2016). *The W.R. Bion Tradition – Lines of Development, Evolution of Theory and Practice over the Decades*. London: Karnac.

ALESSANDRO BRUNI

Panel discussion/group discussion

Chair/Facilitator: James Gooch; with Monica Horovitz, Nanci Carter, Gisèle de Mattos Brito and Avner Bergstein.

The rich experience of the conference gave back to me two emerging "peak" emotions, joy and suffering. Joy, surely, at the Donna Gunther soul dancing that brought all us participants to experience a sort of light group Tantric fusion. Suffering, when the second "tribe" session ended in such a weird and unpleasant way, leaving many colleagues in a state of anger and disappointment.

The atmosphere of the conference renewed the spirit of the 1970s when a new wind of creativity blew from California through the Anglo-Saxon and European world. Even in Psychoanalysis you have had the intelligence to invite many British analysts, among them Wilfred Bion himself.

Thinking around the deep task of our discipline, I believe that Psychoanalysis is the greatest response in human history to the aphorism written above the door of the Delphi oracle.

"γνοθι σε αυτον"
"Know yourself"

Included in this aphorism is the idea that there is a subject who has to deal with an unknown Self. In some way, this was an anticipation of the unconscious. Freud proved that it is not possible to know yourself on your own, alone, without interaction with at least one other human being, ideally an analyst.

Considering the dramatic condition of our planet, Psychoanalysis can offer a chance for help, a "μεθοδος", id est, "a way to proceed beyond". Psychoanalysis is a method for re-integrating the ever-more split and alienated Ego of human beings. From this point of view, the position of the analyst or the position of the patient are not so important in themselves. What is important is that this cathartic method can be activated in Psychoanalysis and group settings.

Finally, I have the impression that the atmospheres of all the three basic assumptions could be detected from the emerging emotions of the conference large group. The dependence basic assumption has been honored by paying homage to our two great masters, James S. Grotstein and James Gooch. The pairing basic assumption has been wonderfully expressed by Barbara Bain and Alan Mandell, performing Samuel Beckett's masterpiece "First Love". The fight-flight basic assumption erupted suddenly with the unexpectedly fast ending of the last "tribe meeting". This reminds us that "O" in some way cannot be contained, because, as Bion claimed, Psychoanalysis is not a "container", but a "probe".

Thanks to all of you.

NANCI CARTER

A formless something – thoughts on the conference experience

I am most privileged to be here with this learned panel of Bion scholars. I want to thank the organizing committee and the facilitators whose expansive thought and vision sought to provide a space for truth – creating a Bionian group experience open to O, and promoting a deeper understanding of O. The play between the small groups and the large community group created a tension that shaped something similar to what happens in the consulting room as the patient and analyst navigate between outer structured reality and inner spontaneous process within the analytic relationship. The Soul Motion Dance sessions added another layer of experience for allowing ourselves to open to what may happen – a sensory, rhythmic experience of self and other. Many I talked with enjoyed this kinesthetic surprise.

In my first contact with Bionian ideas, I was struck by a similar poetic reverence toward the mystery of the unconscious that I appreciated in Jungian analytic psychology. However, especially articulated in this conference, Bion's approach is more personal and grounded in the primacy of emotional connection with thought. I think of O taking many shapes and forms depending on the moment, the connection with the analyst and the analyst's own contact with O. Each time an emotional truth emerges and links what had been unconsciously broken and distant, the potential for realization of O is there.

For me, the excellent papers presented during the conference put words to a *formless something* that cannot be created but something that might be allowed to happen, and reminded me of the obstructions that get in the way of an O experience. As I wondered about the sessions I chose to attend, it seemed they each spoke to elements of preventing or attacking O, bridging toward O or noticing how O might evolve.

The presentation by Dr. Pistiner de Cortiñas concerning lies was illustrative of the − K attacks on linking that can keep us out of reality, from being present, conscious − and certainly away from the possibility of O. Dr. Chuster's ideas made sense of the hypnagogic state, a liminal threshold, as a link to K making possible an approach toward O. Dr. Vermote's discussion of regression focused on a starting point of O for all representations and emotions, the undifferentiated unconscious source. He emphasized that O cannot be wanted or sought after, that it happens as spontaneous contact − "becoming O". Dr. Woolridge said in his paper about work with trauma, "For Bion, faith is the only proper response to catastrophe". He has posited that "faith is one of the essential missing ingredients" that allows for a new something to "take root and grow" in the analysis. And we can all recognize the truth that many of our patients have lost faith.

As I thought about my first Bion Conference experience, a poem that often comes to mind with patients came to mind again. I think T.S. Eliot was speaking − with Bionian insight − about O as a possibility, approachable by not grasping for it. His lines in "Four Quartets, East Coker, III" (1943/1971) remind me that the analyst's emotional holding − without memory or desire, or even hope − is critical in the dark, stuck, suffering places with our patients.

INDEX

"psychoanalytic asceticism" 34
psychoanalytic object 10, 54, 71, 74, 77, 97, 176–177, 232–233, 263, 266
psychotic symptoms 164–165
psychotic transformation 128

Quinodoz, Danielle 297

Racker, Heinrich 49
Ramoneda, Bianca 177
Rangell, Leo 196
Rank, Otto 150
Real (Lacan) 240, 246
Reality 1–2, 4–5, 11–12, 19–21, 23, 26, 31–33, 35–36, 38, 47, 53–55, 58, 60–62, 65–73, 75–76, 81, 83–86, 92, 95, 97, 101, 119, 122, 124–125, 129, 130–131, 139, 156–157, 159, 165–166, 177, 182, 206–208, 212–213, 221, 224, 230, 238–239, 244, 248, 250, 255–258, 264, 266–267, 277, 296, 301–302, 310, 316–317, 323–324
Reality Principle 55, 67, 131, 157, 256
"real psychoanalysis" 56, 251, 254
reciprocal kindling 91–96
regression 32, 240, 263–267, 342
religious states 20
remembering 53, 101, 184; *see also* memory
reparation 93, 301–305
repetition compulsion 196–198
repressed material 113
repression 101, 233–234, 236, 246, 270–271, 304
reverie 6–7, 8, 10, 12, 23, 32–33, 43, 58, 80–82, 84, 86, 93, 132, 140, 181–182, 196, 197, 222, 228–229, 233, 271–272, 297, 301, 308–309, 311–312
reversible perspective 11, 241, 245
Rickman, John 41
Ringstrom, Philip 196
Rito, Lúcia 177
'role responsiveness' 48–49
Rosenfeld, Herbert 42, 46

sacrificial victim 143
Sandler, Jayme 257
Sandler, Joseph 47, 48
satisfaction 65, 68
Schreber case 42, 165–166
scientism versus humanism controversy 195
sculpture 196, 251
secondary repression 234
Second Thoughts (Bion) 6, 43, 66, 72, 73, 75
Segal, Hanna 22, 42, 44, 128, 182, 310
selected fact 35, 37, 43, 47, 157, 169, 181, 193, 265, 278, 279, 301
selective repression 233–234
Self: kinds of selves 263; models of self 198; psychoanalytic concept of 263

self-concept 201
sensations 58, 68, 85, 163–165, 176, 187, 191, 214, 226, 251, 308
"*sensuous-concretization syndrome*" 255
Seven Servants (Bion) 2
Shakespeare, William 128, 250
sign 1, 7, 18–19, 21, 25, 55, 70, 79, 106, 108, 121, 139, 151, 159, 223–225, 241, 251, 265, 271, 273, 280–281, 284, 316
'sleep' 188–189
Socrates 253
Sophocles 202
space 33, 35–36, 49, 55, 57, 67, 76, 82, 84–87, 91–93, 95–98, 101, 114, 121, 123, 128, 132, 187, 189, 191–192, 194, 196, 207–208, 211, 213–215, 217, 223, 228, 235, 238, 246, 249, 251, 285, 287, 291, 294–298, 301, 323
spectrum model 152–153
Stafford, William 34
Starte (TV show) 177
Steiner, John 296–297
Steppenwolf (Hesse) 83
Stevenson, Robert L. 177–178
stories 58–59, 163
Strachey, James 44, 151, 249, 268
subjective self 6, 263
"*subjectivist idealization*" 255
sub-thalamic fears (terror) 8, 140, 164
suggestion 196
supra-system 215
symbol 22, 29, 37, 54–55, 60, 73, 101, 107, 118, 120–121, 196, 221, 223–224, 230, 297, 232, 235, 309
Symbolic 79, 118, 120, 151, 225, 232, 239–243, 245–247, 249–250, 253, 271, 294, 310, 316, 319
symbolic equations 42, 128, 310
symbolization 7, 79, 118, 123, 164, 295, 297
symbolon 79, 118, 224
Symington, Neville 196
Szasz, Thomas 196

Taylor, David 32
terror(s) 8–9, 25, 36–37, 46, 56, 58, 80, 85–86, 98, 101, 124–125, 131, 140, 143, 163–165, 179, 181, 192, 246, 308
"Theory of Thinking, A" (Bion) 65, 308
things-in-themselves (beta-elements) 20, 25, 27–28, 46, 131, 156, 224, 229, 230, 233–234, 245, 251, 271, 277, 285, 309, 311–312
thinking 5, 9–12, 18, 23, 31–32, 42, 44, 46–47, 49, 53, 57, 62, 64, 66–72, 74, 76, 79, 83, 86, 101, 118–124, 132, 142, 144–146, 153, 155, 167, 178, 190, 222, 225, 233–234, 236, 245, 254, 263–266, 272, 277, 279, 285, 287, 291, 295, 297, 302, 304, 308–309, 315–316, 318–319, 321

For Product Safety Concerns and Information please contact our EU
representative GPSR@taylorandfrancis.com
Taylor & Francis Verlag GmbH, Kaufingerstraße 24, 80331 München, Germany

www.ingramcontent.com/pod-product-compliance
Lightning Source LLC
Chambersburg PA
CBHW080227270326
41926CB00020B/4167

9 780367 001346